Palestine–Israel in the Print News Media: Contending Discourses

Palestine–Israel in the Print News Media: Contending Discourses is concerned with conceptions of language, knowledge, and thought about political conflict in the Middle East in two national news media communities: the United States and the United Kingdom.

Arguing for the existence of national perspectives which are constructed, distributed, and reinforced in the print news media, this study provides a detailed linguistic analysis of print news media coverage of four recent events in the Palestinian–Israeli conflict in order to examine ideological patterns present in print news media coverage. The two news communities are compared for lexical choices in news stories about the conflict, attribution of agency in the discussion of conflict events, the inclusion or exclusion of historical context in explanations of the conflict, and reliance upon essentialist elements during and within print representations of Palestine–Israel. The book also devotes space to first-hand testimony from journalists with extensive experience covering the conflict from within both news media institutions.

Unifying various avenues of academic enquiry reflecting upon the acquisition of information and the development of knowledge, this book will be of interest to those seeking a new approach to the Palestinian–Israeli conflict.

Luke Peterson completed his doctoral studies at King's College, Cambridge investigating language, news media, and discourse surrounding the Palestinian–Israeli conflict. His current research includes analysis of the conflict within the context of global, economic neoliberalism.

ROUTLEDGE STUDIES ON THE ARAB–ISRAELI CONFLICT

Series Editor: Mick Dumper, University of Exeter

The Arab–Israeli conflict continues to be the centre of academic and popular attention. This series brings together the best of the cutting edge work now being undertaken by predominantly new and young scholars. Although largely falling within the field of political science the series also includes interdisciplinary and multidisciplinary contributions.

Palestine–Israel in the Print News Media:

Contending Discourses

Luke Peterson

Routledge
Taylor & Francis Group

LONDON AND NEW YORK

First published 2015
by Routledge
2 Park Square, Milton Park, Abingdon, Oxon OX14 4RN

and by Routledge
711 Third Avenue, New York, NY 10017

Routledge is an imprint of the Taylor & Francis Group, an informa business

British Library Cataloguing in Publication Data
A catalogue record for this book is available from the British Library

Library of Congress Cataloging in Publication Data
A catalog record for this book has been requested

ISBN: 978-1-138-78164-1 (hbk)
ISBN: 978-1-315-76975-2 (ebk)

Typeset in Times New Roman
by Saxon Graphics Ltd, Derby

Printed and bound in the United States of America by
Edwards Brothers Malloy on sustainably sourced paper

Contents

Figures

Acknowledgements

Like all books many years in the making, this work owes a great deal to a great many people, without whom it would have been in every way impossible for me to envision or engage, let alone complete. To Drs Bert Vaux and Lori Allen I am indebted to you both for your patience, for your thoughtful approach to my work, for your helpful critique, and for your continuing support of my academic career. To James Logan (Clare College) and Oceane Li-Le-Dantec (Homerton College) I owe a tremendous debt of gratitude for your voluntary assistance with my research. To Andre Hough, Matthew Merrick, Mansour Ahmed, and Morgan Condon, for chats and jokes, for laughter and support, and above all, for true friendship, I am truly grateful and I am forever in your debt.

To my father who taught me the value of hard work and the importance of achievement in all things, thank you. To my mother who turned my gaze outward and taught me to see all the world and all of its people as special, as vital, and as a resource to be valued and protected, thank you. To my brother and my best friend, for being my mentor, for being my guide, for being the model of a man I have long emulated, thank you. To my wife and partner, words fail to express all that you have done for me, and all that is owed yet almost surely can never be repaid. For you in my life I could not be more thankful.

And to my young son, you don't know it yet but you have already saved your father a hundred times over. You give me purpose and direction. You give me insight and wisdom. You give me patience and perspective. But most of all, my son, you give me laughter by the barrel full. Thank you for being my bright boy, my bonny lad. Thank you for being my son.

Luke Peterson
King's College
University of Cambridge

1 Introduction

Discourse, Language and the Printed News Media

This book analyzes the construction and representation of Palestine and Israel and the political, military, and civil conflict that has simultaneously united and divided them throughout decades of their shared history on a small plot of semi-arid land between the Jordan River and the Mediterranean Sea. It is not the representation of conflict within the region itself that concerns this investigation but rather its representation in geographical locales far removed from the sites of the physical conflict: the United States and Great Britain. The constructions and representations of Palestine–Israel of interest here are neither visual nor aural, neither graphic nor ancient, but rather textual, of the kind found in the contemporary and authoritative mainstream print news in both of the aforementioned countries. That is to say, this study offers a comparison of the language used to describe some of the more recent and especially newsworthy events (often as determined by those working within the news media themselves) in the Palestinian–Israeli conflict. As such, this enquiry is not exclusively a history of that conflict per se, nor can it be classified strictly as an explication of linguistic theory. Rather the analysis to follow combines elements of multiple scholarly disciplines (the work of history, the close study of language, and the circumscription of discourse among them) in order to sketch the boundaries of contemporary epistemology. Comparing the formation, distribution, and absorption of language describing Palestine–Israel between the United States and Great Britain, including the similarities of representation as well as the manifold differences therein, is, then, the ultimate goal of this work.

To put it concisely, this study constitutes an investigation into the print news media discourse on Palestine–Israel in the United States and Great Britain.[1] In so doing, I offer a comparison of the variances of representation present in the news media institutions located in each of these two national news media communities. Through this process I seek to identify ideological focus and even political orientation present in the two news media institutions. This study undertakes this comparison with an eye toward the connections between language and thought, and the various ways in which print news media language plays a role in the development of knowledge in two contemporary societies. Conclusions in this book speculate as to the boundaries of the available authoritative knowledge on Palestine–Israel within the United States and Great Britain, suggesting how individual and collective perceptions of the conflict may be formulated in distinct ways in each of these two locales. Given that epistemological developments and discursive constructions within any contemporary society are necessarily ephemeral, however, these conclusions can only hope to be snapshots of language, thought, politics, and place. Nevertheless, it is this author's hope that these conclusions and the methods by which they are reached are as noteworthy as they are informative. It is my further hope that the patterns of language and knowledge here described provide insight into the construction and application of language, into patterns of coverage within the print news media, and into the development of knowledge about Palestine–Israel within two contemporary news media communities.

But while the above introduction suffices to explain what this study is and, to a substantial extent, what it does, none of the above suggests any reason *why* this research project was undertaken. A word on that is in order here. My background is as a student of the history as well as the contemporary social and political circumstances in Palestine–Israel. As such, I have travelled to, lived in, researched in, and explored both sides of the line in this divisive conflict. As an American citizen, I have also sought out information on the region from major news media sources in my home country. As a doctoral student in the United Kingdom (and as the son of an English mother), I have likewise engaged in this pursuit in England, where I sit now as I compose this work. And from within these multiple venues of scholarly investigation into Palestine–Israel, differences in tone, text, perspective, and presumption in the language used to describe the conflict in the pages of the authoritative newspapers distributed throughout each country became increasingly apparent. Those differences did not strike me as surprising within the media products of Palestine or of Israel; each side of a political conflict has always sustained its own narrative. But those differences that appeared between news media publications from within Great Britain and the United States seemed to me to be especially noteworthy.

Upon further investigation into these sources, questions as to the form and content of these representational incongruities began to arise. I speculated as to how it might be possible to investigate these structural and functional deviations, and what social, cultural, and/or historical motivations might be responsible for their appearance in mainstream news media publications. I worked to apply a quantitative methodology in this investigation for the purposes of scholarly objectivity, but I could never fully retreat from my qualitative roots either (the result of this prolonged internal debate was the formulation of the hybrid investigational methodology that appears in this book's case study chapters). Throughout all of these investigations however, what lay at the heart of the questions I was asking was the concept of *discourse* and its manifestation in the print news media of two distinct national news media communities. The resulting study, therefore, provides a comparative sketch of the boundaries of that discourse, and offers speculations as to its impact on the formation of knowledge on Palestine–Israel within the United States and Great Britain.

This study has a cognitive aspect as well, offering a brief and speculative assessment of the effect of language in the news media upon the development of *public knowledge* (alternatively termed *social cognition*—both terms and their application to be explained later in some detail) about Palestine–Israel. This assessment is grounded in the erudite research of those linguists and psychologists who specialize in the production and assimilation of spoken and print language in the "mind/brain."[2] This aspect appears in this project because it is not simply the presentation of events in two national media institutions that is of concern here, but also their interpretation and absorption into the communities in which they circulate. That is, it is not only the words on the page and their arrangement in a news media publication that is of interest, but also the potential thoughts, behaviors, attitudes, and actions that those words and presentations engender.

As mentioned, these elements of this book are, to an extent, exploratory. This author's expertise is as a scholar of the Palestinian–Israeli conflict, a commentator on the politics and dynamics of the contemporary Middle East, and as an analyst of discourse. Nevertheless, in the course of this investigation, aspects of the connection between thought and language (inescapable within the study of discourse) arose so often as to effectively render this research project incomplete without the inclusion of this line of argument. As such, considerations of the connection between language and cognition appear regularly in the pages that follow. And while inroads into the possible connection between print language in the news and the processes of individual and collective thought are provided with ample circumspection, these investigative elements nonetheless comprise an important part of this research project. Ultimately, these aspects serve to shed light onto the social and political influence of authoritative print language in the contemporary news media, and suggest related avenues of research into the connections between the mind/brain, language, thought, media, culture, and society.[3]

Potential scholarly benefits to be derived from this study are many. One value lies in the employment of the aforementioned methodology; the close reading and careful analysis of nearly a thousand print news articles for the purpose of discursive comparison is, to the best of this author's knowledge, a unique undertaking.[4] Historical sketches that precede each news article analysis are likewise valuable as they incorporate the most recent, expert scholarship on the Palestinian–Israeli conflict available at the time of this writing. Further, the delineation and definition of the concept *national news media community*, a term already employed in the introductory explanation above, is also an important innovation. Setting down the role of printed news within contemporary nation-states affirms the irrevocable connectivity between collective, national identities and print publication even in an age of instantaneous access to ostensibly landless, electronic information (more on this topic below). The value of conjecture as to the role of printed news language in the formation of individual and group knowledge has been discussed already as a point of extreme interest and potential academic gain in the study of cognition, speculative though it may be. And finally, the evaluation of the practice of print journalism in the Middle East in the words of those who are occupied by it day after day is, I believe, both valuable and illuminating in any study of the news media and their role in the creation of knowledge in contemporary society.

As such, I hope that what follows below is of interest to scholars of the Middle East, students of discourse, practitioners of cultural and identity studies, linguists and cognitive scientists, and experts in media studies, alike. And though walking a tightrope between disciplines and methodologies throughout the course of this research project has been as humbling as it has been challenging, I sincerely hope that I have done justice to each field of inquiry invoked, and to each erudite scholar cited in the pages below. My innovations, whatever they may be, are a credit to each of them. My mistakes, however, are mine alone.

Print in the electronic age

As stated above, the study to follow gives pride of place to the social and cognitive impact of the printed word present in authoritative news publications over and above the news language provided by its ever-present, ever-expanding electronic counterpart. This practice may seem inherently anachronistic given the increasing propensity of news consumers to preference electronic sources over paper ones. And while it is true that electronic news sources have grown exponentially over the last decade while many of their print partners have perished, this author nonetheless holds that the tradition of the printed word in society has an in-built discursive weight, and that electronic sources, or talking-head news programs cannot be said to occupy the same intellectual space as traditional printed volumes.[5] More will be said on the connections between news, print, knowledge, and identity in the chapters to follow. For now, a brief discussion on the social and intellectual value of the published, printed word in the electronic age is in order so as to situate the linguistic analysis to follow in its rightful context.

The impact of texts created and distributed by the news media is of critical importance to the discussion of public knowledge and social cognition in this work. Indeed it has been suggested that texts themselves as particular forms of transmitted knowledge constitute agents in the development of cognition and can exert agency through the structure of meaning and conditioning of information. It is through words in print, and the news media as text that language and its concomitant social and political importance is transmitted to consumers of the news. Specifically, it is authoritative language in print that conveys meaning and structures thought in considerations of Palestine–Israel in both the United States and Great Britain.

A variety of forms of electronic or online opinion editorials, online commentaries, consumer talk-backs, and published letters to the editor compete with authoritative newspapers for intellectual space and discursive influence in contemporary news media markets. Internet blogs, special-interest newspapers, and informational products from small interest groups or from members of unique subcultures are also examples of this type of political expression. These alternative forms of media exist primarily in the ever-expanding World Wide Web, a free, open, and virtually unregulated electronic universe where it is possible to read and hear news and perspectives on any conceivable topic with the click of a button. The source material to be found in this world is as diverse as it is unpredictable.

News and political information found online might as likely be from educated experts as it is from ignorant, unrepentant bigots. There are methods for the verification of electronic sources and online posts but they are not infallible. Where news is concerned, the internet remains a measureless and wild place.

Existing as they do outside of regulated news agencies and beyond the strictures and conditions imposed by established media conglomerates, alternative sites of news production are modes of communication that work against the institutional news current. They are not bound to conform to the standard, acceptable news narratives embraced and espoused by the authoritative media. Collectively this might make these sources attractive alternatives to the more mundane and predictable narratives touted by their establishment counterparts. Indeed, news consumers often seek out these news sites in order to obtain information that is categorically outside the accepted norm of mainstream political expression. Some of these news providers have become incredibly popular, even to the point of competing with traditional media outlets in the provision of information on certain subjects. As such, these sites and the non-traditional perspectives they endorse occupy an important place when it comes to the provision of news and political perspectives within contemporary media markets.

Still, individual, small-group, highly specialized, and other independent news products are outside of the institutionally-established national news media structure. As such, many scholars of contemporary media believe that these methods of alternative expression do not significantly impact the extent of institutional agency in the creation of the news.[6] Rather it is more often suggested that alternative voices working to counteract expansive institutions of news production are subsumed, marginalized, or otherwise rendered ridiculous by authoritative media. In this way, authoritative news sources are able to use alternative sources to solidify their influence within national news discourse. So while increasing in number and popularity among expanding groups of news consumers, alternative, electronic news sources may in fact be situated to serve the needs of the news media institution by maintaining the existing status quo where massive, conglomerate media corporations condition and distribute information to the majority of the news consuming public.

As such, institutionally vetted, authoritative news text remains a crucial avenue of investigation into considerations of discourse, thought, and language. Distinct from alternative modes of communication, including rapidly shifting electronic publications, items in print retain a more lasting, more substantial impact upon cognition. Often repetitive or recurrent themes—such as the frames of representation identified in the case studies in this book—deepen this cognitive impact. Ultimately, conceptual relations, positive and negative associations, and functional memory is significantly informed in each of these processes. It is this value of print in the construction of knowledge, and the value of text and its influence upon individual and social memory that renders the printed news so influential in the construction and distribution of contemporary discourse. Consequently, items in print receive significant investigative attention over and above electronic media in the discussion to follow.

Sources and method

But of course, not *all* news texts present within these two massive news media institutions are analyzed within this book. Rather this work engages with the authoritative news media and examines the ideological principles upon which its coverage is based. Here, the term *authoritative* describes a minority of print publications that dominate the intellectual landscape and contribute broadly to the structure of news information disseminated in society.[7] As such, the concept of authority that is applicable within this study relates closely to Gramscian hegemony, defined as "intellectual and moral leadership" and is suggestive of authority in intellectual as well as moral products.[8] A more recent and perhaps even more applicable definition of the term hegemony identifies this concept as "that order of signs and practices, relations and distinctions, images and epistemologies—drawn from a historically situated cultural field—that come to be taken-for-granted as the natural and received shape of the world and everything that inhabits it."[9] It is this establishment of an authority "taken-for-granted" as much as actively granted by any individual or institution that characterizes the printed news sources examined for their perspective within the discourse on Palestine–Israel here in this work.

This analysis of the contemporary news media seeks to isolate descriptions of events provided by those news sources responsible for constructing and representing the naturally received order of the world and the events in it. The publications examined here, therefore, are those that originate in the cultural, commercial, and political capitals of the nation-state and which possess a wide circulation across regional boundaries within the nation. They are the recognized and established leaders in the distribution of news and the attribution of meaning within a community and as such retain a very large influence upon a variety of forms of discourse. As such, I deem these sources *authoritative* and I engage this study with a focus upon those media resources in order to examine the output of the *authoritative news media*. In identifying and analyzing these sources in their contribution to specifically political discourse in the United States and Great Britain, then, this study articulates the borders of authoritative discourse construction while at the same time describing the ideological parameters within which discourse shapes news events as they occur in the world.

Based upon these principles of news media analysis, the case studies within this book contain a comparative analysis of news media perspectives on four events in the relatively recent history of the Palestinian–Israeli conflict: the Israel settler relocation of 2005; the Palestinian Legislative Council elections of 2006; the Israeli–Gaza War of 2008–2009; and the Israeli naval attack on the humanitarian aid convoy of 2010. Each case study focuses on the news media coverage surrounding an event by comparing printed news from both the United Kingdom and the United States. This comparison is conducted through close analysis of hundreds of print news media articles per event. In order to conduct an examination of this type, in addition to those press items physically collected over the course of this research project, electronic archives and online databases were utilized in order to develop a substantial data sampling for each event and from each national news media community under consideration. This method typically generated between ninety and one-hundred and twenty news articles per national news media community per media event, each of which were subject to multiple close readings by this author for the purpose of discerning patterns of news narrative presentation. Only main news desk and foreign or international news items were collected. Events related to the topic at hand, though not specifically dealing with the event to be analyzed, were discarded along with newspaper editorials, letters, and commentary. Small, independent, or alternative publications that happened to appear in online searches were not included in the data sets in the case studies to follow.

For each case study, a sampling of articles was gathered for a range of publication dates centered on the days during which the event in question transpired. In addition to bounding the articles analyzed by an applicable date range, a keyword search was employed using electronic archives and/or online databases in order to generate a selectively random sample of news articles pertinent to the topic under investigation from authoritative news publications in the United States and the United Kingdom. The goal in developing samples of this magnitude was not to be able to draw conclusions simply about particular articles or publications, but rather to be able to analyze the coverage of a highly publicized foreign affairs event within a specific national news media community. That is to say this study examines a wide range of ideologically and politically situated news publications from both communities under investigation. The article sampling in the case studies in this work deliberately included this broad range in order to be able to draw effective conclusions about the national media as a whole. The range of political orientations and ideological affiliations within a nation is analyzed for the purpose of developing a focused image of the ways in which the nation as a whole represents conflict in Palestine–Israel, not just its "liberal" press or its "conservative" press.

It is within these parameters, both semantic and methodological, that a specific data set was generated for each news media community, and for each event under consideration. As mentioned, the overriding factor in the selection of the specific news items was not randomness, but rather selective randomness whereby news articles from certain sources produced within a given period of time and focused upon a given news topic were found, collected, and analyzed. In aiming for this type of authoritative, nationally relevant news sampling, the following newspapers provided the majority of the articles in the data sampling analyzed below. In the United States, items from *The Los Angeles Times*, *The New York Times*, *The Christian Science Monitor*, *The Washington Times*, and *The Washington Post* dominate the article sampling. In the United Kingdom, *The Guardian*, *The Independent*, *The London Times*, and *The Daily Telegraph* were most prevalent. Each of these sources reaches a national audience and is granted authority within news media discourse for their contribution to public understanding.[10] This is not to say that some of the sources used do not have an established ideological character in many or most matters that they cover.[11] Nevertheless, they remain examples of authoritative news media for those reasons mentioned above, and by virtue of the general esteem that the ability to describe and define the natural world and the events in it grants them in the communities in which they are based.

Finally, as a matter of academic integrity, it should be mentioned that despite the careful criteria applied in the selection of news sources and products, detecting and classifying frames of representation based upon the presentation of language within a news publication is a subjective process. In reading news items, the news media consumer brings his or her perspectives to bear just as the reporter, editor, and various contributors on the newspaper staff bring their perspectives to the creation of news. In addition, it is highly likely that investigating examples of news media coverage of Palestine–Israel is especially susceptible to the generation of partial results given the highly contested nature of both the histories and the contemporary realities of the region and the conflict it contains. Given the problematic nature of analyzing coverage of events in the region, it is fair to assume that analysis of the particular news coverage to follow might be fraught with bias or polemical positioning. In understanding these potential problems I have made considerable efforts to avoid these pitfalls, including multiple close readings of the texts prior to their judgment or analysis, the juxtaposition of quantitative and qualitative data analysis in each case study, and the provision of excerpts from news articles as appendices as justifications for the identification of journalistic frames of representation presented in each case study to follow. In implementing these steps, I hope that the conclusions to be drawn from the following analysis are fair and justifiable, but more importantly, sustained by the data in their presentation in the case studies themselves.

Palestine–Israel: history and conflict

As has been made evident, this book deals with representations of Palestine and Israel and the conflict in which they have been engaged for decades. As of this point, however, I have not yet suggested what facts on the ground will serve as the baseline for the succeeding discussions of bias, presumption, and perspective in the print news media in its representation of this regional conflict to the outside world. A brief discussion of the region is in order here, then, so as to provide the reader with some historical purchase in the following consideration of print media coverage. And though it is outside the scope of this book to provide a detailed account of the history of Palestine–Israel in full, in order to appreciate contemporary events in the region and their portrayal in the print news media, it is necessary to provide a brief overview of the history of that conflict. Where necessary, I provide references for those assertions included in the following description taken from regional scholars whose specific academic purview is the elucidation of past events. It is upon their careful histories that the following examination of the Palestinian–Israeli conflict is based.[12]

Histories of Palestine–Israel tend to focus on the years during and after the First World War as the seminal moments in the birth of political turmoil in the Middle East, turmoil that shows no sign of abating even now, a century later. The Middle

East, the crossroads of the world, was in clear disarray by the outbreak of that war in Europe.[13] The reigning body politic in the region, the Ottoman Empire,[14] had been steadily losing control of its possessions and its populations during the early years of the twentieth century. Nearby empires with a mind on expansion preyed on increasingly vulnerable sections of Ottoman territory while multiple ethnic groups within the empire began to resist imperial control and enunciate their desire for independence. The result was a state having to contend with both external enemies (Austria-Hungary, Italy, and Russia) and internal opposition who would rather overthrow dynastic rule directly than suffer the indignity of being picked apart gradually by continental foes. So precarious was this empire during the pre-war years that the Ottomans came to be inauspiciously known as the "sick man of Europe" to their anxious rivals on the continent.

Such a vast landmass that was so obviously primed for conquest piqued British interest during the latter nineteenth and early twentieth century. This zeal for territorial expansion was codified by a series of diplomatic agreements in which Great Britain committed itself to providing either military assistance, territory, or both to various European nations and independent Arab interests in return for a measure of autonomy over the remnants of the Ottoman Empire. The Constantinople Agreement between Britain, France, and Russia was written one year after the beginning of hostilities in the First World War and guaranteed territorial acquisitions to participants in the global conflagration (collectively known as the Triple Entente) to be taken from the remains of the Middle Eastern empire. Tsar Nicholas II was promised dominion over the city of Istanbul and the Turkish Straits[15] as well as half of the territory of Persia (the other half going to British control). Of course, neither Tsar Nicholas nor any of the members among the Russian ruling family would make it out of the conflict alive. As a result, all of the territories promised to Russia during the war years were simply revoked and redistributed among the Allies for their administration.[16]

The Sykes–Picot Agreement signed on May 16, 1916 was a continuation of the division of Ottoman territories by allied nations. Upon cessation of the war, the treaty was to provide Russia with the territory in north-eastern Anatolia and France with virtually all of the territory of Syria in *bilad-ash-shams*, the central, mountainous corridor connecting Anatolia with Persia to the east, the Arabian Peninsula to the south, and Palestine, the Mediterranean, and Egypt and North Africa to the west. Great Britain was to be given control over Iraq from the city of Baghdad west to the Palestinian city of Acre which were areas north and west of the French territorial allotment. Sykes–Picot effectively redistributed all of the Ottoman Middle East to allied powers after the war. The various Arab peoples to whom a certain measure of self-government had been granted in the latter years of the Ottoman sultanate were left out of Sykes–Picot altogether. The prevailing powers were determined to extend their imperial control at the expense of the indigenous populations of the Middle East and Africa.[17]

Behind the scene of these ambitious territorial divisions devised by Britain and its allies was a diplomatic correspondence between British High Commissioner in Egypt, Sir Henry McMahon, and Sharif Hussain of Mecca. McMahon arrived in

Egypt in January of 1915 to take over affairs for the British Crown in the Middle East. As High Commissioner, McMahon acted and spoke with the authority of the British government and could therefore enter agreements and commit to agendas as readily as the Prime Minister himself. Similarly, Hussain had a position of rare political influence in the traditionally tribal and fiercely independent communities of Arabia. Hussain was the Sharif of the Hejaz, a province on the Arabian Peninsula located along the west coast and bordering the Red Sea. The Hejaz is a province of distinction throughout the Muslim world being that it contains the two holiest cities in Islam, Mecca and Medina.[18] Only descendants of the Prophet Mohammed himself can govern the Hejaz, which meant that Hussain and his three sons (Amir Ali, Amir Abdulla, and Amir Faysal) were treated with an added measure of respect owed to their sacred lineage. Inasmuch as the diverse Arab community of the early twentieth-century Middle East had a single spokesman to assert their political agenda to the collective military and political powers of the west, Hussain was that spokesman.

Upon the Ottoman commitment to join Germany and the Central Powers in the war, Great Britain had ample justification to pursue its imperial ambitions in that crumbling state. Military and political strategists within the British government had determined that internal strife within the Ottoman Empire would bring about a favorable end to the war all the more quickly and thus would bring about British possession of the territories of the Middle East sooner rather than later. Of further concern to the British in the event of protracted war was the call for *jihad*[19] against Britain and its allies issued by the chief of the Senussi, a powerful political group and tribal union in western Egypt. This call for *jihad*, if supported by Hussain and his followers, would create added difficulties for the British forces operating in the Middle East. Conversely, Hussain's rejection of this call to arms against Britain would effectively end the movement and would facilitate British interests in the region.

For these reasons Hussain was immensely important to Britain's African and Middle Eastern operations in World War I. He alone was in a unique position to provide exactly what Britain needed, but he would do so only at a price. Through a series of letters which began shortly after McMahon arrived in Egypt, the two men negotiated an agreement that has become infamous since its publication. Hussain agreed to take up arms against the Ottoman armies and to encourage Arab communities throughout the region to do the same. In addition, Hussain agreed not to endorse the Senussi call for *jihad*, an act which quashed the movement before it truly began. In return, Hussain sought and received a guarantee from McMahon that Arab territories within the Ottoman Empire would be granted independence and full self-determination after the war. Hussain detailed the boundaries of said territories[20] and presented them to McMahon:

North: The line Mersina-Adana to parallel 37 North and thence along the line Birejik-Urfa-Maradin-Midiat-Jazira Ibn Umar-Amadia to the Persian frontier.

East: The Persian frontier down to the Persian Gulf.

South: The Indian Ocean.

West: The Red Sea and the Mediterranean Coast back to Mersin.

The boundaries proposed by Hussain delineated a region that extended in modern geographical terms from southern Turkey to the Indian Ocean (excepting Aden in the southern Arabian Peninsula which was already a British possession) and from the western border of Iran to the Mediterranean Sea including the Holy Land of Palestine.

Upon review of these boundaries, McMahon responded:

> I am authorized to give you the following pledges on behalf of the Government of Great Britain, and to reply as follows to your note:
>
> That, subject to the modifications stated above, Great Britain is prepared to recognize and uphold the independence of the Arabs in all the regions lying within the frontiers proposed by the Sharif of Mecca.
>
> That Great Britain will guarantee the Holy Places against all external aggression.[21]

McMahon's "modifications" eliminated Palestine from this region asserting that "The districts of Mersin and Alexandretta, and portions of Syria lying to the west of the districts of Damascus, Homs, Hama, and Aleppo, cannot be said to be purely Arab and must on that account be exempted from the proposed delineation."[22] McMahon also asserted that Britain had commitments to her ally France that must be served in the region and that may involve portions of the territory in dispute.

Hussain vigorously protested these territorial omissions. Agreeing to McMahon's adjustment of the original geographical delineation would eliminate Palestine and the holy city of Jerusalem from the proposed independent Arab state or states. Hussain, as a representative of Arabs throughout the Middle East could not endorse this revision. His response clearly stated: "Any concession designed to give France, or any other Power, possession of a single square foot of territory in those parts is quite out of the question."[23] McMahon, an expert bureaucrat, remained noncommittal in his dealings with Hussain while at the same time giving the Arab leader sufficient guarantees and political peace of mind in order to bring about Arab action on behalf of Britain.[24] The two parties came to an agreement and then set about the task of bringing war to the Ottomans, which, thanks in no small part to the efforts of Hussain and his allies, was successful. But that was far from the end of the story where Palestine–Israel was concerned.

To further complicate the wartime land grab in the region, on November 2, 1917, British Foreign Secretary Lord Arthur Balfour wrote a letter to Lord Rothschild, a parliamentary representative which stated in part: "His Majesty's Government view with favour the establishment in Palestine of a national home for the Jewish people and will use their best endeavours to facilitate the achievement of this object." The letter was seen as the culmination of the Zionist[25] movement, a political movement founded and organized by members extending across communities of the old monarchies of Europe which saw the establishment of a state for world Jewry as the only logical course of action in the face of persistent and intense anti-Semitism across the continent in the latter half of the nineteenth and early twentieth century. This document represented a public commitment by the British government under the leadership of Prime Minister David Lloyd George to establish "a national home for the Jewish people" in historic Palestine although somehow without prejudicing "the civil and religious rights of existing non-Jewish communities in Palestine."

Whether or not the government or Great Britain had the political or international authority to issue such a declaration is debatable. Similarly, dispute exists as to the motivation of Great Britain in this matter given that this declaration was preceded by the Constantinople Agreement, the Sykes–Picot Agreement, and the McMahon–Hussain Correspondence meaning that Britain was stretched incredibly thinly as it was in terms of territorial and political commitments in the post-war Middle East. Some scholars have suggested that in issuing the Balfour Declaration Great Britain was trying to persuade Russia into continuing their war effort by pandering to the revolutionaries in that country, most of whom were presumed to be Jewish and Zionist. Another possible, if undemanding, explanation is that key members of British Parliament were themselves Zionists and were able to efficiently push the Balfour Declaration through the diplomatic process because of their commitment to the movement. Conversely, members of the British government, including Balfour himself, may have actually been anti-Semites, motivated to encourage the emigration of Jews out of the British Isles to foreign and distant lands.[26]

Regardless of the British motivation in any of these diplomatic agreements, the fact remains that the years prior to and during the First World War saw Great Britain willfully commit to a chaotic series of completely irreconcilable diplomatic and political scenarios. Inevitably, the contradictory nature of these commitments caused Britain to renege on a number of political promises upon the cessation of global hostilities. Instead, after World War I ended, Britain began to coordinate with other victorious powers in authoring an unprecedented plan for paternalistic management of the leftover Ottoman Empire: the Mandate System. Rather than molding conquered territories into colonies for victorious nations, the League of Nations (the international governing body established at the conclusion of World War I which was responsible for managing global political affairs) established Mandates. These were essentially protectorates to be temporarily administered by European victors in lieu of outright colonial rule. Mandates were created for the territories of Syria, Lebanon, Transjordan, Iraq, and Palestine. Syria and Lebanon were placed under the supervision of France while the remaining territories were ceded to the British. The Mandate System called for the regional powers to promote democratic principles and encourage the indigenous inhabitants to prepare for outright independence when the time came.[27]

In Palestine, British administration took on a unique form. Palestine was considered a special case both because of the religious significance of the territory and because of the competing national claims to it. Not only was Britain charged with governing the indigenous Palestinian population and managing (some would say suppressing) its burgeoning national movement, they were also tasked with the responsibility of fulfilling their own wartime promise to the Zionist movement in the form of the Balfour Declaration. In partial fulfillment of that promise, Britain began a concerted sponsorship of European Jewish immigration to Palestine beginning with the opening of the Mandate Period. The demographic results of these efforts were dramatic. In 1922, Palestine contained 525,000 Arabs (93 percent of the populous) and 40,000 Jewish residents (6 percent of the populous). By 1946, on the eve of the partition of Palestine, the British Mandate contained 1,237,000 Arab citizens (65 percent of the populous) and 608,000 Jewish citizens (35 percent of the populous). This rapid demographic shift was accompanied by substantial land purchase, annexation, and redistribution both officially sanctioned and unofficially orchestrated. The key promise to the Palestinian population of the region contained within the text of the Balfour Declaration not to prejudice "the civil and religious rights of existing non-Jewish communities in Palestine" was largely overlooked during the Mandate Period in favor of adhering closely to the spirit of the Balfour Declaration authored on behalf of the Zionist Movement. The British commitment to Hussain and the implicit promise of a sovereign Palestinian state began to fade rapidly under British administration of Mandate Palestine.

Iraq became an independent kingdom in 1932 under Hussain's son, Amir Faysal ibn Hussain. His older brother Abdullah began rule over newly created Jordan after the end of Britain's Mandate of Transjordan in the same year. Syria and Lebanon would likewise receive their independence from Western administrative rule in the interwar years. Palestine, the most contested territory in the region would remain a mandate until it was officially partitioned by the United Nations (successor to the League of Nations) on November 29, 1947 in UN Resolution 181. The terms of the partition called for the creation of two states within the mandate, one predominantly Arab state to retain the name Palestine comprising 44 percent of the land of the Mandate, and one Jewish state comprising 56 percent of the Mandate. In this partition, the United Nations sought to fulfill both Britain's promise to Zionism and honor its implicit promise to Palestinian nationalism in the form of McMahon's correspondence with Hussain.

The Zionist movement publicly endorsed this solution while Arab leadership across the Middle East rejected it. Palestinians and the majority of their Arab neighbors felt that the UN's establishment of a Jewish state on the land of historic Palestine was the direct product of the swell of Jewish immigration and organized land redistribution during British occupation. They paid no credence to those practices nor to the spirit of the Balfour Declaration that prompted them. On May 15, 1948, the last Union Jack was taken down in Palestine. Hours later the leaders of the Zionist movement proclaimed the birth of the state of Israel.

Within days of the adoption of Resolution 181 fighting broke out between Zionist militias (who equipped and trained themselves during the Mandate Period) and indigenous Palestinians, later supported by a contingent of loosely organized Arab armies from across the region. The circumstances of the 1948 war that created the state of Israel and eradicated the cultural and political integrity of Palestine are significantly conditioned by perspective. In one retelling of this opening salvo of conflict, a group of resilient and determined fighters, refugees or children of refugees from the horrors of the Nazi Holocaust, once released from the shackles of British Occupation fought off five Arab armies to forge a small state for the much maligned Jewish people in their historic homeland. In this narrative, it is commonly assumed that the strength of numbers and materiale in the war favored the rejectionist Arabs who refused to accept the partition of historic Palestine preferring to take up arms against the new Jewish state instead. The victory of the Zionist forces therefore demonstrates the magnitude of the triumph of the Jewish people and possibly even the Divine sanction for their settlement and proliferation within Palestine.

The second retelling of the war of 1948 shifts the balance of power and the military advantage from the one side of the conflict to the other. In this narrative, the Israeli paramilitary was already well developed and highly coordinated upon the opening of hostilities between Jewish and Arab armies in the winter of 1947.[28] As well, both British and international policy had allowed for the stockpiling of substantially more numerous and more functional arms for the Jewish military groups as opposed to the Palestinian fighters. Finally, and perhaps most importantly, new archival work has demonstrated that at no point were the Jewish armies outnumbered by even the coalition of Arab armies.[29] Rather, manpower and war materiale were both on the side of the Zionist militaries. According to this perspective—one generally accepted in most academic circles and substantially sustained by available historical and archival evidence—the myth of the Jewish David meeting up against an Arab Goliath in 1948 is precisely that: a myth. What happened instead was a complete and thorough victory by the larger and better equipped military force.

The armistice that ended the war of 1949 established the internationally recognized "Green Line" border between the new, sovereign Israeli state and the areas that remained culturally and politically Palestinian: the West Bank (including East Jerusalem and the historic and holy Old City) and the Gaza Strip (located on the border of Egypt). These two small pieces of land represent only 22 percent of historic Palestine, the remaining 78 percent having been conquered militarily by the newly organized Israeli army. After the signing of the Armistice of 1949 between Israel and the Arab states (apart from Iraq), Egypt took administrative and civil control over the Gaza Strip while Jordan did the same in the West Bank.[30] Arab rule of the remaining territory in Palestinian hands would not last long, however.

In the summer of 1967, Israel attacked Jordan, Syria, and Egypt, simultaneously dealing a crushing blow to all three armies. The vaunted Egyptian Air Force was destroyed by Israeli air raids while sitting on the runway. Expert Jordanian tank brigades were driven back from the Green Line border and across the Jordan River in surprisingly short order. Within a week, hostilities had ceased and Israel had won an impressive victory. Israel conquered all of the West Bank and the Gaza Strip. In the south, however, the Israeli armored divisions did not stop at the border of Egypt but rather drove through the Sinai up to the Suez Canal, capturing a significant portion of sovereign Egyptian territory. In the north of Israel, military operations seized the strategically valuable Golan Heights from Syria. In under a week, Israel had expanded its territorial possessions significantly while incurring minimal military losses.[31]

The international community was stunned by this attack. While Israel claimed provocation by Egyptian and Syrian forces along its border, the United Nations condemned Israeli actions during this war and the United Nations Security Council passed Resolution 242 which stated, in part, that Israel must return the territories acquired during the week of warfare, and that any and all territory acquired by military force could not legitimately be incorporated into the Israeli state. With the exception of the Sinai Peninsula, which was returned to Egypt piecemeal over the better part of the following decade, Israel has ignored this ostensibly binding resolution since its issuance. The West Bank, the Gaza Strip, and the Golan Heights remain today as they have been since June of 1967, firmly under Israeli military, political, and civil control.

The result of the 1967 war was Israeli autonomy in all matters throughout historic Palestine. Israeli control now extended into areas containing at the time more than 3 million Arab Palestinians. This new political reality marked a turning point in the history of these two peoples. Never before had any Jewish state controlled such a large piece of land; not since the pre-Islamic period had Arab hegemony in the region been so thoroughly undone.[32] And while three-quarters of a million Arab Palestinians were ejected from their homes and made refugees in 1948, for West Bank and Gazan Palestinians, it is 1967 that marks the formal beginning of what is termed the *occupation* of Palestine. Israeli control over all Palestinian land and all Palestinian people had, at this point, become complete.

These were the beginnings of the half-century of strife in the Middle East that has come to be known as the Palestinian–Israeli conflict. British duplicity during World War I fuelled the dispute by giving both Muslim Arabs and Jewish Zionists legitimate claim to lands that they each believe to be rightfully theirs. Based on the specifics of the Hussain–McMahon Correspondence, Palestinians believe that they were duped into serving British interests during World War I without receiving the agreed upon compensation (autonomy in Palestine) for that service; only Zionist interests were truly fulfilled, even surpassed, by British maneuvering in the Middle East. The independent states of Syria, Jordan, Lebanon, and Iraq stand today as testament to Britain's partial fulfillment of Arab aims enunciated by Hussain, yet arguably none of these lands have the religious, historical, or cultural value of Palestine. As a result, an ongoing struggle for independence among Palestinians has defined the region since Britain surrendered the mandate almost seventy years ago.

With this brief history retold for the purpose of establishing a historical footing in this book, this text moves to deal with some of the more theoretical elements implied in this investigation. Specifically, the next chapter will elucidate terms found in this work's title including the term *discourse* which is defined at some length in order to situate my use of this concept throughout this study. Subsequent sections of this book consider the challenges of analyzing the unique form of discourse found in the contemporary printed news to include a discussion of the various and specific forms of communication present within that particular medium. The broader academic tradition of Critical Discourse Analysis (CDA) is likewise explained in connection to this research as is my theoretical assertion of *national news media communities* and their relationships with international news coverage and the coverage of Palestine–Israel. This theoretical discussion will give way to a more practical one in the case study chapters as investigations into the news coverage of recent events in the history of Palestine–Israel are moved to the forefront of this narrative.

Notes

1   Simon Cottle, *Mediatized Conflict: Developments in Media and Conflict Studies* (New York: The Open University Press, 2006).
2   Ray Jackendoff, *Language, Consciousness, Culture: Essays on Mental Structure* (Cambridge, Massachusetts, MIT Press, 2007), 146.
3   See also Douglas Kellner, *Media Culture: Cultural Studies, Identity and Politics Between the Modern and Postmodern* (London: Routledge, 1995).
4   One comparable study that bears mention was the investigation conducted by the Glasgow University Media Group published in 2004 analyzing various forms of media coverage of Palestine–Israel and their subsequent cognitive effects. This method of study, termed by the researchers "Thematic Analysis" assumed, as this study does that "in any contentious area there will be competing ways of describing events and their history … So ideology (by which we mean an interest-linked perspective) and the struggle for legitimacy go hand in hand" (Greg Philo and Mike Berry, *Bad News from Israel* (London: Pluto Press, 2004), 95). This study differs from the analysis of the Glasgow University Media Group, however, by virtue of its exclusive focus on print news language and its discursive impacts to the exclusion of audio, video, or pictorial analysis of representations of Palestine–Israel. Also this study offers a comparison of two national news media communities whereas the Glasgow University Media Group study covered only one region of representation (the UK).
5   The difference being discussed here is between printed news and electronic news sources which otherwise have no dedicated print outlet. In many cases a news source has both a print outlet and an electronic website as is the case with basically all major news publications throughout the US and the UK (and all those whose publications are included for examination within this work's case study chapters). When examining text that appears in both print and electronic formats, I do not claim that the electronic version of the printed source is somehow lessened by virtue of its web-based nature. Rather I am arguing for the trustworthiness and traditional import given to established newspapers over and above independent or untested blogs, news sites, or other alternative media sources.
6   See Edward Herman and Noam Chomsky, *Manufacturing Consent: The Political Economy of the Mass Media* (New York: Pantheon, 1988) and Edward Herman and Robert McChesney, *The Global Media: The New Missionaries of Corporate Capitalism* (London: Cassell, 1997).
7   James Curran and Jean Seaton, *Power without Responsibility: The Press and Broadcasting in Britain* (London: Methuen, 1997 [1985]), 74.
8   Antonio Gramsci, *The Prison Notebooks* (New York: Columbia University Press, 2011) [1938]), 57.

9   John Comaroff and Jean Comaroff, *Of Revelation and Revolution: Christianity, Colonialism, and Consciousness in South Africa, Volume 1* (London: The University of Chicago Press, 1991), 23.

10   Some of the sources mentioned here circulate widely throughout their particular national news media community and are leant credibility in news coverage by virtue of their location in major media markets and their coverage of a variety of local and international news topics (this is true of, for example, *The Los Angeles Times* in the United States and *The Sun* in the United Kingdom). Other sources appeared frequently during the course of data gathering because of their consistent treatment of Palestine–Israel specifically even though their overall circulation may be limited by comparison (for example, *The Christian Science Monitor* in the United States).

11   The media holdings of Rupert Murdoch are among those called into question for established ideological bias in the coverage of the Palestinian–Israeli conflict given his investment in Israeli companies and close friendship with Israeli political leaders: "Sam Kiley, a correspondent for *The [London] Times*, resigned in September 2001, blaming its allegedly pro-Israeli censorship of his reporting. He spoke of Rupert Murdoch's close friendship with Ariel Sharon and heavy investment in Israel" (Philo and Berry, *Bad News from Israel*, 255). Other UK newspapers have been similarly criticized: "The proprietor of *the [Daily] Telegraph* group, Conrad Black, is strongly supportive of Israel and journalists complained that this was affecting editorial policy" (Ibid.). Those papers in the United States who may have similar ideological alignments include *The New York Times* (see Chapter IX, in this study entitled *The Journalistic Perspective*).

12   Many well-documented academic investigations explicate these historical events. Particularly noteworthy works (and those primarily used in this historical synopsis) include Avi Shlaim's *The Iron Wall: Israel and the Arab World* (2000), Tara Reinhart's *Israel/Palestine: How to End the War of 1948* (2002), Norman Finkelstein's *Image and Reality in the Palestinian-Israeli Conflict* (2003), James Gelvin's *The Israel-Palestine Conflict: One-Hundred Years of War* (2005), Ilan Pappe's *A History of Modern Palestine: One Land, Two Peoples* (2005), Don Peretz (1996). *The Arab-Israeli Dispute,* and Rashid Khalidi's *The Iron Cage: The Story of the Palestinian Struggle for Statehood* (2006).

13   The commonly accepted catalyst for the outbreak of war was the assassination of Austrian Duke Francis Ferdinand in Sarajevo on June 28, 1914 by Serbian nationalist Gavrilo Princip.

14   The Ottoman Empire was a dynastic state that was established in the thirteenth century with a capital at Constantinople (formerly Byzantium under Byzantine rule). At its height in the sixteenth century the Ottomans controlled an area extending from the Balkan Peninsula in southern Europe to North Africa including the Middle East.

15   The term "Turkish Straits" collectively refers to the Straits of the Bosporus and Dardanelles which, along with the Sea of Marmara, provided access to the Black Sea from southern Russia. The Constantinople Agreement finally granted Russian access to warm water ports in the southern part of the country which were crucial for Russian trade and commerce.

16   In an addendum to the Constantinople Agreement, and in recognition of the Roman Catholic Church's Mediterranean interests, Italy was provided a share of Ottoman lands later that year in an agreement known as the Treaty of London (Don Peretz, *The Arab-Israel Dispute* (New York: Facts on File, 1996), 11).

17   John Glubb, *Britain and the Arabs: A Study of Fifty Years* (London: Hodder and Stoughton, 1959), 67.

18   The city of Mecca is known as the House of God and is the site of the annual pilgrimage called the Hajj, one of the five Pillars of Islam. Medina contains the tomb of the Prophet Mohammed and as such, has both historical and religious relevance for all Muslims (Glubb, *Britain and the Arabs*, 57).

19   The term *jihad* is often translated as "holy war" meaning to do battle in the name of God for a religious cause. The actual translation is more closely "to struggle" in the name of God or on behalf of fellow Muslims and is an Islamic tradition with roots in the very earliest years of the religion (Munson, *Islam and Revolution in the Middle East*, 80).

20   Although approved by Hussain, the specific boundaries presented to McMahon were actually drawn up by Hussain's youngest son Faysal in coordination with Arab interests represented by two secret societies in Damascus, al-Fatat and al-Ahed. These groups were driven underground during Ottoman Sultan Abdul Hamid II's harsh internal reforms but were nonetheless vital parts of the indigenous Arab resistance to Ottoman rule (Glubb, *Britain and the Arabs*, 59).

21   Glubb, *Britain and the Arabs*, 57–64.

22   Ibid.

23   David Fromkin, *A Peace to End All Peace: The Fall of the Ottoman Empire and the Creation of the Modern Middle East* (London: MacMillan, 2010), 185.

24   A number of scholars have laboured to explain the intricacies involved in this vital correspondence between Hussain and McMahon but few performed a more complete analysis than Elie Kedourie in his work *In the Anglo-Arab Labyrinth: The McMahon-Husayn Correspondence and its Interpretations 1914-1939.*

25   Zionism is the term for Jewish nationalism which was a political movement that sought to establish a homeland for Jews somewhere in the world. Most Zionists felt that the Jewish homeland should be in Palestine in accordance with the Jewish tradition of the covenant between God and Abraham in which God promises the land of Palestine to Abraham and his descendants (Peretz, *The Arab-Israel Dispute*, 12).

26   Balfour cosponsored the 1905 Aliens Act in Parliament that was intended to severely restrict Jewish immigration into Britain.

27   Peretz, *The Arab-Israel Dispute*, 13.

28   Larry Collins and Dominique LaPierre, *O Jerusalem!* (London: Weidenfeld and Nicolson, 1972).

29   Avi Shlaim, *The Iron Wall: Israel and the Arab World* (New York: W. W. Norton & Co., 2000).

30   Pappe, *A History of Modern Palestine*, 142.

31   Jeremy Bowen, *Six Days: How the 1967 War Shaped the Middle East* (London: Simon and Schuster, 2003).

32   Karen Armstrong, *A History of Jerusalem: One History, Three Faiths* (New York: HarperCollins, 1997).

2   Discourse and theory

Discourse defined

In analyzing print language and thought, attitude, and behavior and the dynamic relationships between them, I am engaging in a study of discourse, or of a component of discourse present in a given society or community. As the title of this book suggests, this investigation seeks to illuminate not one but rather two distinct patterns of discourse construction in two distinct, contemporary communities to include the manners in which they might contend or diverge to offer two narratives concerning the same series of events. As such, this study sheds light on a particular aspect of a discourse concurrently produced in two locations: the print news media. In order to flesh out this discussion of discourse to include the connections between language, knowledge, and media, a brief definition of terms must take place in order to focus the present study in terms of scope and discipline for this, and subsequent chapters.

The concept of discourse is most closely associated with twentieth-century French philosopher and psychoanalyst Michel Foucault. In articulating and describing the concept of discourse, Foucault created a vivid theoretical description of the structures and functions of knowledge in contemporary society. Applied to multiple academic disciplines and a variety of social science research, the Foucauldian concept of discourse provides a structured analysis of that which is knowable. The description of this concept bounds modes of production of knowledge (including the mass media) and the restriction of distribution of knowledge in all its forms. At the heart of this description is a consideration for knowledge in society as well as broader considerations for structure of knowledge, language, power dynamics and social agency. Foucault's own description of discourse in his work *The Archaeology of Knowledge* states that:

> discourse [is] that which was produced (perhaps all that was produced) by the groups of signs ... discourse is constituted by a group of sequences of signs in so far as they are statements ... discursive formation really is the principle of dispersion and redistribution ... the term discourse can be defined as the group of statements that belong to a single system of formation[1].

In this definition, Foucault describes discourse as a "system of formation," a combination of any or all statements produced connected to one another by relational content. These relatable statements together compose a discourse with each statement contributing to the broader conceptual formulation of the subject in question.

Discourses are adjustable and fluid constructions, yet it is possible to analyze a discourse by identifying its dynamic borders: what is accepted and what is rejected within a discourse. Discursive borders are culturally determined and often institutionally regulated boundaries constituting what can be authoritatively or legitimately articulated about a concept. These boundaries are influenced by the borders of the constitutive statements within the discourse themselves. Put another way, statements within a discourse *act* upon one another to either promote or restrict each other. The type of the statements and the overall nature of the discourse in question affect the way in which statements within it interact. This in turn influences the formulation knowledge of the subject in question. It is this conception of the agency of the statement that is both unique and influential within a Foucauldian notion of discourse:

> A statement always has borders peopled by other statements. These borders are not what is usually meant by 'context'… the contextual relation between one sentence and those before and after it is not the same in the case of a novel and in that of a treatise in physics; the contextual relation between a formulation and the objective environment is not the same in a conversation and in the account of an experiment. Nor are these borders identical with the various texts and sentences that the subject may be conscious of when he speaks.[2]

The borders of statements create inherent limitations upon discourse which behave as determining factors in the structure of the discourse and its subsequent impact upon the development of knowledge. There is a distinction between the borders of spoken discourse and the borders of written discourse, each being conditioned by a different set of circumstances. Each of these processes affects the reformulation and distribution of discourse in society; the borders of a discourse are equivalent to its particular form of agency. As the discourse is forwarded and reproduced, it interacts with extant systems of power within society and is therefore changed. Articulation of the conceptual borders of statements within discourse in this way explains the processes of production and reproduction of discourse as it disseminates in society.

For Foucault, the structure of discourse involves a great deal of individual agency in the acceptance, rejection, or potential reformulation of a given discourse. However the considerations of a school of thought known as Critical Discourse Analysis spearheaded by Dutch theorist Teun Van Dijk emphasize the influence of large, hegemonic institutions in the construction and distribution of a discourse over and above the agency of single individuals either within or outside of conglomerate institutions.[3] In this way the two schools of thought diverge. The Foucauldian School substantially empowers the individual and puts discourse into the hands of its recipients as much as in the hands of its creators or distributors. Van Dijk's philosophy and that of Critical Discourse Analysis adapts this theory to one that considers the role of institutions and the influence of mass media upon the framing of events and the construction of frames of knowledge. As will become clear throughout this study, it is the second definition of the term discourse that will be preferred throughout this investigation.

Language, discourse, and communication in the news media

The news media is unique within discourse formation. In it, language, text, image, and sound are combined within an expansive, profit-driven, corporate and institutional structure in order to inform a constituent public about events in the world. This institution is as diverse and adaptable as it is powerful; a complex and multi-faceted amalgamation of writers, researchers, producers, editors, and managers cooperate to produce the news. The result is a continuous stream of multi-media messages and rapid-fire information created for public consumption. The news is in the world, but it is also of the world. The aforementioned writers, researchers, managers, and newsmakers do not live in a bubble, hermetically sealed away from that which they describe. They are as affected, influenced, pushed, and changed by unfolding global events as any of the rest of us. As such, analysis of the news is, substantially, analysis of the society that produces it. Analysis of news language and the frames of knowledge that accompany it is a critique of social values, an examination of political priorities, and an unveiling of the ideological predispositions embraced at the site of news media production.

News is communication, it is connection, and it is (re)construction. News reaches out to individuals and communities to explain that which is relevant just like many other forms of media do. Still, several characteristics unique to news media language render this particular type of communication distinct in considerations of discourse analysis. In the first place, "[m]ass media communication is one-sided … participation in the communication does not take place on an equal basis."[4] In the general discussion of discourse above, issues of agency and the application of power in communication were considered with particular consequences for the development of thought on a given topic. But in the case of the news media, agency in language is enhanced due to the authoritative monologue that is inherent to the news. As a corollary, the ability of the consumer to react to the form of the information being delivered is reduced while the capacity of the news to broadly condition knowledge on a given subject is substantially enhanced. The flow of information in this model is substantially unidirectional. With the exception of consumer talkbacks and reader commentary in online publications (or letters to the editor in more traditional print formats), the agency of the individual in reformulating an utterance or an overall discourse is severely restricted.

In addition to expansive agency in the creation of discourse, a second defining feature of news media discourse includes vast distances between addresser and addressee. This occurs in terms of both physical as well as intellectual distance;

huge swaths of geographic and experiential territory can separate the occurrence of an event and the interpretation of a news story about that event. This broad divide between the author/presenter of the news and the news recipient removes an element of exchange from the communicative process that can affect the form of information communicated. As a result, creators and distributors of the news are substantially remade as authoritative mouthpieces providing information for marginally influential recipients:

> The addressees of a mass media text such as a television programme or a newspaper article (that is, its audience) are in a very different relationship with their addressers from, say, the audience in a theatre ... A theatre performance is 'here and now'; performers and audience are all physically present, in the same place and the same time. Everyone present is in a position to affect the communicative event.[5]

As an audience, news media consumers are tasked with receiving information without participating in its construction or disbursement. Distributed news media products subsequently contain "almost no extensional material for discussion" and can therefore be "scanty sources of information on important public issues.[6]" These results contribute to the expanded authority of language as information within the news media. This process occurs in all media used to transmit news as information, particularly the printed word.

The kind of information distributed to the audience by news media language is further restricted by the attribution of specific social and cultural values inherent to news media discussions of stories and events. This occurs as a result of the construction of a presumed audience, that audience that the magazine, channel, or newspapers creates as its demographically and politically idealized recipient group. Such audiences are presumed to possess certain ideological characteristics that conform to the accepted norms of the political and cultural context in which the news is distributed. This has the dual effect of both propagating specific ideological values and in eliminating views that would seriously oppose these view points from the authoritative news media (the alternative modes of media mentioned in the previous chapter): "[i]n having to construct an imaginary person to speak to, media producers are placed in a powerful position ... to attribute values and attitudes to their addressees."[7] As an example, in an analysis of the state of affairs in news media production in the United States, linguist and social critic Noam Chomsky pointed out the absence of any socialist or communist news correspondents within the mainstream, authoritative media.[8] This is a function of the fact that the authoritative news media as an institution does permit those ideological positions within news reportage within the contemporary United States. As a result, those with overtly socialist or communist perspectives either do not attain influential positions with the news media establishment, or find themselves marginalized or excluded from mainstream news media coverage. Taken together, these characteristics afford news media a unique role in the construction and distribution of information in contemporary society.

Orwell's problem: language, agency, and influence

Many would argue, however, that even given the restrictive nature of news media discourse, there exist in contemporary society ample resources through which to discover true and accurate information, in order to provide for oneself an unbounded, ideology-free picture of the world and the transpiring events within it. Yet this supposition encounters substantial empirical evidence to the contrary. We are in the midst of the Information Age. Each of us carries in his or her pocket a computing device (in the form of a mobile phone) more powerful than computers that were able to send men on missions to the Moon. We are saturated with news, text, and up-to-the-minute information. Yet arguably we (in the broadly termed 'West') are more separated by ideological prejudice and more divided political affiliation than at any previous point in our collective history. If we all have access to the same bounty of information, shouldn't we all be reaching the same conclusions about the world and the happenings in it?

The philosophical problem that considers why restrained or limited acquisition of knowledge should exist in a resource-rich environment has been labeled "Orwell's Problem." This intellectual paradigm can be described "as the problem why (in the domain of social knowledge) we know and understand so little, even though the evidence available to us is so rich."[9] As has been discussed, restrained, structured, or otherwise ideologically conditioned information is conveyed to consumers of all media as a result of the historical, political, and social conditions in which that media is produced and distributed. These conditions and restrictions apply especially to productions of the contemporary news. But beyond known and identifiable social, cultural, or political structures imposing restrictions upon the development of unfettered knowledge, Orwell's Problem posits a more fundamental, philosophical question about knowledge and the human condition: why don't more people know more, given practically limitless access to information in the contemporary world? This question poses basic queries about society itself including aspects of knowledge and transmission and issues related to human endeavor in the pursuit of knowledge and the information used to acquire it.

Perhaps the realm of investigation most suited to engaging with Orwell's Problem is the study of language and linguistics. This is because this philosophical paradigm is, at essence, a problem of communication whereby the originator of a given message, or "[t]he *Principal* ... the originator of what is being reported, the one whose views are being expressed"[10] first structures, conditions, or otherwise alters that message before transferring it to a given recipient. The vehicle for this structuring, conditioning, or alteration is language and the process by which this alteration takes place is subtle if not altogether covert. The resultant effect upon language and linguistic structures is not readily or easily recognizable by the recipient. The nature of all languages renders this condition a necessary by-product of the communicative process given that "language is a code that conveys messages through the twin processes of encoding (by the speaker) and decoding (by the listener)."[11] Language, then, is a code through which we learn to communicate, and as all codes, it is by definition representational.

Language functions to extend concepts and ideas from one source location to the next. Beyond that, language allows for, even necessitates "thinking with abstractions," another crucial function of the communicative process.[12] This is because inherent within language is the association of sound with meaning, not simply labeling by necessity; "[a] word without meaning is an empty sound."[13] Within each label posited by language and within each word or combination of words, there is contained directed or implied meaning. It is the study of that meaning—semantics—that seeks to align the components of language with the observable world: "Semantics is about matching words to what exists ... The world has a structure, and language adjusts itself to that structure."[14] It is the identification of and connection to meaning in the observable world that unequivocally relates language, and its component parts, to cognition: "[t]he meaning of a word represents such a close amalgam of thought and language that it is hard to tell whether it is a phenomenon of speech or a phenomenon of thought; meaning ... is a criterion of 'word,' its indispensable component."[15] As a representational code, language then provides not only labels and place holders as we have seen (i.e. "we have a word for cats because cats exist and we need to talk about them and communicate information about them") but provides a system for the construction and the interpretation of meaning.[16] It is meaning's place within cognition that connects language to thought. That connection bears further examination if the true potential of the impact of print news media language upon news readers in the coverage of Palestine–Israel can be discovered.

In language's role as facilitator of the communicative process, it has the ability to set the communicative agenda, serving as an effective screen[17] for the discrimination of information. Effectively, language can hide or eliminate those items that are either unnecessary or do not conform to acceptable social, cultural, or ideological norms. In so doing, language serves as the foundational component for discourse formation and therefore has a unique role in the application of institutional power. In this process, language is a selecting agent, determining what information is to be conveyed and the manner of its conveyance. This function of language provides it with significant agency in processes of structuring and institutionalizing knowledge, and subsequently, cognition:

> Language must first have had something to do with what there is to communicate and with what will be counted as communication. It is not just a means of transferring information, it is also, and far more importantly, the locus of the process of deciding what information is to be, and of instituting the kinds of information that will be available for communication.[18]

Selecting *what* will be communicated is as influential upon the formation of knowledge as the selection of *how* it will be communicated. Though the *how* is often the accepted and assumed component of the role of language in communication, the descriptive *what* and the way in which language screens alternative types of information in any and all processes of communication contribute to an often overlooked source of power in the cognitive process. The net impact is the creation of agency in language and subsequent affect upon cognition termed by philosopher Hilary Putnam in the following excerpt as "understanding:"

> understanding, then, does not reside in the words themselves, nor even in the appropriateness of the whole sequence of words and sentences. It lies, rather in the fact that an *understanding* speaker can *do things* with the words and sentences he utters.[19]

Beyond impacting on cognition and the development of knowledge, political, social, and cultural ramifications ensue from the application of language and the assertion of power or agency in the communicative process. These results stem from the organizational role of language in society and the unifying function it plays in the formation of national, communal, and local identities. So profound is this aspect of language application that this particular role of language has been claimed as constitutive of reality itself within a given political and cultural context: "language is where forms of social organisation are produced, and disputed, and at the same time where people's cultural identities come into existence. In effect, language constitutes realities and identities."[20]

What is perceived is understood. What is understood becomes the norm. What is normalized is acculturated. What is identified, internalized, and publicly or privately expressed depends upon language, its agency, and its application. Beyond theoretical or otherwise intangible structures affected by language, it is this function of language that lends itself to a measure of verifiable observation and social expression in communities and social groups. Putnam classified this function as the most significant among the many roles language plays within society: "If there were *no* 'interaction' between purely linguistic behavior and nonlinguistic events, then language would just be noise-making."[21] Put another way, "Human communication ... is a series of alternating displays of behavior by sensitive, scheming, second-guessing, social animals. When we put words into people's ears we are impinging on them and revealing our own intentions, honorable or not."[22]

These multiple, crucial functions of language make it the focus of a great deal of study and interest in discourse analysis and beyond. In this process of regulation and normalization, language applied to the discussion of Palestine–Israel creates discourse and informs on the accepted parameters of thought, action, and habituation in the process of conceiving of events that take place within the context of that political conflict. The delineated and quantified frames of representation accompanying each of the four case studies to follow are an example of that process of habituation in thought and in action. Taken together, the assertion and reassertion of these patterns of description and narrative perspectives contributes to collective conceptions of Palestine–Israel within each national news media community. This process occurs as a result of language applied in the description of events and its ability to attribute meaning, to discriminate in both the content and the format of information delivery, and to establish cultural norms and social identities. While all of these functions apply within the current study focusing upon linguistic representations of Palestine–Israel in the authoritative news media, the sociological function of language as a normalizing, routinizing, and regularizing agent perhaps deserves greatest consideration.

Language and meaning: Jackendoff's default values

Beyond the crucial function of language as a regularizing, socializing agent, and the functions of text in the development of cognition, another important contribution to the investigation into the relationship between language and knowledge comes from linguist Ray Jackendoff and his theory of Default Values. Jackendoff describes processes of cognition as dependent upon categorization through which effective judgments and collective assessments are formed as mental representations. All of cognition is not limited to this process, but categorization plays an important role in the construction of functional mental associations which themselves serve as vital components in the development of knowledge on a given subject: "[a]n essential aspect of cognition is the ability to categorize: to judge that a particular thing is or is not an instance of a particular category."[23] Put another way: "cognition traffics in essences and reductions."[24]

Inherent in processes of categorization described by Jackendoff are both associative and dissociative functions. The classification of objects, concepts, utterances, or ideas requires both linkages to be created and distinctions to be made. A system of categorization is naturally not complete without the presence of both of these elements. It is this cognitive function—the construction of dynamic and functional mental categories—that reorganizes and redefines both the material and the theoretical within a working system of knowledge and which connects functional, practical definitions with like concepts while distancing them from distinct ones. This practice is enhanced by repetitive exposures to various representations of information, including linguistic expressions of objects, concepts, and types much like those found in the news media. Exposures such as these contribute to the cognitive formulation of words and word meanings, rendering them as "large heterogeneous collection of such conditions dealing with form, function, purpose, personality, or whatever else is salient."[25] In this conception, a term to be recalled and manipulated "shades toward 'encyclopedia' rather than 'dictionary' information inclusive of all relevant associations."[26] Or, as linguist Steven Pinker postulated the relationship between language and knowledge:

> Understanding, then, requires integrating the fragments gleaned from a sentence into a vast mental database. For that to work, speakers cannot just toss one fact after another into a listener's head. Knowledge is not like a list of facts in a trivia column but is organized into a complex network. When a series of facts comes in succession, as in a dialogue or text, the language must be structured so that the listener can place each fact into an existing framework.[27]

For both Jackendoff and Pinker, conceptual structures are tantamount to the associational processes of concepts and their connected and disconnected parts. Once heard and interpreted, they are organized according to mental classification schemes that connect like objects with other like objects, and separate those that do not belong. These new pieces of knowledge are crafted, and are therefore dependent upon, the manner and the frequency of exposure to linguistic presentations, inclusive of the representation of ideas through textual and oral language.

Mental classification based on association and disassociation forms a critical component of the theory of Default Values. In it, Jackendoff describes the manner in which missing information which has been normalized to form part of the regular association with a given term or concept is filled in using those predetermined cognitive associations:

> It is often the case that a particular [TOKEN] (*sic*) is missing certain information from which one wishes to draw an inference. For example, with visual inputs, one generally has no information about the back of an object; but one generally has a strong hypothesis or "best guess" about it, and one is most often not even aware that this hypothesis is an assumption. Similarly, with linguistic inputs, one is constantly disambiguating lexical items and syntactic structures.[28]

Default Values refer to the expression used to describe this "best guess" in cognition regarding a term, utterance, or concept that has been provided and described only partially. It is the remainder of the cognitive picture, the additional pieces of the puzzle necessary to form a complete cognitive form upon which judgments, decisions, and actions are based. The associative information that has been left out of this description is provided not by the text, speech, or dialogue in question, but by existing cognitive associations which have been structured and organized according to previous experience with that term in linguistic presentations. In visual processing, walking into a room and seeing only the back of a chair conditions the viewer to interpret what the front side of the chair will look like. Likewise, in linguistic representations, being provided with a partial description of an object theory, idea, or concept (as is the case in print news media publications) will prompt the reader or audience member to fill in the unknown information with the default value of the concept in question:

> These conditions are used ... to fill in or anticipate information not present in a visual or textual input—for example ... that at a restaurant one often decides what to eat after looking at a menu. One presumably uses this information not just to understand stories, but also to structure one's own action.[29]

Default Values are comprised of derived cognitive provisions built upon previous episodic association, dissociation, and functional manipulation without which a complete determination of the item in question cannot be reached. Similar to the chair that has no conceivable or reconcilable function without a back *and* a front, these values allow for the establishment and manipulation of cognitively complete social, political, or ideological concepts.

From the articulation of the theory of Default Values, further investigation into the development of cognition based upon linguistic input necessarily must contend with the structure and the manner of the input upon which the formation of default values is based. This requires an assessment of a broad and diverse linguistic environment in addition to other forms of conceptual representation as well as consideration of the individual's association with that environment and his/her response to or engagement with it. Practically speaking, this plethora of irreconcilable factors renders this theoretical exercise an impossibility. Still, it *is* possible to assert the existence of a constructed experiential and representational environment in a given community or society. Within such an environment, one in which representational resources are politically or ideologically conditioned, information applied in the construction of Default Values will necessarily be restricted and altered. This conditioned information is used to create organizational frames used in conjunction with many others to fuel processes of cognitive categorization, and ultimately, to form default values. This information, the frames it helps to construct, and the default values that ensue significantly impact individual and collective interpretation of reality, and assist in the normalization of judgments, values, and beliefs on all subjects:

> the essential connection between the frame selection task ... and the use of a frame for its default values ... these two tasks use the *very same* information. For instance, suppose that we were to watch a segment of a movie ... in which people were wearing funny hats, giving someone presents, etc. We would use the same information to decide that we were witnessing a birthday party in such a case (to select the "birthday party frame") as we would to anticipate what would happen at a birthday party to which we had been invited.[30]

Associative/dissociative framing (termed by Jackendoff as Frame/Script theory) and the construction of default values, then, depend upon the same linguistic and/ or visual inputs, that is, the same representations of concepts, terms, events, and occurrences taken in from various media available within a given informational environment. Frames established and the subsequent Default Values they generate consequently impact interpretations and judgments and the decisions and behaviors they engender. Much depends, in this case, upon the form of the information initially posited in this process, and of the type of information provided in the representational environment in question.

Taken together, Jackendoff's Frame/Script theory and the theory of Default Values provide insight into the development of knowledge based upon the representation of external reality in print language. These theories characterize what an individual may know and how that person came to this knowledge through both conscious subconscious processes using stimuli available in their immediate representational environment. The functional evaluation of the truth, therefore, and the distinction of truth from belief are the most critical practical and social consequences of these cognitive processes. In essence, the processes described by Jackendoff construct the bridge between information and knowledge identifying "what a human being knows (largely unconsciously)" and therefore what that human being perceives to be real and more importantly, true.[31] In Jackendoff's own words, the nature of knowledge itself is at the heart of these considerations:

> consider the nature of knowledge ... are we speaking of the theory of (real) knowledge, or of the theory of (projected) [knowledge]? These turn out to be quite distinct endeavors. The former is a problem of cognition—how people form mental representations. The second, by contrast, is the question of what it is that people intuitively ascribe to someone when they say that he knows something; here the answer might well be [justified true belief] (*sic*).[32]

The formation of "mental representations" and their implication for cognition inform as to the extent of the importance of linguistic representations of external reality. These inputs mold frames of information and the subsequent default values in processes tantamount to the mental construction of reality and truth, itself. All elements of knowledge based upon representation are subject to these processes rendering Jackendoff's articulation of these concepts vital in connecting language and linguistic representation to individual knowledge and acquired social cognition.

These theoretical frames are therefore directly applicable to the study of print news language covering Palestine–Israel. Repeated exposures to a partial picture of a group or a culture or indeed of an entire people renders that element as cognitively incomplete. Descriptive focus upon limited aspects of Palestinian politics and/or culture, for example, effectively negates the other aspects of these narrative elements in the mental pictures created by news language. This information can be used to prescribe normative behavior to those consumers of printed news media language based upon the default value of the element of Palestine–Israel being described. Instead a "birthday party frame" posited by Jackendoff in his example, news media categorizations of Palestine–Israel can provided a "terrorist frame" or a "pious, religious frame"; an "aggressor frame" or a "defender frame." These propositions, like the frames of representations within the print news media themselves, contribute substantially to social cognition, and when represented broadly and consistently, provide long-term, lasting mental images of the place, the people, and the events represented in news media language.

Conclusions: language and power in the print news media

To conceive of Orwell's Problem in speculating about limitations on knowledge in an environment of limitless intellectual resources is to ask fundamental questions about the formation of knowledge and the distribution of information in contemporary society. Comprehending and articulating these complex processes in turn leads to an investigation of various manifestations of the communicative process, that process that remains the inescapable, fundamental method for the transmission of concepts, the relation or ideas, the structuring of social norms, and the formulation of individual and collective knowledge. If the communicative process is that unavoidable method by which ideas are relayed and identities are formed, language then becomes the key element connecting each level of exploration to the other and unifying queries about Orwell's Problem under one investigative method:

> Language symbols ... figure prominently in thinking and often determine its direction ... language symbols ... are "tools" of thought in these two senses: (1) They provide at least some of the internal stimuli and stimulus-producing responses that carry forward the sequences of events from the external stimuli initiating the process to the overt responses terminating it. And (2) they represent the organizations of internal processes (acquired through learning or past experiences) that are potentially critical in determining whether a given sequence of thought will eventuate in successful or rewarded overt response.[33]

The use of language, or as it is given here, "language symbols" in an emphasis of the representational quality of language, and the engagement in the communicative process is an act of thinking, an engagement in the cognitive process based upon linguistic signals and associative meanings. Language is both the representation of internal processes and the organization of these processes for function, manipulation, and later application. Language provides internal structure, external expression, and organizational infrastructure that unify each of these processes. Cognition and expression are equally reliant upon and equally related to language. Without it, each process is severely compromised. In short, "Mastery of language affords remarkable power."[34]

As established, however, engagement with language, its agency, and its application is not an engagement with an unconditioned, unrestricted cognitive or expressive environment. In fact, applying language necessitates restrictions; "no individual is free to describe nature with absolute impartiality but is constrained to certain modes of interpretation even while he thinks himself most free."[35] To apply language is to apply restrictions, either at the individual level or at the institutional level. Inclusion or exclusion of certain elements applied structures and conditions the object or event under consideration. The manner of the description itself, including the assertion of particular political or social preferences as well as conditioning according to certain ideological influences structures cognitive boundaries. Structuring, conditioning, or restricting of this type injects power into the relationship between language and thought, ultimately interfering with cognition and altering the development of knowledge based on available intellectual resources.

It is the introduction of the element of power into Orwell's Problem that connects this theoretical investigation into language and its uses to the more particular point of this overall study: the discourse on Palestine–Israel in two national news media communities. It is, in fact, the application of power in an intellectual environment that negates the possibility of unfettered access to resources and unrestricted access to information. Power, in this case, is asserted in the discussion of Palestine–Israel by the news media as an institution, by the social and cultural context in which that institution exists, and by the language that is applied in the description, coding, and categorizing of events on the pages of the print news itself. Power is likewise, a necessary concomitant of language and is therefore fundamental to the communicative process. And while language contains within it provisions for thought and provides for the means of expression, socialization, and identification, it simultaneously and necessarily has the power to structure, condition, bound, and restrict. Deficiencies of access to knowledge arise, then, because of the existence of power in the intellectual environment.

Orwell's Problem posits a reformulation of the inherent difficulties of access to information through the filter of the news media. It reiterates processes of discourse formation and language application in pursuing information about events in Palestine–Israel over the course of the recent history of the conflict. Subsequent chapters in this study will reintegrate conceptions of language and thought with processes of discourse creation in the United Kingdom and the United States and will draw conclusions about the ideological orientation of the authoritative news media in each country. Ultimate conclusions will speculate as to what each national news media community might be expected to know about the region of Palestine–Israel based both upon the theoretical structures delineated here, as well as the extensive data review and linguistic analysis of printed news media products detailed in successive chapters.

From this introductory theoretical discussion on discourse, language, and knowledge this study now turns to a consideration of each of these active social phenomena on a national level, exploring conceptions of the ideas of community, nation, the media, and the functionalities that connect them. The goal in the subsequent chapter is to establish the concept of a contemporary *national news media community* through which identities are structured and reified, and about which conclusions can be drawn about the political and ideological orientation of the institution(s) that creates them. The aim in this discussion is to provide suitable theoretical frames for an academic investigation that will allow for subsequent investigative inroads into the coverage of Palestine–Israel in two news communities, and the comparison of the coverage therein. In authoring this comparison, this investigation employs methods developed by Van Dijk and the critical discourse analysts mentioned above, and in the process presumes an ideological orientation inherent within the printed news. This disciplinary focus constitutes a form of content analysis of the news itself in which "Ideology is seen as encoded in the content of the text [and] Analysis concentrates on topics and themes, the representation of opinions, who is given a voice, who is excluded."[36] In short, if "The daily press is a child of the city,"[37] the subsequent chapter will analyze the nation as family, and will present a critique on the structure, form, and function of the national news media in that community in the process.

Notes

1   Michel Foucault, *The Archaeology of Knowledge and the Discourse on Language* (New York: Harper and Row, 1972), 5.
2   Ibid, 97-8.
3   Teun Van Dijk, *Racism and the Press* (London: Routledge, 1991).
4   Mary Talbot, Karen Atkinson, and David Atkinson, *Language and Power in the Modern World* (Edinburgh: Edinburgh University Press, 2003), 10.
5   Ibid.
6   Samuel Ichiye Hayakawa, *Language in Thought and Action* (San Francisco, CA: Harcourt, Brace, Jovanovich, Inc., (1978) [1939]), 272.
7   Talbot *et al.*, *Language and Power in the Modern World*, 12.
8   Noam Chomsky and Michel Foucault, *The Chomsky-Foucault Debate on Human Nature* (New York: The New Press, 2006), 75.
9   Eric Reuland, "Reflections on Knowledge and Language" in E. Reuland and W. Abraham (Eds.). *Knowledge and Language, Volume I: From Orwell's to Plato's Problem* (Dordrecht, the Netherlands: Kluwer Academic Publishers, 1993), 25.
10   Talbot *et al.*, *Language and Power in the Modern World*, 11 (emphasis in original).
11   John Ellis, *Language, Thought, and Logic* (Evanston, Illinois: Northwestern University Press, 1993), 16.
12   C. A. Lawson, *Language, Thought, and the Human Mind* (East Lansing, Michigan: Michigan State University Press, 1958), 28.
13   Lev Vygotsky, *Thought and Language* (MIT Press: Cambridge, Massachusetts, 1962), 120.
14   Ellis, *Language, Thought, and Logic*, 9
15   Ibid.
16   Ibid.
17   Kenneth Burke, *Language as Symbolic Action: Essays on Life, Literature and Method* (Berkley: University of California, 1966).
18   Ellis, *Language, Thought, and Logic*, 17 (emphasis in original).
19   Hilary Putnam, *Mind, Language, and Reality: Philosophical Papers, Volume 2* (New York: Cambridge University Press, 1975), 4.
20   Talbot *et al.*, *Language and Power in the Modern World*, 1.
21   Putnam, *Mind, Language, and Reality*, 5 (emphasis in original).
22   Steven Pinker, *The Language Instinct* (London: Penguin Books, 1994), 245.
23   Ray Jackendoff, *Semantics and Cognition* (Cambridge, Massachusetts: The MIT Press, 1983), 77.
24   Arthur C. Danto, "Metaphor and Cognition" in Ankersmit, F. R. and J. J. A. Mooij (Eds.) *Knowledge and Language, Volume III: Metaphor and Knowledge* (Dordrecht, the Netherlands: Kluwer Academic Publishers, 1993), 31.
25   Jackendoff, *Semantics and Cognition*, 139.
26   Ibid., 139–40.
27   Pinker, *The Language Instinct*, 243.
28   Jackendoff, *Semantics and Cognition*, 140.
29   Ibid.: 140–1.
30   Ibid.: 141.
31   Ibid.: 7.
32   Ibid.: 34.
33   John Bissell Caroll, *Language and Thought* (Englewood Cliffs, NJ: Prentice Hall, 1964), 111.
34   Frantz Fanon, *Black Skin, White Masks* (New York: Grove Press, 1967), 18.
35   Benjamin Lee Whorf, *Language, Thought, and Reality: Selected Writings of Benjamin Lee Whorf* (Cambridge, Massachusetts: MIT Press, 1956), 214.

36 Meinhof, U. "Double Talk in News Broadcasts: A Cross-Cultural Comparison of Pictures and Texts" in Graddol, D. and Oliver Boyd-Barrett (Eds.), *Television News Media Texts: Authors and Readers* (Avon, UK: The Open University Press, 1994), 221.
37 Hanno Hardt, *Social Theories of the Press: Early German & American Perspectives* (Beverly Hills, CA: Sage, 1979), 20.

3 Nations, publics, and the print news media

Defining the nation

The amount of scholarship devoted to conceptualizing the *nation* and *nationalism* is enormous, their applications in contemporary academic investigations likewise. As such, a complete review of all material relevant to the topic would be both impractical and tangential here. Nevertheless, it is crucial to situate the concept of a *national news media community* within the current study which aims to compare discourses structured and distributed in two different geographic and intellectual locales. As well, in order to effectively assert the existence of a *national news media community*, a functional and sufficiently robust definition of the term *nation* must first be developed. Such a definition, while considering historical applications of the term for the purpose of charting semantic change over time, must inevitably be focused upon contemporary usages and meanings in order to provide the most useful theoretical framework for a discussion of contemporary society. The objective here is to arrive at a functional definition of *nation* and explore its relationship to *nationalism* with an emphasis on mass communication and the news media's role in creating, structuring, and maintaining the nation in the ideological and conceptual sense. In order to compensate for the volume of material that might otherwise be applicable to such a discussion, the emphasis in the pages that follow will be on a selective sampling of highly pertinent research which substantially assists the development of the concept of *national news media communities.*

In detailing the cultural and genealogical history of the Jewish people,[1] historian Shlomo Sand tackles the cumbersome topic of nationhood and identifies the boundaries of the concept of nationality. Sand explains that interpreting the nature of nationhood involves delimiting an otherwise dynamic and abstract concept, and that "Like many other abstract terms ... concepts such as 'people,' 'race,' *ethnos*, 'nation,' 'nationalism,' 'country,' and 'homeland' have, over the course of history, been given countless meanings—at times contradictory, at times complementary, always problematic."[2] Sand offers an important insight into one key strand of meaning in both historical and contemporary usages of the term "nation." Exploring the historical origins of the word itself, Sand suggests that the use of the term nation in a contemporary sense recalls an ancient subtext through which the eternity and sanctity of nations and national groups is implied: "European languages use the term 'nation,' which derives from the later Latin *natio*. Its ancient origin is the verb *nascere*, 'to beget'."[3] Sand here relates the term nation to the idea of spiritual birth suggesting both a wholly natural, pure, even virginal connotation as well as a timeless one. Such a perspective might be termed romantic in that it emphasizes a heroic, if mythical, past over and above a practical, living present. This aspect of the nation is similarly emphasized by philosopher Ernest Renan who unequivocally viewed the nation in this idyllic light:

> A nation is a soul, a spiritual principle. Two things, which in truth are but one, constitute this soul or spiritual principle. One lies in the past, one in the present. One is the possession in common of a rich legacy of memories; the other is present-day consent, the desire to live together, the will to perpetuate the value of the heritage that one has received in an undivided form. ... A heroic past, great men, glory ... this is the social capital upon which one bases a national idea.[4]

Renan's articulate conception of the nation verges on the nostalgic by emphasizing bygone heroes and glorious history. Still, his description does capture an essential element of contemporary nationhood: the powerful influence of myth in the articulation of a common national heritage. Sand asserts that this strand of meaning, though inconstant and subjective from its origins through to the present day, still informs contemporary usage.

Indeed a common element in some contemporary definitions of nationhood is the assertion of nations as organic, ancient, and wholly natural occurrences coterminous in their existence with human society itself. In his foundational treatise on the development of nationalism, *Nations and Nationalism: New Perspectives on the Past*, Ernest Gellner challenges this aspect of nationhood and contests the concept of the nation as timeless:

> nations, like states, are a contingency, and not a universal necessity. Neither nations nor states exist at all times and in all circumstances. Moreover, nations and states are not the *same* contingency. Nationalism holds that they were destined for each other; that either without the other is incomplete, and constitutes a tragedy. But before they could become intended for each other, each of them had to emerge, and their emergence was independent and contingent.[5]

If, in Gellner's view, the idea of the state (which he defines in a Weberian sense as "that institution or set of institutions specifically concerned with the enforcement of order"[6]) can be considered to be contrived or otherwise artificial, then conceptions of nations must likewise be deemed so. For though societies have long organized themselves into particular groups and subgroups, and have established practical and rhetorical justifications for the manner of that organization, such developments need not ever have taken place. In this view, neither states nor national groups were necessary developments, and human society could as easily have adopted alternative forms of social and political organization. Conceiving the nation as timeless is pure romanticism; attempts to justify any nation as immemorial are political by their very nature.

The conundrum present in defining an abstract concept (nation) by attributing to it further abstract notions (e.g. culture and consciousness) is adequately answered by a theoretical perspective that obviates the need for characteristic categorization in the study of nationhood while functionally obliterating all identifiable or quantifiable characteristics of nationhood in virtually a single stroke. This perspective, articulated by Benedict Anderson, establishes the nation as constructed through the common imaginings of its members. Connections of nationality and nationhood exist because they are thought to exist, even despite cultural difference, ethnic variation, or expansive geographic space. The nation is not boundless in its functional capacities, however, given the subjective imaginings of other national groups geographically near and distant: "The nation is imagined as *limited* because even the largest of them, encompassing perhaps a billion living human beings, has finite, if elastic, boundaries, beyond which lie other nations."[7] Anderson expresses an essentially ontological theory; the nation is imagined by some quantifiable group of people, and therefore, it is so. Simplistic upon initial approach, there nevertheless exists a neatness in his articulation of these concepts and a concise uniformity in his theoretical assertions. As such, Anderson's theories on nationhood and community have developed a devoted following.

Within Anderson's conception of nationhood, the external borders and the internal structures of the nation must constantly be developed and maintained. This requires a far-reaching and consistent, regulatory institution. Such an institution must be broad enough in scope to reach all those who conceive of themselves as members of the nation, and must be active enough to reify those conceptions on a regular basis. Anderson is clear on how this is accomplished identifying print as the medium of interchange that establishes and maintains the social and cultural integrity of the nation: "Print-language is what invents nationalism."[8] In prolific distribution, the printed word creates communal values and structure cultural norms. The printed word in this capacity carries an ideological agenda becoming ultimately political in its orientation given that "Above all, the very idea of 'nation' is now nestled firmly in virtually all print-languages; and nation-ness is virtually inseparable from political consciousness."[9] The political nation then is related to the imagined nation through the medium of print. The marriage of the conceptual and the political is arguably Anderson's most significant contribution to the discussion of the nation and community. If nations are indeed the imaginary constructs that Anderson claims them to be, the vehicle for that imagining becomes the broadly distributed printed media and the manner of that imagining, individually and collectively, is remade as a distinctly political and ideological act.

Following Sand, Gellner, and Anderson then, my functional definition of *nation* is that body or entity which, imagined and agreed upon by its constituent members, is bounded by some area of territory (the region of the imagined and the imagining) and is cultivated and/or maintained by the distribution of media—particularly in print—which themselves contribute to the creation and distribution of a normalized culture, value system, and national ideology. Though not without potential pitfalls, this definition nevertheless pinpoints one critical social element present in the phenomenon that is the contemporary nation: the contemporary mass media and the authoritative printed word.

It must be mentioned that despite its theoretical efficacy, Anderson's work on conceptions of nationhood might be considered dated by some. Media as they exist today would have been impossible to envision at the time of the first publication of Anderson's foundational work *Imagined Communities* in 1983. Electronic communication in the twenty-first century allows for the distribution of printed information across vast new territories by an untold number of authors none of whom need be bound by the confines of national boundaries, imagined, geographic or otherwise. Thus, the printed word has an infinitely broader reach, indelibly faster modes of delivery, and an undeniably more numerable and more socially diffuse corps of contributors than could have ever been conceived in the early 1980s. As such, Anderson's argument for the role of print in the conception of the nation might advisedly be viewed with caution. And while the consequences of burgeoning, new, electronic media upon culture, identity, and conceptions of the nation bear extensive deliberation (indeed, many academic publications devoted to precisely this topic are produced every year), in giving Anderson pride of place in the preceding theoretical discussion, I maintain that his innovative connection of the concept of nation to the printed word remains foundational. Furthermore, as my discussion of nation and the national news media hinges upon the role of the authoritative print news media in contemporary society and not upon the influence of new, alternative, electronic media forms, Anderson's contributions to this discussion, and their contemporary impact in the formation of national culture and national ideology, remain vitally important. With Anderson's place in this argument firmly in mind, then, and equipped with the previously articulated definition of nation, I now turn to an explication of a key constitutive element present therein: the print news media. The goal in the subsequent section is to arrive at a precise articulation of the concept of the national news media community, an idea upon which much in the remainder of this study depends.

The mediated nation and public discourse

In the brief definition provided in the previous section, the central role played by the mass media in defining the contemporary nation is evident. The exploration of this connection does not end with the claim that the nation is connected to the media, however. Acting as authoritative arbiters of information within the community, the mass media and the news media in particular contribute to the establishment of conceptual parameters of the nation through the development and distribution of text, sound, and images from home and abroad. This phenomenon has been labeled "flagging" by Michael Billig in his articulation of "banal nationalism" and is so commonplace according to his assessment as to escape the notice of all but the most attentive and mindful of media consumers: "In routine practices and everyday discourses, especially those in the mass media, the idea of nationhood is regularly flagged. Through such flagging, established nations are reproduced as nations, with their citizenry being unmindfully reminded of their national identity."[10] By definition, practices of flagging construct the aforementioned conceptual parameters, not as static and rigid boundaries but rather as fluid and dynamic discourses, daily reified according to media selectivity and representational perspective. As such, many academic discussions on the subject of national identity in both contemporary and historical contexts include analyses of the role played by mass media communication in this process:

> Benedict Anderson, Liah Greenfeld, and Ernest and Gellner all argue that national identity is communicatively constructed … For Liah Greenfeld, nationalism is the core idea around which contemporary human communities are organized, the constitutive element of modernity. Its medium is not force but language.[11]

This conception of contemporary national identity places language in the center of a fluid and constitutive process. In it, the contemporary media is a nationally specific institution possessive of unique attributes, trends, traits, and tendencies particular to a given social and cultural context. These particular cultural and historical contexts are themselves both bounded and distributed by a nation's media outlets through language and in particular, through centers of institutional language production and distribution. It is the national news media, then, that is the foundational, constitutive influence in the construction of both national identity and its inseparable counterpart, social cognition. Through the flagging of ideological values, the promotion of national traits, and through the substantive definition of "self" and "other", authoritative media language contributes substantially to the development of social cognition *nationally.*

Thus, mass media are an institutional, interactive location where national traits are constructed and connective communication and reification daily take place. Mass media, in this sense, are influenced by cultural norms, arising and existing as they do in a specific temporal and cultural context. They also and simultaneously participate actively in the continual formulation and maintenance of those norms. The result of this type of duality and agency is the existence of nationally specific media forms which are able to effectively structure contemporary cultural, political, and ideological realities for a broad and disparate audience. In so doing, the media influence the creation of a functional, national community.

The role of the contemporary mass media in identity construction and knowledge formation has given rise to the concept of the "mediated nation," a term describing the nature of nationhood and envisioned national characteristics as dependent upon active and repetitive representation in a mediated form. At the heart of the concept of the mediated nation is the nature of the relationship between media and citizen. With particular consideration for news media, the concept of a mediated nation considers the position of news makers and distributors as products of a particular national ethos empowered to affect and potentially alter the values and perspectives by which that nation is discursively formulated. In a scholarly analysis of these relationships in Greece, Mirca Madianou describes the complex nature of these associations and analyzes the manner in which the relationship between media and mediated impacts the formation of cultural norms and national identity:

> the media/identity relationship emerges as a multifaceted process that depends on context. The media provide a common reference for some, while for others those references might be experienced as exclusive ... the news is also a bridge to the outside world ... In this sense the media are at the heart of the tension between collective self-knowledge and collective self-representation that define cultural intimacy.[12]

In defining "cultural intimacy," the media, then, are able to represent "self" and "other" to the consuming public. These representations shape domestic and international events for the media consumer and are ideologically particular within each national community. This process is constitutive and regular, leading one scholar to conclude, "The media constitute us as citizens by offering us *processed* insights into an array of significant domains—economic, political, scientific and so forth."[13] Madianou's use of the word "intimacy" to define this relationship is, therefore, rhetorically appropriate; few other institutions have such frequent and close contact with such a large section of the society they represent. Likewise, few other institutions have an equivalent level of influence in the formation and maintenance of the national community. The "Mediated Nation" then becomes an ideological construct, a "creation of symbolic communicative spaces"[14] in which news information is told and retold. Through this presentation and institutionally acted re-presentation, values, norms, and a collective sense of national self is formulated. The media, in this way "assume a priestly obligation to undertake coverage on behalf of the group. Coverage is ... revelatory, providing visions of citizenship and conveying totem will."[15] Though comprised of multiple social and cultural processes, this relationship between media and consumer, to include media's impact upon the construction of nationhood and national identity, suggests the considerable "power of the media to determine the boundaries that affect practices and discourses about 'home' and 'belonging'" within specific national contexts.[16]

The mediated nation, therefore, constitutes the most authoritative, agreed-upon, and nationally accepted form of mediated self-representation within a given national community. Within it, the national news media community is formulated and daily reified through text, image, sound, and various other forms of institutional representation engendered by the nation's authoritative news media outlets: "The media are used to create occasions for consumers to identify with the public positions."[17] In representing self and other,[18] in constructing and fortifying the national news media community consistent with agreed-upon political, cultural, and economic boundaries, the authoritative mass media create "public discourse" that is both limiting and unifying in its outlook. The public discourse is limited in the sense that it accepts consistent representations and assertions while rejecting alternative, radical, or otherwise unacceptable ones. It is unifying in the means by which a community is constructed in this process across vast geographic spaces and, with reification and repetition, over long periods of time: "The social community is effectively united by the production of a shared sense of reality, which is materially inscribed in the dailiness of the newspaper or media broadcast."[19] This public discourse has the potential to be unifying to the point of exerting an all-encompassing inclusion upon the national news media community, overwhelming forms of resistance exacted by various subgroups within the community:

> As the subjects of publicity—its hearers, speakers, viewers, and doers—we have a different relation to ourselves, a different affect, from that which we have in other contexts. No matter what particularities of culture, race, and gender, or class we bring to bear on public discourse, the moment of apprehending something as public is one in which we imagine, if imperfectly, indifference to those particularities, to ourselves. We adopt the attitude of the public subject.[20]

In suggesting an "indifference" to particularities of subculture and identity at work in daily interactions within a mediated nation, this theory postulates the predominance of news media discourse and the formulation of a subject news public despite a multi-cultural, multi-ethnic community of media consumers. This can be understood considering the role of the media as selecting agent, rendering vast and complicated internal realities and external events as condensed snippets, structured portions of information made to represent complexity simply and palatably: "the media present these distant places to us, they simultaneously 'screen' them from us, in so far as the method of presentation inevitably distances us from the images we see."[21] Through this process of selection, the mass media determine what is to be revealed about the community it serves as well as the rest of the world at large. This process serves to influence engagement and structure perspective. The public of the national news media community is thereby created:

> Media channels engage with the problem of societal complexity, constituting new modes of interaction based on *visibility*: media personally occupy the *specialist* role of selecting, processing and producing vast networks of symbols and significant information (they are the gatekeepers and agenda setters), discursively interrogating decision makers (they serve as advocates), and making accessible the world 'out there' (or rather, selecting segments and constructing versions of it) on behalf of a more or less diffuse audience.[22]

Hence, the public discourse structured by the national news media creates a *national news media community* constituted by forms of representation and produced by the institution of the news media. The process of mediating a given nation becomes simultaneous to the process of the conceptual formation of that nation in the sense that formation refers to the establishment of shared perspectives, common values, and conceptual norms discursively created and distributed by the authoritative mass media.

In this theoretical model, the role of the news media in constructing public discourse, and therefore, as asserted, in creating and reifying the conceptual parameters of the nation is foundational to the integrity of contemporary national communities. This process effectively establishes what is public and what representations can be included and instituted as part of the public and what cannot. Public discourse and the media responsible for creating it are, in this sense, highly political agents within contemporary society:

> Once a public discourse [has] become specialized in the Western model, the subjective attitude adopted in public discourse became an inescapable but always unrecognized political force, governing what is publicly sayable— inescapable because only when images or texts can be understood as meaningful to a public rather than simply to oneself, or to specific others, can they be called public; unrecognized because this strategy of impersonal reference, in which one might say "The text addresses me" *and* "It addresses no one in particular," is a ground condition of intelligibility for public language.[23]

The "inescapable but always unrecognized political force" is an agent of substantial power within contemporary social interactions. It is both proscriptive, preventing what is not "publicly sayable" from being said, as well as prescriptive, informing, structuring, and imparting information and representations in a continual stream. This is the essence of public discourse: the power to create community and subsequently, the conceptualized nation.

Conclusion: the structure and function of the national news media community

Fundamental to considerations of publics, nations, and the news media that serves to influence their constitution is the differentiation between a private, or experientially verifiable world, and a public world which is by definition an unconnected, unverified space. Knowledge of the unverifiable depends upon that which is otherwise personally unseen being represented through sound, text, and/ or image by those who have seen it to those who have not. The process of individuals actively orienting themselves to this un-experienced or otherwise unverified world has been called "public connection" and aids the process by which publics are created.[24] The process of individuals, corporations, groups, and institutions representing that which is distant and otherwise unverifiable to individuals is the process of mediation and results in the necessary creation of a "mediated public connection."[25] Much like Madianou's concept of the mediated nation, the mediated public connection describes the relationship between the diverse mass media and the assembled, attentive audience they seek to reach:

> We have introduced the term "public connection" to capture a dimension of daily life: that is, an orientation towards a public world beyond matters of a purely private concern. We talk of "mediated public connection" where that orientation is sustained principally by our practice of consuming media.[26]

The "orientation towards a public world" can be either fleeting or habitual. When fleeting, membership in a public is likewise fleeting. When habitual, realms of specific concern become constitutive of stable publics centered on an active engagement in elements or the entirety of a mediated public world. Even when fleeting, however, the manner of representation of the public world is specific within the bounds of the nation, and therefore is indicative of elements of both national culture and national identity: "the very conception of the newspaper implies the refraction of even 'world events' into a specific imagined world of vernacular readers."[27] These readers are members of one large community, imagined as "solid simultaneity through time"[28] by news media representations of a public world of shared concern. Daily these readers attend to the products of a particular media system. It is under these conditions that the national news media community develops and flourishes in contemporary communities around the world.

Appreciating the idea of the mediated public connection allows a more polished picture of the concept of the national news media community to take shape. It has been argued to this point that the concepts "nation," "public," and "public sphere," are each forms of organized social bodies which are related and relatable to one another. Each is constituted in part based upon distributed cultural productions. Those cultural productions most relevant to the current discussion include items from the printed news media which are sufficiently broad (i.e., national) in their character, and which contain constructed representations of both the local and the international political and social worlds. Items from the printed news media are daily produced and distributed meaning that there is a constant flow of representation and re-representation circulating within a bounded or imagined collective space. This process lies at the heart of the articulation of the national news media community.

The media of a nation and its representation of the outside world within the national space are also highly influential in the structure of contemporary identity by virtue of their role in constructing ongoing discourse and distributing meaningful symbols within the nation. As discourse is concerned, "national identities, as special forms of social identities, are produced, reproduced, as well as transformed and dismantled, *discursively*."[29] But at their essence, these representations are symbolic, and it is the production and distribution of these symbols that renders the news media so very powerful in this process: "The press is central to any discussion of the production and dissemination of symbols, either in the form of political facts or opinions or in commercial messages."[30] Thanks to the national media, these national symbols are now made "part of the life of every individual."[31] Through these processes the national news media not only portrays events in the aforementioned public world for the consuming members of the nation, it structures the ideology and value systems around which the constituent public bases their demand for those very representations. This renders the influence of the national news media a double-edged sword, an active though subtle dual value system through which a bounded national group comprehends world events while demanding verification for the manner and form of their comprehension. Effectively, this reifies the national self and solidifies the national character in the imagined, Andersonian sense:

> If a nation is an imagined community and at the same time a mental construct, an imaginary complex of ideas containing at least the defining elements of collective unity and equality, of boundaries and autonomy, then this image is real to the extent that one is convinced of it, believes in it and identifies with it emotionally.[32]

Belief in the standardized system of news media representation in a given nation along with an arguably even firmer belief in the demand for representation of the public world that is ostensibly individual, independent, and totally organic, makes the national connection between individuals within it much stronger. News events are portrayed according to the parameters of a discursive structure; sustained news stories have restricted, palatable frames which are relied upon when information is distributed for public consumption. In this way, nation, knowledge, culture, and self are all communicated through the national news media, and are daily maintained through the process of repetitive representation and distribution in a given territory.

These representations might be actively addressed and studied within the sphere of their distribution, or then again, might be only passively regarded, or perhaps not regarded at all. Whether passively regarded or actively examined, the products of the authoritative print media within the imagined or political limitations of a national space impact the development of public knowledge within a specific imagined national boundary. They formulate perspectives on the national self and create opposition to that collective association with constructed and/or contrived external others. They posit archetypes and images through language and picture through which the represented world is processed and understood. They unify through overt display as well as passive representation. In short, the national news media present and re-present the wide world to their constituent, consuming public, and as such, play an enormously influential role in the formation of knowledge within a given national community.

As well, the national news media substantially contributes to the national character and irrevocably constructs national culture. The nation, Anderson's imagined community, can therefore be viewed as the community of printed information and the values and ideologies imparted by media products. This renders the impact of the national media as cultural as well as social and ideological. Naturally these roles are complementary and related given that "the culture in which one has been *taught* to communicate becomes the core of one's identity."[33] The national news media is the standard bearer for the manner in which a nation's inhabitants engage with one another while simultaneously defining and circumscribing culture, identity, and ideology. The character of national identity and the conceptual parameters of national discourse are both heavily dependent upon national news media representations.

Following discussions above considering the theoretical formations of discourse, the news media, the nation, and the national news media community, the subsequent chapter will engage in a brief examination of the specific functions of the news media in contemporary society in the United States and the United Kingdom. This discussion will necessarily move away from the theoretical and into the practical in preparation for subsequent case studies investigating print news media representations of Palestine–Israel in the two national news media communities. Where necessary, the discussion to take place will specify divergences in the structure and/or behavior of the news media in each society. In other cases, the structure specified will function as an encompassing one, incorporating the characteristics of both national, commercial media institutions. The goal of the next chapter, then, is to describe the distribution and concomitant consumption of information regarding political conflict in Palestine–Israel, and to connect this particular form of news information with broader news media practices and traditions in two countries. This effort will also highlight relevant characteristics of general public consumption that might serve to illuminate subsequent discussions of linguistic representations in the printed news.

Notes

1   I employ Sand liberally in this section of the study because of his innovative description of the theoretical concept *nation*. And while his primary motivation in exploring these ideas is for the purposes of articulating the ramifications of concepts of nationhood of the Jewish people, that fact, and the fact that this study is partially devoted to considerations of the position of the Jewish nation in contemporary discourse is purely coincidental.

2   Shlomo Sand, *The Invention of the Jewish People* (London: Verso, 2009), 24 (emphasis in original).

3   Ibid., 23 (emphasis in original).

4   Ernest Renan, "What is a Nation?" in Homi Bhabha (Ed.) *Nation and Narration* (London: Routledge, 1990), 19.

5   Ernest Gellner, *Nations and Nationalism: New Perspectives on the Past* (Oxford: Blackwell, 1983), 6 (emphasis in original).

6   Ibid., 4

7   Benedict Anderson, *Imagined Communities* (London: Verso, (2006) [1983]), 7 (emphasis in original).

8   Ibid., 134.

9   Ibid., 135.

10 Michael Billig, *Banal Nationalism* (London: Sage Publications, 1995), 154.

11 Carolyn Marvin and David W. Ingle, *Blood Sacrifice and the Nation: Totem Rituals and the American Flag* (Cambridge: Cambridge University Press, 1999), 25–6.

12 Mirca Madianou, *Mediating the Nation: News, Audiences and the Politics of Identity* (London: UCL Press, 2005), 137.

13 Luke Goode, *Jürgen Habermas: Democracy and the Public Sphere* (London: Pluto Press, 2005), 95 (emphasis in the original).

14 Madianou, *Mediating the Nation*, 5.

15 Marvin and Ingle, *Blood Sacrifice and the Nation*, 145.

16 Madianou, *Mediating the Nation*, 5.

17 Craig Calhoun, "Introduction: Habermas and the Public Sphere" in Craig Calhoun (Ed.), *Habermas and the Public Sphere* (Cambridge, Massachusetts: The MIT Press, 1997) [1992]), 26.

18 For an elaboration on this particular national news media function, see Stuart Hall, "The Spectacle of the 'Other'" in Stuart Hall (Ed.). *Representation: Cultural Representations and Signifying Practices.* (London: Sage, 1997).

19 David Morley, *Home Territories: Media, Mobility and Identity* (London: Routledge, 2000), 109.

20 Michael Warner, "The Mass Public and the Mass Subject" in C. Calhoun (Ed.). *Habermas and the Public Sphere* (Cambridge, Massachusetts: The MIT Press, (1997) [1992]), 377.

21 Morley, *Home Territories,* 183.

22 Goode, *Jürgen Habermas,* 93-4) (emphasis in the original).

23 Warner, "The Mass Public and the Mass Subject," 378-9 (emphasis in the original).

24 Nick Couldry, Tanja Livingstone, and Tim Markham., *Media Consumption and Public Engagement: Beyond Presumption of* Attention (New York: Palgrave MacMillan, 2007), 3.

25 Ibid, 65.

26 Ibid.

27 Anderson, *Imagined Communities,* 63.

28 Ibid.

29 Ruth Wodak, Rudolf de Cillia, Martin Reisigl, Karin Liebhart, *The Discursive Construction of National Identity* (Edinburgh: Edinburgh University Press, 1999), 3-4.

30 Hanno Hardt, *Social Theories of the Press: Early German & American Perspectives* (Beverly Hills, CA: Sage, 1979), 21.

31 Eric Hobsbawm, *Nations and Nationalism since 1780: Programme, Myth, Reality* (Cambridge: Cambridge University Press, 1990), 142.

32 Wodak, et al, *The Discursive Construction of National Identity*, 22.

33 Gellner, *Nations and Nationalism*, 61 (emphasis in the original).

4 Covering Palestine–Israel news media in the United States and Great Britain

The contemporary print news media: history, structure, principles, and practices

An examination of the recent history of the contemporary news media, particularly in the form of printed news in both the United States and Great Britain, reveals a significant shift in the structure, objectives, and organization of that industry, and of news as a product within both societies beginning in the early part of the nineteenth century. During that crucial period, the production of news became a business subsumed within the growth of commercialism and capital-intensive industry in both countries.[1] The organization of news as a product changed in its orientation from issues of local relevance restricted by adherence to a specific political ideology, to a profit-driven production lacking overt political affiliation in order to appeal to the largest number of potential consumers possible. News became big business with ties to and associations with other large commercial firms. Advertising was introduced onto the pages of major newspapers by owners seeking to supplement increasing production costs while expanding markets and driving down the price of their product. As a result, newspapers became substantially cheaper for consumers while at the same time becoming drastically more expensive for capitalists to own and operate. Newspaper ownership therefore became an exclusive proposition precluding the possibility of newspaper ownership by working-class citizens on both sides of the Atlantic. By the mid-nineteenth century changes in ownership, production, and distribution of newspapers made creating the news an endeavor of the elite. By the decades of the 1920s and 1930s, the hegemonic[2] structure of news production in both Great Britain and the United States had been firmly established with the power to present news events and distribute news information firmly in the hands of a distinguishable, elite, and wealthy minority. This minority group, in turn, was able to structure news and distribute information to the recipient public, news-consuming majority.[3]

A century on from these developments in the news industry, today's news products typically adhere to this commercially driven, corporate structure. This fact has changed the manner of the provision of news information irrevocably:

In most western nations the press was at first explicitly political, regulated, and/or censored by the government, and subsidized by the state and/or political parties. As capitalism developed and the profitability of commercial publishing became clear, newspapers tended to come under business control and operate in accordance with commercial principles.[4]

The fact that mainstream news now exists exclusively as a for-profit industry restricts the information appearing within it to a narrow range of what is considered marketable. In fact, global media have become so inundated with pro-corporate messages that they might accurately be called "missionaries of our age, promoting the virtues of commercialism and the market loudly and incessantly."[5] Within this role, news media products can be seen as extensions of corporate interests serving as jewels in the crown of the enormous media empires: "the twenty-nine largest media systems account for over half of the output of newspapers [in the world]."[6] The corporate, conglomerate nature of these expansive industries renders news information as news creation, recasting processes of information delivery to recipient consumers according to the parameters of multinational commercial interests. These interests typically tend toward aggressive commercial expansion and concomitant financial acquisition in accordance with the driving principles of unfettered, free-market, capitalist industry.

In order for news agencies and their parent, conglomerate corporations to be able to produce national and international news containing politically oriented content, close access to the sources of information, particularly national policy makers, their staffs, and other members of government is key. To maintain this type of close access, newsmakers must cultivate positive relationships with individuals and institutions working on issues of national policy. Too much harsh criticism or too little championing of particular policies and the journalist risks having access to the sources of news information reduced or revoked. Speaking specifically about this phenomenon within the news media institution in the contemporary United States, analyst Daniel Hallin suggests that:

> Journalists today have far more intimate and regular contact with government officials than they did in the nineteenth century; this means both that [media consumers] get far more information about what government is doing, and also that the picture of the world the media give us today is far more closely tied to the perspectives of official policy makers.[7]

This close relationship constitutes a second, critical characteristic of contemporary news production and is, like politically unaffiliated and commercially driven news publications, a fairly recent historical development. This feature of the news industry also represents a departure from the principles upon which a free and politically disassociated news media was established, effectively compromising the traditional, idealized values of news journalism within democratic society: "Liberal notions of journalism see the media as watchdogs … paradoxically, of course, the media in liberal capitalist democracies are largely subordinate both to capital and to the state."[8] In essence, these assessments of the role of the news media within "capitalist democracies" reposition news production and information distribution within contemporary Western societies by subsuming these processes firmly within the state agenda, not outside of it as has often been suggested. Contemporary conceptions of Western media systems should account for this theoretical shift and should begin to reimagine the news media within capitalist democracies as an important component of state policy and operations, both domestically and abroad.

If Western media are subordinate to state interests then little separates the output and function of the news media in the national news communities under examination here from those within dictatorial regimes with overtly stated media controls. According to this reassessment, news media in the United States and the United Kingdom should be expected to function as a complicit institution within those states, endorsing state goals in both the political and economic arenas. Journalistic output of members of the contemporary news media should be expected to be partial, especially regarding those issues that are considered to be politically sensitive topics within national policy. As a result, the communicative process within contemporary democratic societies would be severely restricted. According to Hallin, therefore, within the contemporary west "It is wrong, as an empirical matter, to assume that the news media simply provide information. It is a misunderstanding of the nature of human communication to believe that they could do so."[9] Instead, the news media provides its consumers with a framed version of the information at hand, one that is closely aligned with state interests.

The function of the news media in a society where its producers are of the same mind as those residing within the corridors of power is that of reproduction, simply and succinctly, so as to be absorbed by the consuming public in a manner the power elites see fit. But this level of acquiescence and unanimity on the part of journalist and policy maker can fluctuate: "the behavior of the media is closely tied to the degree of consensus among political elites: when consensus is strong, the media play a relatively passive role and generally reinforce official power to manage public opinion."[10] That the degree of consensus among those with substantial political power affects the manner of presentation preferred by the news media is to be expected when members of the active news media are closely tied to members of the national government. Still, in this regard, Hallin leaves open the possibility that the prevalence of multiple, contradictory viewpoints among the political elite would influence and alter the resulting media voice:

> News content may not mirror the facts, but the media, as institutions, do reflect the prevailing pattern of political debate: when consensus is strong, they tend to stay within the limits of the political discussion it defines; when it begins to break down, coverage becomes increasingly critical and diverse in the viewpoints it represents, and increasingly difficult for officials to control.[11]

Public officials and policy makers are aware that a lack of consensus about a particular policy is likely to mean a concomitant lack of control of news information being distributed about that policy. This idea alone may, in fact, serve to encourage a substantial measure of unanimity amongst political elites instead of debate and disagreement. So, although "The mass media are not a solid monolith on all issues ... views that challenge fundamental premises ... will be excluded from the mass media even when elite controversy over tactics rages fiercely."[12] These ideas strongly suggest that the idea role of the news media in society as that of a public champion or highly interested watchdog is an antiquated one. Rather, a more apt analogy might be the press as a very active weather vane alerting the public to the opinions of the policy makers, and contextualizing, justifying, or supporting those opinions to a substantial extent. And while these structures may apply in general terms in considerations of daily news media publications, media scholars Daniel Hallin, Tamar Liebes, Gadi Wolfsfeld, and others have shown that the structural symbiosis of press and politician converge to an even greater extent when political conflict comprises the content of the news media story in question.[13]

These characteristics of contemporary journalism—an adherence to global, commercial interests; a physical and ideological closeness with national policy makers; and a widespread support of the majority view on relevant issues—are significant in political, social, and cognitive terms. These factors significantly quiet alternative or radical points of view in mainstream, authoritative publications while those embracing such views are pushed outside the mediated public connection.[14] Those individuals whose concerns, interests, and/or values are not represented by the mainstream news are also not likely to engage in matters of shared communal concern given that the daily news appears unwilling or unable to address them directly. Restriction of the form of information provided, therefore, and routine support of elite political and economic perspectives potentially affects cognition as well as socialization, and perpetuates media hegemony and unidirectional media influence. At issue then is not simply perception, public opinion, or the extent of basic knowledge held by media consumers; the possibility of involvement, socialization, and the continued viability of an engaged community must also be called into questioned.

US news media coverage of the Palestine–Israel: orientalism and the clash of civilizations

In the United States, journalism as a profession has been called "the primary institution of the American public sphere" and the authoritative news media is considered to be "the major institution outside of the state which performs the function of providing political interpretation and critique."[15] In this role, the news media are responsible for the provision of knowledge about the otherwise unobservable world to the news consuming public within the United States. This public knowledge in turn sustains policy as lawmakers use the support of their constituencies to push forward laws, directives, and policies. In her investigation into the manner in which the mainstream media in the United States covers the Palestinian–Israeli conflict Marda Dunsky elucidates the outcome of this relationship:

even though U.S. Mideast policy has for decades revolved around Israel, the mainstream media seldom examine that policy in a critical light. As a result, alternative and oppositional discourses are effectively stifled, with public challenge to that policy unable to accumulate a critical mass.[16]

According to Dunsky, the absence of a balanced view of the Palestinian–Israeli conflict from the mainstream news media results from consistent US foreign policy support for Israel and is the primary contributor to the lack of development of a "critical mass" among the news consuming US public. As a result, public debate, especially in authoritative forums, is quieted. This lack of public demand for change in US policy in the region is fuelled by media representations of the region and results in the perpetuation of existing policies of successive US governments. The complicity of the press with government policy in this instance contributes to a particular construction of public knowledge and the maintenance of the political status quo. In so doing, the press effectively abandons its role as mediator in favor of a role as mouthpiece for existing political positions. This structure holds true in domestic policy but is especially pertinent in the representation of American foreign policy to news media consumers back home: "foreign news reporting helps the powerful mobilize public opinion (or quiescence) behind the basic goals of policies on which most Americans have little information."[17]

Writing at roughly the same time as Dunsky, in 2007 Stephen Walt and John Mearsheimer, political scientists from Harvard University and the University of Chicago, respectively, published *The Israel Lobby*, an analysis of the unique diplomatic and political relationship between the United States and Israel. Among the many facets this relationship presented, the authors point to a consistent bias within the news media in the United States that serves to frame the Palestinian–Israeli conflict exclusively in terms of Israeli victimhood and Palestinian aggression. According to their assessment:

> A key part of preserving positive public attitudes toward Israel is to ensure that the mainstream media's coverage of Israel and the Middle East consistently favors Israel and does not call U.S. support into question in any way ... the American media's coverage of Israel tends to be strongly biased in Israel's favor, especially when compared with news coverage in other democracies.[18]

Although the majority of *The Israel Lobby* examines the financial and ideological support given to Israel,[19] the authors' candid assessment of the complicity of the authoritative U.S. news media in maintaining a one-sided view of the Palestinian–Israeli conflict within the United States parallels the findings of Dunsky and other scholars. And according to theories of media-establishment relations outlined here, this trend within the US news media institution stands to reason given the ideological alignment between policy and news language present in contemporary democracies. As the history of diplomatic and economic relations between the United States and Israel over the last half-century is one of virtually unfailing support on the part of the former to the benefit of the latter, then the dominant framing within the news media puts forward pro-Israeli perspectives.[20] Though certainly not alone amongst news media topics framed according to specific foreign policy goals, presentation of events in Palestine–Israel within the United States can be seen as a primary case in point of the US "Government's manipulation of the American media and media participation in foreign policy [conditioning] situations where events are often shaped to fit policies."[21]

The generally pro-Israeli perspective of the authoritative news media in the United States is presented to consumers through a variety of different strategies. One of them is explained in detail by arguably the most well-known academic who has worked on explaining the view of the East as it is defined by the West, Edward Said. In his 1978 publication, *Orientalism*, he describes the systematic and wholly pejorative representation of the Muslim, Arab, Persian East at the hands of European scholars, writers, and clergymen beginning in the eighteenth century. Writing a few years later, Said directly addressed issues of Western popular media representation of Muslims and Arabs in his 1981 work *Covering Islam.* Said explains that within the US media "the picture of Islam … is likely to be quite uniform, in some ways reductive, and monochromatic," a representation that was only given more representative fodder by the September 2001 attack on the World Trade Centers and the subsequent US military invasion of Afghanistan and Iraq as well as drone strikes and other military operations in Pakistan, Yemen, and elsewhere in the Muslim East.[22] Furthering Said, political scientist Fawaz Gerges identifies that by the late twentieth and early twenty-first century "Americans ha[d] a rich, full reservoir of negative stereotypes about the Muslim world … perpetuated and reinforced by the mass media."[23] According to this perspective, American attitudes about political actors that were Arab and/or Muslim during the late 1990s were motivated by an innate racism which established a simplistic but useful dichotomy in which Arab/Muslim represented eastern, exotic, illogical, chaotic, and inherently violent as opposed to broadly Western representations of order, logic, peacefulness, and good.

This type of strict cultural divide is at the heart of author Samuel Huntington's oft-mentioned "Clash of Civilizations" theory espoused in his 1996 work *The Clash of Civilizations and the Remaking of World Order.* In it he describes the instability of the latter twentieth century as a direct result of ancient civilizations whose values, ethics, and ideologies were simply incompatible with one another. Among the ancient civilizations Huntington delineates are the Islamic and the Western, two civilizations whose oppositional values are bound to throw them into open and unavoidable conflict. At the heart of this conflict are incompatible value systems and immutable cultural differences which cannot be resolved through peaceable means or diplomatic measures. The increasing levels of interactions of the late-twentieth and early-twenty first centuries have initiated increased hostilities between the two civilizations, the attacks of September 11 being a potent example of this. And, according to Huntington, more hostility is sure to come given the rigid nature of cultural difference—all people within a delineated Huntingtonian "civilization" being colored by precisely the same biases, perceptions, and motivations as all of their civilization-mates—and given the ancient roots of these disputes. Within this frame of thought, there can be no Western hope for reason, peace-making, or logical interaction with the Islamic Civilization. Their civilization is fundamentally different from ours and will remain so into perpetuity. Huntington's broad-brush approach and stereotypical vision of the "World Order" cloaked with academic credibility and a sophisticated language gives weight to further essentializing treatments of the Muslim East of the kind described by Said and Gerges. This perspective adds a convenient academic element to reductive representations in the news media providing further concretization to the narrow frame presented to the news media consumer seeking information about Arabs, Islam, or the East in general.

The stereotypes present for the average news media consumer in the United States directed towards Muslim culture, Arab states, or Arabs in general have become seamlessly transferred onto Palestine and the Palestinians during the latter twentieth and early twenty-first century. One of the most direct and efficient vehicles for the delivery of these stereotypical notions to the public at large was the authoritative mass media and in particular the printed press. The dichotomy created by Huntington and accepted by certain influential scholars as well as many major media outlets became the cultural, historical, and political template by which to view the Palestinian–Israeli conflict. This template was asserted and maintained in various news stories reporting on events in Palestine–Israel where the qualities and character of the broadly framed West were assigned to Israel and in the process remade from Western Christian values into "Judeo-Christian" values while the aggressive, barbaric, and violent character of the Muslim east subsumed the Palestinians. In these renditions of the conflict in the major media outlets in the United States:

> Israel has appeared as a bastion of Western civilization hewn (with much approbation and self-congratulation) out of the Islamic wilderness. Secondly, Israel's security in American eyes has become conveniently interchangeable with fending off Islam, perpetuating Western hegemony, and demonstrating the virtues of modernization. In these ways, three sets of illusions economically buttress and reproduce one another in the interests of shoring up the Western self-image and promoting Western power over the Orient: the view of Islam, the ideology of modernization, and the affirmation of Israel's general value to the West.[24]

Anticipating the clash of civilizations argument, Said already (in 1981) identifies the cognitive outcomes of the ongoing reductive nature of representations of Muslims and Arabs—and later specifically Palestinians—in major media outlets in the United States. In these representations, Israel is attributed with all the qualities of the moral and righteous West. Their political and discursive counterparts, the Palestinians, are imbued with all the aggressive and insidious character of the Muslim East. This includes, as Said instructs, not only images of Islam as violent and unstable but also as inherently anti-modern or backward-looking in its orientation. In this way, when discussing the Palestinian–Israeli conflict, the news media in the United States informs on "cultural interactions in which antagonists promote their own frames of the conflict while the news media attempt to reconstruct a story that can be understood by their audience."[25]

British news media and the Middle East

The history of Great Britain in the Middle East is much longer and much more involved than that of the United States, a relative newcomer in world politics by comparison. It has been suggested that this historical link with the region coupled with the not so distant memory of direct British rule over the area of Palestine–Israel[26] affects the character of contemporary news media coverage of the region. This historical memory may act upon news media coverage, given that political leaders and members of the intelligentsia are more in touch with the social and cultural nuances as well as the historical development of the Middle East than their US counterparts. This sensitivity, if it was to exist, would demand a different type of coverage than that provided in the United States, one which provided more in-depth historical context to unfolding news pieces from the region. Trudy Rubin, former correspondent for the *Christian Science Monitor* in the United States became aware of this distinction between British and US journalistic perspectives on the Middle East during her tenure covering the region: "The British obviously have had long links with the Middle East. They consider themselves involved there and that creates a certain relationship that's more intense, that wants some more in-depth background."[27] As with news media in the United States, Rubin's commentary here connects both journalistic and political practices in the United Kingdom, suggesting that contemporary British coverage of the Middle East is affected ongoing foreign policy in the region. In addition to this political conditioning, British journalists covering the Middle East are able to call upon a large archive of historical material when covering unfolding events in the Middle East. This presumed, in-built consideration and broad historical concern by members of the British political elite combined with extensive archival material available to contemporary British journalists might be responsible for sustaining a more careful, more involved coverage of contemporary events in Palestine–Israel. As a result, British readership may be accustomed to engaging "an amount of material which probably very few American readers would be interested in digesting, and in an analytical way" when it comes to that specific foreign affairs topic.[28] The potential development of a more informed, more practiced, and diligent readership would in turn fuel demand for more in-depth coverage of the Middle East, creating a cognitively profitable cyclical relationship between readership and journalist/coverage.

The historical connection between Great Britain and the Middle East, and the potential cultivation of nuanced information about the region can serve to create a stronger mediated public connection within Great Britain than that which exists in the United States. Mentioned in the previous chapter, the concept of a mediated public connection is based on two assumptions:

The first … is that, as citizens, we share an orientation to a public world where matters of shared concern are … we call this orientation "public connection". The second assumption is that public connection is principally sustained by a convergence in the media people consume.[29]

In assessments of the functions of the popular authoritative media in the United States, the position of the media within the political system as a vital component necessary to sustain the political status quo negates their ability to independently determine and discuss "matters of shared concern." As such, the mediated public connection is significantly altered—if not fractured—for media consumers in the United States. In Great Britain, however, the "orientation to … matters of shared concern" would include wars, conflicts, and political disputes geographically distant from the United Kingdom itself.[30] Attention to issues ahead of or outside of government consideration or intervention within the popular news media in Great Britain generates the aforementioned conscientious readership and sustains the theory of a mediated public connection in Great Britain. According to the existence of both a significant historical connection to the Middle East, and the presence of a viable mediated public connection in the United Kingdom, news media coverage of the Middle East in general, and of Palestine–Israel specifically, can be expected to be generally more contextualized and more historically broad than that found in the United States.

Another reason to anticipate a comparative difference in the coverage of the Middle East when comparing US coverage with popular, authoritative British media outlets is a difference in the character of the British democratic system. Like the deep historical connection with the region and a healthy mediated public connection, a difference in the structure of the democratic system in Great Britain prescribes a qualitatively different role for the popular news media in the country. Couldry, Livingstone, and Markham also comment upon this different character of British democracy and the manner in which it engenders a different participatory role for the citizen than might be found in the United States:

> In Britain the link between citizen engagement and government action has *usually*, not exceptionally, been problematic, and the agenda of "community norms" cannot, automatically, be assumed to encourage "naturally" an agenda of political participation or engagement.[31]

The authors here identify a democratic character in which direct citizen action has not usually influenced policy outcomes and therefore has resulted in a stilted form of citizen engagement and political participation. In identifying a typically problematic link between "citizen engagement" and "government action" in Britain, these authors anticipate an enhanced and a more independent role for the popular news media in the United Kingdom than in other, more participatory democracies where direct and regular citizen engagement is the norm. In this model, popular news media have more freedom to discuss a broad range of issues without sparking consistent citizen reaction. This is not a reflection of a lack of consumption of the public media, but rather a status quo of inaction where citizen engagement is the exception not the norm. In this atmosphere, discussions from various perspectives of a conflict or political dispute generated by the authoritative news media do not directly undermine government policies as they would, for example, in the United States when discussing Palestine–Israel.

Given the presence of a healthy mediated public connection between citizenry and government and the existence of a weak civil society which only rarely sustains collective community action, news media coverage of the Middle East might be expected to be diverse, varied, and balanced. While few would argue that this describes British media engagement with the Middle East in its entirety, these attributes are sometimes true of the British press when compared to their US counterparts. Previous research on this topic has shown that British news media coverage of Muslim communities and of Islam in general demonstrates a "wide diversity of representation than its global image" and that, depending on the news source in question, might even display sympathy or compassion with the plight of the Arab or Muslim minority within Great Britain.[32] It is also clear from other coordinated studies into British media coverage that when exploring conflict within the Middle East, in Palestine–Israel and elsewhere, the British news media presents reports that more closely parallel the position of international law as well as the findings of independent human rights groups.[33] The combination of these factors tends to promote a news media community in which diversity of opinion is valued. In general, these values can be detected in British news media coverage of both domestic and foreign matters extending to and including British coverage of the Palestinian–Israeli conflict as well.

The BBC

The discussion of the BBC and its role in British news media here predicts the subsequent inclusion of a few news articles from the BBC World Monitoring Service in the case study chapters in this book. This marks an important exception to the exclusive analysis of print news media publications in this investigation given that the BBC World Service does not include a newspaper outlet (though like most of the sources investigated in this work, the BBC does produce electronic print articles). The inclusion of the BBC in the data sets to follow might therefore seem inconsistent with the overall approach of this work and might be criticized as deterministic data selection intended to condition a preordained investigative outcome. As explained in detail below, however, the BBC is a unique institution in the news media communities under examination here. It was founded as an instrument of and for the British public, and despite a myriad of institutional, historical, and cultural alterations since its inception, still retains a modicum of that remit today. As a publicly-funded news source, the BBC has no counterpart in the United States which renders its influence in British news making unique on both sides of the Atlantic. As well, it continues to possess a powerful influence in the structuring of information in the UK which renders an investigation of its news publications vitally important in terms of the language present within the contemporary British news. Its impact upon both the structure of news information and public knowledge within the UK, therefore, makes the inclusion of a limited number of these sources in this work's data analysis essential within the context of the current scholarly investigation. A brief discussion of its development and the history of its coverage of the Middle East is engaged here, therefore, within the context of a broader discussion of the history of British political and journalistic engagement with the Middle East in order to provide the background information upon which to base the subsequent analysis of news media language in the US and the UK in the coverage of Palestine–Israel.

Crucial to the promotion of diverse coverage within the British news media community is the publicly funded British Broadcasting Corporation: the BBC. This company was founded as a non-commercial venture in response to the growing commercialism and expanding capitalism of the latter 1920s. Rejecting this expansive commercialism, the BBC was established "with a public service mandate and a certain degree of autonomy from the government."[34] Publicly funded, the BBC is not a for-profit enterprise and therefore devotes only minimal print space to advertising. In view of this level of journalistic freedom, the BBC is more likely to report issues related to the Palestinian–Israeli conflict from a perspective outside the official rhetoric of the British government, which is designed to safeguard British foreign policy in the region. This allows the BBC to employ terminology and commentary more closely aligned with United Nations legislation, and more in line with the position of the international community as regards the ongoing conflict than many publications within the United States.

In an example of this, BBC Middle East Editor Jeremy Bowen commented on the difference between applying terminology preferred by the United Nations and the international community versus terminology that prefers foreign policy precedents as engaged by the United States, and to a lesser extent, Great Britain, "We call the Israeli building in occupied territory 'settlements' … Would we call them neighbourhoods? No we wouldn't. We'd make the point that they're considered by international law to be settlements on occupied land and therefore illegal. We've always made that point."[35] According to Bowen the preferred nomenclature for places, issues, and events surrounding the Palestinian–Israeli conflict is that used by the United Nations and the international community. While criticized as partiality by those preferring an Israeli-centric perspective on regional issues, Bowen went on to state that naming conflict events using appellations preferred by the international community actually reflects the BBC's consistent desire to report events in the Middle East impartially, and in so doing protect itself from the perception of bias as much as possible.

The position of the BBC regarding its coverage of the Middle East and its influence upon public knowledge about the region is heavily influential within authoritative news media discourse inside the United Kingdom. It is nearer to the position of a publicly mandated news organization fulfilling the role of social servant than any rival news agency within Britain (or, for that matter, in the US). According to Bowen, the BBC consciously attempts to build rapport with the British news media consuming public and strives to present itself as a more interested and engaged news agency compared to other, more commercially oriented news producers throughout Great Britain. This attempted public connection is sustained at least in part by the community tax that contributes to the funding of the BBC and ensures that it remains nearly a commercial-free news enterprise. According to Bowen, these factors create and sustain community interest between consumers and the BBC: "people feel they have a stake in [the BBC] and they do because they pay for it directly. It's not indirectly through buying stuff they see in adverts."[36]

And while this community connection is unique to BBC readers and viewers, other news coverage within the country has taken on an avowed, critical character as well. In *The Guardian*, elements of pro-citizen commentary are present in their news coverage, both foreign and domestic. In reporting on tensions within British communities, *The Guardian* is reported to have "greater 'sympathetic identification' with minorities than other papers" and in their reporting therefore are as likely to present the viewpoints of those outside of established British society as of those within the British economic and power elite.[37] Britain's *Independent* has received similar evaluations from news media analysts. Falling very far outside of this group of social critics is *The Sun* whose preference for "populist discourse" renders it all but mute on contemporary political issues, both foreign and domestic, that are otherwise covered extensively by the aforementioned competing news organizations.[38] Unlike the BBC, these publications, while popular as well as authoritative, remain largely bound by the quest for markets, profits, advertising, and adherence to state policy.

Orientalism in the British press

This is not to say that the contemporary news media in Great Britain is free from bias or that it is completely outfitted as a champion of minority, international, or human rights. Like their counterparts in the United States, the authoritative news media in Great Britain comprise a diverse institution incorporating numerous publications and broadcasts structured and developed by thousands of individuals. As such, although the presence of a healthy mediated public connection allows for a wide range of perspectives in reporting, the news media, like their US counterparts, can also distribute coverage that is essentialized and repetitive. In 2002, researcher Elisabeth Poole conducted a study that demonstrated that popular British news media coverage of Islam and Muslim communities within the UK included a number of Orientalist perspectives and was responsible for creating a narrow and pejorative representation of British Muslims. As mentioned in the discussion of US news media tendencies, coverage of Arab communities, of Muslims, or of Islam can affect public perception of Palestine–Israel given the transference of meaning from "Muslim" or "Arab" to "Palestine" or "Palestinian." The elucidation of trends of reporting of Arabs, Muslims, and/or Islam in the authoritative British press is therefore useful in determining similarities between British and US news media communities as it is in appreciating the coverage of issues related to Palestine–Israel.

According to Poole, the late twentieth century saw a spate of events reported in the popular British press involving British Muslims. These events included the Salman Rushdie affair in 1988, the introduction of *halal* meat (meat from animals slaughtered in accordance with Islamic law) into the British primary school system in 1989, the First Gulf War (and British foreign policy during this conflict) in 1991, culminating with likely the most significant of all news media events in British or perhaps Western popular discourse on Islam, the September 11, 2001 attacks in the United States. As a result, news consumers in Great Britain were exposed to representations of this community on a daily basis for months during this period. The frames of representation put forth by the British press in discussing these issues were decidedly narrow. These representations created a wholly negative view of Islam, Arab culture, and the British Muslim community for news media consumers in the UK. Attached to these representations were a restricted number of plausible and intentional meanings that adequately "homogenized" British Muslims as "a negative idea of the Other, an economical and cultural threat."[39] Included among these representations were images and assertions of Muslims as "backward, irrational, unchanging, fundamentalist, misogynist, threatening, manipulative in the use of their faith for political and personal gain."[40] Muslim communities were posed as a general threat to Christian Britain contributing to a "demise of Christian values and thus moral disintegration."[41] Muslim Britain came to be viewed as a Fifth Column of subversive activity inside of the UK.

With representations such as these prevalent in the British press during certain periods of coverage, it is conceivable that British public perceptions of Arabs or of Islam might yet remain largely negative. This opinion would have the power to color British news media coverage of the Palestinian–Israeli conflict, given the discursive alignment of Israel with the broadly conceived west and associated Western Christian-Judeo values. Palestine and the Palestinian, on the other hand, would be cast in the role of the unstable and unpredictable east organized politically and culturally around Islam and its proclivity towards violence and fundamentalist ideology. As evident, the potential for pejorative reproductions of staple stereotypes of the Middle East and of Islam exists in the British print media, as it does in the United States. And while news media in the UK retains a strong public connection in the form of the BBC, the multi-faceted nature of media in a country as culturally and politically diverse as the UK dictates that media coverage in the country will represent a broad spectrum of policy and/or opinion at any given moment. The examination to follow in this book's case studies will work to uncover, therefore, contemporary ideological tendencies of the authoritative press in both the US and the UK and will offer a comparative perspective on each country's media coverage of recent events in the conflict in Palestine–Israel.

Conclusions: media structures and media coverage in the United States and Great Britain

This chapter has examined the news media in both the United States and Great Britain to include considerations of relevant structures, characteristics, influences, and social and political relationships at work in the process of creating the contemporary, printed news. In approaching coverage of the Palestinian–Israeli conflict these particular characteristics have a significant impact. In the United States, a political tenor to news reports confines perspectives on the conflict to a narrow range closely aligning news media reports with US foreign policy interests. In the United Kingdom, the national news media community, influenced by the unique public position of the BBC, reports information from Palestine–Israel with both the consideration for Britain's own historic involvement in the region and with an eye towards international perspectives. In practical terms this means preferring the terms and positions of conflict agreed upon by the international community as opposed to those most in line with existing unilateral political objectives, or with particular strategic alliances. Predictably the disparate nature of this coverage manifests in conflicting news reports about the same events or series of events, and subsequently, encourages the formation of different forms of public knowledge about the conflict within their respective national communities. This is not to say that divergences should be expected to occur in all coverage compared or that similarities won't be found in the analysis to follow. Rather this suggests that structural, cultural, and political specificities should be present when print coverage from the two communities is compared. Elucidation of specific instances of confluence or divergence in linguistic representation of recent events in the Palestinian–Israeli conflict will, therefore, occupy the bulk of the remainder of this study.

Notes

1   Robert McChesney, "Media Convergence and Globalisation" in. Daya Thussu (Ed.) *Electronic Empires: Global Media and Local* Resistance (London: Arnold, 1999), 27–46.

2   In her 1997 analysis of media coverage of the Palestinian–Israeli conflict, Tamar Liebes informs on media hegemony extensively, even using the term in the title of her work, *Reporting the Arab-Israeli Conflict: How Hegemony Works.* In it she describes the development of media hegemony in the coverage of political conflict as "working in the interest of the political establishment to create a false consciousness" (Introduction). The author goes on to illustrate that mere awareness of the potentiality of the development of media hegemony is not enough to prevent its development as "hegemony is almost an unwitting process that supports the status quo and the establishment" despite the fact that "[f]or journalists and reporters, the allegation of hegemonic practices constitutes a most serious condemnation" (Ibid.). Social scientists will recognize the structure of this media hegemony as closely related to Antonio Gramsci's original formulation of the concept of hegemony (or cultural hegemony) in *Prison Notebooks* which describes capitalist states seizing control of methods of cultural production (including the mass media) for the purposes of subduing individual expression in favor of extolling the traditional virtues of the oligarchic state (Antonio Gramsci, *The Prison Notebooks* (New York: Columbia University Press, (2011) [1938]).

3   For an expanded discussion of the corporatization of the news, see also Edward Herman and Robert McChesney *The Global Media: The New Missionaries of Corporate Capitalism* (London: Cassell, 1997) and BarbaraTuchman, *Making News: A Study in the Social Construction of Reality* (New York: Free Press, 1978).

4   Herman and McChesney, *The Global Media*, 11.

5   Ibid., 38.

6   Edward Herman and Noam Chomsky, *Manufacturing Consent: The Political Economy of the Mass Media* (New York: Pantheon, 1988), 4.

7   Daniel Hallin, *We Keep America on top of the World: Television Journalism and the Public Sphere* (London: Routledge, 1994), 5.

8   John Downey, "Full of Eastern promise?: Central and Eastern European media after 1989" in Daya Thussu (Ed.). *Electronic Empires: Global Media and Local Resistance* (London: Arnold), 53.

9   Hallin, *We Keep America on top of the World*, 6.

10   Ibid., 11.

11   Ibid., 55.

12   Herman and Chomsky, *Manufacturing Consent*, xii.

13   In addition to the work already cited by media theorist Daniel Hallin, for additional work on the symbioses between politics and press, see Tamar Liebes, *Reporting the Arab-Israeli Conflict: How Hegemony Works* (1997), Gadi Wolfsfeld, *Media and Political Conflict: News from the Middle East*. Cambridge (1997), and Marvin and Ingle's *Blood Sacrifice and the Nation: Totem Rituals and the American Flag* (1999).

14   For a detailed discussion of this term see Chapter Three in this book entitled *Nations, Publics, and the National News Media Community*.

15   Claus Mueller, *The Politics of Communication* (New York: Oxford University Press, 1973), 124.

16   Marda Dunsky, *Pens and Swords: How the American Mainstream Media Reports the Israeli-Palestinian Conflict* (New York: Columbia University Press, 2007), 378–9.

17   David Paletz and Robert Entman, *Media, Power, Politics* (New York: The Free Press, 1981), 233.

18   John J. Mearsheimer and Stephen M. Walt, *The Israel Lobby and U.S. Foreign Policy* (New York: Farrar, Straus, and Giroux, 2007), 169.

19   In *The Israel Lobby,* Mearsheimer and Walt disclose that "Israel became the largest annual recipient of U.S. foreign assistance in 1976" and that "Israel now receives on average about $3 billion in direct foreign assistance each year, an amount that is roughly one-sixth of America's direct foreign assistance budget and equal to about 2 percent of Israel's GDP" (Mearsheimer and Walt, *The Israel Lobby*, 26). This amount does not include donations by private US citizens which totals "an estimated $2 billion annually" (Ibid., 29).

20   Among the researchers who would disagree with this assessment of the US news media coverage of Palestine–Israel is Stephanie Gutmann. Her 2005 work *The Other War: Israelis, Palestinians and the Struggle for Media Supremacy* argues that the dominant US media institutions are, in fact, biased *against* Israel and have a vested interest in portraying the Palestinian-Israeli conflict as primarily a story of the victimization of the Palestinian people. While this work is not alone in this assertion, it is certainly in a minority opinion when compared with the amount of scholarship demonstrating the US news media's documented record portraying Israel as the primary victim of the conflict and Palestinians as the primary aggressors.

21   Patricia Karl, "In the Middle in the Middle East: The Media and U.S. Foreign Policy" in Edward Ghareeb (Ed.). *Split Vision: Arab Portrayal in the American Media* (Washington, D.C.: Institute of Middle Eastern and African Affairs, 1977), 283–98.

22   Edward Said, *Covering Islam* (New York: Vintage, 1981), 49.

23   Fawaz Gerges, *America and Political Islam: Clash of Cultures or Clash of Interests?* (Cambridge: Cambridge University Press, 1999), 9.

24   Said, *Covering Islam*, 34. For a more recent continuation of the line of argument asserted here by Said, see Morey and Yaqin *Framing Muslims: Stereotyping and Representation after 9/11* (London: Harvard University Press, 2011).

25   Wolfsfeld, *Media and Political Conflict: News from the Middle East*, 31.

26   Great Britain was awarded Mandate status over Palestine by the League of Nations beginning in 1922, just after the cessation of hostilities in First World War. Britain ruled Palestine as a pseudo-colonial power torn between the national aspirations of the Palestinian people and the growing Zionist movement seeking a Jewish homeland in Palestine. In 1947, economically drained, morally exhausted, and militarily harassed by parties on both sides, Britain abandoned rule of Palestine in favor of a United Nations partition of the land. This partition and the resulting conflict that followed it created Israel (78 per cent of historic Palestine) and the Palestinian Territories (the West Bank, East Jerusalem, and the Gaza Strip, totaling 22 per cent of historic Palestine) which were subsequently conquered and militarily occupied by Israel in 1967, an occupation which stands to this day (Tara Reinhart, *Israel/Palestine: How to End the War of 1948* (New York: Seven Stories Press, 2002), 18–20). For a more in-depth discussion of the origins of the Palestinian–Israeli conflict see the historical summary in this book's first chapter.

27   Trudy Rubin, "Trudy Rubin, Special Correspondent of the Christian Science Monitor" in Edmund Ghareeb (Ed.). *Split Vision: Arab Portrayal in the American Media* (Washington, DC: Institute of Middle Eastern and African Affairs, 1977), 270.

28   Ibid.

29   Nick Couldry, Tanja Livingstone, and Tim Markham, *Media Consumption and Public Engagement: Beyond Presumption of* Attention (New York: Palgrave MacMillan, 2007), 3.

30   Ibid.

31   Ibid., 18 (emphasis in original).

32   Elisabeth Poole, *Reporting Islam: Media Representations of British Muslims* (London: I.B. Tauris, 2002), 98.

33   This is especially true when comparing British news reports to those of the United States, specifically regarding the Palestinian–Israeli conflict. The 2007 study conducted by Howard Friel and Richard Falk entitled *Israel-Palestine on Record: How the New York Times Misreports Conflict in the Middle East* describes the manner in which arguably the most authoritative printed news source in the United States, *The New York Times*, consistently omits reference to both international law and human rights violations documented by independent non-governmental groups in their coverage of the Palestinian–Israeli conflict. Although investigating only one source and the history of that source's coverage of the conflict, the impact that *The New York Times* has upon foreign news coverage throughout the United States renders their findings particularly significant. Providing examples of habitual obfuscation of both international law and human rights violations, the authors call into question the competence and impartiality of *the New York Times'* coverage of the conflict: "With all of this illegality, all covered by international law, lying at the center of the conflict, it's simply not possible for the *New York Times* to ignore international law and still cover the conflict impartially and competently, as it claims to do" (Friel and Falk, *Palestine on Record*, 45). Attention to these crucial elements is, however, more prevalent among British news reports about the region.

34   Herman and McChesney, *The Global Media,* 166.

35   Jeremy Bowen, Personal Interview, December 2, 2008. Bowen's commentary on issues related to US versus British coverage was partially included here because of the discussion of the BBC within this process, and because of his role as Editor of the Middle East News Desk within that organization. A more extensive consideration of his views, along with those of many of his colleagues, is included in Chapter 9, entitled *The Journalistic Perspective: Covering Palestine–Israel in their Own Words*.

36 Ibid.
37 Poole, *Reporting Islam*, 122.
38 Ibid., 149.
39 Ibid., 38.
40 Ibid., 18.
41 Ibid., 118.

5 Evacuating Gaza from two sides of the Atlantic

,

Frames of representation within the print news media

This book now turns to an examination and comparison of a series of recent events in the Palestinian–Israeli conflict as they were represented by the popular, authoritative, contemporary print news media in the United States and the United Kingdom, moving forward with the aforementioned characteristics of each of the national news media communities firmly in mind. The scholarly theories investigated to this point are intended to serve as conceptual frames intended to both inform and condition the linguistic analysis to follow. That analysis, an investigation of print news coverage of four events in the recent history of Palestine–Israel, constitutes the main body of this work: the fleshy data completing the skeletal academic theories. After a thorough review of four sets of print news data, the third and final section of this work turns to an explanation of the motivation of journalists who worked to cover Palestine–Israel in both the United States and the United Kingdom during the course of the recent historical events analyzed here. Following this structure, the theoretical informs the analytical which is in turn bolstered by the practical: the testimony and practice of journalists working to relay events in the Middle East to consumers back at home. Conclusions in this book will seek to unify these three complementary approaches by reifying the connected nature of all three aspects of this investigation. It is to textual data and to the specificities of news media language in the coverage of Palestine–Israel that this study now turns.

Upon examining a sampling of articles from the two national news media communities under investigation, certain patterns in the linguistic presentation of news events emerge. These trends—tendencies to present news stories from a particular perspective or based upon particular assumptions about the events that have transpired—come from a journalistic reliance upon an element or set of related elements within a news story asserted over and above a myriad of other possible perspectives. This process constitutes the act of embedding narratives within news stories that convey particular presuppositions, particular judgments, and particular evaluations of the reported event(s). In some social science disciplines, these phenomena are variously called "'paradigms', 'stereotypes', 'schemata' [or] 'general propositions'."[1] For the purposes of this study, these journalistic structures will be referred to as "frames of representation" or more simply "frames." More than the facts and figures reported within the news, the linguistic analysis of the printed news media to follow holds that these frames of representation are the elements within news coverage most responsible for the provision of meaning, for the connection of cognitive strands with previously provided narrative tropes, and for the establishment of the semantic structure of the news.

Frames of representation provide the reader with historical, cultural, moral, and ideological structures upon which to base their knowledge about the event(s) under consideration. These structures are inherent to the production and transmission of news because there are always alternatives to the presentation of events being offered by the news media institution: "[t]here are always different ways of saying the same thing, and they are not random, accidental alternatives."[2] Put another way, "Framing essentially involves selection and salience ... in such a way as to promote a particular problem definition, causal interpretation, moral evaluation and/or treatment recommendation for the item described."[3] The attribution of frames of representation in the coverage of news events allows journalists and editors responsible for the presentation of events to formulate the way in which those events are understood and processed by news media consumers. Whether deliberate or incidental, conscious or unconscious, the frames of representation inherent to journalistic practice significantly impact the interpretation of the news. As such, the process of framing and the selective decision making that it entails itself *makes* news given that alternative presentations and the concomitant alternative manner of their absorption by news readers are always available. Frames of representation, therefore, are always particularistic in nature: "[t]here is no such thing as a correct frame; there are always alternative frames that can be applied to an event."[4]

Framing is also value-laden according to the particular social and cultural context in which the news item is created and according to the particular language and linguistic structures assigned to the news item. The implication of cultural or social value inherent in frames of representation comes from the fact that "the very notion of 'representation' carries within it the qualification of representation *from a specific ideological point of view*."[5] In examining trends and tendencies surrounding specific frames of representation within the printed news media, the case studies explicated here aim to discern what ideological judgments or social and cultural values are being conveyed within print news media coverage on Palestine–Israel during four heavily attended media events[6] in the recent history of the political and civil conflict within that region. This investigation will also emphasize patterns of framing over time in Western news coverage of Palestine–Israel, and will call attention to particular proclivities and journalistic perspectives which are embedded within printed news coverage of the region.

The approach to news media analysis articulated here focuses upon language as the vehicle through which representations of real world events are passed from the news media institution to the news media consumer. In focusing upon language analysis and interpretation, this study conceives of language in the news media as an ideological tool and an indoctrinating force imposing "a structure of values ... on whatever is represented."[7] In other words, it is the language of the news, by virtue of lexical choice, naming rituals, historicization, and other strategies, that creates the aforementioned frames of representation within a given news product. These frames in turn contribute substantially to the parameters of meaning within a news story and establish the cognitive frames according to which the story is absorbed by the consuming public. At the heart of each level of this multi-layered semiotic process is language, including its selection, its application, and its functionality within a given news product. With this understanding of frames of representation, their role in the news media and their relationship to text language firmly in mind, this study can now turn to an explanation of the historical circumstances that inform the creation of news publications that discussed the Israeli settler evacuation/relocation from the Gaza Strip in 2005.

The birth of the settler movement

In the summer of 1967, once control of their new territorial acquisitions had been secured, the Israeli state quickly undertook to permanently settle Jews in the Arab–Palestinian areas they had successfully conquered during the Six Day War. The settlements were created as "Jewish-only spaces ... industrial parks, and military bases, which were strategically dispersed throughout the [occupied territories] and connected by a massive network of highways and bypass roads."[8] Modest in scope at first, and haphazard in organization, these settlements have grown substantially in both extent and capacity since the earliest days of the settlement project. The primary catalyst for this expansion came in the form of a change in government within Israel. The ascension of "the right-wing Likud Party ... in 1977 [saw] Jewish settlement in the Occupied Territories ... accelerated. Massive confiscations of land took place and centres of Palestinian population became more and more cut off from each other, surrounded by a network of Jewish settlements."[9] Subsequent Israeli governments of varying political stripes took up the Likud call of the late 1970s and followed suit in expanding Jewish-only settlements in Palestinian area. Whether officially sanctioned or disorganized and unauthorized, Israeli settlement activity in the 1970s, 1980s, and 1990s saw massive increases in the Jewish settler population in the West Bank and Gaza. This increase brought with them concomitant increases in the planned expansion of existing and future settlement sites. Indeed, settlement construction in areas of strategic importance has, since the 1970s, completely altered the landscape of Palestine and permanently changed the geography of the region: "The story of the settlements and the occupation is huge: complex and elusive in its first years; wild and tragic, and omnipresent as the occupation has deepened."[10]

In his study of the ongoing Israeli occupation of Palestine, Neve Gordon points out that:

> By 1987, Israel had established 110 settlements in the West Bank and an additional 15 in the Gaza Strip, comprising about 85 percent of all the

settlements that existed in 2005 … The estimated amount of money invested in these settlements was more than $8 billion. Thus, during the first twenty years of occupation, Israel had already built most of the settlements, seized over 40 percent of Palestinian land, and had managed to transfer about sixty thousand Jewish citizens to the [occupied territories].[11]

By the 1980s haphazard and unguided settlement activities had largely given way to the organized state-run settlement project that describes Israeli policy in Palestine up to the present day. In fact, the extent of the Israeli commitment to the settlement project (what has also been called a "colonization" project) has been so extensive that settlement construction and expansion has gone forward even during times of peace negotiations between the two sides of the conflict.[12] As such, it has been asserted that "the settlements and the settlers were the factor that dictated more than any other element the positions of the State of Israel in the first official negotiations with the Palestinians on permanent borders."[13] The same might be said about each subsequent negotiation which has resulted in little territorial gain for a future state of Palestine while enshrining massive territorial acquisition for Jewish-only Israeli settlements.[14] As a result, a widespread settlement activity inside Palestinian areas has effectively, possibly irrevocably, changed the facts on the ground in the Palestinian–Israeli conflict.

Part of this change has been strictly demographic. The insertion of Jewish-only enclaves into areas previously exclusive to Palestinians (both Muslim and Christian) blurs both cultural and political borderlines amongst conflicting parties, and has remade Gaza and the West Bank into piecemeal territories, totally eroding the territorial and cultural contiguity of Palestine. In their 2007 study of the settlement phenomenon entitled *Lords of the Land: The War over Israel's Settlements in the Occupied Territories, 1967-2007*, Idith Zertal and Akiva Eldar identify the demographic impacts of this ongoing Israeli policy:

> The number of Jewish settlers beyond the Green Line … continues to rise at a steady rate. At the end of 2006 the number of settlers stood at 270,000 (to this number should be added some 222,000 settlers living in neighborhoods surrounding Jerusalem beyond the Green line), and since the withdrawal from Gaza nearly 20,000 new settlers have been added in the West Bank. Two-thirds of them were babies born in the settlements and the rest were newcomers from Israel or other countries.[15]

The Israeli state invites settlement from all over the world in Jewish-only enclaves situated inside Palestinian cultural areas. This invitation is extended primarily through economic incentives and offers of Israeli citizenship to internationals possessing Jewish heritage.[16] The purpose of these invitations is to challenge the demographic realities present within the political conflict; Israel's various pro-settlement governments have, over the course of the settlement project, attempted to eradicate the cultural and territorial contiguity of Palestine by interspersing Jewish-only settlements through what remains of Palestinian territory. The alteration of these facts on the ground inherent to the settlement project ensures that future peace negotiations between the two parties would have to include considerations for the hundreds of thousands of Israeli citizens living inside Palestinian areas. In effect, the settlement policy ensures that no Palestinian state can ever be created given that sufficient autonomous, contiguous land on which to build such an entity does not exist.

Beyond these demographic and political challenges, the settlements themselves comprise a collective, punitive measure against Palestinians by virtue of the land confiscations, travel restrictions, and physical impositions that they entail. These effects of the settlement policy belie their explanation as natural demographic expansion or non-aggressive territorial extension on the part of the state of Israel. Rather, the settlements and the settler-only roads and passageways that connect them are a manifestation of hostile occupation. Invoking French philosopher and psychoanalyst Michel Foucault (whose theoretical innovations are discussed at some length in the introductory chapter to this work), author Neve Gordon explains that the settlements are an intended act of aggression, subversion, and surveillance designed to weaken, subdue, and/or pacify[17]:

> The settlements are, accordingly, disciplinary artefacts that aim to render the occupied inhabitants visible and docile. They are used to monitor the Palestinians who work in the fields below or who travel on the adjacent roads and in this way function as panoptic towers that encourage the inhabitants to adopt certain norms and practices. Not a single settler needs to be in the settlement, since the mere *possibility* that a settler is standing within one of the overarching buildings and watching is often sufficient to ensure that certain restrictions and prohibitions are observed and specific modes of behavior and comportment are followed.[18]

Seen in this light, the settlements are more than a nuisance for Palestinian commuters in the West Bank, and much more than organic Israeli communities established as a result of demographic or economic necessity. Rather, the settlements themselves embody frontline hostilities in the ongoing political conflict between Israel and Palestine. Further, these planned communities exist in violation of numerous international peacetime agreements to which the state of Israel was a voluntary party: "The process of the settlement of Jewish civilians in the territories in breach of the Geneva Convention, which does not permit the transfer of inhabitants from the occupier's territory to the occupied territory."[19] Yet the illegality of the settlement project based on international statute goes largely unnoticed, even within Israel itself given that the "Israeli government and the Israeli courts refuse to recognize the application of the body of international humanitarian law … to the occupied territories."[20]

Within this climate of hostility and international illegality, the settlement project continues to this day. Best estimates today suggest that there are upwards of half a million Jewish settlers occupying ethnically exclusive communities within Palestinian cultural and political areas: "the number of settlers [has] reached some 270,000 (the 230,000 settlers in East Jerusalem and around it not included)."[21] This number reflects only those settlers occupying West Bank settlements, however. Within the Gaza Strip, a more remote and less strategically valuable region for Israeli settlement, there were, at the height of the settlement project in that region, no more than 8,500 settlers living there. Still, during Israeli settlement activities in the Strip, the small settler population monopolized Gaza's resources—including as much as 80 percent of the water—even as they lived amongst a population of 1.5 million Palestinians.[22] In addition, these Jewish-only communities in Gaza relied on a substantial Israeli military contingent; thousands of Israeli citizens performed their mandatory national service as members of the Israeli Defence Force (the Israeli Army) within the occupied Gaza Strip. This large military presence, in addition to the intense economic and social pressure placed upon the Palestinian population of Gaza as a result of decades of Israeli occupation and restriction has made the Gaza Strip one of the most violent areas within the occupied territories throughout the Palestinian–Israeli conflict.

Israeli settlers no longer occupy Gaza, however. In the late summer of 2005, the roughly 8,500 settlers of Gaza (a number that had swelled to approximately 10,000 with an influx of protesters and squatters) were evacuated by executive order of the Israeli government.

> At midnight on August 14-15, the Israeli Army sealed off the Strip and began to empty it of Israelis. A week later there were no Israeli civilians left in the Strip. Only soldiers remained, loading military supplies onto trucks, dynamiting houses and uprooting trees. Public buildings and synagogues were left intact. On September 12 Israel declared an official end to its occupation.[23]

This political decision was made by Israel unilaterally; no discussions or negotiations with Palestinian leadership preceded this maneuver and few followed it. For some outside the region, it appeared that Israel was finally complying with international law in Gaza. For many settlers as well as many living within Israel, this policy was seen as a betrayal of the duty of the Israeli government to expand the state of Israel to its Biblical proportions, remaking the terrestrial nation into the divine one, *Eretz Yisrael.* Others saw something more nuanced within this political maneuver.

Many commentaries in the news media in the United States, and some in Great Britain, saw the settler removal from Gaza as a step towards peace. The architect of this "disengagement," Israeli Prime Minster Ariel Sharon, was widely lauded for this reason. Ironically, he has also been the man who had championed the settler movement throughout his long military and political career. As such it was suspected that his motivations were far from altruistic. Quoting Sharon himself, Palestinian analyst Azzam Tamimi revealed that "as part of the disengagement plan, Israel would 'strengthen its control over other areas of Greater Israel,' which would become an integral part of the State of Israel in any future agreement."[24] In fact, in real terms, the Israeli settler withdrawal from Gaza was actually an extension of the

Israeli settlement project in Palestine: "the number of new settlers in the West Bank in 2005—15,800—exceeded those evacuated from Gaza as a part of the disengagement—8,475—by almost a factor of two."[25] Seen in this light, the unilateral withdrawal of Israeli settlers from Gaza was, in fact, an aggressive act on the part of Israel designed to re-entrench the Israeli occupation of the West Bank, thereby securing a wider swath of territory for future Israeli concerns.

Regardless of the motivations beyond this highly publicized regional policy, whether from a genuine desire to move towards peace, or whether to further entrench the Israeli settler-colonial occupation in other areas of Greater Israel, "Sharon's decision to extricate the army from Gaza, uproot the settlements there, and return the settlers to Israel proper … was carried out with great drama."[26] Accompanying this high drama was an equally high level of international attention, particularly from representatives of the international news media focused on Palestine–Israel during the summer of 2005. It is to that news coverage, and to the language and accompanying frames of representation presented to news media consumers in the United States and Great Britain before, during, and after the settler removal from Gaza that this chapter now turns.

For the remainder of this case study, two diverse national news media communities will be considered and compared in an investigation that seeks to uncover patterns present within their collective approaches to the coverage of this event. For this particular case study, and in examining both national news media communities under investigation here, this research approach entailed surveying printed news articles covering roughly an eight-month period of time (February to September 2005). This breadth of analysis is intended to uncover patterns of representation organized around narrative frames of representation. In order to compare the presence or absence of the frames of representation between two separate national news media communities, a close analysis of a representative sampling of the authoritative print news media from each of the communities under consideration was engaged. The results of this analysis in both quantitative and qualitative terms appears in the conclusion to this chapter.

Frames of representation in settler withdrawal from Gaza (US and UK)

Although an eight-month period is represented in the news analysis below, the majority of the articles come from a narrower timeframe from roughly August 10, 2005 to September 12, 2005. This period saw a heavy increase in news media coverage of the settler withdrawal in both the United States and Great Britain due to the fact that this one-month period saw the actual implementation of the unilateral Israeli policy. September 12, 2005 was the day on which the last Israeli settler left the Gaza Strip. Upon reading and reviewing the sampling of print news articles in question, a number of frames of representation become evident across the various sources considered; an explication of each takes place below. The frames of representation to be discussed below were developed from a close reading of the articles themselves without prior identification or predetermination on the part of this author. In many cases multiple frames of presentation occurred within the same article and were therefore noted for their appearance in each. In some cases, a single frame dominated the article's presentation and was therefore noted as "dominant" with the particular news article as opposed to simply "present." Graphic representations of this system of notation appear in the concluding sections of this study and appendices to this work contain specific examples of the textual presentations noted within each frame of representation. Appendix A contains these examples for this particular case study; Appendix B contains citations of all articles analyzed in this chapter.

Evacuation of Gaza does not end Israeli occupation. Within this frame of representation, journalists and printed news media outlets emphasized the perpetuation and/or expansion of Israeli occupation in Palestine despite the policy of settler withdrawal from Gaza. The news media's identification of withdrawal as a component of occupation was tantamount to the assertion that "the disengagement plan, which was labelled with fancy phrases like 'partition' and 'an end to the occupation,' ... did almost nothing to change the living conditions for the residents of the Strip."[27] In a textual example of this frame taken from a British article reviewed for this case study, *The Evening Standard* asserted that "Israel will continue to build settlements in the West Bank and will not repeat the Gaza Strip withdrawal elsewhere."[28] A similar assertion was made by *The New York Times* reporting on Israel's planned expansion of settlements in the West Bank, which was pushed forward alongside the 2005 evacuation of settlers from Gaza: "Israel also announced plans to build 50 more homes in a West Bank settlement."[29] The presence of this frame of representation within various news reports suggests that the printed news media was aware of the dubious motives present in the unilateral Israeli withdrawal from Gaza. Though certainly not obligated to report this facet of the evacuation plan in *every* news article covering the Gaza settler evacuation of 2005, the absolute absence of this frame of reference in certain reports covering the region during this period might indicate an institutional preference against declaring the potentially spurious interests motivating this Israeli policy.

Palestinian suffering. This frame of representation focused on the suffering endured by the Palestinian people as a result of the long-running Israeli settlement project, and asserts this narrative trope within the news stories covering the Israeli withdrawal. This frame viewed the withdrawal from Gaza as a palliative measure, one to which the Israeli state was obligated as a result of its persistent engagement in illegal settlement activities within Palestinian cultural and political area. In a textual example from the print news media institution within the United States containing this frame of representation, a *New York Times* article from the summer of 2005 reported on a Palestinian family in Gaza with a three-year-old boy whose hobby is to ""sit drawing a machine gun,"...Tamam said: "When he hears bullets, he cries, 'I don't want to die.' This 3-year-old knows about death. What kind of life is this?"[30] The provision of this testimony from a Palestinian resident of Gaza demonstrates the trauma done to the Palestinian people overall as a result of Israeli military occupation and internationally illegal settlement policies in Gaza. In this case, and in others like it, the provision of quoted material from one side of the conflict or the other is a powerfully influential journalistic tool impacting the formation of knowledge about the issue at hand in the minds of readers (more on this particular journalistic strategy to come). A similar example from the British news media institution focuses on the loss of pride and dignity concomitant with the economic and social restrictions of Israeli occupation as well: "Naim Mahmoud Abu Hanoun is a proud man, but his spirit has been all but broken by the past four years of living on the flour, rice and beans provided by the United Nations and the Saudi government."[31] Within a news item reporting on the settler withdrawal from Gaza, this textual element amply demonstrates Palestinian hardship as a result of Israeli policy and provides a countervailing narrative to presentations of the withdrawal from Gaza as a benevolent Israeli act. This textual presentation provides relevant context to the media event at hand indicating that the sum total of the Israeli occupation of Palestine is much larger, much older, and much more debilitating to the Palestinian people than the settlements in Gaza alone.

Palestinians as violent/terroristic. Examples of Palestinian society as violent abound in print news discourse in both the US and the UK. Palestinians are depicted as embracing "the cult of the suicide bomber" and worshiping "bomb-makers and martyrs."[32] The accusation of violence on the part of Palestinians is typically the accusation of original violence. They are violent as a matter of natural fact; they commit violence because it is in their (Arab, Muslim, eastern) nature to do so. The violence of others is contextualized, routinized, white-washed and defended. Indeed, the violence of state actors (the United States, Britain, Israel, for example) is frequently applauded loudly by news media outlets as prudent and necessary. Violence as a political tool or as a means to an end is not condemned in popular discourse consistently or evenly but rather selectively, purposefully, and with substantial forethought by both media and political elites. There is no more evident example of this highly subjective treatment of political violence than the contemporary Palestinian–Israeli conflict.

During the coverage of the settler withdrawal from Gaza, certain news reports asserted that Palestinian violence was an overriding element within the broader political process. Textual examples of this frame of representation from the US news articles reviewed include: "Israeli military chief Lt. Gen. Dan Halutz … did not specify how much violence Israel would be willing to absorb before stopping the pullout," and "Israel warned that it would not allow violence to hinder the operation."[33] In these examples the threat of Palestinian violence is ubiquitous and reported as endemic even during an Israeli political military operation which would ostensibly benefit Palestinian society. Even though it is not logical that the Palestinians should be violent when Israel is engaging an operation designed to improve their lives, nevertheless news consumers were provided with the looming threat of Palestinian violence throughout this process. This threat came presumably as a matter of routine course, or as a result of some other inherent or natural fact. Palestinians cannot help themselves, they simply *are* violent, political and/or historical circumstances be damned.

From UK articles reviewed the following examples of this frame of representation illustrate this narrative trope: "For the third day running, militant members of Hamas fired salvoes of mortars and home-made rockets mostly at Jewish settlements inside Gaza" and "the *unceasing* assaults on the settlements ... helped force Mr Sharon into pulling out of Gaza (my emphasis)."[34] As evidenced by the examples above, the notation of this frame is not equivalent to the accusation of falsehood or obfuscation on the part of the news media institution. I presume that Hamas members (or other armed Palestinians) *did* fire rockets at Jewish settlements on the day in question as I presume there *have been* examples of Palestinian attacks on Jewish-only settlements within the Gaza Strip. I do not question the accuracy of the reportage in this commentary, but rather, I am interested in both the nature of, and the purpose behind the inclusion of this commentary in a discussion about the settler removal from Gaza in 2005. For example, the declaration that attacks on Israeli settlements in Gaza were "unceasing" over a given period time is a highly deterministic one. The idea that Palestinian violence forced Israeli leadership to remove settlers from Gaza is also highly speculative and therefore telling in this media piece. Indeed, the assertion of Palestinian violence at any point throughout the Gaza pullout process, whether real or perceived, whether dubbed "unprovoked" or "retaliatory," is discursively influential and therefore must be analyzed as such. The ongoing process of investigation here, then, does not hinge on veracity (indeed, does not even question it) but rather *purposefulness* in constructing a narrative about the Palestinian–Israeli conflict during this particular media event.

Palestine as corrupt/backwards. Assertions that Palestinians are corrupt or dysfunctional range from top-down perspectives of governmental fraud, "Mr. Abbas inherited a weak, corrupt Palestinian Authority ... who cared more for struggle than for civil administration" to categorizations of broad-based communal and endemic maladjustment, "Palestinian forces did their best to keep a kind of order, but there was ... chaos."[35] As with descriptions of Palestinian violence, this characterization is frequently asserted as a permanent rather than a transitory condition. Corruption within Palestinian society is presented not as a function of trying political and social circumstances but rather as an irredeemable cultural failing. Through this frame of representation, government officials as well as citizens are impugned with an indelible mark of retarded civil development.

Presentations of this frame within the UK print news media sample analyzed for this study include the categorization of Palestinian society as fragmented and destitute: "thousands of Palestinians swarmed into the forsaken settlements and youths set fire to synagogues and other symbols of the hated occupation."[36] These and other accounts within the article sample analyzed for this case study were marked for inclusion in the frame "Palestine as corrupt/backwards" because of the portrayal of the citizens of Gaza as desperate scavengers. This narrative of the Israeli settler evacuation from Gaza describes Palestinians as opportunists who saw the emptying of Gaza's settlements as a chance to benefit materially from the abandoned infrastructure without any inclination toward a broader vision of the political impact of the policy on their individual or collective futures: "Gaza ... Monday was a carnival of ... widespread *scavenging*" (my emphasis)."[37] Other examples in this data set include assumptions that Palestinians will loot and steal at the first opportunity: "Just before dawn, young men from the Khan Yunis refugee camp went through the settlement, taking whatever they could *scavenge* (my emphasis)."[38]

Portrayals such as these in which the Palestinians greeted the relocation of Israeli settlers from Gaza with dark motives and as looters and "scavengers" serve to adequately describe Palestinian society as undisciplined, destructive, immoral, and existentially corrupt. To label Palestinians as "scavengers" in a land that has been their ancestral homeland for scores of generations until recent memory substantially undermines their claim to occupied lands, discursively separating them from their familial connections to Palestine. Lexical choice here is of paramount importance; one does not "scavenge" or "loot" what one owns or otherwise has *rights* to. One only "scavenges" what rightfully belongs to someone else as might a vulture, an opportunist, or a thief in the night. Inherent in this frame of representation, therefore, are complementary ideas of both backwardness and temporariness. This frame helps to convey a real sense of pervasive, inherent underdevelopment within a Palestinian society which, after all, retains only ephemeral connections to the land on which it lives according to this frame of representation, and steals what it can in order to survive.

Palestinians as celebratory. Depictions of Palestinians as outlandishly celebrant accompanied a number of printed news media articles covering the 2005 Israeli evacuation of Gaza in both the United States and Great Britain as well. Presentation of this narrative trope serves to dehumanize the Palestinian population of Gaza as heartless and cruel especially when this frame is accompanied with accounts of pervasive Israeli suffering as a result of the settler withdrawal from Gaza (see description of frame entitled *Israeli Suffering* below). The following presentations from the US print news media were included for notation within this frame: "At about 2 a.m., they rushed in, leaping over barbed wire and racing up a dirt hill … They waved flags and … shot guns in the air," and "Monday [in Gaza] was a *carnival* of celebration (my emphasis)."[39] Examples of this frame of reference from within the British news media institution include reports that "Palestinians celebrated the clearing of the settlements [with] a prayer of thanks outside a gate leading to [now empty] Peat Sadeh settlement" and "In the southern town of Rafah, hundreds of Palestinians wearing T-shirts with the Palestinian flag bearing the slogan 'Today Gaza, tomorrow the West Bank and Jerusalem'."[40]

Alone or in combination with frames detailing the immense hardship that the settler evacuation from Gaza entailed for the Israeli people, the assertion of the Palestinians as overly celebratory casts a dark pall over conceptions of humanity or even sympathy of Palestinians in the face of the ostensibly prolific suffering of Israelis caused by the relocation policy. The presentation of Palestinian society then becomes a disturbingly unfeeling one in which the misery of others is celebrated and cheered. Through this frame of representation, news consumers learn of the callousness of the average Palestinian and of their potentially cruel social and/or political designs. The picture created is wholly uncomplimentary to Palestine and the Palestinians.

Evacuation ends occupation. In contrast to the frame of representation elucidated at the outset of this section, this frame of representation provides textual evidence which promotes the assumption that the settler evacuation of Gaza meant an overall end to the Israeli occupation of Gaza or the overall occupation of Palestine. This frame is noteworthy for its inaccuracy as much as for its a-historical approach to reporting the conflict; the settler evacuation of Gaza in 2005 in no way caused an end (or even a reprieve) to the ongoing Israeli military, civil, and political occupation of Palestine. Though statistically infrequent in the news articles examined for this case study, the assertion of this frame in any news report during this period is both cognitively and discursively significant given the sheer conceptual distance between this assumption and the facts on the ground in this conflict.

Examples of this frame of representation include the insinuation of the settler evacuation as a solution to territorial conflict. Evidence such as this implies that the settler withdrawal was a keystone to a peace settlement between Israel and Palestine, one which would provide some political entity which might be accurately described as a viable Palestinian state. Other elements within this frame of representation overstate the effects of the settler withdrawal itself. The title of a *Chicago Tribune* article declared "Gaza occupation coming to a close."[41] Other, more subtle turns of phrase conveyed the idea that Gaza—and potentially all of Palestine—would be freed as a result of the settler withdrawal. In the British daily *The Guardian*, the Gaza withdrawal was reported as a measure "which would remove almost 9,000 Israelis from land conquered in 1967, [and] would improve the lives of Israelis and Palestinians."[42] In the first place the assertion that the lives of Gazan Palestinians would be improved by the removal of the settlements was dubious given the continuation of Israeli military control and civil authority over all of Gaza even after settler relocation. Further, the phrase "land conquered in 1967" is a vague reference which may imply the ease of Israeli restrictions on other parts of Palestine (or Syrian) territory seized in the 1967 war, none of which were evacuated or altered in anyway during this period of 2005. Given that military closures, travel restrictions, blockade, and economic suffocation are still very much a part of the daily life of Palestinians living in Gaza at the time of this writing, to say nothing of the brutal, indiscriminate bombardment endured by Gaza at the end of 2008, the beginning of 2009, journalistically assertions such as these seem overly optimistic at best, irresponsible at worst.[43]

Israeli suffering. A significant number of the articles examined in this study presented Israeli suffering as the dominant frame of representation throughout the text. This narrative asserts that the Israeli withdrawal of settlers from Gaza was a great and even an unnecessary hardship. For some this brought about an existential crisis, as the orders of their government contradicted what they believe to be a divine mandate to occupy areas of Gaza. For others, the logistical hardships of moving were overwhelming. Emotional scenes filled with settler angst and pain were included in the presentation of this frame: "tears flowed freely at a farewell party;"[44] "Many of the settlers have known no other home;"[45] "Some people cried out;"[46] "Despite the drama, [and] tears."[47] Examples from the print news media sampling taken from the British news media include similar presentations to those in the US: "Tehila hauls herself on to her prosthetic limbs and looks into the camera: 'I don't understand what kind of soldier will be willing to drag me from my home and ruin my life for the second time'" and "One sobbing settler was seen pleading with a brigadier general not to evict him."[48]

The emphasis in these stories is on the trauma done to Israeli settlers (who occupy their lands, farms, and homes in direct contravention of multiple international laws, as previously discussed) by virtue of their relocation from Gaza to other homes in the occupied West Bank or within the state of Israel. In presenting the suffering of Israelis as heartfelt, somber, and regrettable this frame of representation discursively and cognitively aligns the reader with the Israeli settlers being evacuated. The image created for the reader is one of repeated Jewish/Israeli victimhood in the face of unfair political circumstances. An alliance is created; the reader is placed with the Israeli settlers and set against the Palestinians of Gaza. To reinforce this presentation, the many articles that described settler suffering frequently paid scant attention to the illegality of the settlement project itself or the decades of hardship it has wrought upon Gazan and Palestinian society. Once again, the perspective of the analyst here is not one to question the veracity of the claims made in these reports. Rather the question to ask is why the hardships done to Israeli settlers inside occupied Palestine as a result of their evacuation to homes outside of Gaza was asserted as a focus of news reports during this period amongst all other possible frames which might have been emphasized.

Israel as lawful/moral. According to this frame of presentation, the settler evacuation of Gaza is evidence of the Israeli respect for and adherence to law, especially international statutes that condemn the acquisition of territory by force and which compel occupying states *not* to transfer civilians to areas under military control. Put another way, this frame of representation is asserted as an Israeli awakening: a recognition of the error of their previous ways and a good-faith effort to put things right through the unilateral withdrawal from Gaza. Various news articles analyzed depicted Israeli lawfulness in order to demonstrate this facet of the evacuation as an abiding Israeli concern. Lawfulness was not asserted as a fleeting characteristic or an action engaged only grudgingly. Often Israeli lawfulness was presented as a matter of course or of natural fact. Israel *is* a law-abiding state; Israelis *are* a lawful people.

Oft-asserted within this frame of representation was a familial, fraternal basis for moral measures during the process of settler evacuation. In that process, above all, "somber, careful, and even sensitive behavior of the army and the police toward their fellow citizens"[49] prevailed. By and large, the same sobriety characterized behavior of those ideological settlers who opposed relocation: "The [settlers] ... oppose violence, pointing out that they have relatives serving in the army that will remove them."[50] As well, restraint and adherence to law categorized Israeli actions, even when their own citizens' security was at issue: "Israel will use 'all necessary means' to stop mortars and rockets ... At the same time, Israel promised restraint."[51] Examples of this frame of representation from the news article sampling taken from the United Kingdom include further suggestions of Israeli restraint: "The [Israeli] army has gone to great lengths to avoid confrontation"[52]; "The difficulties that the government has faced in reinforcing its authority have been compounded by the security forces' determination to avoid violent confrontation with the settlers if possible."[53]

The significant statistical presence of this particular frame of representation in each national news media community sampling indicates the importance of this narrative trope as an underlying theme in the broader news story about the Israeli removal of settlers from Gaza in 2005. The emphasis on the lawfulness of this policy was prevalent in both national discourses and would have influenced the social cognition of news media consumers in both communities during this time.

Israelis as pious/religious. This frame of representation constitutes the presentation of Jewish members of Israeli society as reverent, pious, and somber. Jewish prayer, fasting, religious ceremony and celebration all featured prominently within this narrative frame conveying a sense of reverence, respect, and humility in association with the Jewish faith. In the news articles reviewed for this case study, the Jewish faith was presented uncritically and was categorized only in positive terms. The discursive effect of these glowing descriptions is to cast Judaism in an exclusively productive light producing an effect that is the cognitive opposite of characterizations of Islam in the contemporary news media as discussed earlier. Further, these positive attributes carry seamlessly to judgments of Israel and of Israeli policy within the region given that Israel is the self-professed representative of the political expression of the Jewish faith.

Textual examples of this frame include descriptions of prayer meetings, religious ceremonies, and biblical references: "Efrat Weiss, 22 ... said one passage in Lamentations spoke most powerfully to her. 'Remember, Lord, what happened to us, consider and see our misery,' the passage says."[54] Mention of specific holidays in the Jewish calendar, the practices they invoke, and/or their significance likewise fits within this narrative frame: "religious Jews will fast, refrain from laughter and sex and avoid banal conversations to mark Tisha B'Av, the day of mourning for the fall of the Jewish temples."[55] A related component within this narrative is the elevation of the status of the land itself in the eyes of its Jewish occupants to holy or sacred. This view of the land as a divine gift or a miraculous bequest falls firmly within the Israeli/settler narrative of events surrounding their escort out of Gaza in 2005:

> Mr Lopes planted 10 fruit trees ... as a symbol of his faith in the "miracle" he knows is the only chance of stopping Ariel Sharon's plan ... "The planting shows our roots in the land," he explains. "The Torah says that you cannot eat a tree's fruit for its first three years. This act says we will be here to eat the fruit in the fourth year."[56]

The connections between religion, land, faithfulness, and sanctity appeared often in news media descriptions during this period. As an oft-expressed narrative theme within the news media coverage of the 2005 settler evacuation, these discursive connections provide consumers of the news media with a strong image of Israeli sanctity and stewardship over Palestinian political and cultural areas.

This frame is built largely upon identification of the inviolability of the religious practices of the settlers being asked to leave Gaza, as well as the Israeli soldiers charged with carrying out this relocation. Gaza itself, an exclusively Palestinian cultural area for hundreds of years before Israeli occupation, becomes recast as a land imbued primarily with holy significance for the Jewish people. The feelings of the Palestinians of Gaza as regards the same land are not mentioned in these presentations. In this way, this frame ties the Jewish faith to the land Israel occupies suggesting an ancient and righteous Jewish mandate over Palestine. Simultaneously these presentations minimalize the Palestinian relationship with the land by underplaying or ignoring this potential narrative.

Israel as a fractious society. The frame of representation "Israel as a fractious society" was noted in order to identify the journalistic mention of internal contentiousness present within Israeli society amongst different demographic, social, and ideological groups during the summer of 2005. Specifically, this frame of representation identifies the ideological confrontation between Israeli settlers and their sympathizers and Israeli soldiers tasked with removing that group from their homes within the Gaza settlements. This frame specifically references non-violent confrontation between various Israeli groups while the frame identified below, *Israelis as Violent/Aggressive* is concerned primarily with Israeli-on-Israeli violence during this period. Naturally, though, these two frames are connected discursively and often appeared together in news articles during this period.

Protests, debates, and other forms of social friction were noted here, including *The New York Times* report that "the police and the army managed to defuse a mass protest led by the Yesha Council … after nearly four days. About 30,000 protesters gathered on Monday night 10 miles from the Gaza settlements."[57] As well, fringe movements within Israeli society that were mentioned in the gathered news sample invoked this notation: "the "hilltop youth" … is seen as even more extreme than the mainstream settler youth and is regularly involved in the persecution of Palestinian villagers living near West Bank settlements."[58] An example of this frame from the UK news media sampling includes the assertion that "the settler movement is divided. A hard core believes the withdrawal from Gaza can be prevented by causing such mass disruption in the affected settlements."[59] As the primary narrative trope within coverage of the Israeli evacuation of the settlers from Gaza was that of an internal Israeli dispute, and as this presentation of events during the summer of 2005 constitutes an ideologically safe and uncontroversial presentation of events reported in the region, this frame of representation appeared with great frequency in both national news media samplings examined here.

Israelis as violent/aggressive. Many print news articles examined for this case study discussed incidents of violent clashes between Israeli settlers and the military units sent to evacuate them from Gaza. Others selected violent acts perpetrated on Palestinians by Israelis as a narrative focus while still others identified random acts of violence and rage undertaken by disaffected Israeli settlers in protest of the Israeli policy of evacuation. Each of these types of violence were noted in a given news article as containing the journalistic frame of representation *Israelis as Violent/Aggressive*.

Reports from violence between settler and soldier include the example from the US news media sample discussing the removal of settlers from the Gaza settlement Kfar Darom in which "there was a battle involving pikes, razor wire and a caustic liquid."[60] Reporting on violence by Israelis towards Palestinians, an example from the news media sample derived from British sources reported "the second cold-blooded murder of Arabs by Jewish hardliners in recent weeks, Asher Weisgan stopped his car at a checkpoint, grabbed a security guard's gun and opened fire."[61] This is a particularly noteworthy description given the biting language used to describe Israeli action. In an evident example of violence embodied by disaffected, random rage, *The Daily Telegraph* reported that "One middle-aged female settler set herself on fire, causing 60 per cent burns."[62] As violent clashes between soldiers and ideological settlers resisting government orders were the norm in the summer of 2005, this frame of representation was frequent in both national news media samplings. Though somewhat uncharacteristic of descriptions from both news media communities, such text certainly provides discursive substance to conceptions of Israeli aggression in the region. Qualification of this violence through the reporting of Israeli restraint and/or the disinclination toward violence on the part of Israeli soldiers substantially muted scenes of this violence in some news reports, however. Many news items specified that the controlled actions of the Israeli military prevented significant casualties during this process. As such, an indication of the frame *Israelis as Violent/Aggressive* may not, in and of itself, wholly characterize the ideological perspective or narrative tone of a given news piece.

Compensation. This frame of representation was noted throughout the article sampling when mention was made of financial compensation awarded by the Israeli government to the settler families who were relocated during this period. In certain examples, specific amounts of money were mentioned as compensation for settlers asked to relocate to homes within Israel proper or to other illegal settlements within the Palestinian West Bank. In others, mere mention of benefits to cooperative settler families was made without identifying specific sums. Examples of this frame of representation include *The New York Times* article revealing that "most [settler families] already have received at least some financial compensation and found new homes. Many families will receive cumulative payouts in the range of $200,000 to $300,000."[63] In the news article sampling for the United Kingdom, it was reported that "50 per cent of settler families who have entered negotiations with the state on rehousing [will receive] compensation of up to $300,000 (£170,000)."[64] Information about the compensation package offered to settlers was also used as speculation about a peaceful transition between Israeli settlers and soldiers: "Army chiefs believe that most settlers will choose to go without a struggle—not least because each family that remains beyond August 17 will lose compensation of up to £50,000."[65] Statistical evidence reviewed immediately below demonstrates that this frame of representation was to be found only infrequently in print news articles analyzed from both the United States and

Great Britain. This evidence would roundly suggest, then, that in neither national news media community under examination was the substantial financial benefit to Israeli settlers being relocated from Gaza deemed important in the contextualizing of news events reported in Palestine–Israel in the summer of 2005.

Statistical evaluation, the United States

In Figure 5.1 each frame of representation is represented in two of three categories corresponding to the three vertical bars present above the name of each frame in the graph. The left most vertical bar for each frame is the percentage of the sampling in which the frame in questions was *present*, the middle bar indicates the percentage of articles in which the frame in question was *dominant*, and the far right bar constitutes the total percentage of representation (present *or* dominant) of that frame within the article sampling. A notation of a frame of representation in any given news article therefore means that it is represented *twice* in graphic presentation above: once in the present or dominant graph, and once more in the total graph. Cases where a particular frame of representation was never dominant in the sampling are an exception to this graphic structure. In these cases, the total percentage of a frame's appearance as *present* is the equivalent to its combined appearance in the graph depicting presence and dominance combined. In those cases, the right-most bar and the left-most bar are equal while between the two there is no bar (meaning the frame was dominant in *no* articles in the sampling).

In statistical terms, four frames of representation dominated the US print news media presentation of the settler evacuation from Gaza in 2005. In descending order of frequency of appearance they are *Israeli as Fractious*, *Israel as Lawful/Moral*, *Israeli Suffering*, and *Palestinians as Violent/Terroristic*. Among those four, *Israel as Fractious* appeared more than any other, present in 50 per cent of news articles reviewed and dominant in an additional 22 per cent. In total, 72 per cent of the news articles reviewed mentioned, emphasized, or relied upon this frame in reporting the settler withdrawal. The frames *Evacuation Does End Occupation*, *Palestinian Suffering*, and *Evacuation Does Not End Occupation* received the least amount of attention in the US news sampling reviewed. In total, these frames appeared in just 9 percent, 3 percent, and 3 percent of the news articles analyzed, respectively. According to this statistical review, the major narrative themes present within the US print news media coverage of Palestine–Israel in the summer of 2005 were Palestinian violence and Israeli suffering. Equally emphasized was a conception of the fragmentation within Israeli society caused by the policy of settler removal from Gaza. The print news underscored these proceedings with the assertion that the Israeli policy of removal was motivated by legal or moral concerns. Print news consumers in the United States during this period would therefore have understood Israel as a law-abiding state even in the face of internal divisions, unrepentant Palestinian hostility, and the painful sacrifice of its own soldiers and citizens.

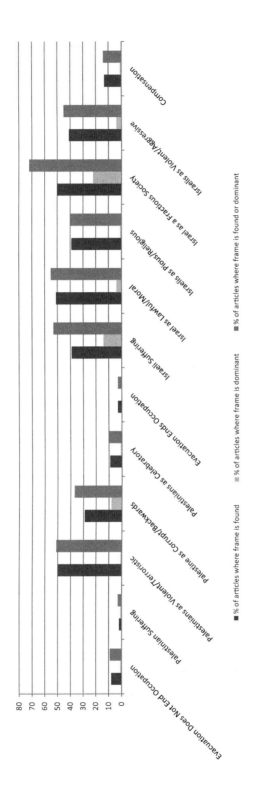

Figure 5.1 US Print News Media: Gaza Settler Withdrawal

Presentations of Israel as a fractious society during this period are sustained by the historical record of the settler relocation from Gaza. Minority elements within Israeli society during this period clearly opposed this policy vocally and vehemently; Israeli efforts to oust their own citizens from internationally declared illegal settlements were massive, constituting the largest mobilization of the Israeli military for any non-combat operation in the state's history.[66] But the emphatic presentation of Israeli lawfulness as well as the profound and ubiquitous nature of Israeli suffering during this same period constitutes an ideological positioning within the US news media more than an evidentiary one. Since 2005, Israel has continually demonstrated its unwillingness to relinquish its hold on much larger settlement areas in the West Bank; the illegal settlement project continues apace within the Palestinian territories, even if Gaza is no longer an integral part of that project. As such, overt expressions in the US news media of Israeli lawfulness during the summer of 2005 are of out step with Israeli policy since this event, and with the rest of the recent historical record.

Some have even suggested that the removal of settlers in Gaza in 2005 was in fact a staged drama primarily designed to divert global attention away from Israeli designs in the Palestinian West Bank which included, among other illegal confiscation policies, the construction of a 700-kilometer, 9 meter high concrete barrier deep inside Palestinian cultural areas: "Sharon's decision to extricate the army from Gaza, uproot the settlements there, and return the settlers to Israel proper (or to settlements in the West Bank) ... which was carried out with great drama ... to a large extent diverted attention both in Israel an abroad from the separation barrier."[67] Scholar and activist Noam Chomsky went a step further in his analysis calling the entire event "transparently fraudulent." In his view:

> It would have sufficed for Israel to announce that the IDF would withdraw, and the settlers who were subsidized to enjoy their life in Gaza would have quietly climbed into the lorries provided to them and travelled to their new subsidized residences in the other occupied territories. But that would not have produced ... [the] welcome propaganda cover for the real purpose of the partial "disengagement": expansion of illegal settlements in the rest of the occupied territories.[68]

Though difficult to substantiate in its entirety, this perspective, one that remakes the entire episode in the summer of 2005 as a choreographed spectacle with premeditated political outcomes, is sustained by certain predominate elements in the news media record during this period. These include aforementioned scenes of settler wailing and weeping, of crying and commiserating that were presented to US news consumers over and above any similar presentation of prolonged Palestinian hardships resulting from the settlement project itself. Similarly, the US news media provided only scant mention of the substantial amounts of compensation that were being provided to settlers leaving Gaza. Presentation of this fact might have mitigated pervasive scenes of Israeli suffering that appeared with frequency in US publications during this time. The determined focus of the

US news media institution on Israeli suffering during the summer of 2005 should likewise, therefore, be categorized as an ideological perspective prioritizing and emphasizing Israeli hardship within the broader news narrative on Palestine–Israel.

Statistical evaluation, the United Kingdom

Two frames of representation dominated the UK presentation of the settler withdrawal: *Israel as Fractious* and *Israelis as Violent/Aggressive*. Contrary to the US presentation, the UK presentation emphasized the notion that the settler withdrawal from Gaza did *not* constitute an end to Israeli occupation, a frame of representation which was present or dominant as a frame in 25 percent of the news articles analyzed. The UK news sampling also included a stronger emphasis on the frame depicting Palestinian suffering and a weaker emphasis on conceptions of Israel legality or morality. The frame *Israeli Suffering* was not as prevalent in the UK news media as it was in the US; the frame of Palestinian violence was likewise emphasized to a much smaller degree within the broader news narrative within the UK.

As in the article sample from the United States, the idea of Israeli fractiousness as a key component of the news narrative from Palestine–Israel in 2005 can be borne out by events on the ground in the region. There did exist within Israel a conflict between ideological settler groups opposed to returning Gaza to the Palestinians, and Israeli government and state officials determined to remove settlers from the region. This conflict manifested itself in protest, dispute, debate, and even violence at various points throughout the summer. The violence described by the UK print media and noted under the frame *Israelis as Violent/ Aggressive* typically involved settler versus soldier action where hard-line settler groups attacked Israeli soldiers in an attempt to prevent them from carrying out evacuations in Gaza. This frame of representation can likewise be sustained by evidentiary and photographic evidence of the interactions between Israeli soldiers and settler groups in Gaza in 2005. As such, the primary narrative focus of the British news media in this description of events during the settler withdrawal constitutes less of an ideological position either in support of or against one side of the conflict, and more of evidentiary reportage from a conflict region. Both of these elements contrast with reports of the same events from US journalists during this period. Direct comparisons between statistical presentations in each national news media community further support this assertion.

Statistical evaluation, comparison

While the frame *Palestinian Society as Violent* of representation was not a dominant feature of many news articles in either national sampling, the US news media demonstrated a greater propensity to include this frame within news stories covering the settler withdrawal. Slightly more than 51 percent of US news articles surveyed for this study represented aspects of Palestinian society as violent

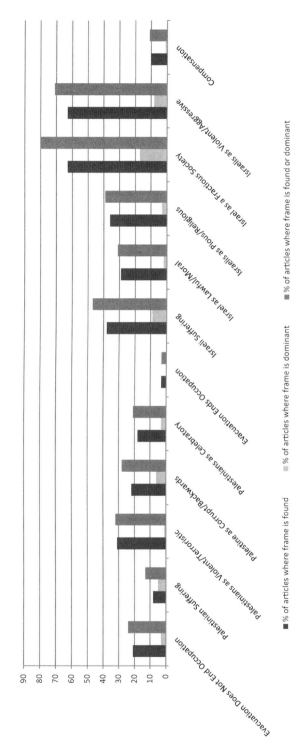

■ % of articles where frame is found   ▨ % of articles where frame is dominant

■ % of articles where frame is found or dominant

Figure 5.2 UK Print News Media: Gaza Settler Withdrawal

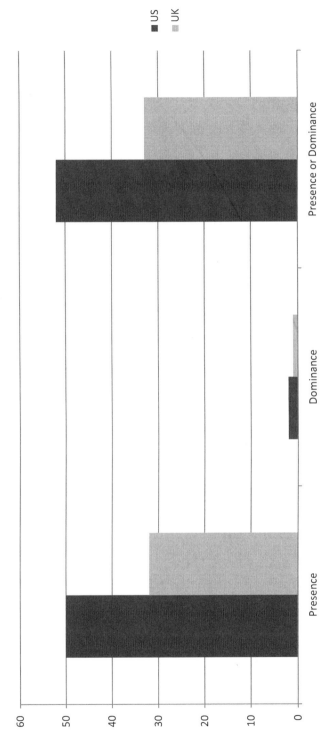

Figure 5.3 US and UK Comparison: Palestinians Society as Violent

compared to 33 percent of British news articles. This suggests that the US news media chose Palestinian violence as a more common narrative trope in the description of the settler evacuation from Gaza than their trans-Atlantic counterparts. This presentation within the US news media comprises a discursive complement to the emphatic presentations of Israeli suffering and Israeli legality. When considered together, a picture of the US news media institution as supportive of recent Israeli policy decisions and largely sympathetic to Israeli perspectives within the Palestinian–Israeli conflict begins to take shape.

According to the statistical evidence in Figure 5.4, the print news media in Great Britain was much more inclined to attribute violent actions or violent motives to Israeli actors in this conflict than were their US colleagues. This frame was present in 63 percent of British news articles sampled versus 41 percent in the US sample (dominant in 8 percent of articles in the UK sampled as compared to 4 percent in the US). This difference is striking given that the events represented by the two news media communities were ostensibly the same. That is not to say that this perspective is *not* present within the US news narrative of 2005, rather it is simply underrepresented as compared with what was reported by the British print news media. This disparity suggests that journalists and editors in the United States, either overtly or subconsciously, have underplayed occasions of Israeli violence during this period of conflict. This difference in narrative focus between the two media communities in the coverage of the same events further evinces an ideological differentiation between the US and the UK. In short, the British news media appeared more willing than the US news media to report Israeli actions as negative or detrimental during this period of coverage.

Finally, the generous US application of the frame *Israel as Legal/Moral* is indicated by its presence in more than 55 percent of the total news articles sampled (present in 31 percent of the UK sample). The presence of Israeli benevolence within the policy of settler withdrawal from Gaza was not typically qualified within US news reports. Rather this action was most often presented as an unequivocal Israeli adherence to international law and social justice. Such descriptions were found less often in British news reports, which more readily classified the unilateral Israeli policy of withdrawal from Gaza as problematic, multi-faceted, and indeed, as a gateway to the entrenchment of Israeli occupation of the West Bank. Criticisms such as these were seen less often within US news reports. This final point provides further evidence of a significant ideological differentiation between the two national news media communities.

Conclusions: framing the settler removal on two sides of the Atlantic

The issue of the settlements within the cultural and political context of the Palestinian–Israeli conflict is a sensitive one. This is due, at least partly, to the fact that Israeli settlement policies have been discursively linked to assertions of the cultural and national survival of the Jewish people: "The call 'to populate or perish' … has been accompanied in the Zionist project with the warning that the survival and prosperity of the Zionist settlement is a precondition for the survival

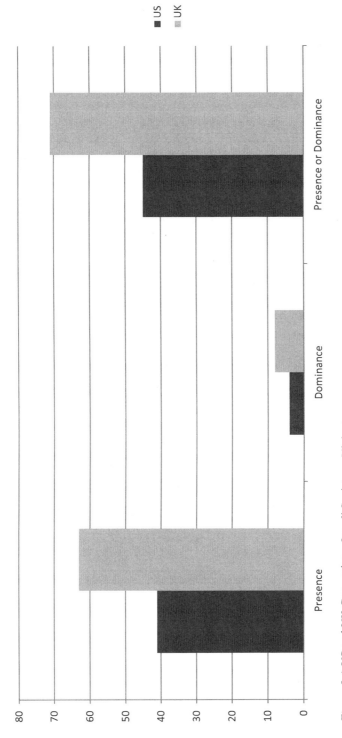

Figure 5.4 US and UK Comparison: Israeli Society as Violent

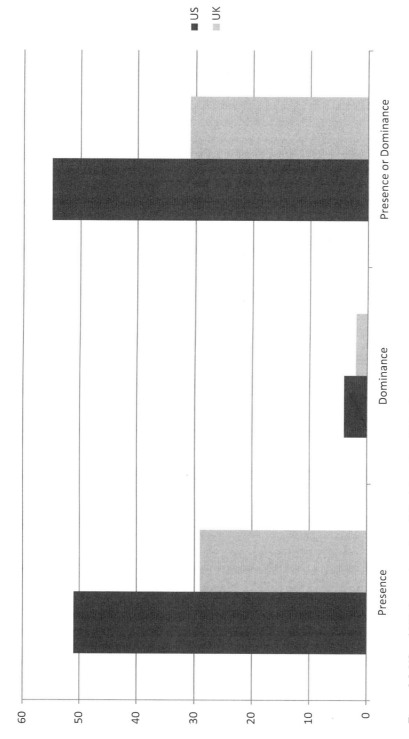

Figure 5.5 US and UK Comparison: Israeli Society as Legal/Moral

of the Jewish people as a whole."[69] As such, evaluating the representations of Israeli settlements and the settler movement itself within the authoritative print media can often arouse controversy and debate. Nevertheless, according to the statistical analysis above, and both the quantitative and qualitative review of hundreds of products from the print news media in the summer of 2005, certain trends in the presentation of the Israeli settler withdrawal from Gaza in 2005 are possible to discern.

While it is true that a variety of frames of representation were asserted in the printed media in the United States as part of their coverage of Palestine–Israel in 2005, it cannot be said that these frames represent a wide spectrum of ideological or political beliefs about the region they discuss. The statistical evidence reviewed suggests that only a portion of the broad canvas that represents the possibility of ideological views and journalistic narratives within this news event were attended by the US news media. The US coverage of this event highlighted Palestinian violence, the suffering of Jewish–Israeli settlers, the legality of settler withdrawal, and the fractious nature of Israeli society. Israeli settler relocation from Gaza was formulated and distributed as a story of a society enduring tremendous suffering and hardship as a result of the Israeli insistence on abiding by international law.

The British press brought a different perspective to bear to these events. In the UK, much less emphasis was placed on Israel's legal position or moral fortitude within the context of the settler removal while much more emphasis was placed upon Israeli soldier and settler violence. Palestinian violence was an underrepresented frame as well when compared to US representations. Statistical evidence also indicates that the British press was more inclined to assert that the unilateral Israeli removal of settlements from Gaza was a method of further entrenching the infrastructure of military occupation in the Gaza Strip and in the West Bank (including East Jerusalem). Criticism of Israeli national policy, descriptions of the history of Israeli occupation of Palestine, and criticism of the settler movement was evident in many news articles taken from the British press. These perspectives were virtually absent in US print news media examples.

It is clear then, from both the quantitative and qualitative evidence reviewed above that the perspective of US news media institution during the coverage of the settler withdrawal from Gaza in 2005 was one of strong identification with, and sympathy for Israeli policy and the Israeli people. Palestinians, on the other hand, were portrayed largely as violent and obstinate while no context of the abuse or subjugation they have endured as a result of the Israeli settlement project was made evident. In the UK, more care was taken to contextualize the settler movement within the broader conflict. News articles pointed to the 2005 settler relocation as, at best, a mild alleviation of Israeli occupation policies. Palestinian suffering as a result of Israeli occupation was more likely to be portrayed in the UK news than in the US. The story within the story, then, focused on Palestine and a narrative of continued occupation within the UK, while in the US the narrative focus was fixed on Israeli suffering, Israeli sacrifice, and the continuing plight of the Israeli people.

Notes

1   Roger Fowler, *Language in the News: Discourse and Ideology in the Press* (New York: Routledge, 1994), 17.

2   Ibid., 4.

3   R. M. Entman, "Framing: Toward Clarification of a Fractured Paradigm," in *Journal of Communication*, 43 (4), 1993, 52.

4   Gadi Wolfsfeld, *Media and Political Conflict: News from the Middle East* (Cambridge: Cambridge University Press, 1997), 36.

5   Fowler, *Language in the News*, 66 (emphasis in the original).

6   The term "media event" refers to an upsurge in the attentiveness of both news producer and news consumer due to a change in the status quo in social, political, and/or historical orientation of the world and the agents within it: "Media events … are live events (organized outside the media itself) that break the normal routines of media broadcasting, are covered by all broadcasters, and create a cultural situation where viewing is a virtually mandatory ritual of citizenship. Media events, which attract larger audiences than any other form of communication media, have tremendous potentials in terms of media power, because they erase the divide between private and public, and also because they dramatize the symbols, narratives, and cultural codes of a particular society" (Alexander, J. C. and Ronald N. Jacobs "Mass communication ritual and civil society" in Tamar Liebes and James Curran (eds.). *Media, Ritual and Identity* (London: Routledge, 1998), 27–28. Media events like the ones to be described in the case study chapters in this work are regular occurrences in the social orientation of the news media consumer/citizen and which constitute a collective spike in intensity, interest, and attention paid by consumers to news media matters and are often accompanied by specific representational strategies within the news media in the description of pressing foreign and international news events. While these events are not fictionalized by the news media institution, they are dramatized so as to enhance the descriptive spectacle while at the same time bolstering news products as profitable commodities, often out of real world tragedy.

7   Fowler, *Language in the News*, 4.

8   Neve Gordon, *Israel's Occupation* (London: University of California Press, 2008), 179.

9   Nahla Abdo and Nira Yuval-Davis, "Palestine, Israel, and the Zionist Settler Project" in David Stasiulis and Nira Yuval-Davis (eds.). *Unsettling Settler Societies: Articulations of Gender, Race, Ethnicity and Class* (London: Sage, 1995), 299.

10   Idith Zertal, and Akiva Eldar, *Lords of the Land: The War over Israel's Settlements in the Occupied Territories, 1967-2007* (New York: Nation Books, 2007), xviii.

11   Gordon, *Israel's Occupation*, 131.

12   For an in-depth discussion on the issue of Israel as a neo-colonial state, see Timothy Mitchell, *Native vs. Settler: Ethnic Conflict in Israel/Palestine, Northern Ireland, and South Africa* (Newport, CT: Greenwood Press, 2000) and Maxime Rodinson, *Israel: a Settler Colonial State?* (New York: Monad, 1973).

13   Zertal and Eldar, *Lords of the Land*, 178.

14   Rashid Khalidi, *Brokers of Deceit: How the US Has Undermined Peace in the Middle East* (Boston: Beacon Press, 2013).

15   Zertal and Eldar, *Lords of the Land*, xiii.

16   There are two types of settlers inhabiting Jewish-only settlements in Palestine: those who are motivated by religious belief and/or ideological nationalism, and those who are supported by economic incentive. But it is economic incentive that is primarily responsible for attracting most settlers to the settlements. Offers that include "subsidies for housing in the West bank (*sic*) … almost 50 percent higher than in depressed areas within Israel [and eligibility] for a 7 percent income tax reduction, and all settlement industrial parks were granted the A+ status for industrial development" see to it that

West Bank settlements remain incredibly attractive areas for permanent settlement (Gordon, *Israel's Occupation*), 139.

17   Michel Foucault, *Discipline and Punish: The Birth of the Prison* (New York, Random House, 1995).

18   Gordon, *Israel's Occupation*, 138 (emphasis in original).

19   Zertal and Eldar, *Lords of the Land*, 345.

20   Mitchell, *Native vs. Settler: Ethnic Conflict in Israel/Palestine, Northern Ireland, and South Africa*, 140.

21   Zertal and Eldar, *Lords of the Land*, 99–100.

22   Gideon Levy, *The Punishment of Gaza* (London: Verso, 2010), 19.

23   Nathan Shachar, *The Gaza Strip: Its History and Politics* (Portland, Oregon: Sussex Academic Press, 2010), 167.

24   Azzam Tamimi, *Hamas: A History from Within* (Northampton, Massachusetts: Olive Branch Press, 2007), 205.

25   Sara Roy, *Failing Peace: Gaza and the Palestinian-Israeli Conflict* (London: Pluto Press, 2007), 327.

26   Zertal and Eldar, *Lords of the Land*, 428–29.

27   Levy, *The Punishment of Gaza*, 19–20.

28   I. Gilmore, "No Fresh West Bank Pullout, Says Sharon," *The Evening Standard*, August 22, 2005.

29   Greg Myre, "Sharon May Delay Gaza Pullout to Mid-August," *The New York Times*, April 19, 2005, 10.

30   Stephen Erlanger, "Will Israeli Settlements Serve Them, Gazans Ask," *The New York Times*, June 14, 2005.

31   Donald Macintyre, "The Gaza Pullout: Caught in a Trap. *The Independent*, August 11, 2005.

32   Stephen Erlanger, "High Risks in a Summer of Statecraft," *The New York Times*, May 1, 2005.

33   Mark Lavie, "Israeli, Palestinian Officials Begin Talks on Gaza Pullout," *The Associated Press*, June 15, 2005.

34   Timothy Butcher, "Gaza Strip Handover Plans under Threat," *The Daily Telegraph*, May 20, 2005; Chris McGreal, "Gaza's Settlers Cannot Believe Sacrifices Are in Vain," *The Guardian*, August 10, 2005.

35   Stephen Erlanger, "High Risks in a Summer of Statecraft," *The New York Times*, May 1, 2005; Greg Myre, "Some West Bank Settlers Leave Quietly, if Tearfully," *The New York Times*, July 8, 2005.

36   Stephen Farrell and Ian MacKinnon, "Gaza Looters Settle Old Scores," *The Times*, September 13, 2005, 29.

37   Stephen Erlanger, "With One Gaza Settlement Left, Sharon Assails Resisters," *The New York Times*, August 22, 2005, 7.

38   Greg Myre, "Some West Bank Settlers Leave Quietly, if Tearfully," *The New York Times*, July 8, 2005.

39   Ibid.

40   Chris McGreal, "Gaza Settlers Cleared Ahead of Schedule," *The Guardian*, August 20, 2005, 2; Donald Macintyre, "Last of the Settlers Leave without a Fight," *The Independent*, August 20, 2005, 24.

41   Joel Greenberg, "Gaza Occupation Coming to a Close," *The Chicago Tribune*, August 14, 2005.

42   Conal Urquhart, "Violence Erupts at Gaza Eviction," *The Guardian*, June 30, 2005.

43   Indeed, it has been suggested that one ulterior motive of the settler relocation from Gaza in 2005 was to pave the way for an uncomplicated and total Israeli military assault of that region. See Chapter 7, *Covering the Gaza War* for further detail.

44   Greg Myre, "Some West Bank Settlers Leave Quietly, if Tearfully," *The New York Times*, July 8, 2005.

45 Chris Canfield, "Israelis, Arabs Reunite at Peace Camp During Gaza Withdrawal," *The Associated Press*, August 16, 2005.

46 Joel Greenberg, "As Gaza Strip Withdrawal Looms, Jewish Settlers Fall Back on Faith," *The Chicago Tribune,* April 22, 2005.

47 Stephen Erlanger, "Last Settlers Leave Gaza Quietly, Ending a 40-Year Era," *The New York Times*, August 23, 2005, 8.

48 Chris McGreal, "Gaza's Settlers Cannot Believe Sacrifices Are in Vain," *The Guardian,* August 10, 2005; I. Gilmore and Joe Murphy, "Gaza on the Brink," *The Evening Standard*, August 15, 2005. 7.

49 Stephen Erlanger, "Gaza Pullout: New Scars for Arabs and Israelis," *The New York Times*, August 22, 2005.

50 Ramit Plushnick-Masti, "Parents and Kids Pour into a West Bank Settlement, Determined to Block an Israeli Pullback," *The Associated Press*, July 17, 2005.

51 Stephen Erlanger,"Israel Defense Chief Opposes Razing Settler Homes After Evacuation," *The New York Times*, May 12, 2005, 9.

52 Timothy Butcher, "Gaza's Foes Unite to Ensure Peaceful Pull-out 50,000," *The Daily Telegraph*, August 15, 2005, 011.

53 Donald Macintyre, "Israeli MPs Take the Sting out of Settlers' Protests by Rejecting Delay to Evacuation," *The Independent*, July 21, 2005.

54 Joel Greenberg, "Israeli Parliament Passes Budget, Removing Hurdle to Gaza Pullout," *The Chicago Tribune*, March 30, 2005.

55 Conal Urquhart and Inigo Gilmore, "After all the Threats, It's a Muted Goodbye to Gaza," *The Observer*, August 14, 2005.

56 Donald Macintyre, "Jewish Settlers Praying for a Miracle to Stop Gaza Pull-out," *The Independent*, August 7, 2005.

57 Stephen Erlanger, "Israel Defense Chief Opposes Razing Settler Homes After Evacuation," *The New York Times*, May 12, 2005, 9.

58 Conal Urquhart, "Youthful Infiltrators Bent on Defying Authority," *The Guardian*, August 18, 2005.

59 Chris McGreal, "Israelis Gather to Fight Removal of Gaza Settlers," *The Guardian*, August 1, 2005, 2.

60 Stephen Erlanger, "Gaza Pullout: New Scars for Arabs and Israelis," *The New York Times*, August 22, 2005.

61 Timothy Butcher, "Tears, Fury and a Death Camp Hymn in Israel's Historic Retreat from Gaza," *The Daily Telegraph*, August 18, 2005, 002.

62 Ibid.

63 Greg Myre, "Defense Chief In Israel Seeks To Preserve Settler Homes," *The New York Times*, April 8, 2005, 16.

64 Donald Macintyre, "Jewish Settlers Praying for a Miracle to Stop Gaza Pull-out," *The Independent*, August 7, 2005.

65 Stephen Farrell and Ian MacKinnon, "Time Runs Out as Samson Gets Ready to Bring the House Down," *The Times,* August 13, 2005, 44.

66 Shachar, *The Gaza Strip*, 2010.

67 Zertal and Eldar, *Lords of the Land*, 428–9.

68 Noam Chomsky and Ilan Pappe, *Gaza in Crisis: Reflections on Israel's War against the Palestinians* (London: Penguin, 2010), 113.

69 Abdo and Yuval-Davis, "Palestine, Israel, and the Zionist Settler Project," 300.

6 The Palestinian legislative council elections, 2006

The Palestinian legislative council elections, January 2006

It is widely believed, by experts and interested lay persons alike, that the general elections held in January 2006 in the West Bank and Gaza Strip for the Palestinian Legislative Council or PLC—"the embodiment of Palestinian political legitimacy in the West Bank and Gaza Strip"[1]—marked an unprecedented turning point in the Palestinian–Israeli conflict. Both within the region and beyond, many analysts argued that the political dynamics of the broader Middle East were irrevocably affected by this election and its results. In it, relative newcomers to Palestinian politics, the Islamic Resistance Movement known more commonly by the acronym "Hamas,"[2] won a thorough and almost completely unforeseen victory over incumbent secular rivals, Fatah:

> The outcome was emphatic. Hamas won seventy-four seats in the 132-seat parliament and Fatah won just forty-five … Hamas won 56 per cent of the seats with just 44 per cent of the national vote, whereas Fatah had 41 per cent of the vote but gained only 36 per cent of the seats.[3]

This sweeping victory for Hamas represented an electoral revolution in the governing body that is "the nearest the Palestinians have to a Western-style parliament."[4] For the first time in history, the Islamic Resistance Movement had actively pursued and achieved expansive electoral power within the Palestinian Authority. The result was the political ascendance of a religiously oriented resistance movement with an active military wing to the majority party in Palestinian parliamentary politics. Experts, analysts, and pundits both within the region and throughout the world were shocked. One scholar presented this event in what might be considered a typical fashion:

> The Palestinian Central Elections Committee *shocked the world* on January 26, 2006, when it announced that the Islamist part had won a majority of seats in the Palestinian parliament. There was no refuting the fact that Hamas has won a legitimate landslide victory.[5]

The global shock was perhaps most profoundly felt by pundits and policymakers within the second George W. Bush Administration in the United States. As the US had had an active interest in Palestine–Israel for decades, and as the Bush Administration was ostensibly working towards opening negotiations for a peace settlement, the parliamentary election of Hamas, considered by Washington to be a terrorist organization, flummoxed a great many. Astonishment in the halls of power in the nation's capital was perhaps best expressed by Secretary of State Condoleezza Rice who "was heard to comment: 'Some say that Hamas itself was caught off-guard by Hamas' strong showing.'"[6]

But other analysts disagreed with the Secretary of State's assessment. Many now believe that perhaps Hamas themselves were the only political force in the world that *wasn't* surprised by its sweeping electoral victory, suggesting that the group had deliberately created subterfuge in the run-up to the election in order to lull its political opponents into a false sense of security. Rumors of strategic deception such as misleading pollsters and organized underreporting of party affiliation have circulated in the Palestinian territories since the 2006 election. If these rumors are true, then Hamas' political approach had been "an artfully choreographed strategy of deception," one that was an unqualified success.[7] This marginalized, under-funded, underdog group had managed to dupe poll-makers, policy specialists, and world leaders along with some of the top intelligence agencies in the world. On the back of this strategic and electoral victory, Hamas' success in the January 2006 elections can rightly be called the "turning point in Hamas's political life."[8] From that point forward, both Hamas and Fatah, along with citizens of Palestine and Israel, had to prepare to face "new realities and challenges" in what amounted to a complete "paradigm shift … across the whole Palestinian political scene."[9]

The 2006 PLC elections marked not only a landslide victory for Hamas, but also a crushing and demoralizing defeat for the front-runner and incumbent majority party, Fatah. Pressing questions were to follow these election results both from within the Palestinian political scene and from abroad, where governments now faced a Palestinian parliament dominated by a political party that most in the international community considered unrepentantly violent. Some analysts wondered aloud how Hamas had won such a stunning majority in their first real foray into the national political scene. Others phrased this quandary pointedly in the negative: how had Fatah failed in this election so thoroughly?

Answers soon followed. Speculation about the outcome of the election centered on several competitive narratives involving different aspects of internal Palestinian politics and social dynamics. In the first explanation, popular among pundits and politicians in the Western hemisphere, the vote for Hamas was quite simply a vote *against* Fatah. Years of corruption, political stagnation, and profound complacency had led to a standstill within the Palestinian government, and had driven the Palestinians themselves to support any alternative. In this narrative, Hamas was elected as the result of a widespread protest vote; the country's political leadership simply had to change. While plausible and compelling, this explanation is not sustained by statistical evidence gathered both before and after the election took place. Analyst Azzam Tamimi suggests that:

The explanation for the result most commonly put forward was the assumption that the electorate voted for Hamas to punish Fatah. In reality, only a fraction of the votes cast was made up of protest votes ... Proportional list voting showed that 44.45 percent voted for Hamas, not much more than the 40 percent that seemed to be Hamas's usual score, while 41.43 percent voted for Fatah.[10]

According to previously calculated percentages of voter preference and party loyalties, the results of the 2006 PLC elections were closely aligned with Palestinian public opinion, if slightly boosted in favor of Hamas. What is evident then is that the baseline level of Hamas' popularity was overall, much higher than had been previously suspected by outsiders to the Palestinian system, as well as regional experts. In a two-party system, this fact, and the election results themselves, perhaps should have been more highly anticipated. Nevertheless, expressed in these terms, the 2006 PLC elections were simply the vehicle through which the Islamic Resistance Movement to the Israeli occupation demonstrated that their popularity within the West Bank and the Gaza Strip was significant and "had been built up over a much longer period than many electoral experts acknowledged."[11]

Viewed through an Anglo-American lens, the PLC election results of 2006 were politically unsettling. Even as these results were explained as a broad protest of incumbent Fatah (an explanation which does not appear to be entirely valid), interested parties in the Western world in general had a difficult time grasping how "the Palestinians could elect an armed extremist faction that made no secret of its main goals – the end of a Jewish state in Palestine—or its means: violence."[12] But at the heart of this perception lies a profound difference in the assessment of the Palestinian–Israeli conflict by Western analysts and observers, Israeli citizens and experts, and indeed, Palestinians themselves: "[w]here Israel's supporters see a small, vulnerable Jewish state surrounded by Arab enemies, Palestinians see a nuclear regional superpower backed by the US which seeks to control, or even expel, them."[13] So, while shock and dismay at the new majority political party in Palestine ran rampant in Israel and in the West, which saw the vote for Hamas as an utter abandonment of any chance at regional peace, "many Palestinians saw no evidence of a peace process, so voted for Hamas."[14] In the final assessment, it can be said that like most voters approaching a ballot anywhere in the world, the Palestinians who elected Hamas did so on the basis of a collection of practical and complementary political and social motivations that included Hamas' "fidelity to the Palestinian dream ... [their provision] of services to the population ... [and] the failure of the peace process."[15]

The profound bewilderment experienced within the Bush Administration in the United States following the election of the Islamic Resistance Movement in 2006 would be followed very shortly by outright rejection of the election results, an election which came about in large part due to the American insistence upon the development of democracy in the Middle East. Subsequent to this official disavowal of the results, the United States cut off foreign aid to the Palestinian

Authority as a punitive measure: "In Jerusalem, Jacob Walles, the US consul general stated that Washington would discontinue its $368 million (£208 million) annual direct aid to the PA. 'I don't see how we would do that if the ministries were controlled by Hamas.'"[16] Several other international bodies and independent states would soon follow suit with implementing significant diplomatic pressure upon the Palestinians in order to bring about an economic crisis in Palestinian government and a practical reversal of the election results:

> Moving quickly, the United States, the United Nations, the European Union, and Russia – the four international powers known as the Quartet – said they would refuse to deal with a Hamas-led government unless it accepted three conditions: renounce violence, recognize Israel and respect previous agreements signed by Hamas's predecessors.[17]

Not satisfied with international condemnation, Israel took matters into their own hands shortly after the election results were finalized. In carefully coordinated raids conducted in June of 2006, Israeli soldiers arrested and detained 65 Hamas-affiliated members of the newly elected Palestinian parliament, "among them eight government ministers, 20 legislators and several mayors."[18] Their detentions spanned various durations and were debilitating in the Palestinian territories given the administrative difficulty associated with running a government from prison.[19] In the handful of years since Hamas' ascent to political power these measures of political and diplomatic obstruction—in particular the international economic boycott of the Hamas-led Palestinian government—have proven disastrous for the Palestinian government and its citizens.

In order to fully appreciate the reasons for this immediate and vehement reaction from officials within the Bush Administration and their international counterparts it is important to first understand Hamas, their origins, their prevailing ideology, and their social, political, and military practices. What follows then, is a brief description of these characteristics for the purposes of establishing historical context and for the provision of a cognitive locus in this chapter. This description provides a backdrop for the analysis that appears later in this chapter of the manner in which Hamas was discussed and represented in both the US and UK print news media in the weeks after their electoral victory of 2006.

Hamas: origins and identity

The Islamic Resistance Movement was founded in Palestine in December of 1987, just after the beginning of the first *intifada* or "shaking off," a movement undertaken by grassroots Palestinian groups to resist the Israeli military occupation of Palestine: "The 1987 *intifada* was mostly a weaponless confrontation, relying instead on mobilizing people, mass demonstrations and throwing stones at Israeli soldiers. Hence it was called the 'stones revolution.'"[20] As reviewed earlier, the Israeli occupation of Palestine developed in two primary phases. The first led to the establishment of the state of Israel in May 1948 on what was 78 percent of historic Palestine. The second phase was the Israeli military conquest of the remaining 22 percent of Palestine in a mere six days of fighting (hence the commonly used name for this battle, the Six Day War). As such, Hamas perceives themselves to be "the immediate victims of a plot hatched by an unjust world order that saw fit to create a Jewish state in the very heart of the Arab and Muslims lands."[21] The first *intifada*, then, was the first indigenous, organized resistance to Israeli military, social, and political control of Palestine. For Palestinians as a collective group and for Hamas in particular, this was the result of four decades of Israeli oppression and domination.

Hamas was born here, at the outset of the 1987 *intifada* and soon rose to prominence in the miniscule Gaza Strip, a narrow coastal area two miles wide by forty miles long that constitutes a small part of the 22 percent of Palestine conquered in the 1967 war. And while the "formation of Hamas almost coincided with the outbreak of the intifada ... the joint eruption of the intifada and emergence of Hamas was the culmination of two parallel, but not separate, curves of changes, one national and one partisan."[22] The group's origins in fact lay with the Muslim Brotherhood, an Egyptian-based organization founded in 1928 by Hassan al-Banna with the purpose of building "an Islamic society by applying Islamic law (*shari'a*)."[23] The primary goal of the Brotherhood (*al ikhwan,* in Arabic) was to align the social and political life of all Muslims more closely with the Qur'an and the *sunnah*—the deeds and sayings of Prophet Muhammad. The aims of the Muslim Brotherhood subsequently evolved more political ends, embracing and inspiring more specifically oriented political and social movements within the Arab world:

> Islamic movements, as demonstrated by Hasan al-Banna's Muslim Brotherhood Association (MB) in Egypt, which became a role model for similar movements across the Arab world, have shown flexibility, adopting mixed elements from these strategies under different social and political conditions.[24]

One such situation-specific movement within the Arab world was the Brotherhood's branch in Palestine. Before adapting a truly independent political and ideological identity, Hamas actually began as the Palestinian branch of the Brotherhood organized in the region in the years preceding the creation of Israel and open conflict between Palestinian and Zionist groups:

> Hamas is an offshoot of the Muslim Brotherhood and considers itself to be a branch of the Brotherhood in Palestine. Yet, Hamas also views itself as a natural extension of the Palestinian resistance—in its various manifestations— to the Zionist invasion.[25]

Ideologically speaking, then, Hamas evolved as a part of a whole: the Palestinian branch of the broader Muslim Brotherhood movement intended as a spiritual and political sojourn for all Muslims in the world. But after two decades of complete

Israeli occupation of Palestine, the vision of the Muslim Brotherhood began to diverge from the path of resistance thought to be most crucial for those with Islamist sympathies within Palestine. Specifically, the failure of the Brotherhood to rank those issues affecting Palestine's Muslims—namely Israeli occupation— as more politically and socially pressing than the reformation of the entire *umma* (the global Muslim community) resulted in a divergence of ideological approach between the parent organization and the Palestinian branch. In his detailed study *Hamas: A History from Within*, Azzam Tamimi explains the nature and import of this ideological divergence:

> It was ironic that the Ikhwan, who sent hundreds of volunteers to prevent the fall of Palestine in to Zionist hands in 1948, had by the early 1970s begun to rationalize their abstention from the jihad in Palestine. What happened in Palestine, they would argue, was nothing other than a symptom of the sickness that afflicted the umma, which had been weakened by the lack of religious observance. The most drastic consequence of wandering away from the path of Islam, they explained, had been they collapse of the project to consolidate an Islamic civilization, which in turn enabled the enemies of Islam to occupy Muslim lands, including Palestine.[26]

According to this perspective, the *ikhwan* saw the occupation of Palestine as a problem within the *umma*, one which was symptomatic of the widespread secularism and corruption that afflicted the politics and societies of the Middle East and North Africa. For them, the solution was Islam (particularly Sunni Islam), its instruction, its propagation, and its strict observance in all parts of the *umma*. Only then would the "sickness" affecting the region be eradicated, resulting in a new flowering of Islamic civilization to include the liberation of Palestine and the return of Jerusalem (*al-Quds*) to the hands of Muslim rulers. For the Muslim Brothers in Palestine, accepting the occupation as but one issue in a range of issues, spiritual, political, and otherwise, affecting the Muslim communities of the Middle East became problematic in the face of continuous and oppressive Israeli occupation measures.

As a result, in December of 1987, twenty years after total Israeli occupation of Palestine had been achieved, Hamas chose to loosen its affiliation with the Egyptian Muslim Brotherhood in order to more directly challenge the aggressive nature of the Israeli occupation of Palestine. The more broadly stated and slow-paced orientation of the Islamist ideology of the Brotherhood could no longer sustain a Palestinian group that was under daily threat from a specific and immediate force:

> The creation of *Hamās* ... in December 1987 or early 1988 was the answer of the Muslim Brotherhood to the popular uprising against the Israeli occupation and marked the turning away from the quietist and reformist approach of the Brotherhood.[27]

This is not to say that the reasons for the outbreak of *intifada* were entirely the same as those for the founding of the Islamic Resistance Movement. Rather, "leaders of the [Brotherhood] in Gaza simply made use of the surge in the frustration and anger of the people of the Strip to bring about the transformation of their organization into a resistance movement."[28]

The outset of *intifada* in the waning weeks of 1987 marks the point in the history of the Palestinian–Israeli conflict when Hamas became the sole representative movement for Islamic resistance to the Israeli occupation of Palestine, a development which can be said to have come directly out of the widespread, popular and civil resistance to the Israeli occupation which spontaneously erupted in the Palestinian Territories in December of that year. In fact, it has been said that the founding of Hamas was the most significant result of the *intifada*, with the most profound and long-lasting consequences for the regional conflict: "without question, the most important by-product of the intifada was Hamas."[29] It seems clear that even in the earliest days of Hamas' existence, their potential to have a significant political and military impact upon the landscape of the conflict was evident. Indeed, their emergence was tacitly welcomed by Israeli officials for the same reason that it was quietly disdained by Palestinian leadership of the day: Hamas represented a potentially powerful counterbalance to the Palestinian Liberation Organization, a group that Israel was actively seeking to marginalize.[30]

Representations of Hamas

Between the years 1987 and 2005, Hamas concerned itself primarily with two activities: charity to the Palestinian people and armed resistance to the Israeli occupation.[31] But, while the paramilitary practices undertaken by Hamas have certainly garnered the lion's share of the debate about Hamas and their role in Palestinian politics and governance, the efforts and energies of the group are, and have been, as varied as they have been exhaustive. Noted Hamas expert Dr. Khaled Hroub comments:

> Hamas, in the eyes of many Westerners … has always been reduced to a mere "terrorist group" whose only function is and has been to aimlessly kill Israelis. On the ground in their own country Hamas … chart[s] parallel and harmonious paths of both military confrontation against the Israeli occupation, and grassroots social work, religious and ideological mobilization and PR networking with other states and movements.[32]

Hroub, among others, challenge the pervasive notion that Hamas is merely "a racist, terrorist group with genocidal intentions against the Israeli people."[33] As these analysts have suggested, the true nature of Hamas as a resistance group, and more recently as a political party and legislative government, is much more complex. Far from denying the fact that Hamas has engaged in terrorist activities and has been responsible for violent acts perpetrated during the course of the Palestinian–Israeli conflict, this point of view posits a bigger picture, one that includes Hamas' work as a charitable organization, and the group's commitment to the provision of the basic needs of the Palestinian people, especially within the isolated and impoverished Gaza Strip. This argument establishes that it was out of a profound commitment to the service of the Palestinian people that Hamas adopted a contemporary political platform and participated in the 2006 Palestinian Legislative Council elections. Their success in these elections reflects this close contact with the people and the consistent success of the group's charitable goals:

> In the West, this aspect of Hamas is often underestimated. To television audiences and newspaper readerships, through images of shrouded Israeli corpses and the gutted shells of passenger busses burned down to their tyre rims, Hamas is understandably defined by its violence … To [Palestinians] Hamas is also the incorruptible social reforming organization, providing an Islamically inspired network of schools and charity organizations caring for orphans and delivering food to widows.[34]

The point to emphasize here is not that the deliberate assault on civilians can be overlooked when a group also endorses charity and service. Nor is it that the one should not be discussed so as to emphasize the other. Rather, the point asserted by Hroub and Milton-Edwards and Farrell among others is that Hamas is a multifaceted organization whose history, ideology, and religiosity cannot be reduced to a single, reductive conceptual notion such as "terrorist" or "militant" no matter how much political utility that notion happens to carry. Rather, a broader understanding of the context in which Hamas exists as a social and religious movement that is "deeply rooted in the Palestinian society in the West Bank and Gaza Strip" to include both long-term and short-term goals is necessary in order to clearly approach political developments in contemporary Palestine.[35]

Frames of representation on the election of Hamas in 2006 (US and UK)

With that brief history of Hamas retold to include its historical origins, its multifaceted nature, and its ongoing role in contemporary Palestinian society, this chapter now turns to a close analysis of the news media language used to represent this group and their electoral victory in regional, parliamentary elections in early 2006. The following analysis represents this author's examination of news articles gathered from major news sources in the United States and the United Kingdom published before, during, and after the PLC Elections of 2006. Upon reading and reviewing each news piece several times over, the news articles were marked to indicate the statistical prevalence of each frame in the two separate samplings. Tables and statistical references at the end of this chapter are derived from these calculations; a qualitative explanation of each frame of representation identified in the data sampling takes place below.

Hamas as terrorists. As mentioned in the discussion of the history of the development of Hamas above, the reductive representation of Hamas as simply a terrorist organization bent on the elimination of Israel holds sway as a convenient and popular trope for journalists covering Palestine–Israel in both the United States and Great Britain: "Hamas is misportrayed as an insular, one-dimensional entity dedicated solely to violence and to the destruction of the Jewish state. It has largely, if not entirely, been defined in terms of its terrorist attacks against the state of Israel."[36] This perspective is often asserted in a blanket fashion indicating the essential nature of Hamas as an organization, one that cannot be overcome or amended. It is a narrative that is both familiar and convenient to journalists working on both sides of the Atlantic. It is also highly palatable to news media consumers in each country and as such took center stage as a relational trope conveying information about the region in a great many news pieces covering the PLC elections of 2006.

A typical assertion of this frame of representation in the print news media coverage of the PLC election in the United States read: "Hamas emphasizes 'the elimination and nonrecognition of Israel.'"[37] A similar report in the United Kingdom explained that the Israeli public was bitterly disappointed with the election results of 2006 due to the fact that "Hamas … is committed to the destruction of the Jewish state."[38] Simplistic representations such as these paint a multi-faceted political organization with a single broad brush ignoring the various layers of Hamas in favor of playing up the aspect of violence associated with the group. Statements of this type present Hamas as an exclusively contrarian organization opposed to non-violence, opposed to Israel, and opposed to peace. They further ignore diplomatic efforts on the part of the organization to create long-lasting *hudnas* with the state of Israel, cease-fire agreements of 10, 20, or 50 years through which an easing of tensions and an end to civilian deaths on both sides of the conflict line might be achieved. In any event, these utterances were liberally applied in the coverage of the 2006 PLC elections in both news media communities under examination. It should be mentioned, however, that in only one of those communities, the UK, was it mentioned that Hamas had, in fact, altered its foundational Charter in order to eliminate its call for the end of the state of Israel. In no US news article reviewed by this author was this fact mentioned.[39]

Hamas as backward. This frame of reference constitutes a pejorative characterization of Arab/Palestinian culture with Hamas presented as the culpable agent responsible for these negative aspects of Arab, Muslims, or specifically Palestinian society. In addition, this frame includes criticism of the Muslim belief system and Islamic ideology present within the Palestinian territories. A UK example describes Hamas as "a party whose women candidates are often so heavily draped they can only be identified in campaign posters by their eyes."[40] Instead of lauding the participation of women on the Hamas ballots, commentary here derides the fact that those candidates cover their hair and face in an adaptation of traditional Arab style of dress. An example from the US news media informs of the:

> Cultural differences [that] could readily be seen between the Hamas and Fatah contingents. A group of Hamas members crouched in prayer inside the

hall during a break in the Gaza session. Female Hamas lawmakers wore head scarves and long robes; the women with Fatah and other secular parties kept their heads uncovered and favored pantsuits.[41]

The point to be made here is not that the simple mention of traditional dress is itself a pejorative categorization. Rather, that the deliberate and frequent association of the *hijab* and Islamic prayer with Hamas serves to provide cognitive distance between the reader and the group itself: "behavior, the body, and dress are treated not as cultural markers but as a kind of moral index, confirming non-Muslim viewers of these images in their sense of superiority and cementing the threatening strangeness of the Muslim Other."[42]

In this way the mention of traditional Arab dress and/or religious behavior, such as prayer, closely associated with the Muslim faith is intended to be distancing and alienating for Western media consumers. Further, frequent reference to cultural practices of the type elucidated above might also be called wholly irrelevant to a political party and its platform on the eve of an important election.[43] Nevertheless such presentations were common and were even used as stock portrayals of Hamas and their candidates in news articles covering the PLC elections in 2006. In light of the discursive associations mentioned in the previous chapter's case study regarding the Jewish tradition and adherents of that faith, a sharp contrast can be seen here with these presentations of Arab culture and Muslim practice and the adherents of Islam in Palestine.

Palestinian voice, rational. Often, in news media presentation describing events in Palestine–Israel, a member of the political or military leadership of one or the other parties involved in the conflict is quoted. Members of the public involved in the conflict might also be provided with the narrative space to assert their community's point of view. This is a powerful tool within printed news media. In this presentation, that voice becomes the embodiment of a national, political, or communal movement; the reader may well interpret this perspective as the defining perspective of the nation or community to which the speaker belongs. As such, this journalistic practice potentially provides substantial authority to the quoted source. In this and in the subsequent three frames of reference described here, then, quotations from parties involved directly with the election of Hamas and/or in the conflict in general were noted for the perspectives they expressed. These frames of reference, then, do not so much evaluate news media perspective using the words of the journalists themselves, but rather evaluate the choices journalists made in including this quoted material.

This particular frame noted Palestinian sources in which rational, sober, and otherwise peaceable sentiments are expressed in the description or evaluation of the election of Hamas. *The New York Times* of March 19, 2006 quoted newly elected Prime Minister Ismail Haniya as declaring "We are committed to the principle of cooperation with Abu Mazen and a dialogue with all the Palestinian factions."[44]Another example of this frame expresses the practical need for cross-border cooperation with the Israelis: "We are ready to negotiate. We are partners with the Israelis."[45] These points of view color the Palestinian camp in these elections as cooperative and moderate, and express the desire to move forward with concrete political solutions in the aftermath of the democratic election of Hamas to the majority of the PLC.

Palestinian voice, radical. The conceptual and ideological opposite of the preceding narrative frame is the presentation of Palestinian voices that are exclusively radical, militant, or violent. These expressions often stand alone within a number of news stories and may, as indicated, represent for the reader the perspective of more than just the lone speaker, but rather the opinion of a great many citizens and politicians within Palestine. According to this frame of representation obstinacy, violence, and negation are the exclusive purview of Hamas, Palestine, and the Palestinians. In this sense, the term "radical" is used here to describe members of a group bent upon violence, destruction, and/or the domination or elimination of another people. Within this frame, Hamas members express their willingness to die or kill, their love for war, and their embrace of endless regional violence. Political compromise is anathema and the recognition of Israel an impossibility: "'Never!' snapped Mahmoud Zahar, a senior figure in the group, when asked Wednesday whether Hamas would recognize Israel."[46] Within this journalistic trope, Hamas' chosen path is clear and any alterations to this path that might be expected as a result of Hamas' democratic successes should not be anticipated. In the UK, examples of this frame appeared in *The Independent* among other publications: "[Hamas candidate] Mrs Mansour ... suggested that ... an interim phase of two states side by side would not deflect Hamas from its goal of 'liberating Palestine from the river to the sea,'" while in the same week, *The New York Times* asserted that from the point of view of Hamas, it is a "political crime is to sit with the Israelis, exchange smiles and say there is progress."[47]

As before, it can be presumed that these quotations have been recorded accurately, and that the speakers introduced here were represented honestly, and without malice of forethought on the part of the journalist or publication. The reason for the demarcation of this frame, however, is to indicate the reliance on these speakers within specific news texts as representatives of Hamas as an entire organization vis-à-vis their violent outbursts and disdain for diplomatic processes. As has been indicated in this chapter, these presentations are, in fact, both incomplete and highly reductive emphasizing only Hamas' policies of negation and destruction within the Palestinian–Israeli conflict.

Israeli voice, rational. This frame of representation involved sober political commentary and astute observation by Israeli politicians and pundits. Any articles containing Israeli voices, official or otherwise, speaking in favor of diplomacy, cooperation, and negotiation with the democratically-elected, Hamas-majority government of Palestine were counted as containing this frame. An example of this perspective from the US news includes the following account: "'The Palestinian Authority still exists – there is no other Palestinian government,' former Prime Minister Shimon Peres told Israel Radio. 'We have no intention of hurting them, starving them, humiliating them.'"[48] Other examples from this frame of reference include the acknowledgement by Israeli officials of the need for Israel to withdraw from all or part of occupied territories in order to secure lasting peace in the region:

"[Ehud Olmert] declared that Israel 'cannot continue to control parts of the territories where most of the Palestinians live.'"[49] These and other quotations present amongst the data were notable for the moderation and spirit of cooperation expressed by Israeli leaders even after the election of Hamas, a period which was largely defined by Israeli (and generally Western) harsh condemnation of the Palestinian election results. The choice to present this moderate, cooperative Israeli voice, then, is significant in the formation of frames of knowledge surrounding this event indicating elements within Israeli society which are pragmatic, reasonable, and willing to cooperate with political counterparts from various ideological stripes, up to and including members of Hamas.

Israeli voice, radical. Alarmist declarations by Israeli spokespeople and officials were peppered throughout the news coverage of this event in both the US and UK, as well. Though less prevalent than similar commentary from their Palestinian counterparts, a certain amount of space was devoted to Israeli commentary depicting the election of Hamas in fundamentalist, racist, or otherwise alarmist terms. In one example from the United Kingdom, the election of Hamas was portrayed as the Middle Eastern equivalent to Hitler's election to the *Reichstag* in pre-war Europe: "[Benjamin Netanyahu] said ... 'When Hitler rose to power, it was said that ruling would moderate him.'"[50] Further voice was given to alarmist sentiment amongst the Israeli people in an *Independent* article which again quoted Prime Minister Benjamin Netanyahu as saying "Sooner or later they will be in the hills over Tel Aviv airport and terrorism could again be a monumental threat to Israel."[51] Similarly, *The Christian Science Monitor* gave voice to Israeli official Dov Weisglass's grim suggestion that the critical food shortage resulting from the Israeli blockade of Gaza was justified: "The idea is to put the Palestinians on a diet, but not to make them die of hunger."[52] It is important to emphasize that the above excerpts appeared in print as quoted material volunteered by Israeli officials and is *not* commentary created from journalists themselves. Nevertheless, the choice to air these perspectives, as with all of those quotations and commentary presented by either Palestinians or Israelis, is a journalistic technique which significantly affects the reader's appreciation of the situation being described. As such, the choice to present quoted material, or alternatively not to include it is a powerful tool in the hands of the news media institution creating and structuring the frames of knowledge and social cognition about a given event.

Hamas as moderates: This frame of representation involved mention of the move of Hamas from an exclusively resistance-oriented group, defining itself primarily in opposition to Israel, to a political actor, seeking legitimacy from within the regional political process. The multi-faceted nature of the group is highlighted here through journalistic and expert commentary. Tellingly, this perspective was taken much further in the news media articles from the United Kingdom reviewed for this analysis. The following examples from the UK were representative of journalistic presentations of Hamas's ideological moderation in the wake of their electoral success.

From *The Guardian*, readers were informed that "Hamas has dropped its call for the destruction of Israel from its manifesto for the Palestinian parliamentary election," and again in *The Independent:* "Hamas has dropped its long-standing call for Israel to be replaced by an Islamic state in its manifesto for this month's Palestinian elections."[53] These representations are especially noteworthy given the comparative absence of this point of view in US news articles. Readers in that country were not informed of Hamas's dramatic shift in policy in preparation for entrance into electoral politics. They were, however, informed by *The New York Times* that "Hamas, running for the first time in Palestinian Authority elections, says that it is prepared to consider a long-term truce with Israel within its 1967 boundaries."[54] Hamas was, therefore, occasionally rendered as moderating its previously stark ideological position in the US vis-à-vis the PLC elections of 2006. But the perspective on Hamas's renunciation of their call for the end of Israel, presumably an eminently noteworthy shift in the organization's regional and global outlook, did not make it to print in the United States in any news article reviewed for this study.

The failure of democracy. A significant amount of commentary reviewing the election results and Hamas' victory in the polls converted this outcome into a sweeping failure of the democratic process. According to this narrative, the fact that Hamas could achieve electoral success in the Middle East or anywhere demonstrated a grandiose failure of democracy and the political bankruptcy of the ideological reliance upon the voice of the people in determining the composition of governments. In the UK, a headline taken from *The Evening Standard* said as much standing alone: "Peace Hopes Shattered by Hamas Win."[55] The assertion in this case is that Hamas will destroy all hopes of peace in the region, a diplomatic aim which was presumed to be irrevocably tied to the emergence of electoral democracy in the region. This assumption was simply false according to this title from *The Evening Standard*. In another example from the United Kingdom, *The Sun* stated that the success of Hamas in the 2006 election was due to the fact that "Palestinians admire Hamas' strength and its dedication to destroying Israel."[56] The picture drawn for the reader is one of democracy run amok, the failure of a system that allows a terrorist group to stand for office.[57] In the US, *The Los Angeles Times* quoted the Director-General of Israel's Foreign Ministry stating "the participation of terror elements in democratic elections ... is a Trojan horse that will destroy democracy from within."[58]

Although representing commentary from an Israeli official as opposed to original text commentary by the journalist, the inclusion this text has the power to convey to the reader perspective, value, morality, and culpability of the kind present in each of the frames of representations discussed herein. According to this narrative frame, in a bizarre reversal of political theory, it is clear that it is not an open electoral process but the ideological character of the candidates that make effective democracy. Indeed, as theorist Daniel Bensaid points out, this narrative asserts a highly particular definition of "democracy," a term which becomes synonymous with "the victorious West, the triumphant United States of America, the free market, and the level playing field."[59] As such, Hamas, a conceptual entity placed well outside the traditional democratic oligarchy in the broadly constructed west, in standing for election, and in fully engaging the democratic, electoral process within their political region in fact mark the end of democracy in Palestine.

The proper function of democracy. Contrary to the frame discussed above, the election of Hamas in 2006 was represented by some journalists as an electoral success, an exercise in uninterrupted, uncorrupted, and the otherwise efficient and laudable democratic process. This frame of reference centered on the declaration of these elections as free and fair with the participation of international observers in the process serving as witnesses to this fact. Among those voices was included former US President Jimmy Carter's group of observers who unequivocally determined that Hamas had been elected without coercion or intimidation, and that the results were the unadulterated will of the majority of the Palestinian electorate. In the United States, Ignasi Guardans, a Spanish member of the European Parliament, was quoted as saying "we cannot push for democracy and then deny the result of free and fair elections."[60] Referring to the newly elected Palestinian government as a new democracy, another piece published in the US asserted that "to destabilize a small, new democracy in the Middle East would send a contrary signal to democracy advocates in … Egypt, Iraq, Syria, and Saudi Arabia."[61] Examples from the sampling examined from the UK likewise contain this evidentiary, narrative trope: "Monitors praised the election process, with the EU monitoring team saying the poll was 'free and fair under severe restrictions'"[62] in reference to the daily restrictions of travel, movement, and access that are part and parcel of the ongoing Israeli occupation in Palestine. Articles that discussed the democratic process of the election in detail, or provided expert analysis from within the region of the type typically associated with other democratic elections throughout the world, were likewise marked for the presence of this frame.

Hamas in history. This frame of representation included efforts by journalists to contextualize Hamas in regional or world history. Typically this contextualization took the form of a comparison between Hamas and another violent, intransigent, or separatist group. *The USA Today* on January 25, 2006, for example, suggested that "Hamas needs to be pushed onto the path taken by the Irish Republican Army (IRA)," a point which serves to connect the Palestinian–Israeli conflict with the Republican struggle for independence from Great Britain in Northern Ireland.[63] Comparisons between Hamas and the IRA were prevalent among those articles containing this frame of representation. Also included within this frame were examples of historical background informing readers about the history of the development of Hamas. Text of this kind sufficiently contextualized Hamas and provided them with an important measure of cognitive depth within the Palestinian–Israeli conflict. One UK news article reported that: "Hamas (zeal in Arabic), is the shorthand version of the group's official title, The Islamic Resistance Movement. Originally moderate, it supported charitable projects and eschewed armed struggle."[64] Each of these strategies was included in the notation of articles containing the frame *Hamas in History* given that they each presented the reader with a distinct vision of Hamas, one that was situated and contextualized in the broader political dynamics of the region.

Statistical evaluation, the United States

Figure 6.1 depicts the prevalence of each frame of representation described in the preceding section in print articles from the United States. Two frames of reference stand out among the data in the table above: *Hamas as Terrorists* and *Palestinian Voice, Rational*. Two other frames are notable for their rarity in this data set: *Israeli Voice, Radical* and *Hamas in History*. The frame *Hamas as Moderates* also never appeared as a dominant frame and surfaced in less than 14 percent of the sample articles. All of the other frames of representation discussed above fall within a range between the prominent *Hamas as Terrorists* frame and the underrepresented *Hamas in History* frame.

Upon examination it seems evident that readers following the coverage of the 2006 PLC elections in the US would have been presented with information depicting Hamas as an exclusively terrorist organization. Despite that fact, many news items contained the frame *Palestinian Voice, Rational* (more than 62 percent of articles reviewed) indicating that quoted commentary from Palestinians included by mainstream US journalists during this period was largely peaceful and reasonable. The prevalence of this frame of representation presents an apparent ideological dissonance with the presence of the frames *Hamas as Terrorists* and *Failure of Democracy* (43 percent) to such a great extent in the article sampling reviewed. Taken together, statistical information from the US sample suggests an ideological positioning by the US news media which sees Hamas as an exclusively terrorist organization and which states that the PLC election results of 2006 were a failure to the democratic process. The Palestinian people are, in a sense, removed from this blanket condemnation, however, as the plentiful inclusion of their rational, sensible, and otherwise sober commentary indicates. The overall picture presented by the frames of representation in this article sampling denies the legitimacy of the Palestinian political process while simultaneously condemning Hamas as a movement and as a political party within regional developments in Palestine–Israel. Crucially, this condemnation includes the total absence, as noted above, of any mention by the US news media of the voluntary alteration of the Hamas Charter to eliminate its call for the destruction of the state of Israel. This critical omission effectively established Hamas as an unrepentant, violent aggressor for US news media consumers, even as the organization sought to change its ideological stripes to a substantial extent in 2006.

Statistical Evaluation, the United Kingdom

As with data reviewed from the US, the two most prominent frames of representation present in the UK were *Hamas as Terrorists* and *Palestinian Voice, Rational*. According to Figure 6.2, the least frequent frames of representation were also *Hamas as Moderate* and *Hamas in History*. Neither *Israeli Voice, Rational* nor *Israeli Voice, Radical* appeared as a dominant frame in the UK data set while *Hamas in History* appeared as the dominant frame in just 2 percent of the

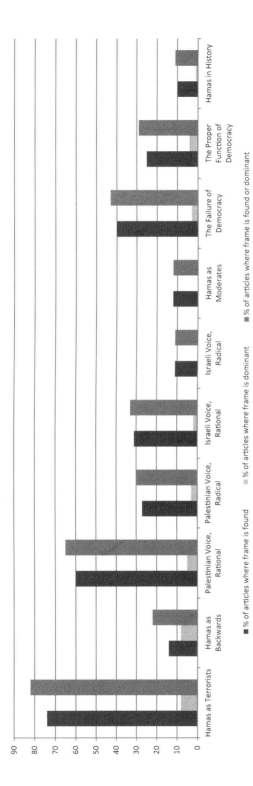

Figure 6.1 US Print News Media: The Palestinian Legislative Council Elections, 2006

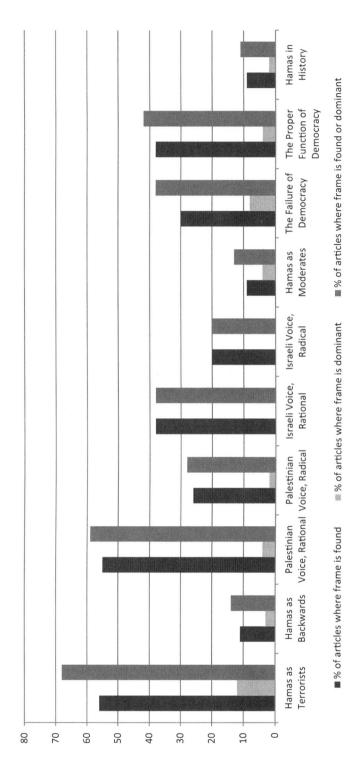

Figure 6.2 UK Print News Media: The Palestinian Legislative Council Elections, 2006

data sampling. All other frames of representation discussed above fall within a range between the prominent *Hamas as Terrorists* frame, and the *Hamas in History* frame.

Initial examination of this statistical evidence leads to the conclusion that the average news reader in Britain in 2006 would, like their counterparts in the United States, have been provided with information about Hamas as an unrepentant terrorist organization. Also as in the United States, many or most of those news pieces would also have contained sober, sensible comments from Palestinian citizens; British journalists in 2006—like their US colleagues—frequently included the opinions of Palestinians in their coverage. Significantly, in a deviation from the patterns displayed by the US data sampling, the second most prominent frame found in British coverage of the PLC elections was the depiction of the election as the *Proper Function of Democracy* (present or dominant in 42 percent of the sample). It is therefore likely that news consumers in the UK during this period would have understood that the PLC elections put a violent, terrorist organization in power in Palestine while hearing sensible and measured testimony about that fact from Palestinians themselves. Nevertheless, this process, according to authoritative news representations in the UK, demonstrated a free and fair democratic procedure.

Statistical evaluation, comparison

As indicated by Figure 6.3 below, the *Proper Function* frame appeared in the UK news sample in 36 percent of articles. This is more than 10 percent higher than in the US sample, in which only 25 percent of the articles contained this frame. Similar trends hold for the dominant column for this frame, where articles from the UK exceeded the rate of dominance of the US sample, 6 percent to 4 percent. The combined percentage of either presence or dominance comes to 42 percent in the UK versus 29 percent in the US.

These statistical variations are significant enough to enable us to draw conclusions about the narrative tropes that framed the coverage of the PLC elections. The British news media had little difficulty evaluating this election in Palestine as legitimate, fair, and above all, democratic. This is evident not only in the presence of the *Proper Function* frame, but also the fact that it provided the dominant narrative focus for more than 6 percent of the articles reviewed. The US news media were reluctant to qualify the election of Hamas to the majority of the Palestinian Parliament as a democratic process. This divergence in perspective may have had more to do with the US news media's evaluation of the *outcome* of the elections rather than their evaluation of the process of the elections given that regional journalists in both countries had equal access to independent findings reporting the very high voter turnout, the very efficient voting process, and the fraud-free election process. In any case, one can conclude that British news readers would have come to appreciate the 2006 PLC elections as a truly democratic process to a significantly greater extent than their American counterparts.

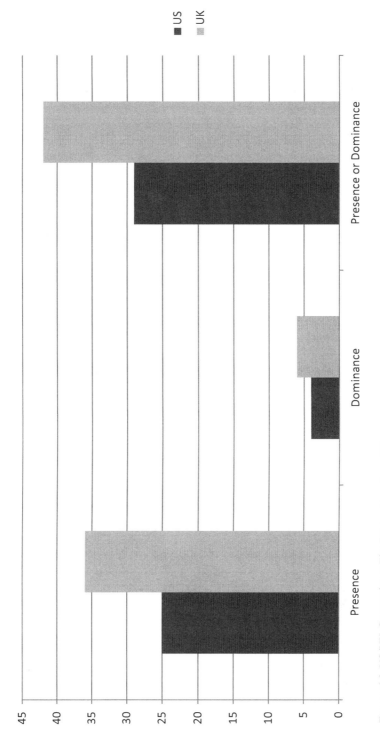

Figure 6.3 US/UK Comparison: The Proper Function of Democracy

The results in Figure 6.4 indicate that the US news media was much more likely to present Hamas as the vanguard of cultural backwardness given that this frame was present in 15 percent of the US sample versus 10 percent of the UK sample and dominant 7 percent versus 3 percent, respectively. While cultural judgments of the sort encoded in the *Hamas as Backward* frame might seem incongruous in news coverage of an election, the comparatively high presence of this frame in US coverage indicates an ideological divergence between the two countries whereby US news media are much more inclined to question cultural and religious attributes of Palestine and the Palestinians than that same institution in the UK.

In all, statistical tendencies in US coverage of the PLC elections may reflect a trend among journalists working in the US news media to view political developments in Palestine–Israel as extensions of religious or cultural differences that are endemic and irrevocable. The same trend may not be as prominent among British journalists covering the conflict.[65] Though these are speculative conclusions, statistical evidence sustains the notion that exposure to a cultural evaluation of Palestine and the Palestinians accompanied US news coverage more often than British coverage. The concluding section of this chapter will investigate the cognitive and discursive consequences of this variance in coverage (among others) and will evaluate the significant quantitative and qualitative differences that appeared between the US and the UK in their national news media coverage of the election of Hamas.

Conclusions: divergent coverage in the US and the UK after the 2006 PLC Elections

As noted in the statistical comparison above, the print news media coverage of the PLC Elections of 2006 in the United States and Great Britain shared certain important similarities. For one, the most dominant frame of representation embedded within both news media presentations was *Hamas as Terrorist*, a frame noted for its emphatic assertion of Hamas as an exclusively violent group, bent on destruction and negation even since their historic move into the political arena. The second most prevalent frame of representation in this statistical review was that of *Palestinian Voice, Rational* (69 percent present or dominant in the US data sampling; 58 percent present or dominant in the UK data sampling). In presenting considered Palestinian testimony to such a statistically significant extent in the coverage of the PLC elections of 2006, British and US journalists demonstrated their willingness to allow the voice of those most directly affected by the election carry the story. In combination, these two otherwise incompatible frames of reference were statistically dominant in both news media communities within the data sampling analyzed here.

The most important similarities between the two news institutions in their coverage of this event end there. One important divergence was the dominant story in both national news media communities, the presence or dominance of the *Hamas as Terrorist* frame, which was statistically more prominent in coverage in the United States, being present or dominant in 82 percent of news articles, than it

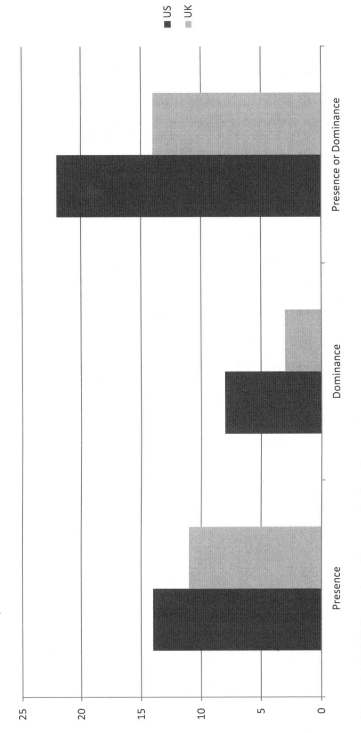

Figure 6.4 US/UK Comparison: Hamas as Backward

was in the United Kingdom, present or dominant in 68 percent of news articles. The British news media was also much more inclined to laud the PLC elections as a legitimate democratic process; *The Proper Function of Democracy Frame* was present or dominant in 42 percent of articles in the UK data sampling but only in 29 percent of articles from the US sample. Additionally, the *Failure of Democracy* frame was present or dominant in 43 percent of US articles, slightly more than the 35 percent of British articles. A final telling point of comparison involves the *Hamas as Backward* frame. The British news media was much less inclined to judge or condemn Arab, Muslim, or Palestinian culture within their coverage of the elections of 2006 than was the US news media which included this frame of representation in 21 percent of articles in the sample reviewed for this case study. In the UK, it was present in just 14 percent of the articles reviewed.

   This statistical evidence leads to the conclusion that the US news media was more inclined to portray Hamas as a threat to democracy, a danger to regional peace, and a harbinger of repressive, fundamentalist culture than was the UK. This presentation conforms to the generally constructed view of the group "invariably associated with the bloody legacy of its military wing" consisting of "cold-eyed, bearded gunmen declaiming in Arabic about the bloodshed that they are ... about to inflict."[66] The story within the story about the PLC elections of 2006, then, was a story not of politicians running for office, but of terrorists unjustly and illegitimately usurping political power. For the US news media, culture, politics, and regional peace were placed at the point of a gun in Palestine–Israel in 2006, and the readership in the US developed their knowledge of the situation accordingly. In the UK, British news media was slightly more willing to present Hamas as a multi-faceted, nuanced political and military organization, more frequently adopting the idea that "Hamas is not a gang" but rather an integral part of the Middle East's "Islamic society."[67] Subsequent public knowledge and social cognition surrounding the election of Hamas and the Palestinian–Israeli conflict within the United Kingdom would have likewise developed accordingly.

Notes

1   Khaled Hroub, *Hamas: Political Thought and Practice* (Institute for Palestine Studies: Washington, DC, 2000), vii.
2   Hamas is the Arabic word for "'enthusiasm' or 'zeal' and ... is the acronym for *Harakat al-Muqawama al-'Islamiyya* [Islamic Resistance Movement]" (Ziad Abu-Amr, Ziad. *Islamic Fundamentalism in the West Bank and Gaza: Muslim Brotherhood and Islamic Jihad* (Bloomington, IN: Indiana University Press, 1994), 66). The group's name was selected both for its identification of the group as the Islamic Resistance Movement in Palestine as well as for the meaning of the original Arabic term.
3   Beverley Milton-Edwards and Stephen Farrell, *Hamas: The Islamic Resistance Movement* (Cambridge, England: Polity Press, 2010), 259.
4   Ibid., 230.
5   Jonathan Schanzer, *Hamas vs. Fatah: The Struggle for Palestine* (New York: Palgrave MacMillan, 2008), 95 (my emphasis).
6   Zaki Chebab, *Inside Hamas: The Untold Story of Militants, Martyrs, and Spies* (New York: I.B. Tauris, 2007), 2.

7   Ibid.
8   Hroub, *Hamas*, 39.
9   Ibid.
10   Azzam Tamimi, *Hamas: A History from Within* (Northampton, Massachusetts: Olive Branch Press, 2007), 219.
11   Ibid.
12   Milton-Edwards and Farrell, *Hamas*, 9.
13   Ibid.
14   Ibid.
15   Tamimi, *Hamas*, 220–1.
16   Milton-Edwards and Farrell, *Hamas*, 262.
17   Ibid.
18   Nathan Shachar, *The Gaza Strip: Its History and Politics* (Portland, Oregon: Sussex Academic Press, 2010), 172.
19   In fact, at the time of this writing, March of 2014, 12 elected officials from the Hamas-led government remain in Israeli prisons.
20   Khaled Hroub, *Hamas: A Beginner's Guide* (London: Pluto Press, 2006), 48.
21   Tamimi, *Hamas*, 3.
22   Hroub, *Hamas*, 36.
23   Abu-Amr, *Islamic Fundamentalism in the West Bank and Gaza*, 1.
24   Shaul Mishal and Avraham Sela, *The Palestinian Hamas: Vision, Violence, and Coexistence* (New York: Columbia University Press, 2000), 113.
25   Hroub, *Hamas: Political Thought and Practice*, 11.
26   Tamimi, *Hamas*, 52.
27   Andrea Nüsse, *Muslim Palestine: The Ideology of Hamas* (Amsterdam, The Netherlands: Harwood Academic Publishers, 1998), 16.
28   Tamimi, *Hamas*, 14.
29   Schanzer, *Hamas vs. Fatah*, 29.
30   In their comprehensive study of Hamas published in 2010, Beverly Milton-Edwards and Stephen Farrell report that Israeli policy was definitely favorable to the establishment of an Islamist group within the Gaza Strip to serve as a potential political foil to the established and intransigent PLO. They base this assertion, in part, on Israel's demonstrated willingness to allow the existence of Islamic societies and social groups (in this case, the Muslim social service group known as the *mujamma* or "society") within the Strip, even going to the extent of granting them official status in the territories: "The Mujamma received a boost in 1978, when it was granted official status by the Israeli authorities ruling Gaza, at a time when it was nigh impossible for secular groups to get the same recognition. Officials in the office of the Israeli Prime Minister, Menachem Begin, gave approval to the registration. Many Palestinians believe, and some former Israeli officials concede, that this happened against the background of an Israeli strategy to produce a counterbalance to the PLO, and to divide secular nationalists by encouraging them to this Islamic alternative ... While the welfare and charity arms of Israel's public enemy number one, the PLO, were compelled to remain clandestine in Gaza and the West Bank throughout the 1970s and 1980s, the Mujamma was able to operate openly and freely" (Milton-Edwards and Farrell, *Hamas*, 44–47).
31   Sara Roy, *Hamas and Civil Society in Gaza: Engaging the Islamist Social Sector* (Princeton, New Jersey: Princeton University Press, 2011).
32   Hroub, *Hamas: A Beginner's Guide*, vii–viii.
33   Tamimi, *Hamas*, 2.
34   Milton-Edwards and Farrell, *Hamas*, 158.
35   Mishal and Sela, *The Palestinian Hamas*, vii.
36   Roy, *Hamas and Civil Society in Gaza*, 1.

37 Stephen Erlanger, "Hamas Leader Sees No Change Toward Israelis," *The New York Times,* January 29, 2006, 1.

38 Inigo Gilmore and Martin Bentham, "Gunfight at Parliament as Hamas Sweeps to Poll Victory," *The Evening Standard*, January 26, 2006, 17.

39 See frame of representation this chapter entitled *Hamas as Moderates* for a further explication of this topic.

40 Chris McGreal, "Hamas Makes Gains against Fatah, But Fails to Win Power: Exit Poll Shows Ruling Party Clinging to Office: Militant Islamist Group Mounts Strong Challenge," *The Guardian*, January 26, 2006, 19.

41 Laura King, "Hamas-Led Parliament Takes Power," *The Los Angeles Times*, February 19, 2006, 6A.

42 Peter Morey and Amina Yaqin, *Framing Muslims: Stereotyping and Representation after 9/11* (London: Harvard University Press, 2011), 3.

43 Though space prevents a more complete discussion on the *hijab* and its potential associations within contemporary discourse, the following works: "Making Sense of the "Islamic Peril" by Karim H. Karim (2002), "(Un)veiled Muslim Women Talk about Hijab" by Ines Hofmann Kanna (2010), and "Troublesome Threesome: Feminism, Anthropology and Muslim Women's Piety" by Christine M. Jacobsen (2011) provide a more in-depth discussion on this issue and were consulted for this section of this study.

44 Greg Myre, "Hamas Completes Lineup for Palestinian Ministries," *The New York Times*, March 19, 2006, 6.

45 Palestinians Go to the Polls, *The Guardian*, January 25, 2006.

46 Laura King, "Hamas Faces a New Struggle: Its political success will call for tough decisions by the Islamist group: whether or not to ally with archrival Fatah and to recognize Israel," *The Los Angeles Times*, January 26, 2006, 6A.

47 Donald Macintyre, "Guns or Politics? Now Hamas Must Choose," *The Independent,* January 23, 2006; Stephen Erlanger, "Hamas Leader Sees No Change Toward Israelis. *The New York Times*, January 29, 2006, 1.

48 Laura King and Ken Ellingwood, "Israel Assesses a New Reality; With its Enemy Hamas Elected to Govern the Palestinians, the Jewish State Treads Lightly," *The Los Angeles Times*, January 29, 2006, 1A.

49 Stephen Farrell, "Pullout Offer on Eve of Election," *The London* Times, January 25, 2006, 37.

50 Donald Macintyre, "Palestinian Funding Hangs in the Balance as International Donors Urge Abbas to Stay On," *The Independent*, January 30, 2006.

51 L. Doyle, "Israelis Fear Hamas 'Terror State'," *The Independent*, January 24, 2006.

52 This quote appear in D. Francis, "What Aid Cutoff to Hamas Would Mean: The US Provides about One-Third of the Nearly $1.1 Billion in Aid to the Palestinians. *The Christian Science Monitor*, February 27, 2006. But it should be mentioned that Mr Weisglass has since denied ever saying that which is attributed to him in this report.

53 Chris McGreal, "Hamas Drops Call for Destruction of Israel from Manifesto," *The Guardian*, January 2, 2006; Timothy Butcher, "Hamas Drops Call for the End of Israel as Poll Nears," *The Daily Telegraph*, January 13, 2006, 18.

54 Stephen Erlanger, "U.S. Spent $1.9 Million to Aid Fatah in Palestinian Elections," *The New York Times*, January 23, 2006, 11A.

55 Isabel Oakeshott, "Peace Hopes Shattered by Hamas Win," *The Evening Standard*, January 27, 2006, 15.

56 Q and A: From Bombs to Ballot Boxes, *The Sun*, January 27, 2006.

57 It is only fair to mention that among a large number of Britons, *The Sun* is considered as little more than a tabloid rag containing naked women (the now famous "page 3 girls"), football scores, celebrity gossip, and little else. Nevertheless, during the period of coverage being discussed here, *The Sun* had the largest circulation of any newspaper in Britain with an average daily circulation of over 2 million copies as recently as

March of 2014. This publication's presentations of events in Palestine–Israel are therefore included in this study, as they are in other case studies in this work.

58   Laura King, "Hamas Faces a New Struggle: Its political success will call for tough decisions by the Islamist group: whether or not to ally with archrival Fatah and to recognize Israel," *The Los Angeles Times*, January 26, 2006, 6A.

59   Daniel Bensaid, "Permanent Scandal" in Giorgio Agamben, Alain Badiou, Daniel Bensaid, Wendy Brown, Jean-Luc Nancy, Jacques Rancière, Kristin Ross, and Slavoj Zizek, *Democracy in What State?* (Colombia University Press: Chichester, West Sussex, 2011), 17–18.

60   Alan Cowell, "Europeans Insist Hamas Must Disavow Terrorism," *The New York Times*, January 27, 2006, 6A.

61   When Freedom's Just Another Weapon, *The Christian Science Monitor,* February 23, 2006.

62   Gabriel Milland. "Terror Group's Shock Poll Win." *The Express,* January 27, 2006, 14.

63   "Ballot Box Gains for Hamas Pose Dilemma for U.S., Allies," *USA Today*, January 25, 2006, 10A.

64   Timothy Butcher, "Hamas Rallies to Election Call from Jail," *The Daily Telegraph,* January 23, 2006, 15.

65   See the section subtitle "Covering Palestine-Israel in the United States versus the United Kingdom: Politics and Culture" in *The Journalistic Perspective*, Chapter 9.

66   Milton-Edwards and Farrell, 2010: 3

67   Chebab, *Inside Hamas*, 225.

7 Covering the Gaza war

Gaza: December 2008–January 2009

On December 27, 2008 the Israeli Air Force, acting in conjunction with Israeli naval vessels located in the Mediterranean Sea, began a coordinated assault on the Gaza Strip, a forty-mile long by two-mile wide area inhabited exclusively by Arab Palestinians and under continuous Israeli military occupation since June of 1967.[1] The Israeli assault was justified by both government and military spokespeople as an overwhelming although righteous military *response* to surface to surface rocket fire emanating from Gaza and threatening Israeli soldiers and civilians in southern Israel. Further justification impugned Hamas,[2] the military and political authority in the Gaza Strip since 2006, as the instigator of the violence and the cause of regional instability. Destroying or debilitating Hamas, therefore, was an oft-stated accompanying objective of the Israeli offensive: "[Israeli] Defence Minister Ehud Barak stated his objectives early on: 'To change the situation fundamentally, until there is no rocket fire'... General Yo'av Gallant, who had planned the operation and now commanded it, wanted to 'Damage Hamas' smuggling routes, its leadership and its tactical options.'"[3] With these stated aims, the Israeli military conducted a three-week bombing campaign and accompanying ground invasion that was as destructive and widespread as it was intense. Writing as an observer from a hill-top position just outside the Gaza Strip itself (a vantage point from which Israeli officials and citizens alike gathered to cheer on the destruction of Gaza), author and historian Nathan Shachar described the escalating violence with the following, descriptive phrases:

> on the last day of 2008, two kilometres from the outskirts of Gaza City, the heavens loom like some latter-day rendering of Biblical prophecy. Plumes of dark smoke billow up from the earth and the sky is crisscrossed by the trails of red tracer bullets. Every now and then, when a blockbuster bomb hits an ammunition depot in Gaza city, the ground shifts under our feet ... A Soviet-style Grad rocket shrieks by on its way to Ashkelon, and an instant later two glowing points appear above, as a Cobra helicopter activates its Hellfire-missiles and steers them towards the launching site of the Hamas rocket.[4]

In a complementary description of regional events, written in the weeks immediately after the assault in their book entitled *Hamas: The Islamic Resistance Movement*, journalists and political analysts Beverly Milton-Edwards and Stephen Farrell described the first day of the Israeli campaign as follows:

> On 27 December 2008 Israel launched airstrikes the length and breadth of the Gaza Strip which destroyed or damaged nearly every Palestinian security installation. Palestinian medical officials said that at least 155 people were killed and 200 wounded in the first strikes, which began without warning shortly before noon as the opening wave of an offensive named "Operation Cast Lead, the IDF's Fight against Terror in Gaza" … At Shifa hospital in Gaza City, scores of dead bodies were laid out in front of the morgue … Many were dismembered.[5]

Milton-Edwards and Farrell describe horrific scenes of a violent episode which was to last three destructive weeks. During that period of hostilities, Palestinian casualties resulting from Operation Cast Lead totaled more than 1,300 with somewhere between 295 and 926 of these casualties counted from among unarmed Palestinian civilians. This vast discrepancy in reported civilian casualties hinges, like in many political conflicts, upon those doing the reporting of the casualties themselves. The number "295" represents an official Israeli military statistic, while the number "926" represents the number of civilian casualties reported by Palestinian sources.[6] According to analyst Michael Gross, this dispute represents a classic consequence of the prosecution of asymmetric war:

> How many civilians died in the Gaza War? … The Palestinians count over 900 civilians among the dead, while Israeli figures number only 300 to 400. Obviously, this makes a huge difference when assessing proportionality. The problem is not one of identification; authorities knew the *names* of most of the dead. Rather, the dispute turns on *affiliation*, who exactly, counts as a civilian or combatant? This is a recurring question of asymmetric conflict and the Gaza War sharpened differences of opinion.[7]

Undoubtedly, the debate about civilian casualties in Gaza is important and has a significant impact upon public perceptions of the regional violence during this period. But regardless of the proportion of Palestinian causalities constituted by civilians, the Palestinian casualty rate, especially as compared to the Israeli casualty rate, can only be said to be alarmingly high. The internationally accepted figure of more than 1,300 Palestinians killed and more than 5,000 wounded speaks to the indiscriminate nature of the Israeli bombardment of Gaza. In addition, these high casualty rates reflect certain practical and political realities of the Gaza Strip itself as well. During the Gaza War of 2008–09, as now, Gaza was under the tight controls of the Israeli government and military; the shipment of goods, the free movement of people, and any and all potential outlets for escape from the Israeli aerial assault were closed off:

Gaza is … a prison … Israel closes them off from the sea, the air and land, except for a limited safety valve at the Rafah crossing. Residents cannot visit their relatives in the West Bank or look for work in Israel, upon which the Gaza economy has been dependent for some forty years. Sometimes goods can be transported, sometimes not.[8]

This combination of circumstances: a militarily sealed zone, 40 miles long by two miles wide, densely packed with over 1.5 million Palestinians and subjected to an extensive three-week bombing campaign could certainly only have produced the aforementioned gruesome results. The Israeli bombing campaign and subsequent ground invasion of the Gaza Strip in December 2008–January 2009 can only be described as a devastating act of war by Israel.

Added to this profound loss of life, Israeli bombardment during Operation Cast Lead was also responsible for unprecedented infrastructural damage within the Gaza Strip: "2,400 buildings destroyed—among them 30 mosques, 121 factories and workshops, and 29 institutions of education. The houses of 350,000 residents were damaged, some beyond recognition."[9] The effect of these damages in an area already economically crippled by prolonged restrictions and closures can scarcely be measured while the financial costs of these damages were predictably astronomical. The repair of Gaza, a parcel of land already debilitated by closures and demolitions prior to December 2008, has yet to make serious progress at the time of this writing, more than five years after the end of the assault. Exceedingly high figures of Palestinian dead and wounded combined with prolific and widespread destruction of property and infrastructure speak to an Israeli campaign that was either calculated in its massive destructive capabilities, or else haphazard in its targeting of legitimate military, security, or paramilitary installations. For residents of Gaza during this period, there was little practical difference between these two scenarios.

The destruction of life and property in Gaza is further amplified by the lack of Israeli casualties on a scale remotely comparable to Palestinian losses. The 1,300 Palestinian dead represent "more than a hundred times the number of Israeli casualties" with comparable ratios amongst the wounded of the two parties."[10] According to reports from both sides, as well reports from international observers, 13 Israelis died in the 2008–2009 war, ten soldiers in urban combat in Gaza, and three civilians as a result of rocket fire from Gaza into southern Israel. Among those ten soldiers who were killed, four died when a misdirected Israeli tank shell landed near their position in an incident of accidental or "friendly" fire. These profoundly imbalanced casualty statistics no doubt reflect the utter superiority of Israeli military capabilities versus those of the Palestinian military and paramilitary groups present inside the Gaza Strip. But more than that, these disproportionate statistics speak to the manner in which Israel conducted this particular military campaign, the latest example of military and political asymmetry of engagement between Israel and its enemies.

Israel's prosecution of Operation Cast Lead—as evinced by the casualty statistics of the war—mandated the protection of its own soldiers and citizens no matter what cost this created in terms of casualties or damage on the other side of the line:

> The Israeli tactic had two objectives: to bring down the number of Israeli fatalities by assuring that no armed resistance came within rage of the soldiers, and to establish a new "price tag" for the firing of rockets against Israel. In other words, the blurring of the civilian/combatant distinction and the overkill volume of fire seem to have been the plan, not an unintended consequence.[11]

In Gaza in 2008–2009, therefore, Israel demonstrated both the will and the capability to cripple an entire society with only the most minimal damage to its own citizens and to its state political and military infrastructure. Though such an effort is highly difficult or else largely unsuccessful in warfare in other theatres around the world, "In Gaza, and in contrast to the conduct of many earlier asymmetric conflicts, the state power … to fight a ground war with zero tolerance for military casualties … was largely successful."[12] The citizens of Gaza were effectively helpless against the Israeli military machine, the fourth largest in the world.

As a result of the inordinately high numbers of dead and wounded among Gazans in December 2008–January 2009, Israel was widely criticized during and after the Operation Cast Lead campaign by human rights groups, pro-peace organizations, and both national and international governmental organizations including the United Nations:

> In September 2009 the UN Human Rights Council's fact finding mission into the operation criticized Israel, accusing its military of using disproportionate force against the civilian population of Gaza, of carrying out a deliberate and systematic policy to target Palestinian industrial sites, water installations and homes, and of using Palestinians as human shields during the conflict.[13]

This is but one example of the multiple, vocal criticisms that were directed at Israel and Israeli political and military officials in the days and weeks following the bombardment. Further criticism was leveled at Israel by various international groups for preventing humanitarian aid from entering Gaza during and after the bombing campaign: "The international Red Cross accused Israel Thursday of 'unacceptable' delays in letting rescue workers reach three Gaza City homes hit by shelling where they eventually found 15 dead and 18 wounded, including young children too weak to stand."[14] According to these condemnations, Israel was either deliberately causing Palestinian civilians (including "young children") to suffer, or else they were facilitating these events by glibly adhering to their ongoing militaristic agenda inside the Palestinian territories.

Israeli spokespeople responded to these allegations by blaming the tactics of Hamas and other Palestinian military groups in Gaza for the suffering of Palestinian civilians. According to these retorts, the high civilian death tolls among the Palestinians of Gaza were due to the Palestinian practice of using human shields during fighting with the Israeli military: "The Israel Defense Forces are engaged in a battle with the Hamas terrorist organization that has deliberately used Palestinian civilians as human shields."[15] In this version of events, Palestinian militants fired rockets and shot guns at Israelis from civilian areas including schools and mosques. In order to eliminate this threat to its own soldiers and citizens, the Israeli military bombed those areas targeting those Palestinian militants who were hiding there. Any civilian death, while unfortunate, was unintended.

The assertion that Hamas provoked civilian casualties by launching rockets from neighborhood streets, schoolyards, and mosques was sustained by international criticism. The United Nations, among other peace-keeping organizations, impugned Hamas for its use of civilian areas to launch rockets into Israel. The Palestinian political and military organization was also criticized by international peace keeping agencies for its disregard for the distinction between enemy soldier and enemy civilian, and for the deliberate targeting of Israeli civilians in southern Israel before and during the three-week war:

> In January 2009 the human rights campaign group Amnesty International warned Hamas that if it was using Palestinian civilians as human shields it would be in contravention of the Geneva Convention: "Hamas fighters also put civilians in danger by firing from homes" it claimed.[16]

In responding to these allegations, Hamas would again invoke the geographic and demographic conditions of the Gaza Strip including realities of space, land, and restricted movement imposed by the prolonged Israeli occupation. According to Hamas, the conditions imposed by Israel in the Strip rendered their military and political options during the 2008–2009 fighting involuntarily finite: "Hamas respond[ed] to the human shield accusations by saying that, with Gaza sealed off from the outside world – by Israel – it has little choice but to wage war in the deeply densely populated city centres and refugee camps where it lives."[17] In effect, Hamas challenged Israeli and international criticisms of its military tactics by claiming that they could only respond to the aggressive military tactics of Israeli occupation from within the environment in which they are forced to live. From this perspective, the conditions created and imposed by Israeli occupation cannot be considered as comprising criminal violations on the part of Hamas and the Palestinians, given that they do not control the political and geographic realities in Gaza.

The essence of this dialogue between Israeli sources, and their sympathizers, and Palestinian sources, and their sympathizers effectively produced two distinct ideological and political perspectives developed during and after the prosecution of Operation Cast Lead. From the perspective of the Palestinian citizens of Gaza, and from news media outlets that shared this view of events, massive amounts of indiscriminate death and structural damage were wrought in the community in order to punish the actions of a few members.[18] From the Israeli perspective, and from news media outlets sharing this view, a consistent risk to Israel's citizens resulting from repeatedly fired surface to surface rockets was forcefully and thoroughly combatted. Israeli spokespeople consistently named Hamas as the group responsible for regional violence and defended Israeli actions as restrained and responsive military tactics designed to weaken the terrorist group.[19]

These accusations and counter-claims in Gaza at the end of 2008 and the beginning of 2009 followed a brutal three-week period. As evinced above, each side of the conflict had justifications at the ready to explain their conduct. These justifications in turn produced a myriad of narrative subplots that were then readily available to journalists working in the region during this period. Within news media coverage of Operation Cast Lead, then, a multitude of embedded perspectives were presented to the consumers of the news. Naturally these perspectives provided within the news media during and shortly after the 2008–2009 Gaza War were not homogenous across news outlets or publications. Rather, through the application of frames of news media representation in the coverage of these events, different aspects of the war and of the broader conflict were elucidated and/or emphasized and different narrative tropes appeared with varying frequency in difference communities of news coverage. Analysis of these variations in representation in two national news media communities comprises the focus for the remainder of this chapter.

Frames of representation in coverage of the war on Gaza (US and UK)

Upon reading and reviewing a substantial sample of print news articles covering the December 2008–January 2009 Gaza War from both the US and British national news media communities, a number of frames of representation embedded within the coverage become evident. The frames of representation to be discussed were identified after a close reading of the news articles themselves and without any specific predetermination before the fact. Those considered here are some of the more statistically significant frames, appearing most often in the article samplings from both national news media communities considered. They are also among those frames whose discursive impact was, in the opinion of this author, potentially greatest in the development of knowledge about the events considered. That is, the frames discussed below each had the potential to significantly influence readers' development of knowledge about the bombardment of Gaza and about the broader Palestinian–Israeli conflict in late 2008 and early 2009.

Palestinian culpability: Crucial to the assessment of culpability, whether identifying Palestinian, Israeli, or joint culpability for the fighting in 2008–2009, is the concept of historicization: the provision of reasonable historical context in the framing of news stories and the reporting of contemporary events. This is not to say that every news article emanating from this coverage should have a historical treatise attached to it in order to situate the scenario being discussed for the reader. Instead the concept of historicization indicates the provision of a small amount of historical context within certain news items can be used to clarify events and identify regional and international actors in theatres of conflict such as

Palestine–Israel. In the majority of examples from US and UK sources, however, political context and/or historical background of Israeli civil and military control of all areas of historic Palestine, including the ongoing Israeli military occupation of East Jerusalem, the West Bank, and the Gaza Strip are unmentioned. At first approach, criticism of news media contending a lack of historical context may seem unreasonable given that "Journalists are [inevitably] fixated on the present."[20] Still, even allowing the "audience-attracting purposes of the press, [and] the need for daily grist"[21] inherent to this process, it is feasible to include historical context especially when covering this region of conflict. Examples of coverage that includes relevant historical information impacting the development of understanding about current events is present within the article sampling analyzed here.[22] These examples from the print news media include a measure of historical background serving to provide the consumer with vital material for the interpretation of events being relayed. This existence of these examples of contextualized coverage indicates the possibility of avoiding the journalistic tendency to "define events from a short-term anti-historical perspective."[23]

Within the article sampling analyzed, the issue of culpability for regional violence was often central in the presentation of events. The assertion of one or the other side of the conflict as culpable for the recent round of violence made its way into most of the publications here examined. In many cases culpability was attributed to one side in the conflict overtly: "Israeli warplanes and helicopters bombarded military targets across the Hamas-ruled Gaza Strip on Saturday and today, *retaliating* for Palestinian rocket fire into Israel."[24] The opening paragraph of this article clearly defines Israeli action as responsive in nature, with the original antagonism attributed to Hamas and the rocket fire originating in Gaza. Other examples of defining Hamas specifically or Palestine generally as the culpable agent in the January conflict include the assertion that "[t]he Israeli offensive is aimed at stopping rocket fire by Palestinian militants"[25] and "[t]he Israeli military said its soldiers fired in self-defense after Hamas fighters launched mortar shells."[26] In this construction the reader is led to believe that were it not for the rocket fire emanating from the Gaza Strip, Israeli military actions would not be taking place. These and other examples from authoritative news sources in both the US and UK led the consumers of printed news media to conclude that culpability in the form of original action lay with Hamas and the Palestinians whereas defense and reaction lay with the Israelis.

Israeli culpability. Other excerpts from printed news coverage openly criticized Israeli military action for its indiscriminate nature, its broad scope, and for the unnecessary cruelty it imposed upon the Palestinians of Gaza. They present a very different perspective to the news media consumer and offer an alternative frame of representation in the potential development of knowledge about this event. Included in this group of articles are those that led with descriptions of Israeli aggression resulting in expansive destruction in the Gaza Strip. In a *New York Times* report from Gaza, the journalist describes the fighting in mid-January of 2009 as a "war [that] comes from the sky: fast, sharp and coldly lethal. And even when it is not crushing a building or collapsing a tunnel, its sounds is always near in the nasal whine of drones and the earsplitting roar of fighter jets."[27] This descriptive prose is clearly meant to invoke the destructive capacity of the Israeli military machine and the ubiquitous fear that it inspires among the Palestinian populous. Other commentaries invoke historical links to the recent conflict and blame Israeli action for prolonged Palestinian suffering. Still others emphasize the arbitrary or indiscriminate nature of the Israeli military offensive: "All road travel is hazardous because Israeli spotters treat any vehicle as a potential threat"[28] and "Israel's bombing campaign in Gaza is the latest in a cycle of military operations dating back to 2006."[29]

In these examples, florid narration of the horrors of war as well as overt condemnation of Israeli actions portray a conflict in which Israeli aggression and militarism cause widespread and unnecessary harm to Gazan Palestinian society. The frame described here has the potential to promote sympathy to the Palestinians and simultaneous judgment of Israeli action on the part of the readers rendering this narrative trope significant in the formation of knowledge among the news consuming public about these events specifically and about the broader conflict as a whole. This frame of representation did not necessarily appear in news articles *without* the previously articulated frame, *Palestinian Culpability*, however. In certain news items each frame was presented alongside the other to indicate culpability and agency in this conflict on both sides of the political divide.

Palestinian suffering. In this frame of representation, significant emphasis was placed upon the hardships endured within the Gaza Strip as a result of the Israeli bombing campaign and subsequent ground invasion of Gaza. In news articles that emphasized Palestinian suffering, various journalistic approaches were used to convey the tribulations endured by the Palestinian people. One strategy, effective for the graphic manner in which it was expressed, was to detail physical injury to Gazans resulting from Israeli action. Included in these descriptions are eyewitness accounts of physical trauma as well as reference to widespread death (particularly of civilians) that resulted from the Israeli military campaign. A January 5 article in the *Los Angeles Times* piece reported "a man lying on the street with both legs severed"[30] while a January 9 piece from *The New York Times* reported "The International Committee of the Red Cross said ... it had discovered 'shocking' scenes—including small children next to the mothers' corpses."[31] Other gripping descriptions of Palestinian trauma at the hands of the Israeli military include depictions of individuals and families whose loved ones perished during the attacks: "women wailed as they searched for relatives among the bodies that lay strewn on the hospital floor."[32] Further descriptions of the decimated infrastructure of Gaza added to the presentations of the degradation of Palestinian society and communal suffering during and after the Israeli military operation: "smoldering remains of a U.N. food warehouse;"[33] "[n]ear two destroyed Gaza City mosques, men spread carpets on sandy ground to prepare for open-air prayers;"[34] and "High-rise apartments shook and smaller, targeted buildings crumbled under the force of Israeli artillery shelling."[35]

Examples of this frame of representation in the British printed news media included the January 2 report from *The Guardian* describing a man "sat in the middle of a Gaza City street … slapping his face, covering his head with dust from the bombed-out building and wailing: 'My son is gone, my son is gone.'"[36] Identifying the indiscriminate nature of Israeli attacks and the subsequently high civilian casualties in Gaza, *The Sunday Mirror* reported that "The first strikes had come as pupils walked home from school, leaving frantic mothers searching the blasted streets."[37] Both the headline and the leading paragraph of the January 5 *Guardian* article entitled "Tanks, Rockets, Death and Terror: a Civilian Catastrophe Unfolding: Incessant Bombardment, No Electricity, No Water, and the Hospitals Hull to Overflowing—How Gaza Was Torn Apart" impart upon the reader the ubiquitous and profound nature of the destruction wrought in Gaza by the Israeli military operation. In its entirety, the opening paragraph reports:

> It has never been like this before. The assault is coming from the sky, the sea, and the ground. The explosion of shells, the gunfire from the tanks and the missiles from planes and helicopters are incessant. The sky is laced with smoke, grey here, black there, as the array of weaponry leaves its distinctive trail.[38]

These vivid descriptions and graphic details impart upon the reader the unrepentantly violent nature of the Israeli attack and the indiscriminate consequences of this military action upon the men, women, and children of Gaza. As with other conceptual parameters identified throughout this study, this frame is not articulated here in order to suggest inaccuracy of representation. Rather it is identified in order to suggest the power of the language applied within this frame in the formation of cognition about Gaza during this time.

Israeli suffering. Palestinians were not the only groups depicted as suffering or endangered by events in Gaza. Israeli civilians were also shown to be terrorized and long suffering before and during the Israeli military operation in the Gaza Strip. In this frame of representation, the print media was able to define Israelis as victims and identify Palestinians as instigators. A description of this type can be found in the December 25, 2008 *New York Times* article entitled "Gaza Rocket Fire Intensifies":

> More than 60 rockets and mortar shells were fired at southern Israel by the afternoon, the Israeli military said. The rockets slammed into the Israeli town of Sderot, the yard of a house and a water park in the coastal city of Ashkelon and an Israeli factory at Nir Oz near the Gaza border, and they hit a house outside the Western Negev town of Netviot. The strikes caused extensive damage and widespread panic among the residents.[39]

In this presentation, the clear emphasis is on the suffering of the Israeli civilians subjected to random but persistent rocket fire from sources within the Gaza Strip. While this article did note that serious injuries sustained by this practice were rare, the article nonetheless emphasized the shocking and debilitating nature of such attacks within the communities of southern Israel and attributed aggression and militancy to the Palestinian communities of Gaza. In particular Hamas and its military wing, the Izz al-Din al-Qassam Brigades were identified as responsible actors in the spreading of fear and destruction among the communities of southern Israel. Other examples of this frame of representation emphasize the cruelty of this rocket fire by identifying child victims or potential victims of this practice: "Twenty rockets and mortar shells fell inside Israel on Sunday; one missile damaged an empty kindergarten in Ashdod."[40] Examples from the printed news media in the UK likewise identify the threat posed by these rocket attacks to the Israeli civilians living in and around Gaza: "Palestinian militants fired about 20 rockets into southern Israel, but there were no casualties. Four Israelis have been killed since Saturday."[41]

It should be noted, however, that this frame of representation was not necessarily presented to the exclusion of the frame describing Palestinian suffering in the news articles examined here. In some print examples from the data sample analyzed, journalists described both communities as victimized and fearful. In juxtaposing the two frames within the same news piece, a certain equivalence is created between the two communities. Other news pieces eschewed this tactic in order to depict an unequivocal story about the suffering of one community while impugning aggression and intransigence upon the other. The frequency of this narrative tendency within each news media community is best seen in the provision of the statistical representations and accompanying analysis of each frame at the conclusion of this chapter.

Palestinian narration, rational. As explained in the previous chapter, this frame of representation presents sober commentary from articulate individuals present in or involved with the Palestinian community during the Gaza War. Through the inclusion of these commentaries, readers are provided with legitimate, sober perspectives from the Palestinian citizenry and may therefore attribute political and/or moral justification to the Palestinian side of the conflict. Examples of this presentation in the British news coverage of the Gaza War include a January 4 article from *The Observer* that quoted Palestinian negotiator and legal counsel to the Palestinian Liberation Organizations, Diana Buttu in discussing the status of Gaza as a continually occupied area:

> When the Israelis pulled out [in 2005], we expected that the Palestinians in Gaza would at least be able to lead some sort of free life. We expected that the crossing points would open. We didn't expect that we would have to beg to allow food in.[42]

Intelligent articulation of the Palestinian perspective such as this conveys to news media consumers conceptions of legitimate political and social hardships endured by the Palestinian community of Gaza during and after the December–January war. Other examples of this perspective include a political analysis of factionalism within the Palestinian government and the way in which it was affected by the recent fighting in Gaza. In a January 20, 2009 *Los Angeles Times* article, Ghassan Khatib, a Palestinian analyst based in the West Bank city of Ramallah explained:

"Hamas will be much less powerful militarily against Israel but significantly stronger against Fatah."[43] Here, Khatib provides an examination of political solutions to the ongoing crisis even when facing open war and destructive, collective punishments. Quotations such as these convey intelligent and thoughtful analysis of the politics of the region despite widespread military conflict. This frame provides a measured image, therefore, of contemporary Palestinian society, one that is careful and nuanced as opposed to essentialized and/or reactionary.

Palestinian narration, radical. Palestinian voices are radicalized when only militant or otherwise aggressive or antagonistic segments of the population are given space to express themselves within the news media. The result is the construction of the general Palestinian perspective as one that embraces violence and destruction and potentially even openly advocates the destruction of the state of Israel. One such expression of violence came from Hamas official Sami Abu Zuhri, who claimed that the war with Israel did not end when hostilities in Gaza came to an end since the Palestinian cause intends to liberate the whole of historic Palestine: "We want to free all Palestine, not just Gaza."[44] Zhuri's assertion using the first person plural pronoun "we" indicates that Abu Zuhri believes that he speaks for a group of people, presumably Hamas or possibly even a broader segment of Palestinian society. As well, in this particular news article, Abu Zuhri is the only Palestinian source provided for the reader. It is conceivable, therefore that readers of this source may interpret Abu Zuhri as speaking for a significant majority of Palestinians or that his opinions are those of the Palestinian people in general. Further radicalization of the Palestinian voice is found in commentaries claiming political or moral victory in the aftermath of the Gaza War despite the widespread death and destruction wrought within Gaza. Such a perspective is provided by an anonymous Hamas official quoted in *The Los Angeles Times* as saying: "[e]very time the attacks increase, our support increases … We won't surrender to the cowardly policies of the Zionists."[45]

These and other presentations of radical Palestinian voices within the authoritative news media suggest that a culture of death and martyrdom underpin the fabric of Palestinian society. From this perspective, the tragedy of civilian death and widespread destruction during Israeli military action in Gaza is an acceptable price for political capital. Such an assertion is likely to be viewed with disdain by audiences for whom any civilian death should be accidental and regrettable and for which there can be no conceivable political or social benefit. As in the previous example the tone and character of this Palestinian perspective is anti-social, violent, and radical. In such presentations, and where no sober or measured Palestinian perspective is to be found in a given news item, none can be attributed to Palestinian society.

Israeli narration, rational. Rational and sober commentary was attributed to various Israeli speakers as coverage of the December 2008–January 2009 Gaza War progressed. In a similar fashion to Palestinian commentaries noted under the frame *Palestinian Voice, Rational*, this frame demonstrates the willingness of the news media to give editorial space, and therefore narrative authority, to intelligent, articulate citizen-leaders within Israel whose perspective may therefore be seen to be loosely equivalent to the perspective embraced by that political or ideological side of the conflict.

Rational narration advocating the Israeli point of view includes commentaries advocating peace and tranquility as well as condemnations of aggressive or indiscriminate violence. Frequently these assertions were provided by military or government officials within Israel lending further credence to their presentation given the tendency among consumers of the authoritative print news media to attribute expansive authority to state structures and to official members of state institutions. Then Israeli Foreign Minister and candidate for Prime Minister of Israel, Tzipi Livni was an oft-quoted government source during the period under examination. Commentary indicating her profound desire for peace even in the midst of an expansive military operation portrays Israel as a considerate, possibly even a passive actor who engages in military solutions only "to give peace and quiet to the citizens in southern Israel."[46] Other assertions from Israeli military officials profess their desire to avoid civilian casualties at all costs, even at risk to their own personnel: "The IDF in no way intentionally targets civilians and has demonstrated its willingness to abort operations to save civilian lives and to risk injury in order to assist civilians."[47] In these examples, the Israeli attempt at the alteration of regional politics by military means is undone. What remains is a transformative Israeli discourse containing official utterances promising restraint, calm, and ultimately, peace. Presented with this narrative frame, news media consumers are led to perceive reluctance or even regret on the part of Israel for their military operation in Gaza.

Israeli narration, radical. Within this frame of representation, Israeli government or military spokespeople express a profound lack of concern for the civilian damage being done to the Gaza Strip. Instead, certain statements reflect their desire to destroy huge swaths of territory, to kill indiscriminately, and to punish the entire Palestinian population for the actions of a few members of their community. Within this frame of representation, Israelis demonstrate little regard for international criticism or public censure for their actions. The frame *Israeli Narration, Radical*, therefore speaks to Israeli self-identification as aggressive, hostile, and militant and demonstrates an overt disregard for the well-being of Palestinians.

This perspective was present in the January 5, 2009 *Los Angeles Times* article by Richard Boudreaux and Rushdi abu Alouf entitled "Conflict in Gaza: At the Scene; Nowhere to Go, Gazans Stay Home." In it, Alex Fishman, an Israeli "military affairs correspondent" is quoted as saying: "we are moving in with full force, shooting everything we have, including artillery ... We'll pay the international price later for the collateral damage and the anticipated civilian casualties."[48] Not only does this spokesperson heartily endorse random, imprecise violence in the Israeli military operation, he expresses knowledge of civilian casualties, calling them "anticipated" but dismisses them as inconsequential. Presented with this quotation, consumers of the news media will interpret official Israeli policy as aggressive, callous, and blatantly destructive. In another, perhaps less incendiary example of Israeli commentary that characterizes this frame of information representation, Israeli Foreign Minister Tzipi Livni, in what might have been a conscious rhetorical alignment, echoed then US President George Bush's earlier assertion of an exclusively bifurcated world view: "These are the days when every individual in the region and in the world has to choose a side."[49] Livni's comments are clearly meant to broaden the regional conflict in which her country is engaged to include "every individual … in the world." While not as openly aggressive or callous as Fishman's declaration, the effect of Livni's comments create a looming, domineering image of Israel, one connected to the Bush Administration's division of the geopolitical landscape into two camps: one good, one evil.

These and other Israeli self-guided narratives lend credence to the view of Israel as an aggressive state and place the onus of conflict and violence upon them. As with the presentation of Palestinian radicalism, when these Israeli voices are the lone commentaries on Israeli policy or perspective presented in the news pieces, they lends particular validity to these representations and postulate a widespread callousness or destructive urge present within Israeli leadership and/ or society as a whole.

Israeli restraint/precision. According to this frame of representation, even in the midst of a violent conflict that cost the lives of more than 1,300 Palestinians, Israel embraced caution, restraint, and precision in both the intent and the execution of military policy. Within this journalistic frame, the reader may attribute reluctance or regret to the Israeli government, military, or spokespeople, even in the midst of a bloody military campaign in the Gaza Strip. From this perspective Israel attacked Gaza out of necessity, not desire.

The description of Israeli distribution of public warnings in the form of leaflets prior to specific air force sorties was marked within this frame of representation, as it portrays Israel as a fair, benevolent actor. This action is described here in an excerpt from a January 2009 edition of *The London Times*: "Leaflets dropped earlier in the day over Gaza City and the border areas urged Palestinians to flee their homes. 'For your safety, you are required to leave the area immediately,' stated the warning from the Israel Defence Forces.[50] Likewise, the expressed mitigation of damage caused by Israel during Operation Cast Lead, or the emphasis on Israeli military technology and targeting systems as precise or even humane warranted notation within this frame of reference: "There had been no carpet bombing of large areas, no firebombing of complete suburbs. Targets had been selected and then hit … but almost always with precision munitions."[51] Other descriptions that prompted the notation of this frame of representation included assertions of Israeli reluctance to fight, disdain for violent solutions to political conflict, or compassion toward their Palestinian enemy-neighbors: "Israel has been avoiding an offensive ever since Hamas overran the Gaza Strip in 2007."[52] As in previous discussions of journalistic frames, degrees of accuracy in the representation of events are not at issue here. What is at issue is simply the inclusion of particular pieces of information as background or context for the retelling of regional events, and the sublimation, suppression, or exclusion of other frames (or potential frames) concomitant in this process.

Palestinian aggression. Within this frame of representation, elements of militancy, aggression, and/or violence on the part of Hamas or Gaza's non-affiliated Palestinian residents is emphasized. This frame of representation (like the frame *Israeli Aggression* discussed below) was noted independently of frames implying culpability by either party for the outbreak of violence. So, whether describing violence by Palestinian parties as retaliatory or in the first cause, whether presented as illegal or as justified, language describing Palestinian violence or aggression in the Gaza War was noted here. Examples from the US news media include this excerpt from *The Los Angeles Times*: "Militants in the Gaza Strip showered southern Israeli towns with rockets and mortar fire Wednesday in the latest sign that the six-month truce between Israel and Hamas has collapsed."[53] Emphasis on Palestinian violence and the profound effect it has upon Israeli society fit naturally within this frame of reference as well: "The Palestinian rocket that hit the Israeli town of Beersheba detonated without causing injuries but the shock waves are still reverberating through the Jewish state."[54] As the news items reviewed for analysis here contain descriptions of a period of open war between Palestinian militants and the state of Israel, the frame *Palestinian Aggression* featured prominently as a narrative trope employed by both media communities during this period. An explanation of the statistical prevalence of this frame of representation, as well an attempted reconciliation between the statistical record presented by the examined sample and the known damage resulting from the Gaza War itself, is presented in the conclusion to this chapter.

Israeli aggression. Like the frame delineated above, *Israeli Aggression* naturally assumed a prominent role in the retelling of regional events from the winter of 2008. Descriptive language was employed in the print news samplings from both national news media communities to discuss violence and aggression on the part of the state of Israel, either as retaliatory action or as action taken in the first instance. General military operations and their destructive consequences were noted for this frame of representation, as were specific instances of Israeli sorties, invasions, or other military maneuvers: "Israeli missiles have wrought unprecedented destruction in Gaza, reducing whole buildings to rubble;"[55] "Mayhem, death and destruction came to Gaza at 11:30 am last Saturday when Israel dropped a first wave of bombs on the Hamas security compounds it was determined to wipe off the face of the map."[56] As may be evident, the notation of this frame of representation was very often found in news media articles along with the presentation of the frame *Palestinian Suffering*. In any case, in the article sampling from both the US and UK, this frame of representation was especially statistically prevalent due to the widespread destruction inflicted upon Palestinian society by the Israeli military throughout the course of this war. A detailed discussion about the particulars of this statistical prevalence follows below.

Palestinian restraint/precision. The logical counterpart to the frame *Israeli Restraint/Precision* identifies the same characterizations of reluctance, resistance, and disinclination towards violence on the part of Palestinian actors or spokespeople during this heightened period of conflict in Palestine–Israel. Language within the print news media sample analyzed for this case study was noted for representing this frame if and when Palestinian actors were described as supporting compromise, as agreeing to a cease-fire, or as accepting a truce with Israel. Examples from the printed news media in the United Kingdom include a January excerpt from *The Mirror* stating that "Last summer, Hamas initiated and accepted the terms of a six-month ceasefire between them and Israel."[57] Also present in a Sunday edition of the January 2009 *Mirror* was this report about Hamas' inclination toward non-violent reconciliation with Israel: "Hamas has offered a one-year, renewable truce on condition that all Israeli forces leave Gaza within a week."[58] Whether because of the unsophisticated nature of military equipment and tactics employed by Hamas, or the consistent attribution of base, violent motives on the part of Palestine and the Palestinians by foreign journalists in the US and UK or indeed, whether by some combination of factors present amongst the news media institution covering the Gaza War, this frame was the least statistically significant frame of all those noted in the article sample reviewed here.

Statistical evaluation, the United States

As indicated by Figure 6.3, in statistical terms, three frames of representation dominated the article US news media coverage of the 2008–2009 Gaza War: *Palestinian Suffering*, *Israeli Aggression*, and *Palestinian Aggression*. In total, they appeared in 73 percent, 71 percent, and 69 percent of the article sampling, respectively. This evidence suggests that consumers of the US print news media during the Gaza War, and in the weeks that followed, were likely to have been presented with a news story depicting Palestinian suffering as a result of the war. Israeli aggression was also a prominent narrative feature of this data sample; violence initiated by Palestinians was nearly equally present. If a news item contained official Israeli commentary, likely that commentary was sober and rational. *Israeli Narration, Rational* exceeded *Israeli Narration, Radical* by a statistical total of 46 percent versus 13 percent in the sample reviewed. Radicalized Palestinian commentary was statistically much more prevalent in this data sample, appearing in roughly 33 percent of articles reviewed whereas rational Palestinian commentary appeared in 39 percent of the sample. When the issue of culpability was addressed by the US print news media, it was attributed to Palestine or the Palestinians in 40 percent of the sample and to Israel in only 18 percent of the sample reviewed.

Some of this journalistic presentation matches with what is known about the prosecution of this war on the ground in Palestine–Israel. Palestinian casualties were widespread and seemingly indiscriminate and vastly outnumbered the casualties on this Israeli side of the conflict line during this war. The evidentiary results of this war then are in keeping with the US journalistic presentation of *Palestinian Suffering* (73 percent) and *Israeli Aggression* (71 percent). What is conceptually inconsistent when comparing the statistical evidenced produced here with the facts on the ground in Palestine–Israel is the emphasis on Israeli casualties in the US printed news (in 47 percent of the sample reviewed) and on the de-emphasis of Israeli culpability for a series of devastating air strikes launched

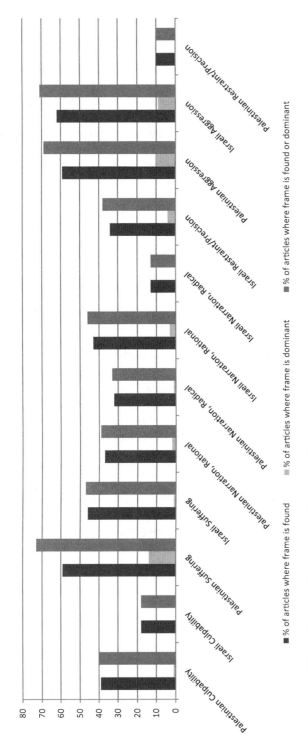

Figure 7.1 US Print News Media: The Gaza War, 2008–2009

■ % of articles where frame is found   ■ % of articles where frame is dominant   ■ % of articles where frame is found or dominant

unilaterally by Israel bombarding large areas of civilian populations and lasting more than three weeks. Instead of focusing upon these narrative elements within this news story, trends within the US print news media during this period were more focused upon Israeli casualties (a total of 13 compared to the more than 1,300 Palestinian dead) while squarely placing the blame for the fighting (and presumably their own casualties) on the Palestinians. These tendencies diverge significantly from both the historical record of this episode of conflict as well as the international assessments of what transpired in Gaza between December 2008 and January 2009.

Statistical evaluation, the United Kingdom

As is evident in Figure 7.2, the UK print news items present two frames of representation to a greater statistical extent than other frames. The frames in question were also prevalent in the US news media sample: *Palestinian Suffering* and *Israeli Aggression*. Unlike the US sample, though, the British news media institution was statistically much more critical of Israel for their culpability for the fighting in December 2008–January 2009; nearly 60 percent of news articles reviewed contained that particular frame of representation. This compares with only 28 percent of news articles which contained the frame identifying Palestinian culpability. The frame demarcating the narrative trope centered on *Palestinian Aggression* also featured prominently, present in over 53 percent of the news articles reviewed here. This frame was outdone by its counterpart, however, as *Israeli Aggression* featured in 75 percent of the British articles analyzed.

The prevailing frames of representation in the British news media during the bombardment of Gaza, therefore, focused on Palestinian casualties and Israeli responsibility. Narration on both sides of the conflict line was relatively even across ideological perspective and the appearance of the *Israeli Suffering* frame was low compared to the US sample appearing in only 26 percent of articles reviewed. According to the UK news media, restraint was not widely exercised by either party to the conflict; only 22 percent of news articles contained the frame *Israeli Restraint/Precision* while 6 percent contained the frame *Palestinian Restraint/Precision*. Overall, the language in the printed news representations of events in Palestine–Israel indicates an episode of unrestrained and imprecise violence for which Israel was predominantly responsible. The results included the widespread destruction of Gaza, extensive civilian casualties, and wide-ranging infrastructural damage.

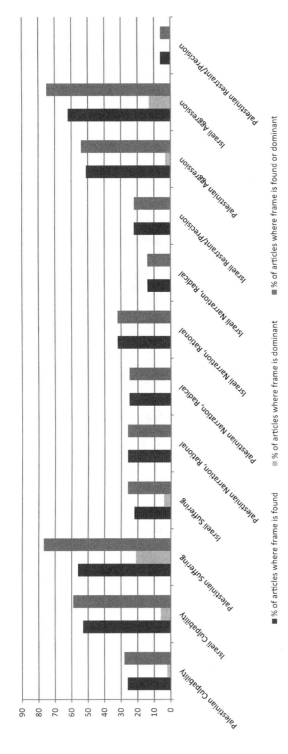

Figure 7.2 UK Print News Media: The Gaza War, 2008–2009

■ % of articles where frame is found or dominant

■ % of articles where frame is dominant

■ % of articles where frame is found

Statistical evaluation, comparison

While the above statistical information is telling in terms of narrative context and journalistic approach to coverage of the 2008–2009 Gaza War within the US and the UK, a direct comparison of particular frames of representation between the two nations also reveals informative patterns. According to Figure 7.3, print news in the United Kingdom was much more likely to include assertions of Israeli culpability for regional violence than their trans-Atlantic counterparts. The difference in the statistical prevalence of the *Israeli Culpability* frame in the given data sample reviewed for this case study is profound. Though dominant as a narrative trope in only about 6 percent of the news British print news articles analyzed here, the frame was in fact present in over half of the printed articles (54 percent) reviewed. This compares to no indication of this narrative as a dominant frame of reference in any news article from the US reviewed for this analysis, and only a very slight presence within that sample: just 18 percent.

According to the language used in the US print news media to describe the unfolding events in Gaza between December 2008 and January 2009, Israel was seldom ever presented as a culpable agent. Institutionally speaking, this perspective carried over a wide geographic and political spectrum of news publications with news articles from Washington DC to Los Angeles contributing items to this data sample. Even those very diverse publications had in common a great reluctance to attribute culpability to Israel for its assault on Gaza in 2008–2009. British journalists covering the same episode in Palestine–Israel showed no such disinclination; nearly 60 percent of their sample coverage analyzed contained significations of Israeli culpability for the fighting. In the UK sample reviewed, 29 percent contained language asserting Palestinian guilt for action in Gaza during this period whereas the US sample contained language indicating Palestinian culpability in 40 percent of the news items. The extremely wide variance in the appearance of this frame of reference in the two media communities indicates not only an institutional divergence in the attribution of guilt or blame in this violent episode of the Palestinian–Israeli conflict. The wide statistical margin indicated by here suggests, once again, an ideological divide between journalists, editors, and publishers working for news media outlets in the two countries.

The point of comparison to be made here is one of context and perspective. In covering the same events, British journalists routinely accused Israel of violence in the first instance; US journalists did not. This disparate perspective within the journalistic investigation of the period was widespread and indicates a critical divergence in language, perspective, and the subsequent discourse developed by the news media during this process. In the final assessment, evaluating evidence for *Israeli Culpability* so differently in the Gaza War would have been highly influential in terms of creating public knowledge and social cognition about this episode and about the broader conflict within the communities being served by the newsmakers in question.

Statistical evidence depicting the presence and/or dominance of the frame *Israeli Suffering* in the two national media communities is likewise institutionally

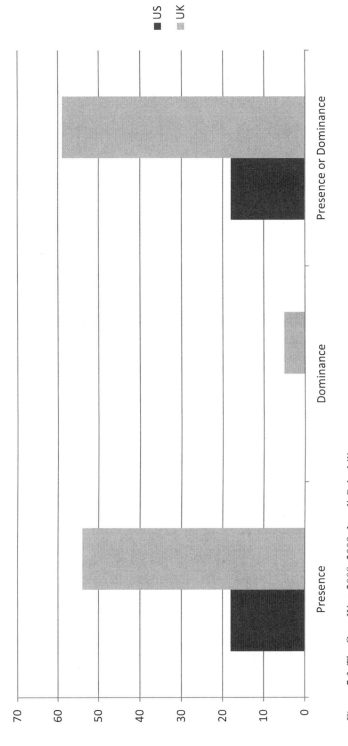

Figure 7.3 The Gaza War, 2008–2009: Israeli Culpability

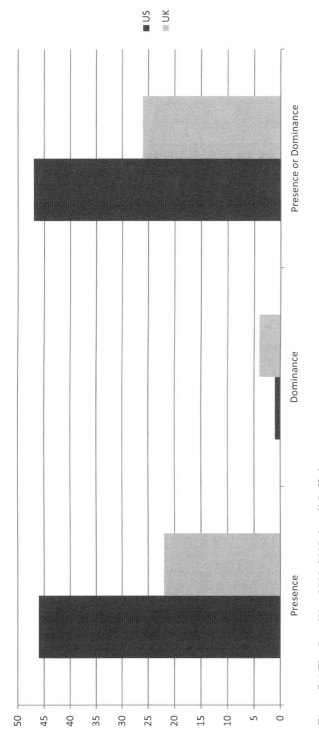

Figure 7.4 The Gaza War, 2008–2009: Israeli Suffering

as well as ideologically informative. Though both parties to the fighting as well as international observers agree that more than 1,300 Palestinians died in this war compared to 13 Israeli casualties, the US print news media was comparatively much more focused on those few Israeli casualties than were their trans-Atlantic colleagues. As evidenced above, the UK print media *did* devote entire articles to the story of Israeli fears, shock, and injury resulting from rockets launched by Palestinian groups from with the Gaza Strip. Plainly, though, these articles represent the minority of coverage. The *Israeli Suffering* frame was dominant in only roughly 4 percent of articles reviewed in this sample. In contrast, representations of Israeli hardships in the US print news media are present in 46 percent of the news articles reviewed for this case study though are dominant in only 1 percent. Overall, the 47 percent of US articles reviewed that contained this frame as either present or dominant is significantly larger than the 26 percent of articles in the UK sample. The US print news media institution was more focused on the small number of Israeli casualties than the UK media was, mentioning, as they did, Israeli suffering in nearly half of the articles sampled here.

This author is not asserting that Palestinian deaths were more important than Israeli deaths during the Gaza War. They were, however, 100-fold greater, according to the best sources available. While the British print news media seemed to reflect that disparate statistic within their coverage, discussing Palestinian casualties much more frequently than Israeli ones, it is clear from the sampling analyzed here that US news media outlets chose a different tack, focusing instead upon the Israeli casualties during this episode. What was relayed in the British print media then was a story of disproportionate suffering with the Palestinians taking on the vast majority of dead and wounded as a result of this violent war. What was relayed in the US print news media was a tale of dual suffering, of two societies equitably struggling and suffering through violent political conflict.

Conclusions: covering the Gaza War

Despite the above focus on the institutional and ideological difference in approach to the coverage of the 2008–2009 Gaza War between the United States and Great Britain, it is important to remember the similarities present in both national news media printed publications as well. The two frames of representation that appeared as statistically dominant within both media samples reviewed were *Israeli Aggression* and *Palestinian Suffering*. From a journalistic perspective, given the widespread damage and destruction of Gaza resulting from the Israeli bombardment and subsequent ground invasion of the region, the dominance of these two frames of representation in both news media communities stands to reason. These two frames combined to narrate news stories from a war zone that were essentially presenting themselves to regional journalists throughout the conflict: bombs dropped, citizens killed. These similarities between US and UK coverage might have been expected.

As noted above, important differences between coverage in the two national news media communities did exist and became evident in the linguistic analysis and statistical review of news article samples taken from the period of the conflict. In certain cases, these differences were important diversions from what was known about the facts on the ground surrounding the war. This was the case with the statistical prevalence of the frame *Israeli Suffering* in the US print media sample to a much greater extent than the UK print news media, and to a greater extent than the evidentiary record. In other cases the statistical prevalence of a particular frame lent ideological weight to one side of the conflict or the other. In the UK sample, for instance, readers would have likely received a narrative context of the conflict which would have included the idea of Israeli culpability. This presentation would have been much less likely in a news article taken from the United States during the same period.

In sum, reading main news desk pieces from within the United States between December 2008 and January 2009, consumers of the print news media would have likely been presented with a story of suffering on both sides of the conflict caused by violence on both sides. The blame for that violence would have been likely understood to fall squarely on the shoulders of the Palestinians, not the Israelis with *Palestinian Culpability* appearing in 40 percent of the US sample versus only 18 percent for the *Israeli Culpability* frame. In the UK, news readers would have been more likely to be presented with the opposite story; *Israeli Culpability* dominated discussions of fault for the conflict present in 59 percent of the sample reviewed and dominant in 6 percent. According to the theoretical frames considering language, knowledge, and discourse previously discussed in this work, it is highly likely that these disparate trends of journalistic presentation would have created substantially different conceptual frames regarding this media event in each community under consideration here. Naturally, subsequent alterations in the development of both individual and social cognition about this episode of violence and about the Palestinian–Israeli conflict in general would have followed within the news media consuming public in both the US and the UK in 2008–2009. The next chapter, the final case study in the overall investigation, will determine whether or not these ideological trends are maintained in the coverage of the 2011 flotilla attack by the Israeli navy.

Notes

1   For a detailed explanation of the historical development of the Israeli occupation of Palestine, see the opening chapter of this book.
2   For a detailed analysis on the origins of Hamas, and their role within contemporary Palestinian politics, see the previous chapter in this study entitled *The Palestinian Legislative Council Elections, 2006*.
3   Nathan Shachar, *The Gaza Strip: Its History and Politics* (Portland, Oregon: Sussex Academic Press, 2010), 183.
4   Ibid., 17.
5   Milton-Edwards and Farrell, 2010: 298–300.
6   Michael Gross, *Moral Dilemmas of Modern War: Torture, Assassination, and Blackmail in an Age of Asymmetric Conflict* (New York: Cambridge University Press, 2010), 255.
7   Ibid., 255–6 (emphasis in the original).

8   Gideon Levy, *The Punishment of Gaza* (London: Verso, 2010), 19–20.
9   Ibid, ix.
10 Ibid.
11 Shachar, 2010: 184.
12 Gross, 2010: 253.
13 Beverley Milton-Edwards and Stephen Farrell, *Hamas: The Islamic Resistance Movement* (Cambridge, England: Polity Press, 2010), 152.
14 Frank Jordans,"ICRC: Israel Delayed Access to Wounded for Days," *Associated Press,* January 8, 2009.
15 Ibid.
16 Milton-Edwards and Farrell, 2010: 151.
17 Ibid.
18 Milton-Edwards and Farrell, 2010.
19 Frank Jordans,"ICRC: Israel Delayed Access to Wounded for Days," *Associated Press*, January 8, 2009.
20 Don Paletz and Robert Entman. (1981). *Media, Power, Politics* (New York: The Free Press, 1981), 21.
21 Ibid.
22 See in Appendix F of this study, Rory McCarthy, "Gaza: Hamas: Struggle for Self-Defence and the Struggle for Palestinian Primacy," *The Guardian,* January 5, 2009, 5; James Hider, "Elite Israeli Forces Cut Region into Three in Drive to Eliminate Hamas," *The London Times,* January 5, 2009, 6–7; and Richard Boudreaux, "Palestinian Authority is Left Weakened: The Moderate Government Appears Ineffective and Marginalized after Israel's Gaza Assault," *The Los Angeles Times*, January 20, 2009, A6.
23 Paletz and Entman, *Media, Power, Politics*, 21.
24 Richard Boudreaux Rushdi abu Alouf, "Israel Pounds Gaza, Pledges More Strikes against Hamas; The Militant Group Urges a New Uprising as 271 Palestinians Are Killed," *The Los Angeles Times,* December 28, 2008, A1 (emphasis added).
25 Richard Boudreaux, "Civilian Toll Grows; Israeli Forces Reach Gaza City; Twenty Children Die and Three Soldiers are Killed by 'Friendly Fire' as Troops Fight their Way into Urban Areas," *The Los Angeles Times*, January 6, 2006, A6.
26 Griff Witte and Sudarsan Raghavan, "Israel Hits U.N.-Run School in Gaza; 40 Die at Shelter That Military Says Hamas Was Firing From," *The Washington Post*, January 7, 2009, A01.
27 Sabrina Tavernise, "In Home and on Streets, a War that Feels Deadlier," *The New York Times*, January 18, 2009, A14.
28 Timothy Butcher, "Palestinians Able to Strike Deeper into Israel," *The Daily Telegraph*, January 1, 2009, 13.
29 Rory McCarthy, "Israel Considers Ground Attack as it Mobilises More Troops; Olmert: Fighting in Gaza Will Be 'Long and Painful,'" *The Guardian,* December 29, 2008, 1.
30 Richard Boudreaux and Rushdi abu Alouf, "At the Scene; Nowhere to Go, Gazans Stay Home; Some Scrambled to Stock up Supplies as Israeli Troops Neared; Five Died When Shells Hit a Main Market," *The Los Angeles Times*, January 5, 2009, A4.
31 Alan Cowell, "Gaza Children Found with Mothers' Corpses," *The New York Times*, January 9, 2009.
32 Taghareed El-Khodary and Isabel Kershner, "Israel Keeps up Assault on Gaza; Arab Anger Rises. *The New York Times*. December 29, 2009, p. A1.
33 Ashraf Khalil, "UN Chief Tours Gaza, Israeli Town; Ban Calls Destruction in Palestinian Territory 'Shocking'. In Sderot, He Calls Rocket Attacks on Civilians 'Appalling',"*The Los Angeles Times*, January 21, 2009, A3.
34 Alfred de Montesquiou, "Guns Silent as Gaza Edges Back to Normalcy," *The Associated Press*, January 23, 2009.

35   Richard Boudreaux and Rushdi abu Alouf, "Israeli Offensive; Injuries Linked to Incendiary Shells; Israelis Hit Gaza City on 3 Sides; the Drive is Met by a Fierce Hamas Response," *The Los Angeles Times*, January 12, 2009, A6.

36   Guardian Reporters, "Assault on Gaza: Israel Vows to Fight Hamas 'to bitter end': Jets Target Official Buildings, 'Weapons Stores' and University," *The Guardian*, January 2, 2009, 10.

37   Karen Rockett, "Gaza's Grief: 205 Dead in Biggest Israeli Raid in 40 Years," *The Sunday Mirror*, December 28, 2008, 8.

38   Hazem Balousha and Chris McGreal, "Gaza: Tanks, Rockets, Death and Terror: A Civilian Catastrophe Unfolding: Incessant Bombardment, No Electricity, No Water, and the Hospitals Full to Overflowing—How Gaza Was Torn Apart," *The Guardian*, January 5, 2009, 2.

39   Isabel Kershner, and Taghreed El-Khodary, "Gaza Rocket Fire Intensifies," *The New York Times*, December 25, 2008.

40   Richard Boudreaux and Rushdi abu Alouf, "Israeli Offensive; Injuries Linked to Incendiary Shells; Israelis Hit Gaza City on 3 Sides; the Drive is Met by a Fierce Hamas Response," *The Los Angeles Times*, January 12, 2009, A6

41   Rory McCarthy, "Israeli Bomb Kills Hamas Leader and Six of His Family," *The Guardian*, January 2, 2009, 1.

42   Chris McGreal, "Why Israel Went to War in Gaza," *The Observer*, January 4, 2009, 19.

43   Richard Boudreaux, "Palestinian Authority is Left Weakened: The Moderate Government Appears Ineffective and Marginalized after Israel's Gaza Assault," *The Los Angeles Times*," January 26, 2009, A6.

44   Alfred de Montesquiou, "Guns Silent as Gaza Edges Back to Normalcy," *The Associated Press*, January 23, 2009.

45   Ashraf Khalil, "UN Chief Tours Gaza, Israeli Town; Ban Calls Destruction in Palestinian Territory 'Shocking'. In Sderot, He Calls Rocket Attacks on Civilians 'Appalling'," *The Los Angeles Times*, January 21, 2009, A3.

46   Taghareed El-Khodary and Isabel Kershner, "Israel Keeps up Assault on Gaza; Arab Anger Rises,".*The New York Times*, December 29, 2008, p. A1.

47   Frank Jordans, "ICRC: Israel Delayed Access to Wounded for Days," *Associated Press*, January 18, 2009.

48   Richard Boudreaux and Rushdi abu Alouf, "Conflict in Gaza: At the Scene; Nowhere to Go, Gazans Stay Home, " *The Los Angeles Times*, January 5, 2009.

49   Chris McGreal, "Why Israel Went to War in Gaza," *The Observer*, January 4, 2009, 19.

50   Marie Colvin and Uzi Mahnaimi, "Israeli Tanks Roll Gaza to Crush Hamas; Calls for Ceasefire," *The Sunday Times*, January 4, 2009.

51   Timothy Butcher, "Gaza Has been Hit Hard, but Has it Made Any Difference?" *The Daily Telegraph*, January 21, 2009, 22.

52   Joshua Mitnick, "Israel Postures to Reshape Truce; Troops Line Gaza Border, Slam Hamas for Third Day," *The Washington Times*, December 30, 2008, A01.

53   Ashraf Khali and Rushdi Abu Alouf, "Palestinian Attacks on Israel from Gaza Intensify," *The Los Angeles Times,* December 25, 2008.

54   Timothy Butcher, "Palestinians Able to Strike Deeper into Israel," *The Daily Telegraph*, January 1, 2009, 13.

55   Kiran Randhawa, "Navy joins bombardment of Hamas terrorist bases: (1) Israel blasts Palestinian militants for third day (2) 'This is the beginning of a successful operation. The idea is to change realities on the ground' Israeli Foreign Minister Tzipi Livni," *The Evening Standard*, December 29, 2009, 4.

56   Guardian Reporters, "Assault on Gaza: Israel Vows to Fight Hamas 'to bitter end': Jets Target Official Buildings, 'Weapons Stores' and University, *The Guardian*, January 2, 2009, 10.

57   Sir Jeremy Greenstock, "Shooting Must Stop, Talking Must Start; after 18 Days of Siege, Israel Prepares Final Assault," *The Mirror*, January 13, 2009, 6.
58   Rupert Hamer, "War is Over; Israel Halts Onslaught, but Can Gaza Peace Last?" *The Sunday Mirror*, January 18, 2009, 7.

8 The flotilla attack

Blockade

As has been made evident in the case studies reviewed to this point, the Israeli occupation of Palestine is executed through various forms of strict control in which the vast majority of civil, social, and political decisions affecting Palestinian citizens are taken out of the hands of their elected leadership, and are transferred to clerical offices in Tel Aviv and West Jerusalem. The Palestinian Authority, which serves as the ostensible governing body of the Palestinian people, has an incredibly limited capacity to provide for its own society. Palestinians do not control their own water resources nor their own airspace above what is internationally designated as their sovereign territory. The PA does not control border crossings with their Arab neighbors (nor indeed, with Israel itself) and they cannot regulate their own commerce and shipping into and/or out of their territory (more on this below). Israeli-only settlements are daily expanded within Palestinian territory confiscating hundreds of acres of Palestinian land every year while the PA observes the situation entirely unable (or as has been alleged by some critics, unwilling) to stop or even slow the process. They do not control waterways in the Mediterranean off the coast of Gaza and they have incredibly limited access to fishing rights in that body of water. Palestinians cannot travel out of their own towns and villages without express permission from the Israeli government to do so, a formal application process which requires up to six months or longer for an official word of response which is invariably "no." Students who might be able to study abroad, family members who would vacation with distant relatives, pilgrims who would travel to regional holy sites are prevented from doing so by the strictures of Israeli occupation. This is life in Palestine today.

Nowhere is the lack of Palestinian self-determination more evident than in the impoverished and besieged Gaza Strip. While the West Bank has developed a modicum of independent civil and cultural institutions, allowing its citizens to engage marginally with the outside (particularly the Arab) world, citizens of the Gaza Strip have been largely denied this opportunity by virtue of suffocating Israeli controls on all aspects of Palestinian life. This control of life is cultural, social, and societal, but most pressingly for Gaza's young and growing population, it is also economic. In this arena a series of repressive controls keeps the Gazan economy dependent and developmentally retarded.[1] Goods imported to and exported from the Strip must be approved and inspected by the Israeli authorities. This prolonged process of inspection on goods designated for export frequently causes perishable goods to spoil, damaging the productive capacity of Gazan farmers and manufacturers significantly. In attempting to bring goods into the territory, additional inspections on imports greatly restrict the multitude of staple consumer products which might otherwise ease daily life in Gaza. These strict controls leave Palestinians who work the land in the region, or who fish its waters, all but bereft of economic opportunity:

> The Israeli government controls much of the Strip's access to water, limits the use of the land closest to the separation fence and the use of all but a small stretch Gaza's traditional fishing waters. Israel also controls the airspace of the Strip, its import and export terminals, and the possibilities of its inhabitants to travel. Even without those impediments, it would be a challenge to organise sustainable development with the growing population pressure on resources and the environment.[2]

Taken together, these policies comprise a daily Israeli assault on the Gazan economy. These measures are comprised of equal parts restriction, control, limitation, and deliberate repression that have, over decades of Israeli control of Palestinian areas, stunted the potential economic growth of Gaza irrevocably and irretrievably. As a whole, these policies comprise the ongoing Israeli blockade of Gaza.

For several years before, and for more than a year following Israel's bombardment of the Gaza Strip, its residents found themselves under this economic siege. In protest of the 2006 Palestinian Parliamentary Elections which saw Hamas rise to a majority position within the Palestinian government, Israel, in coordination with regional allies, instituted the economic blockade described above of the already severely depressed Gaza Strip. The blockade continues to the time of this writing, and remains as strict in its implementation as it arbitrary in its application: "Among the banned products are diapers, poetry, and candy."[3] At least in part, the efficacy of this blockade was made politically feasible by the Israeli settler withdrawal and relocation process which took place in 2005;[4] the lack of Israeli citizens placed permanently within the Strip meant that the economic strangulation of the region would affect only Palestinians. Seen with the benefit of nearly a decade of political developments within the region, the settler withdrawal from Gaza in 2005 can now be largely viewed as a method to further entrench Israeli occupation given that it did nothing at all to mitigate occupations measures in Gaza or elsewhere. Rather the policy was used as a means for Israel to disengage from meaningful negotiations with the Palestinian leadership and abandon the internationally sanctioned Road Map for Peace authored by the so-called Quartet of diplomatic allies. The settler withdrawal, then, furthered Israeli occupation and extended the region's political conflict despite consistent Israeli protestations to the contrary:

For the Palestinians, the withdrawal did not end the conflict ... although Israel withdrew both troops and settlers, it nonetheless continued to maintain a tight grip on the borders of the Gaza Strip, controlling the movement of persons and goods into and out of it ... The restrictions also covered medical supplies, educational materials, fuel, and all sorts of other essential commodities. The entire Palestinian population of the Gaza Strip, nearly 1.2 million people, became prisoners.[5]

From the settler withdrawal of Gaza and the subsequent implementation of Israel's blockade onward, the Palestinians of Gaza became completely reliant upon Israeli beneficence in the transfer of goods and aid to the Strip. As a result, the quality of life for Palestinians living in Gaza decreased in every measurable way *after* the settler withdrawal. Commenting on this perspective in her economic study of the Israeli occupation in Palestine, author and activist Sarah Roy classified the population of the Gaza Strip as one "approaching a state of total economic exhaustion. As individuals become increasingly impoverished, their ability to withstand continued economic pressure will diminish, particularly in the absence of an acceptable political situation."[6] The tightening of the Israeli hold on Gaza that was facilitated by the settler withdrawal has, in every measurable way, further jeopardized the possibility of political compromise within the regional context of contemporary Palestine–Israel.

The blockade policy and its implementation had international support as well as substantial political backing within Israeli political circles. Israel's insistence on framing the democratically elected Hamas in the language of violence and terrorism rendered the Palestinians themselves as responsible agents for their own depressed economy and building humanitarian crisis. In particular, the Israeli presentation of themselves as a state under siege defending against a global network of irrational terrorists during this period had particular resonance among the American political elite and the supports of the Bush Administration. In presenting Hamas and the politics of the Gaza Strip within the global context of the War on Terror, and with the increasing rhetorical polarization of democratic West versus fundamentalist East, Israel effectively isolated Hamas as a political movement within the destitute Gaza Strip while at the same time positioning itself even closer to Washington and to the unipolar American agenda. As such, the election of Hamas and the imposition of economic siege in Gaza brought the US and Israel even closer together in terms of political, military, and perhaps most importantly for the Israeli state, economically. Although a more thorough analysis of this confluence of strategic language and political influence between the US and Israel during this period of time is not possible here, suffice to say that the policy interests of these states remain closely aligned even after national elections, governmental changes, and shifts in party dynamics in both locales.[7]

So, in spite of the fact that the 2006 Palestinian Parliamentary Elections were widely observed as fair and legitimate by international observers, the Israeli government saw fit to punish the Palestinian people for the outcome of those elections, "And it did so with the explicit support of the U.S. and the international community and its domestic constituency, the latter perhaps most importantly of all."[8] The resulting punitive blockade has been as intentional as it has been effective. The resulting economic crisis has had profoundly adverse effects on Gaza society and likewise substantially impacts future prospects for economic freedom and prosperity in the future, "Israeli proposals calling for self-rule in the Occupied Territories, therefore, envision an economic future for the Gaza Strip and the West Bank that is essentially no different from their economic past."[9] Owed to this blockade policy and its associated, repressive occupation measures, Gaza is often referred to as an open-air "prison, [whose] inhabitants are still doomed to live in poverty and oppression."[10] In fact, Israeli policies in Gaza have been so strict as to attract international attention as well, not only from interested activists and human rights organizations, but also from international governmental organizations including the United Nations. These fundamental, international concerns about the economic crisis in Gaza growing led some of these groups to plan a direct intervention in the region. In doing so they were planning to take the humanitarian crisis in the Gaza into their own hands.

Flotilla

The deepening crisis in the lives of Gazans became more than a point of critique among government agencies observing the situation from afar, it became a rallying cry for activists working in Palestinian solidarity movements around the world. From within these groups developed a plan to challenge this most suffocating and prolonged of Israeli occupation policies in Gaza. In its infancy, this plan was modest in scope. It first involved the purchase of a few sea-worthy liners to carry donated goods through the Israeli blockade and directly to seaports in Gaza. Through this mission, the group that came to be known as the Free Gaza Movement, intended to bring aid to those in need while simultaneously undoing what they saw as an unjust and unnecessary collective punishment instituted by the Israel government. Early attempts were only marginally successful. The Free Gaza Movement achieved the transfer of aid to the blockade Gazans but only through Israeli ports; on two separate missions their vessels were commandeered by the Israeli navy before they could reach the Gaza shore and escorted to Israeli ports for offloading and inspection. Some goods were transferred in to Gaza from these aid ships, other goods were confiscated and/or destroyed. Decisions about what was let in or kept out, however, remained firmly in the hands of Israeli policy makers. The blockade could not be broken.

Frustrated by the impenetrability of the Israeli blockade of Gaza, May of 2010 saw the most ambitious flotilla project undertaken to that point. In that month, nine ships carrying more than 700 activists and over 10,000 tons of aid materials valued at over $20 million set sail for the Gazan coast from various Mediterranean ports in a coordinated move to break the Israeli-imposed deadlock. In the early morning hours of the morning of May 30 in international waters near the coast of Gaza, those flotilla ships were approached by Israeli military vessels. Chaos ensued. According to most reports, a number of vessels were fired upon with live ammunition, and subsequently boarded by Israeli naval commandos from water-borne swift boats as well as circling attack helicopters. On one ship, the Turkish vessel Mavi Marmara, gun shots directed at passengers accompanied this boarding procedure leading to the deaths of nine activists and the wounding of scores more. The activists were arrested, taken to the Israeli port city of Ashdod, and thrown in prison. Their possessions were confiscated or destroyed and all aid materials intended for Gaza were taken into custody. Once in control of all individuals involved in this event, the state of Israel became the sole arbiter of the information surrounding it. A prolonged period of radio silence was followed by the slow release of snippets of information. The international press, kept in the dark for hours, even days after these events, scrambled to interpret these events. Had Israeli soldiers opened fire on unarmed, aid-carrying civilians? Or was there more to the intentions of this group than had been reported that point in time? Who were the members of the flotilla, really? What happened aboard the flotilla ships? And what really happened on board the Mavi Marmara?

Disputes quickly surfaced at virtually all levels of investigation of this story as to the manner, form, and intent of the cargo and passengers aboard the aid flotilla. According to some perspectives, those on board were humanitarians in the truest sense, carrying aid and supplies to a much beleaguered population and risking their own safety in the process. The passengers aboard represented a wide swath of politicians, journalists, activists, and artists including Israeli Knesset member Hanin Zoabi (one of the few Arab representatives ever to sit in Israeli parliament), Nobel Peace Prize winner Mairead Corrigan, and Denis Halliday, the former UN Assistant Secretary-General. These and other members of the group were entirely peaceable and entirely non-violent as was the aid they were bringing into Palestine: "The cargo ships are carrying an array of donated goods not allowed into Gaza, including cement, prefab homes, lumber, window frames, paper for printing school books, children's toys, a full dentist's office, electric wheelchairs and high-end medical equipment."[11] Their peaceful intentions and loud declarations of the same were ignored by Israeli soldiers upon their approach to the aid vessels. When they boarded the ships, Israeli soldiers charged these peace activists aggressively, shooting first and asking no questions. As they boarded the boats from sea and air, they opened with live fire on all those on deck, evidence of which can be gleaned from holes in the tops of the heads of a number of the flotilla victims.[12] The Israelis killed a number of activists quickly, including a number of them by execution. In order to rescue themselves from this brutal attack, and in order to protect the women and children aboard the boats, a number of activists fought back against the Israeli attack with what they had to hand including sticks, pikes, cooking knives, and in one case, a deck chair. Despite this horrific attack, a number of activists administered aid to injured Israeli soldiers who had been hurt in the retaliation from ship passengers. In this version of events describing the participants and the action on the Free Gaza Movement flotilla in May/June of 2010, the onus of violence and the responsibility for the death of nine civilians on board the Mavi Marmara rests squarely on the shoulders of the Israeli military who assaulted an unarmed group of peace activists suddenly, brutally, and with intent to kill.

In other versions of events, the flotilla activists comprised a headline-grabbing wolf in sheep's clothing: an ill-intentioned and armed outfit determined to seek out confrontation with Israeli soldiers. They were carrying arms and bomb-making materials and were intent upon equipping the most violent elements in Palestinian society to help them cause maximum number of Israeli casualties. Further, many members of the flotilla were widely known to be connected to some of the most malfeasant terrorists in the world: "a Turkish passenger vessel that was carrying about 600 activists under the auspices of Insani Yardim Vakfi, an organization also known as I.H.H. Israeli officials have characterized it as a dangerous Islamic organization with terrorist links."[13] Following this line of determined discourse, the activists on board the ships in question attacked peaceable Israeli soldiers well before they had reached the decks of the ships whose broadcast warnings to the vessels to stop their engines and for their passengers to show their hands had been ignored. Flotilla members attacked first with pikes, swords, knives, and batons. Israeli soldiers found themselves under siege as they rappelled from helicopters onto the waiting deck of the Mavi Marmara, many sustaining injury before they reached the ship's deck. No shots were fired by the Israelis until they came under violent attack from those waiting below. When compelled to fired, Israeli soldiers first used nonlethal ammunition in order to subdue the violent passengers. They were forced to use live ammunition when they could not otherwise gain control of the situation. The activists on board represented terrorists groups or were themselves terrorists with totally nefarious intentions toward Israel, the state object of their hate. The deaths that resulted on board the Mavi Marmara are, therefore, predominantly the fault of the activists/terrorists on board the flotilla vessels who had intended to provoke a fight with the Israelis from the beginning of their voyage.

This chapter—the final case study in this work—explores those versions of events along with many others in the proliferation of news coverage that came out of the US and the UK in the months that followed the flotilla attack. As before, what is of interest is information that is both presented as assumed fact as well as that which is cast as dubious or uncertain by the authoritative print news media. Through the exploration of this coverage, patterns of investigation and of reportage surrounding this media event is highlighted and analyzed in concluding comments to this chapter. Through this analysis, and as with previous case studies in this book, the goal is to find an ideological orientation in the authoritative print news media covering Palestine–Israel in each country. This ideological tendency is suggested by the revelation of statistical tendencies in the presentation of the aforementioned frames of representation in the article samplings reviewed from each community. The form of these frames of representation and their statistical expression in the news article sampling investigated for this chapter is described immediately below.

Frames of representation in print news media coverage of the flotilla attack (US and UK)

The articles examined in this chapter range over a period of time from May through July of 2010. This timeframe spans print news coverage reporting on the sudden and violent flotilla attack, as well as the long aftermath attempting to describe precisely what happened and why, many parts of which are not agreed upon by parties sustaining conflicting narrative even to this day. However, my review of the news article sampling from each community grappling with this highly attended media event elucidated particular frames of representation, themes, and narrative tropes applied and reapplied by the journalists and editors covering this story during this period. The following discussion first defines those frames of representation then demonstrates their statistical prevalence in a news article sampling taken from both the United States and the United Kingdom.

Gaza blockade as legal, legitimate. This frame of representation is equivalent to a journalistic defense or justification of the long-standing Israeli policy of blockading Gaza. Within this perspective, journalists assert Israeli security concerns as a top priority in the engagement of this policy. Journalistic narratives within this frame also suggest that a reversal of the blockade policy would open Gaza's borders to a flood of weapons to eventually be used against the Israeli state and its citizens. Such a perspective distinctly underplays the element of human suffering endemic in the Israeli blockade of Gaza's 1.5 million Palestinians, as much as it suggests that the policy is a necessary measure to prevent the perpetration of violence or terrorism against the state of Israel: "the blockade prevents terrorists in Gaza acquiring illicit weapons and civilian materials used to attack its forces."[14] This frame of representation also includes defense of the Israeli policy goal of politically and economically debilitating the democratically-elected ruling party in Gaza, Hamas, as a legitimate political tool in the hands of Israeli policy makers: "One of the primary rationales for the blockade... is the need to create a material and political gap between the West Bank, run by the Fatah-dominated Palestinian Authority, and Gaza, run by Hamas."[15] In certain news articles analyzed in this chapter, justification of both of these political goals—Israel's pressing need for security and their desire to destabilize Hamas— occurred within the same news piece: "Israel's blockade of Gaza is aimed both at preventing weapons from entering the narrow coastal strip and weakening Hamas with crippling economic restrictions."[16] The presence of this frame of journalistic representation therefore constitutes a rhetorical defense for Israeli state policy and action in perpetrating the blockade of Gaza, and subsequently, a justification for the Israeli attack of the aid flotilla determined to break it.

Gaza blockade as illegal, illegitimate. According to this frame of representation, journalists reporting on the 2010 Flotilla Attack of Israeli naval forces against ships carrying humanitarian aid to Gaza included the perspective that the blockade itself constituted a collective punishment against the Palestinian people and was therefore not a legitimate political tool being applied by the Israelis. Overt criticism of the Israeli blockade and/or descriptions of its detrimental effects indicated the presence of this perspective within a given print news article. The presence of this narrative trope likewise indicated a criticism of Israeli occupation as a whole given that the long-running Israeli blockade was instituted as part and parcel of military and political strategy intended to prolong the ongoing Israeli civil and military control over Gaza, to marginalize domestic political elements within Gaza society (namely Hamas), and to extend the occupation of Palestine itself. This frame of representation within the US included the assertion that "it was unlikely to halt international outrage [over the attack against the flotilla] and demands that Israel lift or at least loosen the devastating closure that confines 1.5 million Palestinians to a small sliver of land and only allows in basic humanitarian goods."[17] This frame also included criticism of the blockade impugning Israel's allies as responsible parties in contributing to the ongoing suffering of Gaza's Palestinians: "Aid groups say the blockade imposed by Israel and Egypt has done little to weaken Hamas and has devastated Gaza's economy, leaving 80% of the territory's 1.5 million residents dependent on international aid."[18] Journalistic perspective highly critical of the blockade of Gaza was also found within the UK sample: "the Quartet's Middle East peace envoy, Tony Blair ... has demanded an end to Israel's economic blockade of Gaza, which this naval convoy set out with the intention of challenging."[19] This frame of representation further criticizes Israeli action in implementing the blockade of Gaza and simultaneously criticizes the assault on the humanitarian aid flotilla. Given the harsh and collective nature of this particular policy, as well as the wide-ranging international critique of it, this frame was fairly common among news media reports of this media event.

Flotilla/activists as legal, humanitarian. According to this perspective, the flotilla and its participants were indeed peaceful and humanitarian in their purpose. This frame included mention of the various humanitarian supplies that were confirmed to be onboard the various ships in the flotilla, as well as protestations of peaceful and benevolent intent by activist members themselves. This narrative perspective was also noted if and when journalists covering the flotilla attack labeled the flotilla as a "humanitarian" project or mission. An instance of providing a listing of the humanitarian manifest aboard the ships came from a *Christian Science Monitor* article from the US that stated: "The cargo ships are carrying an array of donated goods not allowed into Gaza, including cement, prefab homes, lumber, window frames, paper for printing school books, children's toys, a full dentist's office, electric wheelchairs and high-end medical equipment."[20] Also found within the US sample was the labeling of the flotilla as a humanitarian project, as in a *New York Times* article indicating that international "uproar was ignited when Israel sent its commandos into international waters to stop the flotilla carrying humanitarian aid, including construction materials, toys and used clothes, to Gaza."[21] Similar treatments of the flotilla activists and their cargo appeared in the British sample, some going so far as to indicate that Gazan children would have greatly benefitted from the efforts of the flotilla activists: "Besides building materials, medical supplies, the ships are carrying paper for schools as well as a complete dental surgery. Crayons and chocolate are also on board for Gazan children."[22] In this and other presentations of the legitimacy of the flotilla mission, the Israeli attack on the humanitarian convoy seems all the more cruel and unjust given the potential aid the ships would have provided to Gaza's most innocent and vulnerable population.

Flotilla/activists as illegal, provocative, violent. The opposite narrative trope suggests that participants in the flotilla were violent anarchists with connections to well-known international terrorist groups who blatantly and openly attacked the Israeli soldiers who peacefully boarded their boats. Within this revised conception of events, Israeli soldiers were forced to defend themselves from armed and aggressive flotilla activists whose cargo included pikes, knives, metal rods and other offensive weaponry which had been stowed on-board in anticipation of a violent confrontation with Israeli personnel. Violent action, therefore, was the sole purview of the members of the flotilla; Israeli action occurred only in response. In the United States article sample, *The New York Times* reported that "[Israeli] soldiers were dropped into an ambush and were attacked with clubs, metal rods and knives"[23] while *The Daily News* informed that "[Israeli soldiers] were mobbed, they were clubbed, they were beaten, stabbed, there was even a report of gunfire."[24] Similarly, the British news media reported that members of Israeli boarding party were completely shocked by the use of violence by flotilla members and simply reacted accordingly: "Israel's navy commandos found themselves being beaten by Turkish civilians when they stormed an aid ship bound for Gaza."[25] In these and other representations, the attribution of violence in the first instance to members of the flotilla substantially remakes the mission's intent from a peaceful one into a provocative one. Violence in the first instance is attributed to the passengers aboard the aid vessels and the entire conceptual frame of the story is shifted for news media consumers. The two diametrically opposed points of view immediately above were not necessarily mutually exclusive in news reports during this period. In certain articles reviewed for this study, both views sometimes appeared together within a single news article presenting conceptually opposed versions of events within a single news piece.

Israeli violence, aggression. Given that the primary action involved in the Israeli attack on the humanitarian flotilla was a violent encounter with clearly disproportionate consequences, the frame of representation that included descriptions of Israeli violence featured prominently in both article samples reviewed for this chapter. This frame was noted when Israeli actions were critiqued, as well as when violent actions of individual Israeli soldiers were mentioned independent of editorial judgments. As such, this was a staple of news descriptions during coverage of this highly attended media event, typically only avoided when superseded by descriptions of diplomatic events surrounding the violent naval encounter, or when news descriptions focused heavily on the blockade and its consequences as opposed to violence in this engagement in international waters. A typical description from the US described the Israeli assault on the flotilla: "Israeli warships ... attacked the ships, killing at least two and wounding an unknown number of people on board"[26] as well as references to the 2008–2009 Gaza War: "Most of the 12,000 homes damaged or destroyed by Israel's 22-day military offensive against Gaza in the winter of 2008-2009 have not been rebuilt."[27] *The London Times'* description of the Israeli naval assault was slightly more graphic: a "bloodbath that ensued when Israeli commandos pulled their guns on the Turkish ferry Mavi Marmara."[28] British descriptions of the flotilla attack also included instances of Israeli violence in the first instance provided as background information further to the contemporary situation in Gaza: "A three-week assault on Gaza in 2008 saw up to 1,300 Palestinians lose their lives."[29] Although examples from the UK news media institution tended to be more florid in their presentations than those presented by the US print news, typical news coverage in the sample reviewed from both news communities contained at least some reference to Israeli violence as a means of conveying information about what occurred on board the flotilla vessels.

Hamas/Palestinian violence, aggression. The opposite frame of representation within a discussion ostensibly of Israeli violence committed against members of an aid flotilla in international waters posits Palestinian—and particularly Hamas-led—violence against Israelis. This frame was asserted as substantive background often to contextualize, in some cases to the point of rhetorically justifying, Israeli actions. Within this frame, Palestinian violence is violence in the first instance; Israeli action is a response. Even when the consequences of violent actions inflict much greater damage on victims of Israeli action, this frame justifies Israeli violence. This perspective exists for historical action provided as contextual background for presentation of the flotilla attack such as the Gaza War in 2008–09: "Israel said it launched the offensive in response to rocket attacks against its southern towns."[30] Other examples included reports that: "There has been sporadic rocket fire from Gaza into Israel since last week's attack on the Gaza aid flotilla."[31] The prospect of future Palestinian violence can also be used as justification for Israeli violence today presented in the guise of a security priority. This was the case in a *Los Angeles Times* presentation of events during and after the assault on the flotilla which speculated that Israeli security "would be at risk if rearmed Hamas militants began launching rockets from Gaza into Israeli territory."[32] As the assertion of Palestinian violence, real and documented, or futuristic and projected, provides substantial contextualization for Israeli actions and their often devastating human consequences, the presence of this frame in news articles ostensibly reporting on Israeli violence can be considered as evidence of an ideologically determinate presentation of events.

Israeli restraint, generosity. Within this frame, Israeli military and/or political actions are represented overtly as legal, moral, and benevolent. Frequently noted within articles that also contain representations of Israeli violence, this frame of representation was often used to mitigate perspectives of Israel as culpable, aggressive, or in violation of international law. As such, this narrative trope often appeared in conjunction with assertions of the *Gaza Blockade as Legal, Legitimate* elucidated earlier in this chapter. Descriptions of Israel opening their ongoing blockade for humanitarian reasons were counted as examples of this frame, as was the inclusion or suggestion of official discourse from Israeli state officials purporting to value restraint and legality above political expediency. In the United States, this included the assertion that "[Israeli Prime Minister Benjamin]

Netanyahu also instructed the military to act with sensitivity in preventing the Rachel Corrie from landing and avoid harming those on board the ship."[33] Other descriptions informed of Israeli soldiers going to great lengths in order to adhere to the standards of international law, despite being insulted, assaulted, or otherwise injured: "Despite its soldiers sustaining gunshot and stab wounds and other injuries, Israel has already begun transferring the ships' humanitarian contents to Gaza as originally offered."[34] Similar descriptions within the British news media portrayed Israeli commitments to relaxing the blockade of Gaza as benevolent, humanitarian policies: "Israel announced yesterday it would 'liberalise' the flow of goods to Gaza."[35] The presence of this frame of representation, therefore, indicated the journalistic assertion of Israeli rationale and sobriety of action even within news descriptions of an Israeli naval assault on civilians which left nine dead and many more injured. This rhetorical strategy would sufficiently contextualize Israeli violence for the average news media consumer.

Humanitarian crisis in Gaza. Unlike the previous frame of representation, the *Humanitarian Crisis in Gaza* frame amounts to a narrative identification with the besieged Palestinian population who are the targeted victims of Israel's blockade policies. This theme identifies specific deprivations suffered by Gaza's Palestinians as a result of these policies and indicates the legitimacy associated with regional and international aid efforts designed to counteract them. Among key efforts designed to alleviate the suffering of Gaza's population would naturally be non-governmental aid efforts such as the kind organized by the Gaza Freedom Flotilla.

Within the UK news sampling this perspective was noted when the presence of statistical information on the ongoing suffering in Gaza appeared, such as: "UN statistics show that around 70% of Gazans live on less than $1 a day, 75% rely on food aid and 60% have no daily access to water"[36] and "[t]he number of people defined as the 'abject poor' – completely unable to feed themselves or their families – has increased over the past year from 100,000 to 300,000."[37] Within US articles, this type of specific statistical documentation was difficult to unearth, making the indication of this frame of representation very rare in the US news sampling covering this media event. As such, this frame of representation was noted as present in a news article given even the *suggestion* of undue hardship directed towards Gaza: "International organizations working in Gaza have warned of growing hardship. Deprived of raw materials, local industry has been severely damaged, and the Gaza economy has collapsed."[38] While it may well be argued that the suggestion of hardship without the statistical measures to demonstrate it transparently constitutes a qualitatively different presentation of this narrative frame, both forms of mention were noted in the statistical analysis of the data given that they both report on the growing humanitarian crisis in Gaza. In any case, the statistical frequency of this frame of representation was decidedly low in the US article sampling even with consideration of general expressions of hardship such as those indicated above.

No humanitarian crisis in Gaza. A dialectically and ideologically opposite frame to that discussed above is the presentation of the humanitarian situation in Gaza during and after the Israeli attack on the aid flotilla as something other than a crisis. In the data sampling analyzed here, this presentation often took the form of suggestions that there is no crisis in Gaza according either to official opinion or purported statistical evidence. Often these presentations came in the form of quotations from Israeli officials themselves, defending Israeli policy by claiming that wide-scale suffering was not the result of Israeli political or military actions in Gaza. In these cases, the news article was marked as containing this frame as a result of the journalistic choice to include these official assertions as opposed to simply ignoring these rhetorical justifications from official Israeli sources. In the US, this frame was asserted in multiple *New York Times* articles in the weeks that followed the Israeli attack on the aid flotilla such as: "Israeli officials say there is no humanitarian crisis in Gaza because the Defense Ministry makes sure that enough food and medicine reach the population"[39] and "In Israel, officials say there is no humanitarian crisis in Gaza because the Defense Ministry makes sure that enough food and medicine reach the population.'[40] British sources included these official protestations as well, defending Israeli action as moral and humanitarian even as the blockade was carried on in the weeks after the flotilla attack: "There is no humanitarian crisis in Gaza ... Israel is conducting itself in the most humanitarian manner, and is allowing the entrance of thousands of tons of food and equipment into Gaza."[41] The presence of these and similar statements decrying the existence of humanitarian struggle in Israeli-blockaded Gaza serves to substantially contextualize Israeli policy and would potentially contribute to the ideological orientation of news pieces towards an Israeli-centric perspective.

Hamas/Palestinian corruption, culpability for Gaza crisis. Within this frame of representation, Palestinians themselves, and specifically the majority political party in the Palestinian Parliament, was impugned as culpable for the Israeli blockade and the ongoing Gaza crisis. According to this narrative perspective, the situation in which Gaza's Palestinians find themselves is one of their own making. Specifically, the election of Hamas to the majority party in government in 2006 forced Israel to blockade Gaza because of the military and political threat represented by Hamas. All negative aspects that follow from this policy are, therefore, the fault of Hamas directly, and the fault of their electorate for placing them in legislative power with the elections of 2006. Language explicitly describing Hamas as a terrorist organization, and/or as the instigator of regional violence was noted within this frame: "Israel has led a land and sea blockade of the Palestinian enclave since Hamas, the Islamic militant group that Israel, the United States and the European Union view as a terrorist organization, seized full control of the territory three years ago."[42] Likewise, reportage indicating that Israel's blockade of Gaza was a political necessity because of Hamas's militancy was counted as an instance of this frame, as in: "Israel ... needs to control the flow of goods into the enclave to prevent the militant Hamas group, which is in government in the area, smuggling in weapons."[43] A final narrative theme within this frame includes descriptions of Hamas turning away Israeli and international aid for the purposes of gaining political capital: "The de facto Hamas government in Gaza has refused to accept truckloads of aid offloaded from the flotilla raided by Israeli forces."[44] News language of this type lends weight to conceptions of

Israeli morality and legality in their treatment of the Palestinian populations under occupation. The presence of this frame undermines the validity of the Palestinian narrative and substantially orients the news piece to an Israeli-centric world view.

Diplomatic crisis, Israeli culpability. Within this frame of representation, Israel was presented at the center of a diplomatic controversy as part and parcel of their attack on an international humanitarian convoy to Gaza. Not least of the diplomatic difficulty raised by this event were the deaths of nine people, eight Turkish citizens and one with dual US–Turkish citizenship. Language describing this diplomatic tension, and impugning Israel for creating the situation, was noted within this frame. Language within this frame typically described the deteriorating state of diplomatic affairs between Israel and Turkey, but other states were occasionally mentioned for their participation in diplomatic protests directed at Israel.

An example in *The Los Angeles Times* described protest movements, both civil and diplomatic, from around the world: "Anti-Israel protesters marched through London on Saturday. Swedish dockworkers are threatening to boycott Israeli ships in a weeklong protest. Vietnam canceled a scheduled visit by Israeli President Shimon Peres."[45] Other examples of language in this frame of representation include reviews of past diplomatic transgressions committed by Israel which were often presented as forming part of a pattern discursively connected to events aboard the Gaza aid flotilla: "Micheál Martin, the minister for foreign affairs, is expected to report to Wednesday's cabinet meeting on the use of fake Irish passports by Israeli agents in last January's assassination of Mahmoud al-Mabhouh."[46] In these and other presentations, news media language alluded to the state of Israel as a violator, sometimes habitually so, of numerous diplomatic relationships and international agreements to which they are legally bound. These descriptions focused upon the ongoing international consequences of that state's tarnished diplomatic record impugning Israel itself as the culpable party in these disputes. Articles that included this frame of representation as dominant typically appeared several days after the violent events on board the aid flotilla had occurred and contributed to the description of the aftermath of the Israeli naval assault upon the aid vessels and their crews.

Diplomatic crisis, Turkish culpability. This frame involved placing the blame on states other than Israel itself for the diplomatic crisis between Israel and other regional or international actors. In other words, this frame of representation marked reporting that criticized or chided states for their criticism of Israeli policy as regarding the blockade of Gaza and the flotilla attack on the humanitarian convoy. Depictions of the aid group IHH, Turkish activists, or other members of the aid flotilla as responsible for the violence aboard the boats was counted as an example of this frame given that the convoy left from Turkish ports, and was sanctioned by the Turkish government. Other descriptions of overt diplomatic or military hostility towards Israel by Turkey, Iran (among other states) were likewise marked as examples of this narrative frame. One such example from the UK described aggressive posturing by Turkey on the eve of the deployment of another aid convoy to Gaza: "Turkey, which bore the brunt of the death toll, is considering sending its own navy to escort the ships. Israel's naval chiefs warned the new threat will be treated 'as if it was a war.'"[47] Another example more generically impugns Turkey's "eastward shift" in recent diplomatic endeavors as responsible for the cooling of relations between Turkey and Israel: "Secular but Muslim Turkey, a Nato member, was Israel's most significant Middle Eastern ally, but the relationship has been battered by Israel's recent wars against Hezbollah and Hamas and by an eastward shift in Turkish foreign policy."[48] As the Israeli naval commandos were most commonly blamed for the violent nature of the flotilla attack in both national news media communities, language impugning Turkey or other states for diplomatic tension involving Israel as a result of the flotilla attack was not widespread in the articles reviewed for this study. In all this frame was statistically infrequent in the news sampling reviewed here.

Statistical evaluation, the United States

As indicated by Figure 8.1, the statistical presentation of these frames of representation in the United States shows a single, dominant frame: *Israeli Violence, Aggression*. This frame appears in 57 percent of articles and was dominant in 4 percent for a total presence in over 61 percent of the sampling. The next most common frame was *Israeli Restraint, Generosity*, which appears in 40 percent of articles and is dominant in 15 percent of them for a total presentation in 55 percent of articles. The frame *Flotilla/Activists as Violent* is also statistically prevalent, showing a presence and a dominance of 36 percent and 8 percent, respectively. *Humanitarian Crisis in Gaza*, *No Humanitarian Crisis in Gaza*, and *Diplomacy Crisis, Turkish Culpability* are the three least prevalent frames in the article sampling appearing in 15 percent, 7 percent, and 6 percent in total, respectively. All other frames of representation fall on a statistical range between the two extremes of *Israeli Violence, Aggression*, and *Diplomacy Crisis, Turkish Culpability*.

This statistical evidence provides telling information about the US print news media as an institution and its coverage of the Israeli blockade of Gaza, the Israeli naval assault on the aid flotilla attempting to break that blockade, and the diplomatic fallout that occurred in the aftermath. The fact that the frame *Israeli Violence, Aggression* dominated the US print news presentation of these events is not out of line with the indisputable events of the summer of 2010. The Israeli naval boarding and seizure of the flotilla vessels *was* a violent act, one that resulted in nine deaths and scores of injuries to Turkish, American, British, and other international civilians. A frequent journalistic narrative presenting Israeli violence as part of the retelling of the events surrounding the flotilla seizure can therefore be seen as an apolitical narrative; the dominance of that frame does not inform news readers substantially as to the ideological positioning of the US news media during this period. More telling in that regard is the prevalence of narrative frames that are not as obviously revelatory. The second-most prevalent frame, for instance, that one which puts a narrative focus on Israel as a restrained and/or generous actor is a case in point. The statistical prevalence of this frame is incongruous with a consistent presentation of Israeli violence and serves rather to qualify the violence in question. Likewise, the high incidence of descriptions of

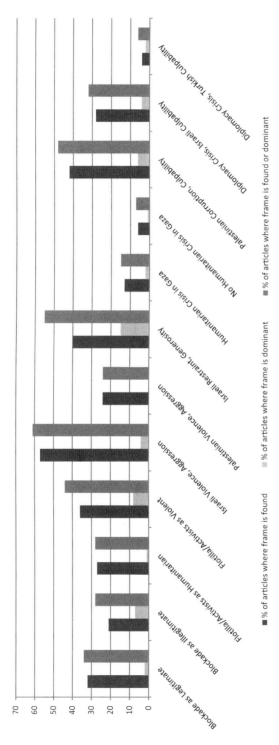

■ % of articles where frame is found   ■ % of articles where frame is dominant   ■ % of articles where frame is found or dominant

Figure 8.1 US Print News Media: The Flotilla Attack

crew members of the flotilla as violent and aggressive toward the Israeli naval commandos depicts a different causality in the appreciation of the events in question. Finally, descriptions of Palestinians as culpable agents, authors of their own blockade and subsequent humanitarian crisis (48 percent in total) contribute to this alternative reading of the events in question, one in which the need for a blockade-breaking convoy is, in and of itself, cast as needless at best, reckless and dangerous at worst. This news media presentation of the Israeli blockade of Gaza and its naval assault on the humanitarian aid convoy sent to break that blockade reveal an institution whose orientation in the recounting of regional events shows a close similarity with official Israeli perspective on these issues. Such a perspective embraces the idea of Israel as a generous state, one willing to give humanitarian aid to the very groups that threaten it, both discursively and militarily. Israel, when violent, only behaves in such a way because it is threatened with violence, as reportage on the violence intentions of the activists aboard the humanitarian flotilla demonstrates.

Statistical evaluation, the United Kingdom

Frames of representation employed by the UK print news media in coverage of the flotilla attack (represented in Figure 8.2) differ significantly from the presentation of the event by its US counterpart. In the first place, though the frame of representation *Israeli Violence, Aggression* is the most prevalent frame in the UK sample as it was in the US, its percentage of frequency is noticeably higher in the UK sample: 77 percent in total versus 61 percent in total. Other, arguably more significant differences exist. The UK sample shows a strong statistical presence of the frame *Gaza Blockade as Illegitimate* (64 percent in total versus 29 percent in the US sample) as well as for the frame *Diplomatic Crisis, Israeli Culpability* (42 percent in total versus 32 percent in the US sample) but few other frames rate substantially in that article sampling. This presentation is visually stark in the graphical evidence above. Two frames soar into the 60–70 percentile mark, one frame reaches the 40 percentile mark, but no other frame tops 30 percent. The UK presentation of the flotilla attack was evidently centered on two journalistic narratives: the Israelis as violent and the blockade as illegitimate. The majority of these news stories came from these two themes and included few other elements with significant narrative weight. In ideological terms this perspective is, like the visual and statistical evidence, a stark departure from the US print news narrative which substantially qualified Israeli action and presented the Israeli blockade as legitimate more often than not. Points of closer comparison between the ideological perspectives evident in the news coverage of both of these national news media communities follow below.

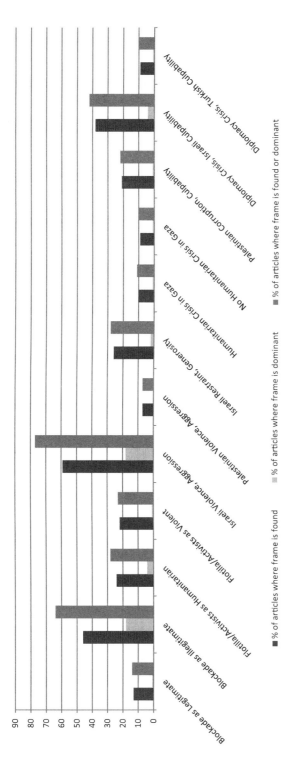

Figure 8.2 UK Print News Media: The Flotilla Attack

■ % of articles where frame is found   ■ % of articles where frame is dominant

■ % of articles where frame is found or dominant

Statistical evaluation, comparison

One of the most glaring differences between the two national news media communities and their presentation of events surrounding the flotilla attack in May of 2010 is the frame of representation *Israeli Restraint, Generosity* (compared in Figure 8.3 below). Recalling that this frame portrays Israeli actions and policies in the region as helpful and beneficial either to the Palestinians or in more general terms, it seems an incongruous narrative focus for news articles ostensibly discussing the hostile boarding of aid vessels, their seizure, and the killing of several members of their crews and the wounding of dozens more. Yet this frame was emphasized in the US news media presentation of the flotilla attack to such an extent as to appear as the dominant frame surrounding the discussion of events in more than 10 percent of news articles surveyed for this study (appearing in total in more than half). This indicates a determined institutional tendency to present Israeli policy in a positive light, even when its actions could be considered violent and unnecessary. Within the UK print news media, this frame of representation was substantially less frequent, present in 25 percent of articles, dominant in 2 percent, and given in total in 27 percent. For the purposes of practical interpretation of events surrounding the flotilla attack in 2010, this means that consumers of the printed news media in the United States would have been much more likely to read qualifying commentary about Israel's role in the matter, those reading British dailies, much less likely so.

A second frame appearing to a much greater extent in the US news media presentation of the flotilla attack (and compared in Figure 8.4 below) was *Palestinian Corruption, Culpability*. Within this frame of representation, Palestinians themselves, often government officials or Hamas party members, were responsible for the growing humanitarian crisis in Gaza. This resulted from obstinacy in cooperation with the delivery of Israeli or international aid, as well as the insistence on importing arms or materials that could be used to manufacture weapons and threaten Israeli citizens. This frame of representation appeared more than twice as often in the US news media sample than in the sample from the UK (48 percent versus 22 percent). In two article samplings of the same size covering the same period of time, this disparity indicates an institutional focus on a particular narrative theme. In this case, the narrative trope in question places culpability for the deprived situation in Gaza on the victims of that situation themselves, the Palestinians. In the same moment, this perspective alleviates Israeli culpability for the creation of a humanitarian crisis in Gaza and mitigates Israeli policy in the ongoing humanitarian blockade of the Gaza Strip. From an ideological perspective, this statistical evidence indicates that the print news media institution in the United States is collectively interested in pursuing lines of narration that impugn Palestinians for regional strife, while forgiving Israel and/or Israelis for the same. By the same token, the British news media institution seems content with attributing blame for the crisis in Gaza somewhere other than onto the Palestinians.

Unlike the previous two comparative illustrations, a final point of comparison illustrates a frame of representation that was emphasized to a much greater extent in printed news in the UK. This comparison (Figure 8.5) depicts a comparison of

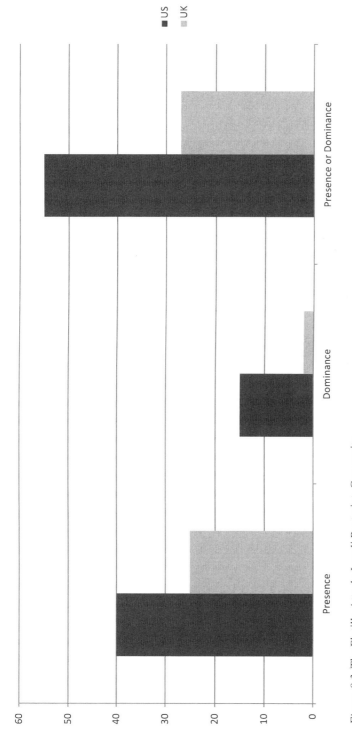

Figure 8.3 The Flotilla Attack: Israeli Restraint, Generosity

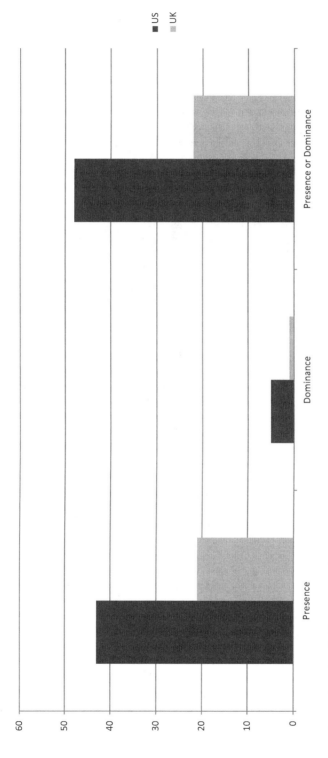

Figure 8.4 The Flotilla Attack: Palestinian Corruption, Culpability

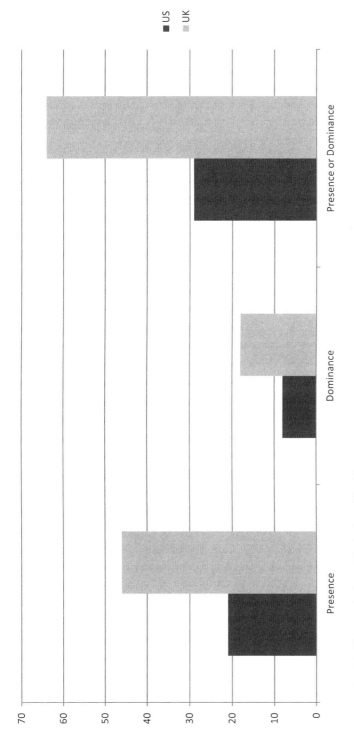

Figure 8.5 Flotilla Attack: Gaza Blockade as Illegitimate

the frame *Gaza Blockade as Illegitimate*; it appears with more than twice the statistical frequency in the UK news sample as compared to the US. In the US, this frame appeared only as 21 percent present, 7 percent dominant, and 29 percent in total. These rates more than double to 45 percent, 18 percent, and 64 percent, respectively, in the UK sampling reviewed during the same time period. As before, the difference between these two statistical presentations indicates a difference in institutional orientation towards the events in question, but more broadly, a difference in perspective on the Palestinian–Israel conflict itself. In presenting the Gaza blockade as an illegitimate conflict policy in nearly two-thirds of articles dealing with the spring 2010 flotilla attack, the print news media institution in Britain delivered a directed critique of Israeli policy spanning the period of the blockade. The violence that erupted when Israel stopped an aid flotilla from breaking that blockade is thereby also impugned as Israeli folly. The explicit criticism of Israeli policy is noticeably lacking in the US news media sample indicating an institutional reluctance to author this manner of criticism. The US news media institution shies away from criticizing Israeli policy; the authoritative print news media in the UK does not.

Conclusions: covering the flotilla attack

US and UK coverage of the Israeli attack on an aid flotilla in late May of 2010 which intended to break the Israeli blockade of Gaza shared some important narrative trends. The most prominent among them was the focus of both communities on incidents of Israeli violence both in explaining the events on board the flotilla, as well as explaining the recent history of interactions between Israel and Palestine in the years of conflict leading up to the flotilla assault. In analyzing for an ideological or political perspective within that coverage, however, this statistical evidence reveals little. A series of political and diplomatic events set off by a violent assault which cost the lives of nine civilian activists and wounded scores more could not but refer to that violent occasion. In informing that all of the dead and the vast majority of the wounded were victims of an organized, professional military assault by the Israeli navy, the print news media engaged primarily in factual reportage (though the US news media did attribute violent intent to the part of the flotilla activists much more than the UK news media did). In the final analysis, this overarching commonality provides scant evidence about institutional news media perspectives to these events in either news community.

Discarding these similarities for the moment and moving to the core of the differences that separate these two national coverages, however, does provide telling insight into institutional ideology. Each of the three points of statistical and graphical comparison above was identified explicitly because of the overarching political and ideological pattern they form in the news communities from which they derive. In the case of the United Kingdom, representations of Israeli violence were paired with condemnations of Israeli policy, namely the ongoing blockade of Gaza that necessitated humanitarian aid and provoked the flotilla mission to begin with. The perspective of the British news media during this period, then, included ample criticism of Israeli policy with little else offered in narrative terms to mitigate this criticism. The overall perspective of the US print news media took the ideologically opposite tack. Along with recounting the violent acts committed by Israel in assaulting the flotilla, the US news media provided substantial contextualization of this violence and the Israeli policies behind it. This included perspectives asserting the validity of the blockade of Gaza more often than those asserting its illegality along with regular assertions of Israel's generosity in regional humanitarian matters, and restraint in military matters.

The next chapter in this study is comprised mainly of interviews this author conducted with journalists who have covered the Palestinian–Israeli conflict (and whose work accounted for substantial portions of the news data analyzed in the previous four chapters). The goal in including their commentary within this investigation is to pursue a clearer picture of the daily work undertaken by journalists from the US and the UK in their coverage of Palestine–Israel. More specifically the following chapter will examine the personal and institutional perspectives of professional journalists in their coverage of recent conflict events. Their professional and personal perspectives—and my commentary on those perspectives—is included at this point of the study in order to connect the thematic strands of media theory, discourse analysis, and print news language that have been running concurrently throughout the course of this study. Beginning with the conclusion of the subsequent chapter, issues of language, text, reception, and cognition are explored leading to a final assessment of ideological trends in print news media coverage of Palestine–Israel in the US and the UK in the concluding chapter of this study.

Notes

1   Sara Roy, *Hamas and Civil Society in Gaza: Engaging the Islamist Social Sector* (Princeton, New Jersey: Princeton University Press, 2011).
2   Nathan Shachar, *The Gaza Strip: Its History and Politics* (Portland, Oregon: Sussex Academic Press, 2010), 186.
3   Ibid., 187.
4   See Chapter 5 in this book: *Evacuating Gaza from Two Sides of the Atlantic.*
5   Azzam Tamimi, *Hamas: A History from Within* (Northampton, Massachusetts: Olive Branch Press, 2007), 222
6   Roy, *Hamas and Civil Society in Gaza*, 43.
7   Among the many texts investigating the nature and consequence of the very close political, military, and economic alliance between the US and Israel, Mearsheimer and Walt's seminal text *The Israel Lobby* (2003), already cited in this work, remains at the forefront of unraveling these important diplomatic connections.
8   Roy, *Hamas and Civil Society in Gaza*, 328.
9   Ibid., 122.
10 Gideon Levy, *The Punishment of Gaza* (London: Verso, 2010), 20.
11 Erin Cunningham, "Large Aid Flotilla to Test Israeli Blockade of Gaza," *The Christian Science Monitor*, May 26, 2010.
12 "Gaza Flotilla Activists Were Shot in Head at Close Range," *The Guardian*, June 4, 2010.

13   Isabel Kershner, "Deadly Israeli Raid Draws Condemnation," *The New York Times*, p. May 31, 2010, 1A.

14   Joe Murphy, "Gaza Blockade Is Close to Being Lifted, Says Blair," *The Evening Standard,* June 14, 2010.

15   Ethan Bronner, "U.S. Taking Gaza Deaths as Cue for Policy Shift; New Approach Is Needed, Aides to Obama Sat, as Israel Warns of Conditions," *The International Herald Tribune*, June 4, 2010, 1.

16   Michael D. Shear, "Obama Seeks New Approach on Gaza; He Calls for Israeli Blockade to Consider Aid as Well as Security," *The Washington Post*, June 10, 2010, 9A.

17   Kristen Laub, "Israel Seizes Ship to Gaza; Nonviolent Takeover Contrast to Previous Raid; Aid Vessel Carrying Nobel Laureate, Activists," *Newsday*, June 6, 2010, 30A.

18   Alexandra Zavis, "Israel Supporters Rally in L.A.; Crowds Back the State, Saying Criticism of Its Raid on a Gaza-Bound Flotilla Is Unfair," *The Los Angeles Times*, June 7, 2010, 1AA.

19   "This Cruel and Ineffective Blockade of Gaza Must Be Brought to an End," *The Independent*, June 5, 2010, 42.

20   Erin Cunningham, "Large Aid Flotilla to Test Israeli Blockade of Gaza," *The Christian Science Monitor*, May 26, 2010.

21   Michael Slackman, "In Bid to Quell Anger Over Raid, Israel Frees Detainees," *The New York Times*, June 2, 2010, 4A.

22   Harriet Sherwood, "Gaza Aid Flotilla to Test Israel's Blockade," *The Guardian*, May 26, 2010, 17.

23   Isabel Kershner, "Deadly Israeli Raid Draws Condemnation," *The New York Times*, May 31, 2010, 1A.

24   Eric Silverman and J. Martinez, "Botched Raid Riles World. Israeli Commandos Kill Nine in Gaza Flotilla. Bibi Defends Actions, But Protests Mounting," *The Daily News*, June 1, 2010, 2.

25   Tom Coghlan and James Hider, "Women Armed with 'Faith' Plan Aid Voyage," *The London Times*, June 25, 2010, 3.

26   Isabel Kershner, "Israel Intercepts Boats Heading to Gaza; Violence is Reported," *The New York Times*, May 31, 2010, 8A.

27   Edmund Sanders, "Showdown Looms As Aid Flotilla Heads toward Gaza," *The Los Angeles Times*, May 30, 2010, 4A.

28   Tom Coghlan and James Hider, "Women Armed with 'Faith' Plan Aid Voyage,"*The London Times*, June 25, 2010, 3.

29   "Bloody Blockade," *The Mirror*, June 14, 2010, 24.

30   Edmund Sanders, "Showdown Looms As Aid Flotilla Heads Toward Gaza," *The Los Angeles Times*, May 30, 2010, 4A.

31   Mark Bluden and Ross Lydall, "Gaza Activists Tell of Terror as Israelis Let Off Gas and Bombs," *The Evening Standard*, June 2, 2010.

32   Paul Richter, "Gaza Flotilla Raid; Raid Throws a Wrench in U.S. Agenda," *The Los Angeles Times*, June 2, 2010, 6A.

33   Sebnem Arsu, "New Ship Heads to Gaza, and Israel Vows to Stop It," *The New York Times,* June 4, 2010, 8A.

34   J. Peled, "A Bloody PR Stunt," *USA Today*, June 2, 2010, 8A.

35   Donald Macintyre, "Israel Urged to Do More as Gaza Blockade is Eased," *The Independent*, June 18, 2010, 28.

36   Ian Black, Afua Hirsch, and Haroon Siddique, "Gaza Flotilla Assault: The Blockade," *The Guardian*, June 1, 2010, 5.

37   "Gaza: In Numbers," *The Guardian*, June 5, 2010, 28.

38   Hiram Cooper and Isabel Kershner, "Obama Pledges New Aid for Gaza and West Bank," *The Washington Post*, June 10, 2010, 14.

39   Ethan Bronner, "U.S. Taking Gaza Deaths as Cue for Policy Shift; New Approach Is Needed, Aides to Obama Sat, as Israel Warns of Conditions," *The International Herald Tribune*, June 4, 2010, 1.

40   Ethan Bronner and Isabel Kershner, "New Israeli Tack Needed on Gaza, U.S. Officials Say," *The New York Times*, June 3, 2010, 1.

41   Harriet Sherwood, "International: Israeli Navy Prepares for Action as Activists' Flotilla Nears Gaza: Organisers of Eight-Ship Fleet Predict Standoff: Protesters on Board Face Detention and Deportation," *The Guardian*, May 29, 2010, 36.

42   Isabel Kershner, "Second Set of Activists Steams Toward Gaza," *The New York Times*, June 4, 2010, 7A.

43   "Bloody Blockade," *The Mirror*, June 14, 2010, 24.

44   Harriet Sherwood, "Gaza Flotilla Assault: Where Did the Aid Go?" *The Guardian*, June 4, 2010, 15.

45   Edmund Sanders, "Israel Acts Cautiously in Round 2; Fallout From a Deadly Raid Continues, Though Another Ship Is Seized Without Incident," *The Los Angeles Times*, June 6, 2010, 3A.

46   Phillip Connolly and John Paul McCarthy, "Israelis to Deport Gaza Aid Crew," *The Sunday Times*, June 6, 2010, 1, 2.

47   Chris Dixon, "Gaza Britons Dumped in Turkey With No Cash," *The Express*, June 3, 2010, 15.

48   Ian Black, "Turkey Bans Israeli Military Flight from Airspace as Freeze Deepens, *The Guardian*, June 29, 2010, 18.

9 The journalistic perspective

Covering Palestine–Israel in their own words

Introduction: the anthropology of journalism

A comparative study of the presentation of recent news events in Palestine–Israel by the print news media in the United States and the United Kingdom would be incomplete without an examination of the motivations, perceptions, and experiences of those individuals responsible for the creation of the news itself. In order to be effective, such an examination should include considerations of the personal and/or institutional obstacles faced by journalists working in the Middle East, their professional, personal, and perhaps even their political motivations, and their own valuation of the role they play in defining Palestine–Israel for their readership. Such an investigation, the examination of the practice of journalism in Palestine–Israel by members of both the UK and the US news media institution, is the focus of this chapter.

The discussion to follow centers on the views of regional journalists in their own words (with additional expert commentary interwoven in the narrative) and is provided in excerpts from interviews conducted by this author over a period of roughly a year between London and Jerusalem. The journalists selected for interviews were employed by the authoritative news media in either the United States or the United Kingdom during this period, were willing to speak on the record about issues related to covering Palestine–Israel, and were available to do so according to restrictions of their very busy work and travel schedules. Journalists who produced news articles which were represented in the data analysis in each of the preceding case studies were optimal choices for the interview aspect of this research project, though unfortunately time, narrative space, and the peculiarities of this author's own schedule prevented the inclusion of more opinions than those presented here. Those commentaries that are included, however, come from some of the most notable members of the press who have worked in the Middle East on either side of the Atlantic: Middle East Editor for the BBC, Jeremy Bowen; the former Jerusalem Bureau Chief for the BBC, Jo Floto; the former Jerusalem Bureau Chief for ABC, Simon Macgregor-Wood; and the former Jerusalem Bureau Chief for *The New York Times*, Ethan Bronner. Each journalist interviewed has at least a decade of experience covering the region; most of them spent the better part of their careers focused upon Palestine–Israel.

Accessing the story: on sources and perspective

During the course of each interview conducted throughout this author's research, the issue of journalistic access was raised as a central concern among the myriad of issues confronting the both British and American members of the press covering Palestine–Israel. All of the journalists interviewed confirmed that access to reliable sources is important in all journalistic endeavors, but is of particular importance in conflict zones where perspectives on current events differ so markedly from one side of the battle line to the other. According to each of them, the party to the Palestinian–Israeli conflict who is demonstrably more eager to provide information is undeniably the Israeli side. As described by former Jerusalem Bureau Chief for ABC News, Simon-Macgregor-Wood, when his office needs information about any regional event from an official Israeli source:

> the spokesmen from the Israeli [side] come to us. We don't even have to leave our offices. The Prime Minister's Office with whom we have a very friendly and professional relationship, will call and say … "Mark Regev or Dori Gold" or whoever's available "can be with you at 9:30. He's doing CNN at 9:20," et cetera. It's a very, very slick operation.[1]

Naturally, this state of affairs can tip the balance of story-telling in the favor of the Israeli perspective given that official Palestinian sources do not have the same level of organization or efficiency as officials on the other side of the conflict line. London-based Middle East Editor for the BBC, Jeremy Bowen, concurs with Macgregor-Wood's assessment of Israel's "slick operation":

> The difficulty the Palestinians have in trying to get their message across in a sense is that the Israelis have got a polished and professional [public relations] network. They'll send you emails with information. They'll give you the mobiles and home numbers of spokespeople—and not just the spokespeople, sometimes the Ministers.[2]

This openness and accessibility described by Macgregor-Wood and Bowen as fundamental to the Israeli side in the conflict is noticeably lacking when it comes to accessing Palestinian sources. As a result, most often, journalists don't have two well-crafted stories to choose from in the retelling of regional events, but rather one polished and highly produced story, and one partial or incomplete version of events containing little or anything at all to counteract or contradict the polished story. This in-built dilemma to covering Palestine–Israel was summed up succinctly by Simon MacGregor-Wood who said: "if you're lazy, you can get the Israeli position on a developing story delivered on a plate. You have to go and find the Palestinian one."[3]

The difficulty of narrative access described here exists in this conflict region partially because Israeli efforts to present their story to the foreign press far outstrip Palestinian ones, and partially because the physical elements and restriction endemic to Israeli occupation prevent Palestinians from matching resources and time devoted by Israel in public relations efforts. Though within this structure of journalistic access there is another, possibly counterintuitive result that may work against the ongoing Israeli narrative. Speaking to author Marda Dunsky for her 2007 book *Pens and Swords: How the American Mainstream Media Reports the Israeli-Palestinian Conflict*, reporter Ethan Bronner (former Jerusalem Bureau Chief for *The New York Times* also interviewed as part of this author's research) described the potential harmful impact to the seemingly unchecked Israeli agency in the retelling of regional events:

> while there is a slick, professional press relations operation in Israel, that is sometimes seen as something to pierce through, not to accept at face value. Israel might be subject to greater scrutiny by journalists, in fact, than Palestinians are. It works as you'd expect, which is to say that the Israeli side gets its story out better and faster. But it also has this paradoxical or counterintuitive effect of pushing journalists to sometimes write off the Israeli side as just a PR machine and to try to go seek the real story.[4]

In this sense, Bronner expresses the idea that there is an inherent distrust that exists when journalists are presented with the quick and polished version of events generated by Israeli sources. Bronner speaks of seeking "the real story" beyond what official Israeli sources provide. This implies that there will only ever be slanted or biased information coming from a packaged, polished version of events: the Israeli side of the line. From his perspective at the BBC, Jeremy Bowen agreed with Bronner's assessment: "we don't necessarily give Israelis great credence just because they're better at PR. We don't. We're conscious that it's important not to do that actually."[5]

Nevertheless, even an avowed reluctance not to presume complete accuracy in a packaged Israeli narrative can be overwhelmed by difficulties of access which can prevent Palestinians from being able to express their narrative at all. So, while Bronner and Bowen express cautiousness in handling Israeli source material, the sheer volume of that material from Israeli sources, and the ease with which this material can be found bring about the journalistic tendency to eradicate a narrative viewpoint that is sympathetic to a Palestinian perspective. This imbalanced structure of access, efficiency, and information distribution can substantially inform the manner in which events within Palestine–Israel are related to British and American news audiences.

But the struggle to present a Palestinian viewpoint in the retelling of events in the conflict might be due as much to Western cultural bias as to Israeli public relations efficiency. On this issue, author and journalist Chris Hedges spoke of an operating preference within the US news media establishment in favor of Israeli areas within the conflict zone, and against the Palestinian territories:

> most reporters are uncomfortable working in the Palestinian areas, so they will drive down from Jerusalem to Gaza with a precooked story, stay two or

three hours, get the few requisite quotes, and leave. They don't understand the nuances of Palestinian society at all, or the factual disputes … So Palestinians are painted as a monolith.[6]

Here Hedges highlights another important issue impacting regional coverage amongst Western journalists in Palestine–Israel: cultural affinity. As elucidated, Palestine remains largely *terra incognita* for many foreign news professionals working in the region. Jerusalem, split between the Israeli west and the Palestinian east, is as far as many journalists are willing to travel in order to investigate conflict events, or issues relevant to Palestinian society.[7]

Former BBC Bureau Chief in Jerusalem Jo Floto agrees that sameness or perceived sameness in attitudes, values, language, and habits between Westerners and Israelis readily connects the Israeli side of the conflict with Western audiences. At the same time, these cultural aspects make it that much more difficult for a Palestinian perspective to be heard in the West:

If you look over there [in west Jerusalem] that is a massive shopping mall full of people who look like most of my viewers, full of people speak English with American accents. Most of those people do the kind of stuff that my audience does … if you're looking at a far off part of the world in which you're trying to summarize a conflict in your own mind, you're seeing mall shoppers against people who behave very differently, look very differently, don't speak English and who aren't represented as speaking English. So that is a gap ... I think here it is made more challenging because you are not just talking about Palestinian culture or Arab culture because the background noise on the other side is so familiar, or at least seems so familiar. And again you can see the way that we look at events through an Israeli frame of mind.[8]

The existing similarities between contemporary Israeli culture and broadly described "Western" culture thereby create a starting point for an understanding of the conflict in the US and the UK which automatically prefers an Israeli-centric view of the region. The fact that official Israeli commentary frequently comes in unaccented English and from Western-educated spokespersons makes their message resonate that much more clearly with audiences situated in the West. Additional cultural crossover between Israel and Western countries can be attributed to the fact that "there are a million American passport holders on [the Israeli] side of the fence."[9] So while these factors might substantially explain the Western audience's identification with the Israeli message, it may additionally help to explain the baseline comfort level felt by most journalists working inside Israel, and the inherent discomfort felt by those same journalists while working for prolonged periods inside Palestine.

Part of the reluctance on the part of the news media to travel to and within Palestine also result from security issues, as Jeremy Bowen explained in 2008: "we had a guy based—an expatriate reporter, foreign reporter—based permanently in Gaza and he was kidnapped."[10] Though beyond security issues, and even though, in principle, Bowen feels that "in any kind of reporting, you should narrow the distance between yourself and the story," much of the journalistic isolation that obscures Palestine is, he admits, self-imposed:

> Having lived there myself, as a reporter in Jerusalem ... The thought of going to Gaza was sometimes ... You would think "Oh God, I can't face it" because you ... There would be a big hassle to get in. In Jerusalem, you're there, everything's there. You're in your comfort zone in a sense and sometimes Gaza, it would be a bit of a struggle to go down to be honest because of the hassle factor, mainly getting in there.[11]

Ethan Bronner shares a similar opinion:

> on the Israeli side, physical access [is] easier ... [western journalists] tend to live in Israel, and there aren't military checkpoints stopping you from getting there ... On the Palestinian side, it's less easy to get to the spot because the Israeli military is likely to close the area off.[12]

Though both journalists tell a similar story of the inaccessibility of the Palestinian side of the conflict, Bowen's commentary here is especially telling given his institutional, and what is often presumed to be, his personal predisposition. Bowen's position is as at the Editor of the Middle East desk at the BBC and both Bowen's personal critics as well as critics of the BBC have alleged a profound pro-Palestinian bias in regional coverage, by him in particular.[13] Still, Bowen admits hesitancy in traveling to cover stories from within the Palestinian territories, and in particular in Gaza, as a result of the logistical and structural difficulties that this coverage entails.

New York Times Bureau Chief in Jerusalem Ethan Bronner expressed an inherent preference for the relative comfort of Israel and for the Israeli version of events. In Bronner's estimation, even when accessible, information provided by Palestinians, either as eyewitnesses to an event, or as a narrative description of the regional history, is inherently unreliable. According to Bronner the pre-eminent narrative of the average Palestinian is one of victimhood, a victimhood which is often perceived rather than actual. As such, from his perspective, Israeli sources deserve to carry the day in his retelling of regional events:

> I mean we know that Israel and the IDF feels very much under attack, globally and that any admission of error, or excess, they think is going to come back to haunt them with show trails in Spain or something. So they are very much in a "closed down, bullshit, nothing went wrong" mode ... At the same time, generally, when there's been an attack or a set of events or something and you say to the [Israeli] army "I need to know what happened" and they give you an answer, I would say more times it is true than false. I don't know what the percentage is but I don't feel that they systematically lie to me. I don't. And there have been a number of occasions in the last year and a half when ... somebody was killed in Gaza from something. And the instant story that

comes out of the place is that the IDF has killed seven people. And then the IDF will more than likely provide you with video tape and it will turn out that that is really not quite right. Okay? And there is another problem here which is that the victim which is the Palestinians, they tend to be the victims, they are so involved in being victims that they basically view that every day they get up they are getting slapped by the Jews. And so every day they get up and whether they have been slapped or not they say "I have just been slapped by the Jews." And it's a very big problem because their relationship to facts is not a very deep one. It's true. There's a lot of lying that goes on the Palestinian side. There is. More than on the Israeli side. There is lying on the Israeli side, but there's more of it on the other side. And that's very problematic. So you can't get to them, and when you get to them, they don't tell you anything, and if they tell you anything, it might not be true. That's a big problem.[14]

Quoted earlier in this piece from a previous interview, Bronner expressed an awareness of the "slick, professional press relations operation" working in Israel and described it as an added layer of cover for newsworthy information which journalists had to "pierce through."[15] When interviewed for this project, however, Bronner expressed a different perspective, one that viewed Palestinian testimony in an entirely derogatory light. From Bronner's perspective, the different "relationship to facts" on the Palestinian side condemns their testimony of events and regional histories automatically. Therefore, even if Israeli restrictions concomitant with occupation can be overcome, and Palestinians can be accessed, their version of events will not likely yield newsworthy information and will be presumed to be prevarication more often than information presented by Israelis. Given this admission of bias in sourcing, and given Mr Bronner's very important role as a frequent contributor to the discussion of events in the region, this level of partiality is significant. Within this journalistic environment, it is surprising that any of Mr Bronner's work, or indeed any of the reporting of *The New York Times* generated in Jerusalem, contains an articulated Palestinian perspective. As it is, *The New York Times*' documented Israeli-centrism and decided anti-Palestinian slant can no longer be said to be surprising.[16]

None of the other journalists interviewed for this research project confessed such a distrust of the Palestinian version of events. Undeniably though, problems of access to Palestine and the Palestinians remain for all journalists who participated in this study. As Simon Macgregor-Wood described, the quick and professional packaging of information about current events by Israeli officials may indeed be irresistibly attractive to regional journalists. Or, as described by Floto, preferences for the Israeli perspective may exist about which the journalists themselves are unaware but simply adopt out of desire for a shared cultural and linguistic experience while working in the Middle East. Alternatively, as described by Jeremy Bowen, restrictions on travel, military checkpoints, and closures and diversions may, in fact, isolate Palestinian sources and/or frustrate Western journalists attempting to gain access to those sources to the point that they effectively give up this effort altogether, though in this scenario, the extent of the efforts and motivations on the part of the individual journalists themselves to access Palestinian sources could fairly be called into question. Finally, although likely a minority perspective, Ethan Bronner's assessment of the dubious "relationship to facts" possessed of the Palestinians themselves may make the journalist's effort to seek out their perspective seem like a waste of time. Individually or in combination, these factors clearly contribute to a journalistic environment surrounding the Palestinian–Israeli conflict that heavily favors the Israeli version of history and current events over the version shared by the Palestinians. This conclusion is readily sustained by the statistical evidence rendered in the preceding chapters.

Language, terminology, and the definition of reality

Different procedures guide the selection and application of language in the coverage of Palestine–Israel within different news media organizations. In the BBC, a standard manual informs journalists working in the region which terms are to be applied to what ends and why. Jeremy Bowen explained: "we have a guide. We have training modules that all journalists have to do here…which will give at least some idea of the complexity of the [situation]."[17] The standardized nature of language instruction for journalists covering the conflict at the BBC speaks to the importance that that organization places on language in the reportage of regional events. Bowen's colleague in Jerusalem concurs with this assessment and characterizes the attention paid to language at the BBC as nothing short of intense: "[l]anguage is a massive issue …"occupation," "settlements" all these things have been hammered out … those are the tools which we use."[18] Through these strict systems of control, and only after intense scrutiny and extensive review of applicable terminology, the BBC maintains exacting control over the application of language in the description of events in Palestine–Israel.

Not so at *The New York Times*. Ethan Bronner's description of the application of language in the coverage of the conflict reflected no less the importance with which *The Times* treats the issue, but only after a much more informal process of discovery and development: "There really isn't a specific process … it [is] usually some kind of discussion between the correspondent and the desk where we … come to some conclusions."[19] Bronner emphasized that the informal, "purely collegial" nature of these discussions and conclusions is based primarily on the fact that *The New York Times* is a "multi-faceted animal" with a variety of publications being produced by a variety of journalists and editors.[20] While it is not clear that *The Times* is more or less centralized than the BBC which does have established guidelines and procedures regarding terminology, Bronner nevertheless emphasized that such uniformity in language would be difficult at *The New York Times*:

> the fact is that the *New York Times* is a multi-faceted animal and it could be that in the book review or the magazine or an editorial, they don't [use the same terminology]. They say "wall" or they say "fence" and they don't pay

attention to us. There is no, sort of, language maven at the top of the institution saying "never use the following word."[21]

So, while Bronner identified the importance of attending to particular language and terminology in the coverage of regional events, institutionally speaking, *The New York Times* appears less regimented in their treatment of language issues than the BBC. This would apparently leave a great deal more to the discretion of the individual journalist working at *The New York Times* and would open regional coverage to the perspective of the individual journalist to a much greater extent there than at the BBC. The results of this structural difference between these two news media institutions, two of the most influential in their respective news media communities, are significant.

A case in point of this difference in the structure and format of language used at the BBC versus that used at *The New York Times* is the issue of Israeli settlements in the Palestinian West Bank. Of the many contentious issues in the Palestinian–Israeli conflict, the issue of Israeli settlements built on Palestinian land in contravention of numerous international legal statutes is arguably the most divisive. "Settlement" is the legally recognized term used to describe construction on land inside the Green Line border established after fighting between Israel and a coalition of Arab armies ended in 1967. Settlement activities in the newly conquered West Bank and in the Gaza Strip[22] increased pace throughout the 1970s and 1980s. Nevertheless, that Israeli settlements in East Jerusalem are illegal and internationally recognized to be so does not prevent *The New York Times* from softening their illegality by referring to them as "neighborhoods." This shift in terminology represents these areas as communal parts of the Israeli state instead of expansive, illegal structures confiscating Palestinian land. Commenting on this distinction, Ethan Bronner declared that:

> the *New York Times* has—I am not sure if never—but more or less never referred to Jews living in East Jerusalem as settlers. So we don't do it now either. If someone asks me to explain it, I can't really explain it except to say "we don't." We limit the settlements and settlers to outside the boundaries of Jerusalem and then we talk about Jews living in East Jerusalem and then referred to it as also being conquered land and so on. And then when Har Homa was being built in the last ten years [in Bethlehem] I think it posed a difficulty because, is it a settlement or is it a neighbourhood?[23]

The language policy adopted by *The New York Times* is, in this instance, quite different from the terminology used by the BBC in order to describe precisely the same regional phenomenon. According to Jeremy Bowen, all Israeli building on land conquered in the 1967 war is considered illegal settlement activity, and is named as such:

> We call the Israeli building in occupied territory 'settlements'... Would we call them neighbourhoods? No we wouldn't. We'd make the point that they're

considered by international law to be settlements on occupied land and therefore illegal. We've always made that point. I know Israelis don't like hearing it but it's true.[24]

Likewise, the British-born head of the ABC in Jerusalem disagrees with Bronner's approach in this regard. In this instance an important US news media outlet finds itself more in line with the standard linguistic approach in Britain than that within the news media as an institution in the United States. According to Simon Macgregor-Wood, the failure to call settlements in Palestinian East Jerusalem "settlements" is, in and of itself, the adoption of the Israeli narrative of regional events. What exists at *The New York Times*, then, is a partial view of this important aspect of conflict from within the US news media establishment:

> I have never referred to settlements in East Jerusalem as anything other than settlements for the clear reason that if you do so you are adopting the narrative of one side and that's clearly not what I am here to do… Once you start telling people in America that a certain place is just a "neighbourhood," clearly it's a cleansing word, isn't it? … A neighbourhood is nice. That's where my friends live, neighbourhoods. If you live in a settlement, if you have any contextual knowledge of the conflict and the issues that relate to it you understand a different kind of person.[25]

It is noteworthy that Macgregor-Wood expressed his careful choice of language in terms of the personal rather than the institutional. The central point here is that even though he works within the US news media, Macgregor-Wood's perspective on this issue may be colored more by his British heritage than by his present employment status. So, while Macgregor-Wood's expressed attention to "sensitivities of the language … and the influence that it may have" he may actually be placing himself outside the mainstream perspective of the authoritative U.S. news media as it has been catalogued here.[26]

The issue of Israeli settlement in East Jerusalem is a telling case study of the difference in language and terminology embraced institutionally, and expressed practically, by members of the US and UK news media institution. Though it is not advisable to draw sweeping conclusions based upon the testimony of a handful of journalists, nevertheless, based upon the conversations related in part here, it is evident that both the cultural and political context within which these reporters are situated weighs heavily on individual perspective when it comes to events within the conflict. Further, it is clear that those individual perspectives are given much broader room for expression at a news organization like *The New York Times*, for instance, as opposed to the approach taken by the BBC. As these respective news organizations are two of the best known and most representative in their respective news communities, then, it seems reasonable to conclude that the news media communities in which each of these organizations are situated approach the language of the conflict in very different ways from one another.

Covering Palestine–Israel in the United States versus the United Kingdom: politics and culture

In addition to a consensus on the importance of language in reporting the conflict, each reporter interviewed agreed that, for a variety of historical and political reasons, the institutional and/or ideological approach toward covering Palestine–Israel differs between the contemporary news media in the United States and United Kingdom. As mentioned, uniquely situated to either confirm or disconfirm this assertion, Simon Macgregor-Wood was born and raised in the United Kingdom but now works within the US news media. He suggests that the great cultural affinity that exists between the United States and Israel today was formerly present in Britain as well "[a]s a child I remember my household and households like mine were sympathetic to Israel." The existence of the British affinity for Israel did not last, however, bur rather "shifted dramatically because of the occupation."[27] As a direct result of Israeli policies in and against Palestine over the course of the last 30 to 40 years, the general public attitude in Britain toward Israel has grown more critical toward Israel and more sympathetic to the plight of the Palestinians living under Israeli occupation. Jo Floto expressed the difference between US and British perceptions in this way:

> I think in Britain much more so than in America … there is a sympathy for the Palestinian side and that is more freely expressed in British society than it would be in American society. That middle-class people won't buy Israeli avocados, for instance, it's that kind of low background noise.[28]

In general terms, this perception was shared by all of the journalists interviewed for this study. As well, each identified the obvious existence of a close political and cultural connection between Israel and the United States. What is less clear, however, is whether the sympathy felt for Palestinians in Britain informs contemporary British cultural practices, or vice versa. Macgregor-Wood, for one, suspects that cultural representations in the United States and the United Kingdom are influenced by political policies and public attitudes and not the other way around. He noted that the depiction of Palestinians specifically, and Arabs or Muslims generally, does not come with the same pejorative stereotypes in Britain that it does in the United States.

> I mean Hollywood and its characterization of Arabs or Muslims … I'm not a left-wing firebrand but you go to mainstream movie products that portray Arabs, it's a joke. And I think I do connect on that issue as being British, where there is a far greater sensitivity to cultural diversities and, critically, their portrayal. You know it's just not acceptable in the British mainstream media to present an Arab as a kind of squawking loony, whereas you look at a Hollywood film that's very often how they are.[29]

Here, Macgregor-Wood speaks to the existence of cultural sensitivities and accompanying taboos which seem not to be present in the United States. He is not alone in this opinion. Speaking to this issue some years earlier, John Cooley, then of ABC-TV News in London, said of American representations of Arabs that "Arabs are probably still the only group in the U.S. that anyone dares to portray in pejorative terms. This kind of thing would never be tolerated by other ethnic groups in the United States."[30] If in fact Macgregor-Wood and Cooley are correct, the pervasive negative representation of Arabs, Muslims, and/or Palestinians in the United States would certainly influence the perspectives of US journalists working in the region, and would therefore affect their coverage, and the way in which relevant information was being relayed back to their audience, either subtly or overtly. British audiences to news of the Middle East might conversely be insulated to an extent from these perspectives and may well develop knowledge of the Middle East from the authoritative news media in a manner more respectful to practices and traditions of Arabs and Palestinians. Still, it would be difficult to quantify the way in which the pervasive negative portrayals of Arabs and Palestinians in the United States, or indeed, the lack of this type of portrayal in the UK, impacts upon journalists covering the Middle East. The point here is not to simplify these dynamic relationships, but rather to point out possible reasons for the divergence of perspective on Palestine–Israel that exists in the United States and Great Britain, and the concomitant divergence of news media coverage of the region that has already been identified in this study.

If cultural representations in the United States serve to enhance the cognitive distance of that public from Palestinians, the opposite is true of the contemporary American approach to Israel. On this topic, Macgregor-Wood argues that the affinity felt between the American public and the Israeli people, much like that embraced by the British in the early moments of the history of the state of Israel, derives from a perceived sameness and an assumed cultural continuity:

> Israelis have a head start on American public opinion from here because they are "more like us"… [there are] huge number of American Jews who are also Israelis who live here and who are eloquent and articulate and who communicate the language in a manner in which people in the Midwest can understand.[31]

Ethan Bronner commented on this issue as well, suggesting that the presumed sameness which emotionally connected many Americans with the state of Israel was based on fundamental similarities to include a shared value system, a shared historical experience, and a shared work ethic: "the affinities of the two countries are great. The fact that both have many immigrants, there is a very strong "can-do" attitude in both places, people work hard in a similar way. There's a lot that binds the two."[32] But Bronner also expressed the differences in approach to covering the conflict between the UK and the US as more specifically a product of differing American versus European political agendas whereby institutional acceptance of questioning the right of Israel is present Europe while absent in the United States:

in the United States, broadly, the legitimacy of Israel is not questioned. Its policies totally opened to being questioned. But the legitimacy of there being a state for the Jews in some portion of Palestine is accepted ... Apparently in Europe, when you talk about the Israel-Palestine conflict, the base question is "why is there an Israel?" That's the base question that feeds the coverage of the *Independent* and *Le Monde*, you see it. It does not feed our coverage. That's the biggest difference.[33]

In anticipation of an alternative perspective, another way to frame Bronner's evaluation of the status of Israel in news coverage might be to suggest that European, or specifically British coverage takes an approach to the conflict which is open to all perspectives on the issue, and closed off to none. This might occasionally include questioning the historical vagaries of whether or not Israel—or any state for that matter—should exist today. In the United States, speculation about contemporary as well as historical realities is very often left out of the authoritative news. Among such speculation would be included, as Bronner points out, the facts surrounding the creation of Israel inside historic Palestine. So while the existence of political conflict in the region today can be given suggestive or speculative historical context in British and European representations, the past—and its enumerable potential repercussions—is very much left behind by American journalists. The existence of this singular perspective within such a vital arm of free expression as the press within a nation itself borne from genocide and ethnic cleansing might not, in fact, be very unusual.

A final consideration of the issue of the difference in the coverage between the United States and the United Kingdom comes from Jeremy Bowen. To his mind, the approach to the conflict by the journalistic community is similar to the approach to all foreign news in both national news media communities. The relevant factors guiding this approach are primarily geopolitical; the resulting coverage in turn creates disparate social realities within each national community:

I would say that people [in Britain] are a bit more outward looking. America is its own continent. We're a small island off a continent so you have be a bit more outward looking and the agenda too is ... The news agenda here is, even if you only watch the news once a week is going to be a bit more outward looking, frankly. If you try and get your view of the world through American network newscasts, you'd think that there was one big America and a tiny few places around it because it is not really covered.[34]

Bowen relates that the UK is a small part of a large cultural and political area whereas the United States sits perched atop the community of nations as the lone agent of *hyperpuissance*. As such, cultural and political outlooks within the two nations should be expected to diverge. And as cultural products of those nations, in addition to being writers generating information for them, journalists should be expected to be, at least in some part, beholden to these very influential political and social forces.

Concluding thoughts

Among the journalists interviewed for this project, none was more candid or less guarded about his beliefs and opinions than Ethan Bronner, former Jerusalem Bureau Chief for *The New York Times*. For Mr Bronner, facts, sobriety, and evidentiary truth are on the Israeli side of the conflict. Exaggeration, misrepresentation, and outright lies reside with the Palestinians. Evidence of these biases surfacing within the printed reports about Palestine–Israel from *The New York Times* abounds (and has been covered at some length in preceding chapters) and substantially conditions that paper's reportage of the contemporary political conflict.[35] This includes, but is not limited to, adopting place names aligned with the Israeli point of view, underrepresenting Palestinian voice in regional reports, and contextualizing Israeli narratives of events, but not Palestinian ones. In fairness to journalists working in this region still today, this author could find no other journalist to testify in kind as Mr Bronner did as to his preferences or warm personal feelings about one side of the conflict or the other. Not to overstate the matter, but these personal sentiments here recorded may go some distance to explaining the statistical variances and tendencies toward preferential coverage among the papers-of-record in the United States and the United Kingdom.

Notes

1 Simon Macgregor-Wood. Personal Interview by Author, September 2, 2009.
2 Jeremy Bowen, Personal Interview by Author, December 2, 2008.
3 Macgregor-Wood. Personal Interview by Author, 2009.
4 Ethan Bronner Interviewed in Marda Dunsky, *Pens and Swords: How the American Mainstream Media Reports the Israeli-Palestinian Conflict* (New York: Columbia University Press, 2007), 329.
5 Bowen, Personal Interview by Author, 2008.
6 Chris Hedges in Marda Dunsky, *Pens and Swords: How the American Mainstream Media Reports the Israeli-Palestinian Conflict* (New York: Columbia University Press, 2007), 357.
7 There are some important exceptions to this truism, chief among them, Israeli reporter and author Amira Hass who not only frequented the Palestinian West Bank and Gaza Strip in researching news articles for the Israeli daily *Ha'aretz*, she in fact lived in Gaza, and later Ramallah, for a number of years beginning in 1993 being possibly the only Israeli woman not affiliated with the Israeli military or civil occupation of Palestine to do so (Amira Hass, *Drinking the Sea at Gaza: Days and Nights in a Land under* Siege (New York: Holt and Company, 1996), 3–10.
8 Jo Floto. Personal Interview by Author, August 13, 2009.
9 Ibid.
10 Bowen, Personal Interview by Author, 2008.
11 Ibid.
12 Bronner in Marda Dunsky, *Pens and Swords*, 320.
13 There is at least one website, bias-bbc.blogspot.com, devoted exclusively to this idea.
14 Ethan Bronner. Personal Interview by Author. September 10, 2009. Bronner here is reiterating a widely held negative stereotype about the Palestinian people which has appeared throughout this political conflict in a variety of media. In his assessment of the US news media and its relationship with the Palestinian people, analyst Azmi Bishara pointed out that "in 2002, former Prime Minister Ehud Barak drew on

long-standing stereotypes of Arabs to contend in an interview published in the *New York Review of Books* that [PA President Yasser] Arafat and his people were naturally inclined to lie" (Amahl Bishara, "Watching U.S. Television from the Palestinian Streets: The Media, the State, and Representational Interventions," *Cultural Anthropology*, *23(3)*, 2008, 492).

15 Ethan Bronner Interviewed in Marda Dunsky, *Pens and Swords: How the American Mainstream Media Reports the Israeli-Palestinian Conflict* (New York: Columbia University Press, 2007), 329.

16 On the 25 of January of 2010, the electronic magazine *The Electronic Intifada* (or E.I.) reported that Mr Bronner's son had voluntarily joined the Israeli Army (formally the Israeli Defence Force) and would be completing the three-year mandatory service imposed upon all Israeli citizens (even though the Bronners are US citizens). The entrance of Mr Bronner's son into the Israeli military was asserted to be a conflict of interest by E.I. who suggested that Mr Bronner should be removed from his post at the paper, given the evident compromise of even a pretense of journalistic impartiality upon the revelation of this information. *The New York Times* was quick to defend their Jerusalem Bureau Chief, however, and suggested that a reporter of Mr Bronner's professionalism and integrity would be able to suspend his judgment of the situation even in the event of his son's involvement on the Israeli side of the conflict (New York Times Fails to Disclose Jerusalem Bureau Chief's Conflict of Interest, *The Electronic Intifada*, January 25, 2010, http://electronicintifada.net/content/new-york-times-fails-disclose-jerusalem-bureau-chiefs-conflict-interest/8644). One cannot but wonder whether *The Times* would have mustered the same vehement defense for a correspondent whose son had become directly involved in the Palestinian-Israeli conflict by voluntarily joining a Palestinian paramilitary unit.

17 This language guide is presently available on the BBC website.

18 Floto, Personal Interview by Author, 2009.

19 Bronner, Personal Interview by Author, 2009.

20 Ibid.

21 Ibid.

22 The 21 Israeli settlements in the West Bank with some 8,500 settlers in them were evacuated unilaterally by Israeli Prime Minister Ariel Sharon in the late summer of 2005. See Chapter 5, *Evacuating Gaza from Two Sides of the Atlantic: Comparing Frames of Representation in the Print News Media* in this work for more information.

23 Bronner, Personal Interview by Author, 2009.

24 Bowen, Personal Interview by the Author, 2008.

25 Macgregor-Wood. Personal Interview by Author, 2009.

26 Ibid.

27 Macgregor-Wood. Personal Interview by Author, 2009.

28 Floto, Personal Interview by Author, 2009.

29 Macgregor-Wood. Personal Interview by Author, 2009. Here Macgregor-Wood speaks to an aspect of representation of Arabs within contemporary media that has recently received some scholarly attention. For further information see Jack Shaheen's 2009 work *Reel Bad Arabs: How Hollywood Vilifies a People.*

30 John Cooley, "ABC-TV News in London," in Edmund Ghareeb (ed.). *Split Vision: Arab Portrayal in the American Media* (Washington, DC: Institute of Middle Eastern and African Affairs, 1977), 211.

31 Macgregor-Wood. Personal Interview by Author, 2009.

32 Bronner, Personal Interview by Author, 2009.

33 Bronner, Personal Interview by Author, 2009.

34 Bowen, Personal Interview by Author, 2008.

35 Howard Friel and Richard Falk, *Israel-Palestine on Record: How the New York Times Misreports Conflict in the Middle East* (New York: Verson, 2007).

10 Conclusion

Contending discourses

Two discourses contend for dominance in print news media presentations of Palestine and Israel in the United States and Great Britain. In the United States, news media perceptions hold close to an official Israeli version of events. The four case studies examined in this dissertation suggest that the authoritative news media in the United States is reluctant to criticize Israeli occupation, Israeli policy, or Israeli military intervention in the ongoing political dispute in the region. Official Israeli sources are employed with greater frequency and are sustained with more vehemence than Palestinian ones. Palestinian voices are more likely to appear as radical or marginal, if at all. Palestinians are most often presented as agents of violence in the region and are most often seen as guilty of violence in the first instance. Palestine's cultural and political world is often impugned as backward or strange, its customs and practices held up to a microscope of judgment and branded, in Said's terms, as foreign, eastern, oriental, and ultimately, other.[1] Similar judgements are not levelled against Israel, a people and culture identified by the journalists interviewed in the previous chapter as a more familiar and sympathetic national group. In short, US print news media discourse closely aligns with official Israeli policies and perspectives.

The printed news in the United Kingdom presents information in a somewhat more nuanced manner than their trans-Atlantic colleagues. In the case studies reviewed above, the British media were as willing to declare Israel at fault for regional violence as they were Palestinian actors. In terms of assessing damage, British news evaluations adhered more closely to statistical realities reported from areas affected by violence; no one community had a monopoly on suffering in the conflict. Finally, in terms of approach to cultural differences, the British print news media were more likely to ignore Western norms of cultural representation than the US media were. In all, the British news media presented a version of events more closely in line with the evidentiary proceedings in the recent history of the Palestinian–Israel conflict, the so-called "facts on the ground," than those presentations examined in the print news media in the US.

Through these trends, two distinct discourses emerge in two distinct national news media communities. As a result, the two national communities exposed to their respective discourses have come to know and view the Palestinian–Israel conflict in qualitatively disparate terms. These differences incorporate not only cultural and historical perceptions but also factual ones, as verifiable evidence of events in the region is changed, obfuscated, or otherwise misrepresented. Such discursive distortions have substantial impact on public cognition as well as on the collective national identities constructed and maintained in each news media community based in part upon the foundational role of the news media in this process in each dynamic national community. Specific trends in these two divergent discourses can be analyzed based upon the presence/absence of linguistic elements within the case studies reviewed in preceding chapters. Whereas those case studies highlighted differences in discourse as they occurred within delineated media events, the discussion below generalizes these distinctions, examining trends in the discourse on Palestine–Israel as they appeared across the time span of all of the case studies presented. In this chapter's final remarks, I situate the present study within existing perspectives on Palestine–Israel in discourse and offer suggestions for further research going forward.

The quality of suffering: the Israeli Soul versus the Palestinian Body

Coverage of Palestinian suffering of the kind noted in Chapter 7, *Covering the Gaza War: The Printed News in the United States and Great Britain*, typically deals with loss of life, liberty, and/or property as was seen on a widespread scale in Gaza in late 2008/early 2009. Depictions of Israeli suffering often go beyond the loss of life or the loss of material goods. In the case of the settler evacuation from Gaza, this was depicted most clearly in the descriptions of the existential crisis brought about by the removal of Jewish-only settlements. In this case, Israeli settlers *did*, in fact, lose property that they owned legally according to Israeli law, but this aspect of loss was not the one emphasized by the news media. Rather, the focus of the story was the spiritual loss of the Jewish people and the crisis of faith within Israel brought about by then Prime Minister Sharon's unilateral policy. Presentations such as these convey to the reader the depth of the Israeli actor in the news story, and the profound sense of suffering experienced by that actor on a deep, emotional, and otherwise spiritual level. Further, as evidenced by the statistical evaluation of that case study, this journalistic perspective was not nearly as common in presentations within the British print news media. The reliance upon this narrative element substantially differentiates between the discourses present in the two national news media communities.

Commenting on contemporary conflict reporting, philosopher Slavoj Zizek addresses the distinction made in the contemporary press between images of the so-called First versus the Third World:

> in … reporting on Third World catastrophes… the whole point is to produce a scoop of some gruesome detail: Somalis dying of hunger, raped Bosnian men with their throats cut. These shots are always accompanied by an advance warning that 'some of the images you will see are extremely graphic and may upset children' … Is this not yet further proof of how … the distance which

separates Us from Them, from their reality, is maintained: the real horror happens there, not here?[2]

As evidenced from the qualitative analysis in this work, Zizek's argument readily applies to coverage of Palestine–Israel in the US news media. Gruesome detail of death and dismemberment often accompany the Palestinian story; Israeli loss is measured in a spiritual or existential sense. This narrative strategy in contemporary print coverage of the region serves precisely the purpose indicated here by Zizek, that of further distancing "Us" from "Them" and informing the consumers of the news where the "real horror" is occurring: there, not here. Palestinian suffering and loss can be understood through US news presentations typically only in the physical sense: they lose their limbs, they lose their life, they lose their house. Palestinians can be killed or dismembered; Palestinians can weep for loved ones and bemoan the bombing of their homes and neighbourhoods. But, according to the majority of presentations analyzed in this study, Palestinians do not feel metaphysical loss, existential crisis, or spiritual angst over the loss of land, hearth, and home. This level of pathos requires attribution of a depth of character and feeling to Palestinians that is rare in the news in the United States. Only one actor in the ongoing conflict is discursively constructed with depth, presented as pensive, thoughtful, and sincere in their existential loss and suffering: the Israelis. The Israeli sense of loss comes from some deeper cultural reservoir, a pool of feeling and spirituality apparently exclusive to Israelis within the context of this political conflict. Palestinians are thus represented as aspiritual, an exclusively corporeal and therefore ephemeral people. In the same manner, Israelis become remade as the soulful, eternal, and therefore righteous group.[3]

It should be mentioned that physical loss and physical damage to the Palestinian community were also presented in the British print news media in the case studies reviewed here. In this sense, the British presentation of the Palestinian communities was not significantly different than those US presentations asserted by their US counterparts. Rather, the difference came in the presentation of the Israeli community, which was the central focus in the US news and which was presented with a depth of purpose not attributed to the Palestinians. This presentation was consistent across the case studies examined here, and shows a journalistic effort on the part of the US news media to demonstrate the complexity of the Israeli community and the challenges that it faces, while eschewing a parallel effort in their representation of the Palestinians.

In sum, the presentation of loss, suffering, and feeling by the US media creates a picture of one society that is thoughtful, spiritual, far-sighted, and ancient opposed to another society that is oriented exclusively in the present and is entirely corporeal and material: the Israeli soul versus the Palestinian body. By appreciating the essential difference between these two representations we can approach an understanding of representations of legitimacy itself—social, cultural, and political—in the news media presentation of Palestine–Israel. If depth of feeling and spiritual loss can be found in descriptions of only one group within the conflict, then the clear implication is that that group possesses the more developed culture, and are the more entitled people. If Palestinians are seen only as living ephemerally with concerns based only in the present, the depth of their culture, their historical experience, and their political claim within the context of conflict is lost. These representations structure knowledge about the conflict; they contextualize and historicize. Consistent representations such as these can only leave news readers with a sense of the depth, spirituality, and righteousness of the Israeli cause, and an equally acute sense of the dilapidated, materialistic, and secular nature of the Palestinian one.

Religion as bastion, religion as weapon

In presentations of culture in the case studies in this work, the US print news media often made mention of the religious traditions of both Palestinian and Israel communities. For many US journalists covering the region, Islam and Islamic custom provided a focal point around which the discussion of Palestine takes place. Likewise, Judaism provides a substantial narrative focus in the telling of regional events for American news consumers. In representing Islam, the US news media attributes pejorative characteristics, and portrays the religion as a negative or detrimental force within Palestinian culture and society. Islam is actively represented as a harmful force within Palestinian politics and society:

> Muslim women wear the hijab, men appear bearded, praying, or both. In each case, dress, beards, and acts stand in for the whole person, denoting cultural orientation, religious commitment, and thus, to secular society, Otherness.[4]

Conversely, the US media's portrayal of Judaism within Israeli society poses qualitatively different attributes to religion and culture. Unlike Islam, Judaism is described with reverence and seriousness. Specific holidays are named and dated and their commemoration practices discussed. Motivations of soldiers, settlers, politicians and citizens are cast in a spiritual context; religion in Israel is salve to repair conflict and division in Israeli culture or politics. Israeli society is uplifted and strengthened by the long tradition of Judaism substantially present within it.

   The national news media in the UK likewise portrayed the religiosity of the Jewish people in a positive light. In our case studies reviewed above, the British press discussed religious holidays and provided details of religious celebrations in some detail. These elements were presented as interwoven within Israeli society and were described in terms that make this practice and belief seem a natural, constructive force within society. However as in the US, Islam was portrayed in a different light. While mention was sometimes made of Muslim practices in the Palestinian community, few judgments were made by the British press in presenting these elements one way or the other. Islam in the British news media representations therefore adapted a rather neutral social position; it was neither good nor bad, it simply was there, and as such, was unavoidable. This sterility of presentation contrasted with often florid discussions of the role of Judaism in Israel. Though not a distinctly pejorative portrayal of Islam as such, the British discussion of religion did indeed differ depending on which religion, and upon which society was under discussion. The impact of the presentation of both national news media communities, then, shows a similar distinction, and sustains a common conclusion about the print news media discourse concerning Islam and Judaism in the coverage of Palestine–Israel.

What can be concluded from these presentations is that only Judaism can serve as a force for good within the conflicting communities. The depth and detail of presentation of Jewish holidays and ceremonies compared to the distinct lack of a similar presentation of events in the Muslim community bears this out. Further to the specific manner of presentation in the US print news media, only one of the two religious traditions in the affected communities can be a force for the perpetuation of violence: Islam. In print news media language describing the presence of Islam in the Palestinian communities, various pejorative references indicate the religion's profoundly dangerous character. Islam's association with terrorist elements, its connection to suicide and cultism, and its odious view of women in society are all elements of this presentation. As such, to approach news presentation of the Palestinian–Israeli conflict is to approach a disparate assessment of the role of religion in society. In the first case, religion as a force within Israel is tried and tested, a deep tradition with positive consequences for its practitioners. In the second, Islam is strange and inherently problematic. It motivates conflict and it provides the excuse for violence. In the hands of the Palestinian community, it is a cruel and aggressive political force. Though exceptions to these generalizations certainly do exist in both news communities, the bulk of the many news items analyzed for this study sustains these conclusions.

The psychology of trauma: home and landscape

In covering the settler withdrawal/relocation from Gaza, the print news media in the United States devoted considerable time and energy detailing the suffering to the settler community as a result of this policy. The British print news media contained the same frame of representation within their coverage, though it appeared to a much lesser extent. Recall that in this frame of representation in both news media communities, the trauma of the move caused settlers to wail, cry, and weep bemoaning an Israeli policy decision that they felt was unjust and unfair. Through these textual images, news media consumers were able to absorb a visceral description of the trauma of Israeli loss, about the agony of removal from the land they hold dear, and above all, about their detachment from home engendered by this regional political manoeuvre. Yet scarcely a mention was made of this sense of loss, of this displacement from home, and this detachment from physical and geographical space within the Palestinian community, either as a result of contemporary war or historical trauma. In this imbalanced presentation of the two conflicting communities, authoritative print news media products in comparison here portray a vision of love, faith, and allegiance to the land in dispute within one community in conflict only. Within this vision, the land of Palestine–Israel is home to one community, but merely as habitable space to another. As with the other points of discursive comparison above, depth of feeling and complexity of emotional connection become the purview of only one of the two feuding communities; cognition about the conflict develops based upon this pillar of discourse.

This narrative technique linking home to the Israeli community substantially conditions elements of loss and trauma within discourse on Palestine–Israel. The effect is to render Israelis as a complete and full nation, a substantial people with all of the recognizable and attendant cultural characteristics that this distinction entails. Palestinians, on the other hand, remain partial within discourse; they are physical and material but not spiritual or historical. When describing injuries resulting from violence, for instance, only the Israeli communities subject to shelling from Palestinian militias within the Gaza Strip are presented as traumatized or shocked. Palestinian injuries, as indicated above, are measured in the physical sense, but scarcely in the print news in either the US or the UK, in a psychological one. It is as if the stress of war and the shock of bombs and bullets falling nearby affect only one party to conflict, if print news representations are to be taken as a reliable measure. These presentations connect the notion of the spiritual nature of loss experienced by Israelis discussed above. The picture provided is that of a whole; a whole people suffer mental, emotional, and psychological injury. Whereas a partial people suffer only physically; soul, spirit, and psyche remain unmentioned and therefore unaffected.

The suffering involved in this discursive trope is one which emotionally connects the land to the Israeli while only physically connecting it to Palestinians, if there is any connection at all. Through print news media discourse, elements of the partiality and transitivity of the Palestinians are carried forward in text encompassing both Palestinians as individuals when they suffer exclusively bodily destruction, as well as Palestinians as a collective community whose dislocation from the land is subsumed within the emotionally and psychologically deeper Israeli narrative. Beyond individual frames of representation, these discursive staples in the ongoing textual discourse on Palestine–Israel create an idealized image of the land, the people, and the conflict that contains them. Though identified here in four specific and relatively recent events, the same imagery can be discerned in textual presentations from within US and UK print news publications at any point in the conflict. Much like frames of representation mark time in news discussions of up-to-the-minute events in this region today, these common signposts serve to connect text and meaning in coverage of the Palestinian–Israeli conflict by contributing to the formation of knowledge, cognition, and constructed social discourse on the conflict.

Final words

This study has offered a comparison of the contemporary print news discourse on Palestine–Israel between the news media institutions of the United States and the United Kingdom. It has included comparative elements of form, function, and overall social and cognitive effect in an attempt to define the pliant borders of discourse as it circulates in each national news media community. As an analysis of the contemporary news media, this study has attempted a unique form of investigation by compiling news products produced over a fixed period of time and comparing them, word by word, in a process of close reading and linguistic assessment. Through this process, the coverage of four major news events in Palestine–Israel developed in two distinct locations was evaluated under close scrutiny. Further to that comparison, the producers themselves were engaged in conversation in an effort to discern their perspectives, motivations, and biases in the production of news, bringing to the fore their (often illuminating) cultural preferences and professional attitudes in the coverage of the conflict. As a study in language, this dissertation connected elements of thought—in so far as this phenomenon is critically understood—to the printed word, and demonstrated the pertinent distinctions between what a news reader in Sunderland in northeast England with *The London Times* in hand might know about Palestine–Israel versus what his or her counterpart would know reading the Middle East section of *The New York Times* in Portland, Oregon. These efforts have collectively led to critical conclusions about institutional perspectives on religion, on culture, on nationhood, and on homeland in the Palestinian–Israeli conflict present within each news community under comparison.

In critiquing the printed news media and the discourse on Palestine–Israel, this study in effect offers a critique of a social reality, a critique which has been observed and pondered through the investigative lens of the linguist, historian, and anthropologist, among others: "Social realties form the cement with which we construct our conception of what is real and what is not, what is important and what is not."[5] This inevitably is both a highly personalized and highly subjective process; my conclusions may not necessarily resemble other investigations of this type. Anthropologist Nadia Abu El-Haj provides valuable comment on the issues of scholarship and subjectivity. In her seminal text on the discursive value and academic appropriation of archaeology in Palestine–Israel, she speaks about the manner of academic investigation as indicative of the ideological bias of the investigator him/herself. Abu El-Haj speaks of the earth itself as a known quantity, as a given component in the investigative equation. But it is in the manner of dissecting that earth, of uncovering what lies beneath it, that a particular investigational approach or bias can be discerned:

> The earth has to be carved up in particular ways in order for the objects of archaeology to become visible, not simply by transforming absence into presence, but, more specifically, by creating particular angles of vision through which landscapes are remade. *How* one goes about hewing the land tells us something about what *kinds of* objects archaeologists deem to be significant (to be worth of being observed).[6]

What is present in this study might be considered as a form of hewing as well, a hewing of language, a dig through words, a search for some greater meaning beyond simply what appears on the surface of the page. If this is so, then my determined strikes upon the face of language must surely leave an indelible impression, the examination of which might uncover further meaning about the process of investigation which took place here. And as Abu El-Haj aptly put it, the "*kinds*" of objects unearthed in this research project certainly do indicate what it is that this researcher deems to be "significant."[7] Undoubtedly, this is so. Nonetheless, even as the products discovered and revealed here may be open to critique and even censure by those who do not share my point of view, the process of unveiling these discoveries of language remain of critical import in the study of our understanding of news events and the world they purport to describe. It is my hope, therefore, that that investigative pursuit, and the axe marks upon the earth that it left behind, will be well-received, even if the resulting artefacts of discovery are subject to critique, debate, and further questioning.

Notes

1 Edward Said, *Orientalism* (New York: Random House, 1978).
2 Slavoj Zizek, *Welcome to the Desert of the Real: Five Essays on September 11 and Related Dates* (London: Verso, 2002), 13.
3 Stuart Hall "The Spectacle of the 'Other'" in Hall (ed.) *Representation: Cultural Representations and Signifying Practices* (London: Sage, 1997), 223–79.
4 Peter Morey and Amina Yaqin, *Framing Muslims: Stereotyping and Representation after 9/11* (London: Harvard University Press, 2011), 115.
5 Nachman Ben-Yehuda, *Sacrificing Truth: Archaeology and the Myth of Masada* (Amherst, New York: Humanity Books, 2002), 189.
6 Nadia Abu-El Haj, *Facts on the Ground: Archaeological Practice and Territorial Self Fashioning in Israeli Society* (Chicago: The University of Chicago Press, 2001), 131 (emphasis in original).
7 Ibid.

Appendix A
Evacuating Gaza from two sides of the Atlantic, in-text frames of representation

N.B.: In all Appendices, italics highlight that specific segment of text present in each news article evincing the frame of representation in question.

US print news media

Frame of Representation	Examples from Article Sample
Evacuation NOT an End to Occupation	"*Israel also announced plans to build 50 more homes in a West Bank settlement*, a week after President Bush urged Mr. Sharon to stop the expansion of settlements, as stipulated by the Middle East peace plan known as the road map." Greg Myre. "Sharon May Delay Gaza Pullout to Mid-August." *The New York Times*. April 19, 2005.
	"In an interview published yesterday, *Prime Minister Ariel Sharon said the Jewish state would continue building major settlements in the West Bank* over U.S. and Palestinian objections." –Staff and Wire Reports. "Palestinian Revelers (sic) Tear Up Gaza Settlements." *The Daily News*. September 12, 2005.
Palestinian Suffering	"Muhammad pointed to his son, Zidan, 3. *'This kid will sit drawing a machine gun,'* he said with disgust. Tamam said: *'When he hears bullets, he cries, 'I don't want to die.' This 3-year-old knows about death.* What kind of life is this?" Steven Erlanger. "Will Israeli Settlements Serve them, Gazans Ask." *The New York Times*. June 14, 2005.
	"For Hani Alser, who attended Seeds of Peace in 1999, the withdrawal could have profound implications. *Alser, 21 grew up in Gaza but hasn't been back home for three years because of travel restrictions on the area* since he began studying in Jordan." Clarke Canfield. "Israelis, Arabs Reunite at Peace Camp during Gaza Withdrawal." *The Associated Press*. August 16, 2005.
Palestinians as Violent	"*Palestinians fired two mortar shells on Wednesday at Morag, a Jewish settlement in the southern Gaza Strip*, but no one was hurt, the Israeli military said." Greg Myre. "Israeli Legislators Approve $870 Million for Settlers Who Quit Gaza." *The New York Times*. February 17, 2005.
	"Tension mounted after *an Islamic Jihad suicide bombing killed four outside a shopping mall in the Israeli coastal city of Netanya* last week." Joshua Mitnick. "Exiting Gaza, Israel Fights on Two Fronts." *The Christian Science Monitor*. July 18, 2005.

Frame of Representation	*Examples from Article Sample*
Palestinians as Corrupt, Factional, Backward, Poor	"Egyptian mediators sought to diffuse *a standoff between Hamas and Palestinian President Mahmoud Abbas*, who used force over the weekend for the first time against the Islamic militants to stop the rocket attacks, spurring rare *internal clashes that left two Palestinians dead in Gaza*." Joshua Mitnick. "Exiting Gaza, Israel Fights on Two Fronts." *The Christian Science Monitor.* July 18, 2005.
	"*Young men carried off everything they could take from the debris in the 21 settlements, including chairs, tables and shopping carts. They tore down electricity poles to pull off the wires, ripped out toilets and walked off with doors and window frames.*" Staff and Wire Reports. "Palestinian Revelers (sic) Tear Up Gaza Settlements." *The Daily News.* September 12, 2005.
Palestinian Celebration	"Convoys of yellow minibuses cruised the city's streets Monday, honking their horns and flying the Palestinian flag *in celebration of the end of 38 years of Israeli occupation.*" Martin Patience. "Palestinians Celebrate Pullout as 'Turning Point' in Conflict." *USA Today.* August 16, 2005.
	"As Isaeli forces pulled out of the Gaza Strip today after 38 years of occupation*, joyful Palestinians charged into the ruins of former settlements, planting flags, burning synagogues and firing guns in the air.*" Staff and Wire Reports. "Palestinian Revelers (sic) Tear Up Gaza Settlements." *The Daily News.* September 12, 2005.
Evacuation Ends Occupation	"Gaza occupation coming to a close." Joel Greenberg. "Gaza Occupation Coming to a Close." *The Chicago Tribune.* August 14, 2005.
Israeli Suffering	"Most settlers in the West Bank have single-family homes with gardens, which are much less common in Israel, where apartment living is the norm. *Settlers say they hate the thought of giving up their gardens.*" Greg Myre. "Some West Bank Settlers Leave Quietly, if Tearfully." *The New York Times.* July 8, 2005.
	"Ta'el wandered back into the kitchen and asked, "*Mommy, why isn't there a roof?*" All the tiles had been stripped from the roof and loaded into containers." Joseph Berger. "One Mom Packs, Another Resists; Both Try to be Strong for the Kids." August 12, 2005.
	"'*The little ones are supposed to start school on Sept. 1, but we don't know where we'll be living then. At home they could run free outside, but here we're in a city and they can't leave the hotel. Some don't even know how to use the elevator,*' Goldstein says. 'No one in the government cares about us. No one cares.'" Michele Chabin. "Some Displaced Settlers Refusing Offer of Housing." *USA Today.* August 24, 2005.
Israel as Legal, Moral	"Soldiers received a booklet that told them, *'We stand before some of the most difficult and sensitive tasks ever faced by the state of Israel. ... In our capacity as security personnel it is required by us to defend the public.*'" Andrea Stone. "Israeli Soldiers Brace for Day of Forced Removals." *USA Today.* August 17, 2005.
	"Over the past few days, the world has witnessed a stunning spectacle in Israel: *the government of the Jewish state unilaterally, voluntarily, giving up land in Gaza* – and forcing Jewish residents to leave, involuntarily." "The Gaza Gamble." *The New York Post.* August 19, 2005.

Frame of Representation	*Examples from Article Sample*
Israeli/Jewish Religiosity	"But at a cabinet meeting on Sunday, Yonatan Bassi, the official overseeing the withdrawal, raised the possibility of *waiting until the end of the annual three-week mourning period that commemorates the destruction of the First and Second Temples in Jerusalem*. This year the period runs from July 24 through Aug. 14." Greg Myre. "Sharon May Delay Gaza Pullout to Mid-August." *The New York Times.* April 19, 2005.
	"*The original date falls in the period of Tisha B'Av, a Jewish day of mourning for the destruction of the two Temples in Jerusalem,* when Jews are not supposed to move to a new house." Steven Erlanger. "Israel May Speed Gaza Pullout to Head Off More Protests." *The New York Times.* July 22, 2005.
Israel as Fractious	"Jewish settlers began a new round of protests on Monday and warned *that large numbers of Israeli soldiers could refuse to follow orders to remove settlers from the Gaza Strip later this year.*" Greg Myre. "Jewish Settlers Stage New Protests against Planned Gaza Removal." *The New York Times.* January 4, 2005.
	"*Nine Israeli soldiers refused orders to take part in breaking up the demonstration, joining a small number other (sic) soldiers who have taken similar action. Two of the soldiers deserted their unit and fled to the Gush Katif settlements,* the Israeli newspaper Haaretz said on its Web site." Greg Myre. "Heavy Israeli Armor Presses Gaza Border." *The New York Times.* July 18, 2005.
Israelis as Violent	"*several dozen settlers threw stones and scuffled with Israel security force members* as they removed two mobile homes from an unauthorized settlement outpost in the West Bank near the Palestinian city of Nablus." Greg Myre. "Jewish Settlers Stage New Protests against Planned Gaza Removal." *The New York Times.* January 4, 2005.
	"The West Bank man, Asher Weisgan, said the reason *he seized a guard's gun, killed four people and wounded another* was to create a crisis that would halt the Gaza pullout." Uri Dan. "Settlers' Shalom; They Hit the Road in Peace." *The New York Times.* August 18, 2005.
Compensation	"On Tuesday, *Parliament debated a second reading of a bill to compensate settlers who would leave Gaza,* with a vote expected Wednesday." Steven Erlanger and Greg Myre. "In New Gesture to Palestinians, Sharon Will Discuss Withdrawal." *The New York Times.* February 16, 2005.
	"In Ganim, most *already have received at least some financial compensation and found new homes. Many families will receive cumulative payouts in the range of $200,000 to $300,000.*" Greg Myre. "Some West Bank Settlers Leave Quietly, if Tearfully." *The New York Times.* July 8, 2005.

UK print news media

Frame of Representation	Examples from Article Sample
Evacuation NOT an End to Occupation	"The Palestinian fear is that the Gaza pullout is a convenient ruse for the Israelis to consolidate their grip on the West Bank. *Despite withdrawal from four of its more remote settlements, Israel's Central Bureau of Statistics has reported that 3,981 new 'housing units' are under construction there.*" Uzi Mahnaimi and Aviram Zino. Psychologists on Hand for Army's Nightmare Eviction of Settlers. *The Sunday Times.* August 14, 2005.
	"*Israel will continue to build settlements in the West Bank and will not repeat the Gaza Strip withdrawal elsewhere,* the country's prime minister said today." Inigo Gilmore. "No Fresh West Bank Pullout, says Sharon." *The Evening Standard.* August 22, 2005.
Palestinian Suffering	"Naim Mahmoud Abu Hanoun is a proud man, *but his spirit has been all but broken by the past four years of living on the flour, rice and beans* provided by the United Nations and the Saudi government." Donald Macintyre. "The Gaza Pullout: Caught in a Trap." *The Independent.*August 11, 2005.
	"Experts also say that much of the territory [in Gaza] will have to be used for agriculture and nature reserves around the sand dunes to preserve *the aquifer, which is in severe need of repair because of unrestricted use of it by the settlements with resulting seepage of salt water and even sewage into Palestinian supplies.*" Donald Macintyre. "Abbas Signs Historic Agreement for Control of Gaza Settlement Areas." *The Independent.* August 21, 2005.
Palestinians as Violent	"*For the third day running, militant members of Hamas fired salvoes of mortars and home-made rockets mostly at Jewish settlements inside Gaza,* undeterred by Israeli countermeasures including missile strikes from an attack helicopter." Tim Butcher. "Gaza Strip Handover Plans under Threat." *The Daily Telegraph.* May 20, 2005.
	"But weak as the Palestinians were, they did not go away, *and the unceasing assaults on the settlements that helped force Mr Sharon into pulling out of Gaza* also ensured that Kfar Darom was forced to live up to its motto: 'Perseverance above all.'" Chris McGreal. "Gaza's Settlers Cannot Believe Sacrifices are in Vain." *The Guardian.* August 10, 2005.
Palestinians as Corrupt/ Backward	"[Violence on the part of Hamas] *fits into a pattern of growing reluctance by Hamas to obey Mr Abbas' leadership. Less than a fortnight ago, his ruling Fatah faction was badly bruised in Palestinan municipal elections* by Hamas which made important gains." Tim Butcher. "Gaza Strip Handover Plans under Threat." *The Daily Telegraph.* May 20, 2005.
	"Pillars of fire lit up the night sky even before the last Israeli tanks rolled out before dawn yesterday, *as thousands of Palestinians swarmed into the forsaken settlements and youths set fire to synagogues and other symbols of the hated occupation.*" Stephen Farrell and Ian MacKinnon. "Gaza Looters Settle Old Scores." *The Times.* September 13, 2005.

Frame of Representation	*Examples from Article Sample*
Palestinian Celebration	"*In the southern town of Rafah, hundreds of Palestinians wearing T-shirts with the Palestinian flag bearing the slogan 'Today Gaza, tomorrow the West Bank and Jerusalem'*, joined a demonstration organised by the dominant Fatah organisation which is seeking to wrest credit for Israel's withdrawal from Hamas, which claims it has 'driven' Israel out." Donald Macintyre. "Last of the Settlers Leave without a Fight." *The Independent.* August 20, 2005.
	"The Palestinian Authority said that it would open the door *to jubilant Gaza residents* today by organising a celebration in Neve Dekalim." Stephen Farrell. "Israeli Flag Lowered as Settlements in Gaza are Abandoned." *The Times.* September 12, 2005.
Evacuation Ends Occupation	"Mr Sharon's adviser, Brigadier General Eyval Giladi said yesterday that the withdrawal, *which would remove almost 9,000 Israelis from land conquered in 1967*, would improve the lives of Israelis and Palestinians by removing points of confrontation and may lead to a resumption of peace negotiations with the Palestinians." Conal Urquhart. "Violence Erupts at Gaza Eviction." *The Guardian.* June 30, 2005.
	"Israel completed its pullout from the Gaza Strip today, *ending 38 years of occupation*." Inigo Gilmore. "Synagogues on Fire as Last Israeli Troops Leave Gaza." *The Evening Standard.* September 12, 2005.
Israeli Suffering	"*In the film, Tehila hauls herself on to her prosthetic limbs and looks into the camera: 'I don't understand what kind of soldier will be willing to drag me from my home and ruin my life for the second time.'*" Chris McGreal. "Gaza's Settlers Cannot Believe Sacrifices are in Vain." *The Guardian.* August 10, 2005.
	"Throughout yesterday a steady stream of heavily-laden cars and lorries arrived, bringing settler families, *many in tears*, to their new life in Nitzan New Town." Tim Butcher. "After the Evictions, a Life in the World's Most Lavish Refugee Camp." *The Daily Telegraph.* August 17, 2005.
Israel as Lawful, Moral	"*Israel's response to the current crisis has been relatively mild.*" Tim Butcher. "Gaza Strip Handover Plans under Threat." *The Daily Telegraph.* May 20, 2005.
	"The difficulties that the government has faced in reinforcing its authority have been compounded by *the security forces' determination to avoid violent confrontation with the settlers if possible*." Donald Macintyre. "Israeli MPs Take the Sting out of Settlers' Protests by Rejecting Delay to Evacuation." *The Independent.* July 21, 2005.

Frame of Representation	*Examples from Article Sample*
Israeli/Jewish Religiosity	"Mr Lopes planted 10 fruit trees, pomegranate, peach and lemon, as a symbol of *his faith in the 'miracle'* he knows is the only chance of stopping Ariel Sharon's plan to take the 8,500 settlers out of Gaza. *'The planting shows our roots in the land,' he explains. 'The Torah says that you cannot eat a tree's fruit for its first three years. This act says we will be here to eat the fruit in the fourth year.'"* Donald Macintyre. "Jewish Settlers Praying for a Miracle to Stop Gaza Pull-Out." *The Independent.* August 7, 2005.
	"Today in Gush Katif the religious Jews will fast, refrain from laughter and sex and avoid banal conversations to mark Tisha B'Av, the day of mourning for the fall of the Jewish temples in 586BC and AD70 and the expulsion of the Jews from Spain in 1492." Conal Urquhart and Inigo Gilmore. "After all the Threats, It's a Muted Goodbye to Gaza." *The Observer.* August 14, 2005.
Israel as Fractious	*"Militant Jewish settlers have disrupted traffic on Israel's main highway and clashed with troops* in Gaza to protest against the government's pull-out plan." "Gaza Settler Chaos Strikes Israel." BBC. June 29, 2005.
	"Soldiers today clashed with hundreds of hardline Jewish settlers who set up barricades in protest over Israel's withdrawal from the Gaza Strip." Inigo Gilmore. "Troops Clash with Hardline Settlers." *The Evening Standard.* August 18, 2005.
	"One extreme segment of the settler youth has been called the 'hilltop youth' by the Israeli press. This group is seen as even *more extreme than the mainstream settler youth and is regularly* involved in the persecution of Palestinian villagers living near West Bank settlements." Conal Urquhardt. "Youthful Infiltrators Bent on Defying Authority." *The Guardian.* August 18, 2005.
Israelis as Violent	"a minority of *hardline settlers set fire to their homes* rather than leave them to Palestinians while others painted slogans on their walls denouncing prime minister Ariel Sharon as a traitor." Inigo Gilmore. "Time's Up, Soldiers Tell Gaza Settlers." *The Evening Standard.* August 17, 2005.
	"Meanwhile, *eight masked Jewish extremists slashed the tyres of an army tractor and set it on fire* near the settlement of Kedumim. They fled after a soldier got out and pointed his gun at them." Inigo Gilmore. "No Fresh West Bank Pullout, says Sharon." *The Evening Standard.* August 22, 2005.
Compensation	"Even among settlers he is a hardliner in the sense that he has refused on principle to join the 50 per cent of settler families who have entered negotiations with the state on rehousing and *compensation of up to $300,000 (£170,000)*" Donald Macintyre. "Jewish Settlers Praying for a Miracle to Stop Gaza Pull-Out." *The Independent.* August 7, 2005.
	"The settlers are receiving a compensation package worth an average of $450,000 (£251,000) to provide help if they build their own homes, and even more if they move to the development areas of the Negev desert and the Galilee." Donald Macintyre. "Last of the Settlers Leave without a Fight." *The Independent.* August 20, 2005.

Appendix B

Print news media articles analyzed in *evacuating Gaza from two sides of the Atlantic*

US print news media

Anderson, J. W. (2005, February 17). Israel Approves Funds for Settler Pullout; Victory for Sharon Follows Debates, Protests, Threats. *The Washington Post*, p. A21.

Bennet, J. (2005a, August 18). For Palestinians, Joy and Some Hints of Sympathy. *The New York Times.*

Bennet, J. (2005b, August 21). Abbas Talks Of Future Of Enclaves. *The New York Times*, p. 13.

Bennet, J. (2005c, August 21). Hamas Pushing For Lead Role in a New Gaza. *The New York Times*, p. 1.

Berger, J. and Robin Shulman. (2005, August 14). American Jews Sharing Pain of Gaza Pullout. *The New York Times*, p. 29.

Brinkley, J. and Steven R. Weisman. (2005, August 18). Rice Urges Israel and Palestinians to Sustain Momentum. *The New York Times*, p. 8.

Bumiller, E. (2005, May 27). Bush Praises Palestinian; Tells Israel It Has Duties. *The New York Times,* p. 6

Canfield, C. (2005, August 16). Israelis, Arabs Reunite at Peace Camp During Gaza Withdrawal. *The Associated Press.*

Chabin, M. (2005, August 24). Some Displaced Settlers Refusing Offer of Housing. *USA Today*, p. 8A.

Dan, U. (2005a, February 23). Israel Will Take Guns Off Settlers. *The New York Post*, p. 16.

Dan, U. (2005b, June 27). Troops and Settlers in Gaza Clash. *The New York Post*, p. 8.

Dan, U. (2005c, June 29). Israel Jails 'Mutineer' – Refuse to Fight Settlers. *The New York Post*, p. 27.

Dan, U. (2005d, August 10). Hamas Turns Dead Ear to Abbas on Gaza. *The New York Post*, p. 29.

Dan, U. (2005e, August 12). It's a 'Go' in Gaza; Israel Seals Off Strip in Prep for Pullout as Foes Eye March. *The New York Post*, p. 22.

Dan, U. (2005f, August 18). Settlers' Shalom; They Hit the Road in Peace. *The New York Post*, p. 4.

Dan, U. (2005g, August 19). The Temple of Gloom – Troops Take Settlers from Synagogues. *The New York Post*, p. 4.

Erlanger, S. (2005a, May 1). High Risks in a Summer of Statecraft. *The New York Times.*

Erlanger, S. (2005b, May 12). Israel Defense Chief Opposes Razing Settler Homes After Evacuation. *The New York Times*, p. 9.

Erlanger, S. (2005d, June 14). Will Israeli Settlements Serve Them, Gazans Ask. *The New York Times*.

Erlanger, S. (2005e, August 22). Gaza Pullout: New Scars for Arabs and Israelis. *The New York Times*.

Erlanger, S. (2005f, August 22). With One Gaza Settlement Left, Sharon Assails Resisters. *The New York Times*, p. 7.

Erlanger, S. (2005g, August 23). Last Settlers Leave Gaza Quietly, Ending a 40-Year Era. *The New York Times*, p. 8.

Erlanger, S. and Tagreed El-Khodary. (2005, May 19). Israel Vows Tough Stance, With Restraint, in Gaza. *The New York Times*, p. 8.

Erlanger, S. and Dina Kraft. (2005a, August 10). Abbas Says Calm in Gaza Pullout Would Aid Statehood *The New York Times*, p. 1.

Erlanger, S. and Dina Kraft. (2005b, August 18). Tearfully but Forcefully, Israel Removes Gaza Settlers. *The New York Times*, p. 1

Erlanger, S. and Greg Myre. (2005a, February 16). In New Gesture to Palestinians, Sharon Will Discuss Withdrawal. *The New York Times*, p. 8.

Erlanger, S. and Greg Myre. (2005b, July 22). Israel May Speed Gaza Pullout to Head Off More Protests. *The New York Times*, p. 6.

Erlanger, S. and Greg Myre. (2005c, August 8). Israeli Minister Quits as Pullout from Gaza Nears. *The New York Times*, p. 1.

Erlanger, S. and Greg Myre. (2005d, August 19). Soldiers Evict Gaza Resisters in 2 Synagogues. *The New York Times*.

Erlanger, S. and Michael Slackman. (2005, September 13). Gazans Revel as They Sift Through Ex-Settlements. *The New York Times*.

Frankel, R. and Corky Siemaszko. (2005, August 23). Settlers All Gone from Gaza. *The Daily News*.

Gaza Pullout Begins with Extremists Poised for Trouble. (2005, August 15). *USA Today*, p. 12A.

Greenberg, J. (2005a, March 9). Israel to Hand Over 2 West Bank Cities to Palestinians. *The Chicago Tribune*.

Greenberg, J. (2005b, March 30). Israeli Parliament Passes Budget, Removing Hurdle to Gaza Pullout. *The Chicago Tribune*.

Greenberg, J. (2005c, April 22). As Gaza Strip Withdrawal Looms, Jewish Settlers Fall Back on Faith. *The Chicago Tribune*.

Greenberg, J. (2005d, August 14). Gaza Occupation Coming to a Close. *The Chicago Tribune*.

Greenberg, J. (2005e, August 15). Israel Seals Gaza. *The Chicago Tribune*.

Gutman, M. (2005a, August 5). Palestinian Troops Face Biggest Test during Pullout. *USA Today*, p. 7A

Gutman, M. (2005b, August 12). One Mom Packs, Another Resists; Both Try to be Strong for the Kids. *USA Today*, p. 4A.

Gutman, M. (2005c, August 16). 'Army of Activists' Sets Up Camp in Support. *USA Today*, p. 7A.

Harboush, M. and Corky Siemaszko. (2005, August 19). Hand-to-Hand Fight in Gaza. Israelis Use Force, Empty Settlements. *New York Daily News*.

Harboush, M., Corky Siemaszko, and Michele Green. (2005, August 17). Tears & Jeers in Gaza. Israeli Troops Begin Moves to Evict Settlers. *The Daily News*, p. 7.

Israeli Forces Clear Last of Settlements. (2005, August 28). *The Washington Post*, A03.

Kessler, G. (2005, June 19). Cooperation on Gaza Is Urgent, Rice Says; Palestinians Pressed to Improve Security. *The Washington Post*, p. A24.

Kraft, D. (2005, August 16). For a Basketball League in Gaza, It's the Finals. *The New York Times*, p. 7.

Lavie, M. (2005, June 15). Israeli, Palestinian Officials Begin Talks on Gaza Pullout. *The Associated Press.*

Mitnick, J. (2005a, June 13). Orange Revolt? Settlers See Spectrum of Support. *The Christian Science Monitor*, p. 07.

Mitnick, J. (2005b, June 18). Exiting Gaza, Israel Fights on Two Fronts. *The Christian Science Monitor*, p. 01.

Mitnick, J. (2005c, July 21). History Foreshadows Gaza Pullout. *The Christian Science Monitor*, p. 06.

Mitnick, J. (2005d, August 16). Sharon Acknowledges 'Pain and Tears' of Settlers; Gaza Residents Keep Police from Serving Eviction Notices. *The Washington Times.*

Mitnick, J. (2005e, August 17). Israel Begins Evacuation of Gaza; Army Takes out Settlers. *The Washington Times*, p. A01.

Mitnick, J. (2005f, August 18). Settlers in Gaza Resist Removal; Sharon Hits Slaying of 4 Palestinians in West Bank. *The Washington Times*, p. A01.

Mitnick, J. (2005g, August 19). Soldiers Subdue Gaza Holdouts; Overcome Protests, Clear 17 Outposts. *The Washington Times*, p. A01.

Mitnick, J. (2005h, August 22). West Bank Settlers Clash with Soldiers: Outsiders Aid Ouster Resistance. *The Washington Times*, p. A01.

Myre, G. (2005a, February 17). Israeli Legislators Approve $870 Million for Settlers Who Quit Gaza. *The New York Times*, p. 5.

Myre, G. (2005b, April 8). Defense Chief In Israel Seeks To Preserve Settler Homes. *The New York Times*, p. 16.

Myre, G. (2005c, April 19). Sharon May Delay Gaza Pullout to Mid-August. *The New York Times,* p. 10.

Myre, G. (2005d, July 8). Some West Bank Settlers Leave Quietly, if Tearfully. *The New York Times.*

Myre, G. (2005e, July 12). Israel Seeks $2 Billion in U.S. Aid for Gaza Withdrawal. *The New York Times,* p. 3.

Myre, G. (2005f, August 18). For a Family Unmoved by Talk, a Move by Force. *The New York Times.*

Myre, G. (2005g, August 20). Israeli Troops and Police Clear All but 5 Gaza Settlements. *The New York Times*, p. 3.

Myre, G. (2005h, August 23). Many Evicted Gaza Settlers Go To West Bank, at Least at First. *The New York Times*, p. 8.

Myre, G. and Steven Erlanger. (2005a, August 15). Thousands of Settlers Remain in Gaza, Defying Israeli Orders; Military Moves In. *The New York Times*, p. 9.

Myre, G. and Steven Erlanger. (2005b, September 12) Israel Lowers its Flag in the Gaza Strip. *The New York Times*, p. 10.

Myre, G. and Dina Kraft. (2005, July 1). Israeli Troops Drag Pro-Settler Protesters from Stronghold. *The New York Times*, p. 8.

Myre, G, Taghreed el-Khodary, and Dina Kraft. (2005, July 18). Heavy Israeli Armor Presses Gaza Border. *The New York Times*, p. 1.

Myre, G., Steven Erlanger, and Dina Kraft. (2005a, August 15). Thousands of Settlers Remain in Gaza, Defying Israeli Orders; Military Moves In. *The New York Times*, p. 9.

Myre, G., Steven Erlanger, and Dina Kraft. (2005b, September 12). Israel Lowers Its Flag in the Gaza Strip. *The New York Times.*

Newman, A. (2005, June 5). Group to Visit Gaza Strip to Oppose Israeli Pullout. *The New York Times*, p. 42.

Newman, A. (2005, August 18). How Old Friends of Israel gave $14 Million to Help the Palestinians. *The New York Times.*

Palestinian Revelers Tear up Gaza Settlements. (2005, September 12). *The Daily News*, p. 36.

Patience, M. (2005, August 16). Palestinians Celebrate Pullout as 'Turning Point' in Conflict. *USA Today*, p. 7A.

Patience, M. (2005, September 22). What's in a Name? History, Emotion for Palestinians. *USA Today*, p. 8A.

Perspectives on Gaza. (2005, August 18). *The Dallas Morning News*, p. 17A.

Plushnick-Masti, R. (2005, July 17). Parents and Kids Pour into a West Bank Settlement, Determined to Block an Israeli Pullback. *The Associated Press.*

Rabinowitz, G. (2005, August 16). Settlers Recall Pioneering Days as they Get Ready for Evacuation. *The Associated Press.*

Slavin, B. (2005, June 20). Settlers' Homes to be Razed after Gaza Withdrawal. *USA Today*, 8A.

Stone, A. (2005, August 17). Israeli Soldiers Brace for Day of Forced Removals. *USA Today*, p. 5A.

Stone, A. (2005, August 18). Gaza Settlers Reluctantly Let Go. *USA Today*, p. 10A.

The Gaza Gamble. (2005, August 19). *The New York Post*, p. 30.

Vick, K. and Samuel Sockol. (2005, August 24). Israeli Forces Complete Settlement Evacuation; Holdouts in West Bank Overwhelmed. *The Washington Post*, p. A12.

Wadhams, N. (2005, September 20). After Gaza Withdrawal, Israel Seeks Better Relations with Arab States. *The Associated Press.*

Weisman, S. and Greg Myre. (2005, July 20). Israelis and Palestinians Agree on Demolishing Houses in Gaza. *The New York Times.*

Wilson, S. (2005a, July 1). Israeli Police Push Settlers from Hotel; 150 People Hoping to Prevent August Pullout Evacuated From Gaza Strip. *The Washington Post*, A21.

Wilson, S. (2005b, August 16). Eviction Notices Are Served in Gaza; As Pullout Begins, Israeli Army Blocked From Entering Some Settlements. *The Washington Post*, p. A01.

Wilson, S. (2005c, August 17). Troops Enter Settlements In Gaza Strip; Israeli Army Urges Evacuation As Hour Nears for Use of Force. *The Washington Post*, p. A01

Wilson, S. (2005d, August 18). Soldiers Use Persuasion, Force In Evacuation of Gaza Settlers Duty Exacts Emotional Toll on Troops. *The Washington Post*, p. A01.

Wilson, S. (2005e, August 20). Gaza Evacuations Suspended for Sabbath; Operation to End Early Next Week. *The Washington Post*, p. A11.

Wilson, S. (2005f, August 22). Israeli Troops in Gaza Prepare To Clear Remaining Settlements. *The Washington Post*, p. A11.

Wilson, S. (2005g, August 23). After 38 Years, Gaza Settlers Gone; Last Families Leave Peacefully; Troops Begin West Bank Evacuations. *The Washington Post*, p. A01.

UK print news media

Al-Mughrabi, N. (2005, July 17). Abbas in TV Peace Plea as Violence Puts Israel's Gaza Withdrawal at Risk. *The Observer.*

Bishop, P. (2005b, August 27). Hamas Cashes in on its Gaza Victory. *The Daily Telegraph.*

Bishop, P. and Tim Butcher. (2005, August 19). Snatch Squads End Resistance in Gaza. *The Daily Telegraph*, p. 014.

Butcher, T. (2005a, May 20). Gaza Strip Handover Plans under Threat. *The Daily Telegraph.*

Butcher, T. (2005b, July 1). Settlers on Rampage as 1,000 Troops Begin Gaza Evacuation. *The Daily Telegraph*, p. 014.

Butcher, T. (2005c, August 13). Israelis Leave Gaza in Exchange for Peace. *The Daily Telegraph.*

Butcher, T. (2005d, August 15). Gaza's Foes Unite to Ensure Peaceful Pull-out 50,000. *The Daily Telegraph*, p. 011.

Butcher, T. (2005e, August 16). Palestinians are too Divided Even to Agree on How to Celebrate. *The Daily Telegraph*, p. 004.

Butcher, T. (2005f, August 17). After the Evictions, a Life in the World's Most Lavish Refugee Camp. *The Daily Telegraph*, p. 011.

Butcher, T. (2005g, August 18). Tears, Fury and a Death Camp Hymn in Israel's Historic Retreat from Gaza. *The Daily Telegraph*, p. 002.

Coughlin, C. (2005a, August 18). A Bitter Finale in Gaza. *The Daily Mail*, p. 10.

de Quetteville, H. (2005, August 21). Forgotten Family is Left Behind in Exodus from Gaza. As the Army Declares the Settlements Cleared, the Rozens Remain Strained in No-Man's Land. *The Sunday Telegraph*, p. 24.

de Quetteville, H. and Patrick Bishop. (2005, August 24). Settlement Protesters Mount Last Stand against Police. *The Daily Telegraph*, p. 10.

Derfner, L. (2005, August 14). Sharon's Day of Destiny: Will the Gamble Work? *The London Times.*

Edwards, R. (2005, August 16). Armed Soldiers Prepare to Remove Gaza Rebels. *The Evening Standard*, p. 16.

Ellis, M. (2005a, August 17). Fury in Gaza as First Settlements are Cleared. *The Mirror*, p. 2.

Ellis, M. (2005b, August 23). Gaza Stripped: Last Settlers Weep as Troops Bus Them Out. *The Mirror*, p. 14.

Farrell, S. (2005a, August 5). Lost Land of Hope Foretells Gaza Settlers' Broken Dream. *The Times*, p. 41.

Farrell, S. (2005b, August 20). Last Settlers Are Ready to Leave Gaza Ghost Towns. *The Times*, p. 44.

Farrell, S. (2005c, September 9). Abandoned Synagogues Test Resolve over Gaza. *The Times*, p. 54.

Farrell, S. (2005e, September 28). Five Years on, Hope Starts to Grow. *The Times*, p. 41.

Farrell, S. and Donald Macintyre. (2005, August 23). Gaza Settlers Build Right Up to the End. *The Times*, p. 28.

Farrell, S. and Ian MacKinnon. (2005a, July 14). Militants Locked Out as End Nears for Jewish Settlements. *The Times,* p. 38.

Farrell, S. and Ian MacKinnon. (2005b, August 13). Time Runs Out as Samson Gets Ready to Bring the House Down. *The Times,* p. 44.

Farrell, S. and Ian MacKinnon. (2005c, September 12) Israeli Flag Lowered as Settlements in Gaza Are Abandoned. *The Times*, p. 38.

Farrell, S. and Ian MacKinnon. (2005e, September 13). Gaza Looters Settle Old Scores. *The Times*, p. 29.

Gaza Settler Chaos Strikes Israel. (2005, June 29). BBC News. Retrieved from: http://news.bbc.co.uk/1/ hi/world/middle_east/4633265.stm

Gaza: Start of Withdrawal. (2005, August 15). *The Guardian*, p. 19.

Ghazali, S. (2005, August 20). Gaza's Upstairs, Downstairs World of the Occupation Worldwide: Palestinian Family has Israeli Troops on Top Floors. *The Daily Telegraph*, p. 15.

Ghazali, S. and Tim Butcher. (2005, September 12). Night Withdrawal from Gaza Ends 38 Year Occupation. *The Daily Telegraph*, p. 13.

Gilmore, I. (2005a, April 21). Israelis Start Army Move from Gaza Strip. *The Daily Telegraph*, p. 016.

Gilmore, I. (2005c, August 16). 500 Protesters Held as Gaza Tensions Mount. *The Evening Standard*, p. 8.

Gilmore, I. (2005d, August 17). Time's Up, Soldiers Tell Gaza Settlers, *The Evening Standard*, p. 2.

Gilmore, I. (2005e, August 18). Troops and Police Storm Synagogue. *The Evening Standard*, p. 10.

Gilmore, I. (2005f, August 18). Troops Clash with Hardline Settlers. *The Evening Standard*, p. 10.

Gilmore, I. (2005g, August 22). No Fresh West Bank Pullout, Says Sharon. *The Evening Standard*.

Gilmore, I. (2005h, September 12). Synagogues on Fire as Last Israeli Troops Leave Gaza. *The Evening Standard*, p. 14.

Gilmore, I. and Joe Murphy. (2005, August 15). Gaza on the Brink. *The Evening Standard*, p. 7.

Gozani, O. (2005, August 1). Israel vows to crush Palestinian attacks on Gaza pullout. *The Daily Telegraph*, p. 012.

Israel's Gaza Withdrawal Must be Only a First Step. (2005, August 15). *The Independent*.

Leapman, B. (2005, August 17). One Settler's Desperate Stand over Gaza Pullout. *The Evening Standard*, p. 2.

Macintyre, D. (2005a, July 21). Israeli MPs Take the Sting out of Settlers' Protests by Rejecting Delay to Evacuation. *The Independent*.

Macintyre, D. (2005b, August 7). Jewish Settlers Praying for a Miracle to Stop Gaza Pull-out. *The Independent*.

Macintyre, D. (2005c, August 11) The Gaza Pullout: Caught in a Trap. *The Independent*.

Macintyre, D. (2005d, August 16). Withdrawal from Gaza: Settlers Greet Soldiers with Angry Chants of 'Gestapo'. *The Independent*.

Macintyre, D. (2005e, August 17). Dozens are Arrested in Gaza Protests as the Israeli Army Moves into Settlements. *The Independent*, p. 22.

Macintyre, D. (2005f, August 17). Gaza Protesters Arrested as Israeli Army Moves in to Dismantle Settlements. *The Independent*, p. 22.

Macintyre, D. (2005g, August 17). We're Not Packing. The Army Must Take us Out. *The Independent*, p. 23.

Macintyre, D. (2005h, August 18). Exodus from Gaza: It is Impossible to Watch This without Tears in my Eyes and my Heart. *The Independent*, p. 1.

Macintyre, D. (2005i, August 19). Soldiers Storm the Synagogues to Remove Gaza's Hardline Settlers. *The Independent*, p. 24.

Macintyre, D. (2005j, August 20). Last of the Settlers Leave without a Fight. *The Independent*, p. 24.

Macintyre, D. (2005k, August 21). Abbas Signs Historic Agreement for Control of Gaza Settlement Areas. *The Independent*, p. 15.

Macintyre, D. (2005l, August 23). Sharon Pledges to Expand West Bank Settlements as Last Israelis Leave Gaza. *The Independent*, p. 19.

Macintyre, D. (2005m, August 24). Israeli Troops Smash Their Way into Last Two Settlements. *The Independent*, p. 22.

Macintyre, D. (2005n, September 12). Handover of Gaza Complete but Synagogues are Left Standing. *The Independent*, p. 22.

MacKinnon, I. (2005a, July 20). Tens of Thousands Join Long March to Save the Settlements. *The Times*, p. 29.

MacKinnon, I. (2005b, July 21). Jewish Settlers Show Signs of Defeat. *The Times*, p. 43.

MacKinnon, I. (2005c, August 18). Gaza Settlers' Resistance Wanes as Pullout Begins. *The Times*, p. 2.

MacKinnon, I. (2005d, August 22). Violence Feared as Radicals Rally at Fort for Last Stand. *The Times*, p. 25.

MacKinnon, I. (2005e, August 24). Kitchen Missiles Mark End of Final Settler Strongholds. *The Times*, p. 37.

MacKinnon, I. and Martin Patience. (2005c, August 15). Hundreds of Protesters Ready to Defy Soldiers over Gaza Eviction. *The Times*, p. 4.

Mahnaimi, U. and Aviram Zino. (2005, August 14). Psychologists on Hand for Army's Nightmare Eviction of Settlers. *The Sunday Times*, p. 21.

MacKinnon, I. and Stephen Farrell. (2005, August 17). Clashes as First Gaza Settlers are Removed. *The London Times*, p. 2.

Many Gaza Settlers Agree to Move. (2005, May 26). BBC News. Retrieved from: http://news.bbc.co.uk/1/ hi/world/middle_east/4583705.stm.

McGreal, C. (2005a, August 3). Israelis Gather to Fight Removal of Gaza Settlers. *The Guardian*, p. 2.

McGreal, C. (2005b, August 10). Gaza's Settlers Cannot Believe Sacrifices Are in Vain. *The Guardian*.

McGreal, C. (2005c, August 15). Gaza Settlers Defy Sharon Evacuation Deadline. *The Guardian*.

McGreal, C. (2005d, August 16). Gaza Withdrawal: The Deadline for Evacuation is Tomorrow, but Many Israelis Still Cling on to the Disputed Land. *The Guardian*, p. 10.

McGreal, C. (2005e, August 17). Emotions Run High as Army Enforces Pullout of Gaza Settlers: Young Activists Plan Sabotage to Delay Evacuation. *The Guardian*, p. 2.

McGreal, C. (2005f, August 18). Defiance, Anger and Tears … Then the Inevitable Farewell to Gaza. *The Guardian*, p. 10.

McGreal, C. (2005g, August 18). Sharon Breaks Covenant with Settlers. *The Guardian*.

McGreal, C. (2005h August 19). Israeli Troops Storm Synagogues: Sharon Says Gaza Protests being Cleared Quickly and Final Pullout Would be Early. *The Guardian*, p. 2.

McGreal, C. (2005i, August 20). Gaza Settlers Cleared Ahead of Schedule. *The Guardian*, p. 2.

McGreal, C. (2005j, August 20). Speed of Gaza Pullout Boosts Sharon: As Evicted Settlers Lick Their Wounds, Opponents of the Withdrawal Policy have been Left Reeling. *The Guardian*, p. 16.

McGreal, C. (2005k, August 22). Sharon Says Settler Leaders Playing Politics. *The Guardian*, p. 13.

McGreal, C. (2005l, September 10). Gaza's Hated Landmarks Go. *The Guardian*.

McGreal, C. (2005m, September 12). Hamas Celebrates Victory of the Bomb as Power of Negotiation Falters. *The Guardian*, p. 17.

McGreal, C. (2005n, September 12). Israel Hands Settlements to Palestinians. *The Guardian.*

McGreal, C. (2005o, September 13). Glittering Sea is the Most Precious Treasure for Many in Regained Land: Armed Palestinians Raise Flags over Ruined Towns. *The Guardian,* p. 15.

Milland, G. (2005a, August 16). Gaza Withdrawal Now Gives Jews and Arabs a Real Chance of Peace. *The Express,* p. 12.

Milland, G. (2005b, August 18). The Gaza Struggle: Bloodshed as Soldiers Drag Jewish Settlers from their Homes. *The Express,* p. 9.

Milland, G. (2005c, August 20). First Gaza Homes are Torn Down. *The Express,* p. 10.

Milland, G. (2005d, August 23). Gaza's Tearful Exodus; Last Settlers Pull Out But Fears Grow in West Bank. *The Express,* p. 19.

Patience, M. (2005, August 18). Rooftop Refugees Watch the Eviction. *The Times,* p. 31.

Reynolds, J. (2005, June 4). Digging in For the Long Fight. BBC News. Retrieved from: http://news.bbc.co.uk/ 1/hi/programmes/from_our_own_correspondent/4607021.stm

Settlers Protest at Gaza Pullout. (2005, August 15). BBC News. Retrieved from: http://news.bbc.co.uk/1/hi/ world/middle_east/4150028.stm?tr=y&auid=1629982

Silver, E. (2005b, August 22). Focus Shifts to West Bank as Gaza Empties. *The Independent,* p. 20.

Silver, E. and Donald Macintyre (2005, August 15). Israeli Army Masses as First Deadline for Gaza Pull-out Passes, *The Independent.*

Urquhart, C. (2005a, June 5). Settlers Turn Hotel into Gaza Fortress. *The Observer.*

Urquhart, C. (2005b, June 30). Violence Erupts at Gaza Eviction. *The Guardian.*

Urquhart, C. (2005c, August 16). 'We Forced Them to Leave but They Can Still Seal us Off and Strangle us Economically'. *The Guardian.*

Urquhart, C. (2005d, August 18). Evacuated Families Bed Down in Cheap Hotels – Or Five-Star Luxury. *The Guardia*n, p. 19.

Urquhart, C. (2005e, August 18). Youthful Infiltrators Bent on Defying Authority. *The Guardian.*

Urquhart, C. (2005f, September 8). Killing of Arafat's Cousin Triggers Turmoil. *The Guardian,* p. 15.

Urquhart, C. and Inigo Gilmore. (2005a, August 14). After all the Threats, It's a Muted Goodbye to Gaza. *The Observer.*

Urquhart, C. and Inigo Gilmore. (2005b, August 21). Evicted Settlers Plan West Bank Move to Defy Sharon. *The Observer,* p. 16

Urquhart, C. and Chris McGreal. (2005, August 24). Pullout of Israeli Settlers Complete. *The Guardian,* p. 12.

White, S. (2005a, February 21). Israel to Pull Out. *The Mirror,* p. 12.

White, S. (2005b, August 15). Gaza Tension Mounts. *The Mirror,* p. 2.

Williams, D. (2005, August 18). Exodus from Gaza: The Israeli View: "It's Like we Live in Different Worlds, Tel Aviv versus Gush Katif." *The Independent,* p. 3.

Appendix C

The palestinian legislative council elections, 2006, in-text frames of representation

US print news media

Frame of Representation	Examples from Article Sample
Hamas as Terrorists	"The group *best known for its military wing's suicide bombings and other attacks against Israelis* has emerged as the strongest challenger to the dominant Fatah movement once run by Yasser Arafat." Ken Ellingwood. "Hamas Shows a New Face in Campaign." *The Los Angeles Times.* January 24, 2006.
	"Nor is any Hamas leader on record as expressing a willingness to disarm or to stop attacks on Israel and Israelis, or to make a distinction between Israeli soldiers and civilians, especially settlers living on occupied land, however defined." Steven Erlanger. "Hamas Leader Sees No Change Toward Israelis." *The New York Times.* January 29, 2006.
	"Hamas, which advocates the destruction of Israel, remains on U.S. and EU lists of terrorist organizations." John Daniszewski and Laura King. "West Takes Firm Stand on Hamas." *The Los Angeles Times.* January 31, 2006.
Hamas as Backward	"Female campaign workers from Hamas, *swathed in head-to-toe black veils*, knocked on doors offering to escort women to polling places." Ken Ellingwood and Laura King. "Hamas Makes Major Inroad in Balloting." *The Los Angeles Times.* January 26, 2006.
	"Here, an array of behavior that strict Islamists deem deeply impious is an elementary part of ordinary life – moviegoing, mingling of the sexes, unveiled women with fashionable coiffures, bars and restaurants that serve up alcohol along with jazz and French-accented bistro fare." Laura King. "Palestinians Ponder Life Under Hamas." *The Los Angeles Times.* February 6, 2006.
Palestinian Voice, Rational	"'Ali Jarbawi ... said it was possible the two Fatah groups would come to terms before party slates are closed to changes Jan. 1. From now until the end of this month, they have the possibility to reunify and the hard-core attempts to compromise are going to be in the next couple of weeks,' he said. *'I think there's a good possibility this will come to an agreement.'*" Ken Ellingwood. "Fatah Split Could Benefit Hamas in Palestinian Poll." *The Los Angeles Times.* December 16, 2005.
	"But Nader Said, a Palestinian pollster at Birzeit University's Development Studies Program, said many of those voters would return to Fatah once the race took on a national scope. *'People are using the local elections to punish the Palestinian Authority, but they won't abandon Fatah,'* he said in an interview this week." Ken Ellingwood. "Israel May Block Palestinian Balloting in East Jerusalem." *The Los Angeles Times.* December 22, 2005.

Frame of Representation	Examples from Article Sample
Palestinian Voice, Radical	"*'Never!'* snapped Mahmoud Zahar, a senior figure in the group, when asked Wednesday whether Hamas would recognize Israel." Laura King. "Hamas Faces a New Struggle." *The Los Angeles Times.* January 26, 2006.
	"*'We will never recognize the legitimacy of the Zionist state that was established on our land,*' Khaled Meshaal, the external head of the political and military wings of the militant Islamic group, wrote in the Palestinian newspaper, al-Hayat al-Jadida." Paul Martin. "Hamas Tells West to Take its Aid and 'Get Lost'." *The Washington Times.* February 4, 2006.
Israeli Voice, Rational	"'The Palestinian Authority still exists – there is no other Palestinian government,' former Prime Minister Shimon Peres told Israel Radio. *'We have no intention of hurting them, starving them, humiliating them.*'" Laura King and Ken Ellingwood. "Israel Assesses a New Reality; With its Enemy Hamas Elected to Govern the Palestinians, the Jewish State Treads Lightly." *The Los Angeles Times.* January 29, 2006.
	"*'The mentality of engagement is still the rule,*' says Shmuel Bar, a Middle East expert at the Herzlyia Interdisciplinary Institute just outside Tel Aviv." Joshua Mitnick. "Russia and France Reach Out to Hamas." *The Christian Science Monitor.* February 13, 2006.
Israeli Voice, Radical	"says Yossi Klein Halevi, a fellow at the Shalem Center, a Jerusalem-based research institute. 'That's because we're not talking about handing over territory to a *corrupt, anarchic, terror-supporting Fatah*, but to an Iranian proxy that's far more dangerous.'" Joshua Mitnick. "Israeli Right May Gain Ground." *The Christian Science Monitor.* January 30, 2006.
	"On Tuesday, the Likud leader, Benjamin Netanyahu, described Hamas as part of the 'worldwide jihadist movement' that seeks to *'eliminate the state of Israel, but not merely the state of Israel – it seeks to fight this mad historical battle with the West.*'" Greg Myre. "Hamas Is Formally Asked to Form a New Government." *The New York Times.* February 21, 2006.
	"*'The idea is to put the Palestinians on a diet, but not to make them die of hunger,*' Dov Weisglass, an adviser to Israeli Prime Minister Ehud Olmert, told the Israeli media." David Francis. "What Aid Cutoff to Hamas Would Mean." *The Christian Science Monitor.* February 27, 2006.
Hamas as Moderate	"Hamas, running for the first time in Palestinian Authority elections, says that *it is prepared to consider a long-term truce with Israel* within its 1967 boundaries." Steven Erlanger. "U.S. Spent $1.9 Million to Aid Fatah in Palestinian Elections." *The New York Times.* January 23, 2006.
	"*Hamas says it wants to work with Fatah and other Palestinian factions* to form a broad, inclusive government." Greg Myre. "Fatah Protesters Demand Resignation of Faction Leaders." *The New York Times.* January 29, 2006.

Frame of Representation	Examples from Article Sample
The Failure of Democracy	"A strong showing by Hamas would underscore one of the biggest risks in promoting democracy in the Middle East: *Radical Muslims can win elections*." "Ballot box gains for Hamas pose dilemmas for U.S., allies." *USA Today*. January 25, 2006.
	"'For Israelis, *this is the definitive end of the illusion of a comprehensive peace,*' said Yossi Klein Halevi, a senior fellow at the Shalem Center, a policy research organization in Jerusalem. *'There is no more credible hope of Palestinian moderation.'*" Steven Erlanger. "Victory Ends 40 Years of Political Domination by Arafat's Party." *The New York Times*. January 26, 2006.
The Proper Function of Democracy	"said Ignasi Guardans, a Spanish member of the European Parliament. *'But we cannot push for democracy and then deny the result of free and fair elections.'*" Alan Cowell. "Europeans Insist Hamas Must Disavow Terrorism." *The New York Times*. January 27, 2006.
	"*Ziad abu Amr, a prominent political scientist and onetime Fatah strategist who won a seat as an independent, has been mentioned as a potential foreign minister. Other lawmakers from smaller parties include Hanan Ashrawi, who is considered a moderate and is well known as a spokeswoman for the Palestinian cause.*" Laura King. "The Face of Hamas Rule May Not Include Its Own." *The Los Angeles Times*. February 11, 2006.
	"But *to destabilize a small, new democracy in the Middle East would send a contrary signal to democracy advocates in the more important Arab nations of Egypt, Iraq, Syria, and Saudi Arabia.*" "When Freedom's Just Another Weapon." *The Christian Science Monitor*. February 23, 2006.
Hamas in History	"*Hamas needs to be pushed onto the path taken by the Irish Republican Army (IRA),* which over time split into a military and political wing, the former slowly overwhelmed by the latter." "Ballot box gains for Hamas pose dilemmas for U.S., allies." *USA Today*. January 25, 2006.
	"*Hamas emerged in the late 1980s and was tolerated by Israel as a counterweight to Yasser Arafats Palestine Liberation Organization, then considered a greater threat to Israel.*" Barbara Slavin. "Groups Victory Hinders Mideast Peace Process." *USA Today*. January 27, 2006.
	"*Founded in 1987 in Gaza, Hamas* – the Arabic acronym for Islamic Resistance Movement – focused on two main tasks: eliminating the state of Israel and filling the social and educational needs of impoverished Palestinians." Matthew Gutman. "Hamas voters fed up with Fatah." *USA Today*. January 27, 2006.

UK print news media

Frame of Representation	Examples from Article Sample
Hamas as Terrorists	"*[Hamas] is best known for the suicide bombings it has mounted against its Israeli enemies.*" Guardian Leader. "Between Zeal and Pragmatism." *The Guardian.* January 23, 2006.
	"There was bitter disappointment in Israel, which has ruled out negotiations with *Hamas, which is committed to the destruction of the Jewish state, until it renounces violence.*" Inigo Gilmore and Martin Betham. "Gunfight at Parliament as Hamas Sweeps to Victory." *The Evening Standard.* January 26, 2006.
	"Q WHO or what are Hamas? A *HAMAS are terrorists on the scale of al-Qaeda and the IRA. Their suicide bombers have slaughtered thousands of innocent Israelis.*" Not Given. "Q and A. From bombs to Ballot Boxes." *The Sun.* January 27, 2006.
Hamas as Backward	"*The clan wars are the most visible sign of the disintegration of the Palestinian political and social order in the narrow, hemmed-in urban crush that is Gaza.* As Palestine's politicians prepare to go to the polls on 25 January, their supporting groups are also preparing for a political war." Peter Beaumont. "Palestinians at War as Blood Feud Follows Israeli Pullout." *The Guardian.* January 15, 2006.
	"It would not have drawn a second glance outside Gaza, but *this was for a party whose women candidates are often so heavily draped they can only be identified in campaign posters by their eyes.*" Chris McGreal. "Hamas Makes Gains against Fatah, but Fails to Win Power." *The Guardian.* January 26, 2006.
	"*But many women here are already fully covered.* And there is no denying the deep vein of support that Hamas tapped into in the Gaza Strip." Harry de Quetteville. "The Regretful Fatah Voters who Took Poll 'Game' Too Far in Gaza." *The Daily Telegraph.* January 27, 2006.
Palestinian Narration, Rational	"'We have to run very effective self-defence *and take responsibility economically, politically and socially through cooperation with the Arabs,* not with the Israelis,' [Mahmoud az-Zahar] said." –Chris McGreal. "Hamas Swaps Bullets for Ballots in Attempt to Sweep Away Old Guard." *The Guardian.* January 18, 2006.
	"'*We are ready to negotiate. We are partners with the Israelis,*' he told Israeli reporters in the West Bank city of Ramallah. 'They don't have the right to choose their partner. But if they are seeking a Palestinian partner, this partner exists.'" Staff and Agencies. "Palestinians Go to the Polls." *The Guardian.* 25 January 25, 2006.
Palestinian Narration, Radical	"Mr Abu Tir replied that he saw the two dead brothers as 'sons' and added: '*They did their duty. The blood of martyrs is precious to us.*'" Donald Macintyre. "Hamas Support Grows after Israelis Shoot Militant Leader." *The Independent.* January 18, 2006.
	"'It's our land,' said Dr Zahar. '*Nobody among our sons and grandsons will accept Israel as a legal state.* Historically, they occupied this land as the British occupied it. Israel is a foreign body. Not in this generation, not in the next generation, will we accept it here.'" Chris McGreal. "Hamas Swaps Bullets for Ballots in Attempt to Sweep Away Old Guard." *The Guardian.* January 18, 2006.
	"But in Tulkarem, one of several West Bank cities where protests erupted yesterday, a Fatah gunman, Ibrahim Khreisheh, told Reuters: '*Whoever will participate in a government with Hamas, we will shoot him in the head*'" Donald Macintyre. "Hamas: The hardliners Appear Ready to Share Power, but Will Their Rivals Believe It?" *The Independent.* January 29, 2006.

Frame of Representation	*Examples from Article Sample*
Israeli Voice, Rational	"'*Israel will follow the same policy as in the 1996 elections, which means it will allow people to vote at five post offices in East Jerusalem,*' Mr Mofaz said in a statement. The decision will be ratified by a cabinet meeting on Sunday." Chris McGreal. "US Pressure Forces Israel to Relent and Allow Jerusalem's Palestinians a Vote in Election." *The Guardian.* January 11, 2006.
	"Israel's former defence minister, Binyamin Ben-Eliezer, was more hopeful. '*We will be ready to talk with anyone who acknowledges our right to live in peace and safety,*' he said. 'If it will be Hamas – so be it.'" Chris McGreal and Brian Whitaker. "Israeli Politicians Rush to Condemn Hamas Win." *The Guardian.* January 29, 2006.
Israeli Voice, Radical	"An Israeli official told Reuters that Hamas's involvement was unacceptable because its constitution calls for the destruction of the state of Israel. '*It's like allowing al-Qaida to open a polling station in London,*' the official said." Conal Urquhart. "Palestinians May Delay Poll Over Voting Ban." *The Guardian.* December 22, 2005.
	"Hamas, [Benjamin Netanyahu] said, was stockpiling weapons: '*Sooner or later they will be in the hills over Tel Aviv airport and terrorism could again be a monumental threat to Israel.*'" Leonard Doyle. "Israelis Fear Hamas Terror State." *The Independent.* January 24, 2006.
	"Comparing Hamas's victory to the rise of Nazi Germany, [Benjamin Netanyahu] said the money should not be transferred and added: '*When Hitler rose to power, it was said that ruling would moderate him.*'" Donald Macintyre. "Palestinian Funding Hangs in the Balance as International Donors Urge Abbas to Stay On." *The Independent.* January 30, 2006.
Hamas as Moderates	"Hamas has *dropped its call for the destruction of Israel from its manifesto for the Palestinian parliamentary election in a fortnight,* a move that brings the group closer to the mainstream Palestinian position of building a state within the boundaries of the occupied territories." Chris McGreal. "Hamas Drops Call for Destruction of Israel from Manifesto." *The Guardian.* January 2, 2006.
	"The organisation *does seem to have tempered its extremist position before the elections. Its manifesto makes no mention of destroying Israel but refers instead to 'defeating the occupation'*" Richard Beeston. "Ballot Box Frees Islamist Genie." *The London Times.* January 14, 2006.
The Failure of Democracy	"WHEN the Bush Administration embarked on its ambitious policy to spread democracy across the Middle East, *it never imagined that the main beneficiaries of the ballot box would be the militant Islamic groups most strongly opposed to America and its ally Israel.*" Richard Beeston. "Ballot Box Frees Islamist Genie." *The London Times.* January 14, 2006.
	"Q: HOW did [Hamas] manage to pull off a sensational win? A: *PALESTINIANS admire Hamas' strength and its dedication to destroying Israel.*" Not Given. "Q and A. From bombs to Ballot Boxes." *The Sun.* January 27, 2006.

Frame of Representation	*Examples from Article Sample*
The Proper Function of Democracy	"*Hamas's participation in the Jan 25 election is a breakthrough*, as the group has previously refused to take part in parliamentary and presidential elections organised by the Palestinian Authority." Tim Butcher. "Hamas Drops Call for the End of Israel as Poll Nears." *The Daily Telegraph.* January 13, 2006.
	"With most Palestinians due to vote on Wednesday, *a poll by the Jerusalem Media and Communications Centre showed Fatah capturing 32.3 per cent of the vote, compared with Hamas on 30.2 per cent. This was well within the margin of error of 3.5 per cent, underlining how tight the race will be.*" Donald Macintyre. "Hamas set to break through in polls." *The Independent.* January 22, 2006.
	"*Monitors praised the election process*, with the EU monitoring team saying the poll was *'free and fair under severe restrictions'*, referring to Israeli measures to limit voting in East Jerusalem." Gabriel Milland. "Terror Group's Shock Poll Win." *The Express.* January 27, 2006.
Hamas in History	"Moderate origins of the fanatics: *Founded in 1988, Hamas (zeal in Arabic), is the shorthand version of the group's official title, The Islamic Resistance Movement. Originally moderate, it supported charitable projects and eschewed armed struggle. Became radical in 1990s under leadership of wheelchair-bound Sheikh Ahmed Yassin. Its founding charter warns that Islam will "eliminate" Israel. Israeli warplanes killed Sheikh Yassin as he left a mosque in Gaza in March 2004. His successor, Abdel Aziz al-Rantissi, was assassinated by Israel a month later. In January 2005 newly-elected, moderate leader Mahmoud Abbas agreed ceasefire.*" Tim Butcher. "Hamas Rallies to Election Call from Jail." *The Daily Telegraph.* January 23, 2006.
	"*Both Hamas and the old IRA were formed as hard-line armed resistance movements, but both have subsequently been persuaded of the wisdom of engaging in democratic politics.* There are other similarities too. *The IRA and Hamas have both been perceived at various times as 'protectors' of their respective communities, and have taken an interest in grass-roots social welfare issues.*" Unknown. "Hopes – and Fears – for the Palestinian Election." *The Independent.* January 23, 2006.

Appendix D

Print news media articles analyzed in *the palestinian legislative council elections, 2006*

US print news media

Ballot Box Gains for Hamas Pose Dilemma for U.S., Allies. (2006, January 25). *USA Today*, p.10A.

Brinkley, J. (2006, February 23). Saudis Reject U.S. Request to Cut Off Aid to Hamas. *The New York Times*, p. 12.

Cowell, A. (2006, January 27). Europeans Insist Hamas Must Disavow Terrorism. *The New York Times*, p. 6A.

Daniszewski, J. and King, L. (2006, January 31).West Takes Firm Stand on Hamas Aid. *The Los Angeles Times*, p. 3A.

Dinan, S. (2006, February 25). Bush Sees Mideast at a Crossroads; Says Freedom Will Be "The Work of Generations". *The Washington Times*, p. 03A.

Ellingwood, K. (2005a, December 16). Fatah Split Could Benefit Hamas in Palestinian Poll. *The Los Angeles Times*, p. 5A.

Ellingwood, K. (2005b, December 22). Israel May Block Palestinian Balloting in East Jerusalem. *The Los Angeles Times*.

Ellingwood, K. (2006c, January 24). Hamas Shows a New Face in Campaign. *The Los Angeles Times*, p. 1A.

Ellingwood, K. (2006d, January 30). Palestinian Authority President Confronts Crises on Many Fronts. *The Los Angeles Times*, p. 3A.

Ellingwood, K. (2006e February 22). Premiership Offered to Hamas Leader; Ismail Haniya is Expected to Accept the Post and Form the New Palestinian Government. *The Los Angeles Times*, p. 3A.

Ellingwood, K. and King, L. (2006a, January 23). Voter Discontent Boosts Hamas. *The Los Angeles Times*, p. 1A.

Ellingwood, K. and King, L. (2006b, January 26). Hamas Makes Major Inroad in Balloting. *The Los Angeles Times*, p. 1A.

Ellingwood, K. and King, L. (2006c, January 27). Vote Puts Hamas In Control Palestinians Shift Casts Doubt on Peace Process, U.S. Aid. *The Los Angeles Times*, p. 1A.

Erlanger, S. (2006a, January 4). Palestinians Campaign for an Election That May Not Be Held. *The New York Times*, p. 3A.

Erlanger. S. (2006b, January 23). U.S. Spent $1.9 Million to Aid Fatah in Palestinian Elections. *The New York Times*, p. 11A.

Erlanger, S. (2006c, January 26). Victory Ends 40 Years of Political Domination by Arafat's Party. *The New York Times*.

Erlanger, S. (2006d, January 29). Hamas Leader Sees No Change Toward Israelis. *The New York Times*, p. 1.

Erlanger, S. (2006e, February 23). Iran Pledges Financial Aid to Hamas-Led Palestinians. *The New York Times*, p. 12.

Erlanger, S. (2006f, March 12). Lacking Mandate on Hamas Policy, Mideast Envoy May Quit. *The New York Times*, p. 10.

Erlanger, S. (2006g, March 18). Hamas to Propose Palestinian Cabinet that Excludes Other Parties. *The New York Times*, p. 5.

Finn, P. (2006, February 1). Putin Says Russia, U.S. Differ on Hamas Win; News Conference Is Wide-Ranging. *The Washington Post*, p. 19A.

Forced to Deal with Hamas, U.S. and Allies Walk Tightrope. (2006, February 20). *USA Today*, p. 10A.

Francis, D. (2006, February 27). What Aid Cutoff to Hamas Would Mean: The US Provides about One-Third of the Nearly $1.1 Billion in Aid to the Palestinians. *The Christian Science Monitor*.

Frankel, R. (2006, January 4). After Israel, who can run Gaza? In the wake of Israel's pullout and Yasser Arafat's death, militants have taken control. *The Christian Science Monitor*.

Gutman, M. (2006a, January 24). Palestinian Elections May Bring Shake-Up; Even in the Minority, Militant Hamas Could Derail Fatah's Plans. *USA Today*, p. 8A.

Gutman, M. (2006b, January 27). Hamas voters fed up with Fatah; Election More About Corruption than Terrorism, Some Indicate. *USA Today*, p. 6A.

Gutman, M. (2006c, March 20). Hamas Present Cabinet to Palestinian President; Veterans of Militant Group Dominates List of 24. *USA Today*, p. 12A

Hamas Victory Ushers in a Dangerous Time … (2006, January 30). *USA Today*, p. 10A.

Hamas Wins Majority in Palestinian Parliament. (2006, January 29). *The Washington Post*, p. 03A.

Hearn, K. (2006, February 4). Hamas Courting South American Governments for Support. *The Washington Times*, p. 06A.

Kessler, G. (2006, January 26). Vote Complicates Area's Diplomacy; Hamas Emerges as Significant Force Despite U.S. Efforts. *The Washington Post*, p. 19A.

King, L. (2006a, January 26). Hamas Faces a New Struggle: Its political success will call for tough decisions by the Islamist group: whether or not to ally with archrival Fatah and to recognize Israel. *The Los Angeles Times*, p. 6A.

King, L. (2006b, January 27). Can the Gunmen Now Govern? *The Los Angeles Times*, p. 1A.

King, L. (2006c, January 28) Enraged Fatah Members Riot After Defeat. *The Los Angeles Times*. p. 1A.

King, L. (2006d, February 6). Palestinians Ponder Life Under Hamas. *The Los Angeles Times*, p. 1A.

King, L. (2006e, February 11). The Face of Hamas Rule May Not Include Its Own. *The Los Angeles Times*, p. 1A.

King, L. (2006f, February 19). Hamas-Led Parliament Takes Power. *The Los Angeles Times*, p. 6A.

King, L. (2006g, February 26). Israel Fears an Alliance of Two Enemies. *The Los Angeles Times*, p. 5A

King, L. and Ellingwood, K. (2006, January 29). Israel Assesses a New Reality; With its Enemy Hamas Elected to Govern the Palestinians, the Jewish State Treads Lightly. *The Los Angeles Times*, p. 1A.

Kralev, N. (2006a, February 15). Officials in U.S. Deny Plot on Hamas; Want Cabinet to 'Succeed'. *The Washington Times*, p. 01A.

Kralev, N. (2006b, February 23). Rice Denied United Front Against Hamas; Tehran, Riyadh will Provide Palestinian Aid. *The Washington Times*, p. 11A

LaFranci, H. (2006a, January 27). Is Democracy Empowering Islamists? *The Christian Science Monitor*, p. 1.

LaFranci, H. (2006b, February 21). US Dilemma: Dealing with Hamas: Rice is Traveling to the Middle East to Keep Pressure on the Militant Group. *The Christian Science Monitor*.

Li, X. (2006, January 31). Win Blamed on Voter Anger against Fatah. *The Washington Times*, p. 12A.

Mainville, M. (2006, February 17). Russia to Host Hamas Leaders; Reassures Wary Western Allies. *The Washington Times*, p. 16A.

Martin, P. (2006a, January 31). Hamas Won't Yield on Jewish State; Charter Seen as Inviolable Despite New Responsibilities. *The Washington Times*, p. 12A.

Martin. P. (2006b, February 4). Hamas Tells West to Take its Aid and 'Get Lost'. *The Washington Times*, p. 06A.

Mazetti, M. (2006, January 30). Senators Back Bush's Stance on Hamas. *The Los Angeles Times*.

Militants Win Palestinian Vote. (2006, January 27). *The Dallas Morning News*, p. 4.

Mitnick, J. (2005a, December 16). Expanding Hamas Embraces Female Candidates. *The Washington Times*, p. 17A.

Mitnick, J. (2005b, December 19). Vote Propels Militant Hamas. *The Christian Science Monitor*, p. 6.

Mitnick, J. (2006c, January 20). Can Moderate Abbas Weather Hamas's Rise? *The Christian Science Monitor*, p. 6.

Mitnick, J. (2006d, January 26). Fatah Edges Hamas in Polls; Abbas' Party Fails to Win Majority; Islamic Militants Make Big Gains. *The Washington Times*, p. 01A.

Mitnick, J. (2006e, January 27). Prime Minister Resigns After Hamas's Victory; Militants Shun Calls to Disarm. *The Washington Times*, p. 14A

Mitnick, J. (2006f, January 28). Young Palestinians ponder future under Hamas; Election win brings anxiety to Ramallah. *The Washington Times*, p. 06A.

Mitnick, J. (2006g, January 30). Israeli Right May Gain Ground: Hamas Victory Likely to Influence Parliamentary Elections Slated for March. *The Christian Science Monitor*.

Mitnick, J. (2006h, February 9). Palestinians Probe the Depth of Graft: Hamas's Campaign to End Corruption May Have Spurred the Inquiry into Millions in Stolen Aid. *The Christian Science Monitor*.

Mitnick, J. (2006i, February 13). Russia and France Reach Out to Hamas. *The Christian Science Monitor*, p. 1.

Mitnick, J. (2006j, February 18). Hamas to Take Over Reins of Palestinian Parliament. *The Washington Times*, p. 06A.

Mitnick, J. (2006k, February 19). Hamas Takes Control of Parliament; As it Takes Power, the Group Rejects an Appeal from Abbas for Peace Talks with Israel. *The Washington Times*, p. 01A.

Mitnick, J. (2006l, March 9). Hamas Aims to Bid Up Islamic Aid; Targets Shi'ite-Sunni Rivalries. *The Washington Times*, p. 16A

Myre, G. (2006a, January 13). Israeli Says Any Official Hamas Role Dooms Peace Talks. *The New York Times*, p. 8A.

Myre, G. (2006b, January 24). Palestinians Wrap Up Campaigns As Vote Nears. *The New York Times*, p. 6A.

Myre, G. (2006c, January 29). Fatah Protesters Demand Resignation of Faction Leaders. *The New York Times*, p. 6.

Myre, G. (2006d, January 31). Both Fatah and Hamas Leaders Urge West to Continue Aid to Palestinians. *The New York Times*, p. 8.

Myre, G. (2006e, February 5). Palestinians Set Meeting of Parliament. *The New York Times*, p. 10.

Myre, G. (2006f, February 6). Israel Makes Payment to Palestinians but Says it Could Be the Last. *The New York Times*, p. 3.

Myre, G. (2006g, February 9). Hamas Tells Abbas Not to Act on His Own. *The New York Times*, p. 10.

Myre, G. (2006h, February 20). Hamas Tries in Gaza Talks to Broader its Cabinet. *The New York Times*, p. 11.

Myre, G. (2006i, February 21). Hamas is Formally Asked to Form a New Government. *The New York Times*, p. 10.

Myre, G. (2006j, February 27). Israeli Official Says Hamas Has Made Abbas Irrelevant. *The New York Times*, p. 7.

Myre, G. (2006k, March 6). Hamas Legislators Strip Palestinian President of Wider Powers. *The New York Times*, p. 7.

Myre, G. (2006l, March 19). Hamas Completes Lineup for Palestinian Ministries. *The New York Times*, p. 6.

Myre, G. (2006m, March 20). Hamas, Failing to Find Partners, Proposes Cabinet. *The New York Times*, p. 8.

Myre, G. (2006n, March 23). P.L.O. Rejects Platform of Hamas, Now Set to Take Power. *The New York Times*, p. 5.

New Equation Shocks Mideast. (2006, January 27). *USA Today*, p. 1A.

Pisik, B. (2006a, January 28). Fatah Faithful Cast Blame; Demonstrate Against Those Who Led Party to Election Ruin. *The Washington Times*, p. 01A.

Pisik, B. (2006b, January 29). Election Victors Now Must Rule. *The Washington Times*, p. 01A.

Pisik, B. (2006c, February 3). Hamas Alarms Bethlehem's Christians; Constitution Embraces Islam. *The Washington Times*, p. 1A.

Protecting Free Elections for Palestinians. (2006, January 27). *The Christian Science Monitor*.

Prusher, I. (2006a, January 31). After Victory, Hamas Faces Money Crunch. *The Christian Science Monitor*, p. 1.

Prusher, I. (2006b, February 27). Hamas Leader Rolls Israel Debate: Ismail Haniyeh Appeared to Suggest that Peace Could Be Made with Israel Under Certain Conditions. *The Christian Science Monitor*.

Prusher, I. (2006c, March 14). The Revolutionary Matriarch of Hamas: Mariam Farhat, a Newly Elected Palestinian Legislator, Advocates an Islamist Vision. *The Christian Science Monitor*.

Prusher, I. (2006d, March 20). Key Hamas Cabinet Posts Go to Hard-liners: Moderate Politicians Refused to Join the Organization's New Government Sunday. *The Christian Science Monitor*.

Richter, P. (2006, February 13). Hamas Poll Victory Tears at a Key Bush Alliance. *The Los Angeles Times*, p. 6A.

Roumani, R. and Wilson, S. (2006, January 29). Hamas Is Resolute on Fighting Israel; Militants to Form Army, Leader Says. *The Washington Post*, p. 21A.

Sammon, B. (2006, January 27). U.S. Won't Deal with Hamas; Terrorist Group Surprising Palestinian Election Victors. *The Washington Times*, p. 1A.

Sands, D. (2006, January 28). Muslim States Wary of Hamas' Success. *The Washington Times*, p. 1A.

Slavin, B. (2006a, January 25). Mideast Democracy Boosts Islamists; U.S. Pushes Elections; Fundamentalists Gain. *USA Today*, p. 1A.

Slavin, B. (2006b, January 27). Groups Victory Hinders Mideast Peace Process. *USA Today*, p. 6A.

Sullivan, K. (2006, January 30). Rice Rules Out Aiding Hamas-Led Government; Secretary to Map Strategy with U.N., Europeans. *The Washington Post*, p. 10A.

The Rise of Hamas. (2006, January 28). *The Dallas Morning News*, p. 11A.

Weisman, S. (2006, February 15). U.S. and Israel Deny Plans to Drive Hamas From Power. *The New York Times*, p. 8.

When Freedom's Just Another Weapon. (2006, February 23). *The Christian Science Monitor*.

Williams, D. (2005, December 17). Hamas Wins Control of 3 West Bank Cities; Militant Group's Surprise Victories Shatter PLO Monopoly in Palestinian Politics. *The Washington Post*, p. 19A.

Wilson, S. (2006a, February 10). Putin to Issue Invite to Hamas Leaders. *The Washington Post*, p. 15A.

Wilson, S. (2006b, February 17). Hamas to Choose Top Gaza Figure as Prime Minister. *The Washington Post*, p. 14A.

Wilson, S. (2006c, February 19). Hamas Assumes Control of Parliament; Palestinian Group Holds Firm on Not Recognizing Israel. *The Washington Post*, p. 01A.

Wilson, S. (2006d, February 26). Some U.S. Aid to Palestinians Will Continue, Diplomat Says; Humanitarian Funds Won't Stop Despite Role of Hamas. *The Washington Post*, p. 12A.

Wilson, S. (2006e, February 27). Abbas Not 'Relevant,' Israeli Official Says; Views at Odds With U.S., E.U. Stance. *The Washington Post*, p. 11A.

Wilson, S. (2006f, March 7). Hamas Picks a First-Day Fight; Palestinian Parliament Reverses Law Bolstering Fatah Leader. *The Washington Post*, p. 14A.

Wilson, S. (2006g, March 29). Hamas-Led Cabinet is Approved. *The Washington Post*, p. 15A

UK print news media

Abbas Considers Delaying Palestinian Elections. (2006, January 3). *The Guardian*.

Agha, H. and Malley, R. (2006, January 24) Hamas Has Arrived—But There Are Limits to its Advance: The Palestinian Islamists Will Tomorrow Reap the Rewards of Nationalist Failure, Sharon's Policies, Discipline, Integrity. *The Guardian*.

Beaumont, P. (2006a, January 15). Palestinians at War as Blood Feuds Follow Israeli Pullout. *The Guardian*.

Beaumont, P. (2006b, January 22). Israel on Alert as Hamas Leads Poll. *The Observer, Sunday*.

Beeston, R. (2006a, January 14). Ballot Box Frees Islamist Genie. *The London Times*, p. 53.

Beeston, R. (2006b, January 26). Ballot Box Power May Tame the Extremists. *The London Times*, p. 4.

Between Zeal and Pragmatism. (2006, January 23). *The Guardian*.

Black, I. (2006, January 24). The Road to Legitimacy: The Stunning Electoral Rise of the Palestinian Group Hamas is Set to Break the Mould of Middle East Peacemaking Writes Ian Black. *The Guardian*.

Butcher, T. (2006a, January 13). Hamas Drops Call for the End of Israel as Poll Nears. *The Daily Telegraph*, p. 18.

Butcher, T. (2006b, January 23). Hamas Rallies to Election Call from Jail. *The Daily Telegraph*, p. 15.

Butcher, T. (2006c, January 26). Poll Leaves Hamas Close to Breaking Fatah's Monopoly. *The Daily Telegraph*, p. 17.

Butcher, T. (2006d, January 27). Terrorists Voted into Power: West Tells Palestinian 'Pariah' to Renounce Violence: Hamas Victory Sends Shockwaves across Mid East. *The Daily Telegraph*, p. 1.

Butcher, T. (2006e, January 28). Cars Burn as Anger at Fatah Poll Defeat Turns to Violence. *The Daily Telegraph*, p. 14.

Butcher, T. (2006f, February 6). Hamas Vows to Defend Itself after Three Die in Israeli Air Strike. *The Daily Telegraph*, p. 14.

Butcher, T. (2006g, February 9). Hamas Offers Deal if Israel Pulls Out. *The Daily Telegraph*, p. 18.

Butcher, T. (2006h, February 11). Israeli Fury as Moscow Plans Talks with Hamas. *The Daily Telegraph*, p. 13.

Butcher, T. (2006i, February 17). Hamas Names Popular Pragmatist as Palestinian Prime Minister. *The Daily Telegraph*, p. 23.

Butcher, T. (2006j, February 20). Israel Announces Sanctions on Hamas. *The Daily Telegraph*, p. 15.

Castle, S. and Penketh, A. (2006, January 31). Hamas Told To Recognize Israel in Return for Aid Promised if Violence is Renounced. *The Independent*.

De Quetteville, H. (2006a, January 27). The Regretful Fatah Voters Who Took Poll 'Game' Too Far. *The Daily Telegraph*, p. 5.

De Quetteville, H. (2006b, January 27). Fatah Anger Boils Over as Rivals Take Reins of Power. *The Sunday Telegraph*, p. 8.

De Quetteville, H. and Sherwell, P. (2006, February 26). We Need Help from Everyone, Not Just Iran, Insists Abbas. *The Sunday Telegraph*, p. 30.

Doyle, L. (2006a, January 23). Hamas on the Brink of Political Breakthrough. *The Independent*, p. 2.

Doyle, L. (2006b, January 24). Israelis Fear Hamas 'Terror State'. *The Independent*.

Farrell, S. (2006a, January 24). Hamas Tries to Exploit its Pariah Status at Ballot Box. *The London Times*, p. 39.

Farrell, S. (2006b, January 25). Pullout Offer on Eve of Election. *The London Times*, p. 37.

Farrell, S. (2006c, February 3). Hamas Starts Fundraising Tour of the Arab World. *The London Times*, p. 53.

Gilmore, I. (2006a, January 26). Palestinian Terror Group Hamas in Shock Win at the Polls. *The Evening Standard*, p. 17.

Gilmore, I. (2006b, January 26). Palestinians Elect Hamas Terror Group. *The Evening Standard*, p. 8.

Gilmore, I. and Bentham, M. (2006, January 26). Gunfight at Parliament as Hamas Sweeps to Poll Victory. *The Evening Standard*, p. 17.

Goldenberg, S. and MacAskill, E. (2006, January 27). Palestinian Elections: Reaction: Bush Demands Renunciation of Violence and Recognition of Israel. *The Guardian*, p. 18.

Hamas Deals Blow to Fatah in Local Elections. (2005, December 17). *The Guardian.*

Hamas Faith Call. (2006, January 20). *The Sun.*

Hamas Wins West Bank Elections Landslide. (2005, December 16). *The Guardian.*

Hopes—and Fears—for the Palestinian Election; Hamas. (2006, January 23). *The Independent*, p. 30.

Israel to Allow Palestinians in Jerusalem to Vote. (2006, January 10). *The Guardian.*

Jeffrey, S. (2006a, January 3). Q & A: Palestinian Elections. *The Guardian.*

Jeffrey, S. (2006b, January 26). Hamas Celebrates Election Victory. *The Guardian.*

LaGuardia, A. and Rennie, D. (2006, January 31). Israel Cuts Funds as Hamas Refuses to Give up Violence. *The Daily Telegraph*, p. 2.

MacAskill, E. (2006, January 26). Hard men to Deal with: Hamas's Apparent Election Success Brings Problems, but Raises the Prospect of a More Binding Peace Agreement. *The Guardian.*

MacAskill, E., Steele, J. and Watt, N. (2006, January 31). US Urges Arab States to Fund Palestinians after Hamas Victory; White House Fears Chaos if Support is Cut Off: Danger of Cash Vacuum Poses Dilemma for West. *The Guardian*, p. 14.

Macintyre, D. (2005a, December 22). Palestinian Election in Jeopardy as Israel Moves against Hamas. *The Independent.*

Macintyre, D. (2005b, December 29). Fatah Unifies for Poll while Israel Bombs Gaza Zone. *The Independent.*

Macintyre, D. (2006a, January 11). Israel Lifts Threat of Voting Ban in East Jerusalem. *The Independent.*

Macintyre, D. (2006b, January 4). Bush Pushes for Palestinian Poll Despite Row over Jerusalem Vote. *The Independent.*

Macintyre, D. (2006c, January 18). Hamas Support Grows after Israelis Shoot Militant Leader. *The Independent.*

Macintyre, D. (2006d, January 22). Hamas Set to Break through in Polls. *The Independent.*

Macintyre, D. (2006e, January 23). Guns or Politics? Now Hamas Must Choose. *The Independent.*

Macintyre, D. (2006f, January 24). Fatah Invokes Memory of Arafat as Campaign Closes. *The Independent.*

Macintyre, D. (2006g, January 25). Divisions in Fatah Give Hope to Hamas as Palestinians Go to Polls. *The Independent*, p. 20.

Macintyre, D. (2006h, January 26). Palestinians Show Support for Hamas Elections. *The Independent.*

Macintyre, D. (2006i, January 27). Hamas Scores Stunning Win—But What Happens Now? *The Independent.*

Macintyre, D. (2006j, January 28). Hamas under Pressure to Recognize Israel as Fatah Protest Turns Violent. *The Independent*, p. 30.

Macintyre, D. (2006k, January 28). Will This Mean a Path to Peace or a Road to War? *The Independent*, p. 30.

Macintyre, D. (2006l, January 29). The Hardliners Appear Ready to Share Power, but Will Their Rivals Believe It? *The Independent.*

Macintyre, D. (2006m, January 30). Palestinian Funding Hangs in the Balance as International Donors Urge Abbas to Stay On. *The Independent.*

Macintyre, D. (2006n, January 30). Women of Gaza Fear for their Freedoms under New Religious Regime. *The Independent*, p. 29.

Macintyre, D. (2006o, February 15). U.S. and Israel "Try to Force New Elections by Starving Hamas". *The Independent*.

Macintyre, D. (2006p, February 18). Israel Mulls Sanctions as Hamas Takes Control. *The Independent*.

Macintyre, D. (2006q, February 21). UN Criticises Israel's Move to Withhold Palestinian Cash. *The Independent*.

Macintyre, D. (2006r, February 25). Abbas Threatens to Resign if He Fails to Reach Hamas Deal. *The Independent*, p. 30.

Macintyre, D. and Castle, S. (2006, February 28). Israeli Anger at Europe's Aid for Palestinians. *The Independent*.

MacKinnon, I. (2006a, February 1). Hamas Special Brew—It's Very Dry. *The London Times*, p. 38.

MacKinnon, I. (2006b, February 18). Israel Threatens to Wage Economic War as Hamas Takes Over. *The London Times*, p. 48.

McGreal, C. (2006a, January 2). Hamas Drops Call for Destruction of Israel from Manifesto. *The Guardian*.

McGreal, C. (2006b, January 11). US Pressure Forces Israel to Relent and Allow Jerusalem's Palestinians to Vote in Election. *The Guardian*.

McGreal, C. (2006c, January 18). Hamas Swaps Bullets for Ballots in Attempt to Sweep away Old Guard: Islamist Party Poised to be Second Largest Party and Win Gaza Outright. *The Guardian*.

McGreal, C. (2006d, January 20). New-Look Hamas Spends £100k on an Image Makeover: Spin Doctor Admits He Has "Work Cut Out" with Group Known for Suicide Attacks. *The Guardian*, p. 17.

McGreal, C. (2006e, January 23). Palestinian Elections: Lawless in Gaza: Leaders Try to End Chaos by Taking Guns Off the Street. *The Guardian*, p. 3.

McGreal, C. (2006f, January 24). Fatah Struggles with Tainted Image: Corruption and Incompetence in Yasser Arafat's Faction are Helping Hamas to Win Support in Run-up to Palestinian Elections. Elections: Lawless in Gaza: Leaders Try to End Chaos by Taking Guns Off the Street. *The Guardian*.

McGreal, C. (2006g, January 24). Surge in Support for Hamas as Voters Prepare to Reject Fatah at Polls. *The Guardian*, p. 13.

McGreal, C. (2006h, January 26). Hamas Makes Gains against Fatah, But Fails to Win Power: Exit Poll Shows Ruling Party Clinging to Office: Militant Islamist Group Mounts Strong Challenge. *The Guardian*, p. 19.

McGreal, C. (2006i, January 28). US Threat to Hamas Over $400m Aid: Islamists Told They Must Renounce Terror. *The Guardian*, p. 1.

McGreal, C. (2006j, January 26). Hamas Shock Victory Poses New Middle East Challenge. *The Guardian*, p. 1.

McGreal, C. (2006k, February 3). Israel and Allies Urge Hamas to Renounce Past: Palestinians Go Unpaid as Tax Revenues Are Held Back: Election Victors Ponder Next Move to Avoid Crisis. *The Guardian*, p. 26.

McGreal, C. (2006l, February 20). Israel Halts Funds to Palestinian Authority: Block Announced After Swearing in of Parliament: Hamas Hopes Iran Will Sponsor Administration. *The Guardian*, p. 17.

McGreal, C. and Paton, N. (2006, February 11). Moscow Invitation to Hamas Angers Israel. *The Guardian*, p. 16.

McGreal, C. and Whitaker, B. (2006, January 28). Israeli Politicians Rush to Condemn Hamas Win: Minster Says Window of Peace Slammed Shut: Nearly Half of Public Still Want Talks to Go Ahead. *The Guardian*, p. 1.

McGreal, C., Urquhart, C. and Goldenberg, S. (2006, February 15). US and Israel 'Trying to Destablise Hamas': Report Claims West Plans to Block Palestinian Funds: Islamist Group Defiant as Government Takes Shape. *The Guardian*, p. 17.

Milland, G. (2006, January 27). Terror Group's Shock Poll Win. *The Express*, p. 14.

Oakeshott, I. (2006a, January 27). Middle East Peace Process in Balance after Hamas Victory. *The Evening Standard*, p. 2.

Oakeshott, I. (2006b, January 27). Peace Hopes Shattered by Hamas Win. *The Evening Standard*, p. 15.

Page, J. (2006, February 17). Moscow Courts Hamas in Effort to Revise Middle East Influence. *The London Times*, p. 44.

Palestinian Elections: After the Hamas Earthquake. (2006, January 27). *The Guardian*, p. 36.

Palestinian Go to the Polls. (2006, January 25). *The Guardian*.

Peace Hopes Shattered by Hamas Win. (2006, January 27). *The Evening Standard*, p. 15.

Pekneth, A. and Silver, E. (2006, February 11). Putin's Hamas Overture Provokes Storm of Outrage from Israel. *The Independent*, p. 26.

Q & A: From Bombs to Ballot Boxes. (2006, January 27). *The Sun*.

Rennie, D. (2006, February 27). France and EC Push for Palestinians to Get Pounds 23m Blocked Aid. *The Daily Telegraph*, p. 14.

Silver, E. (2006a, January 16). Hamas Banned from Jerusalem Campaigning. *The Independent*.

Silver, E. (2006b, February 20). Hamas Unrepentant as Israel Imposes Sanctions. *The Independent*.

Silver, E. and Ghazali, S. (2006, February 19). Abbas: Hamas Must Honour Oslo. *The Independent*.

Toolis, K. (2006, January 27). A New Chance to Find Peace?; In Palestine, Hamas Has Scored a Stunning Poll Victory … When Gunmen Embrace Democracy It's Time to Take Notice. *The Mirror*, p. 6.

Urquhart, C. (2005, December 22). Palestinians May Delay Poll over Voting Ban. *The Guardian*.

Urquhart, C. (2006a, January 16). Palestinians Allowed to Vote in East Jerusalem but Israel Bars Hamas from Election. *The Guardian*, p. 23.

Urquhart, C. (2006b, January 27). Euphoria Turns to Shock as Palestinians Ask 'What Now?' *The Guardian*, p. 23.

Urquhart, C. (2006c, February 27). Abbas 'Will Quit' if Hamas Make Job Impossible. *The Guardian*, p. 26.

Appendix E

Covering the Gaza War, in-text frames of representation

US news media

Frame of Representation	Examples from Article Sample
Palestinian Culpability	"Israel launched a massive air assault on Hamas targets throughout the Gaza Strip *in retaliation* for a spate of rocket attacks" Joshua Mitnick. "Israel Hammers Hamas in Gaza." *The Washington Times.* December 28, 2008.
	"Israel—as every country—has a right to defend itself." "Israel Gambles in Gaza." *USA Today.* December 30, 2008.
	"Israel pulled its soldiers and settlers out of Gaza in 2005 but maintained control of its borders, sea and airspace. *Hamas shot rockets at Israel soon after is departure."* Ethan Bronner. "Israeli Attack Splits Gaza." *The New York Times.* January 5, 2009.
Israeli Culpability	"Israel is behaving like a capricious jailer to Gaza's Palestinians. *Besides controlling air and sea access, Israel won't open border crossings into Israel with any consistency—as a result, Palestinians don't have access to the regular trade and jobs that can make their economy viable."* "Israel Gambles in Gaza." *USA Today.* December 30, 2008.
	"Palestinians *hit back*; Hamas shows mettles with *counterattack* after days of Israel bombs." –Ibrahim Barzak and Jason Keyser. "Palestinians Hit Back." *The Chicago Sun Times.* December 30, 2008.
	"Israel resumed its Gaza offensive Wednesday … *Hamas responded* with a rocket barrage." - Ibrahim Barzak and Steven Gutkin. "Israel, Hamas Hurry up Attacks." *The Chicago Sun Times.* January 8, 2009.
Palestinian Suffering	"Abu Wadi said he said nothing *since seeing their neighbour carrying the body of his child, killed in an airstrike Saturday."* Ibrahim Barzak. "Israel Calls Gaza Assault a 'War to the Bitter End'." *The Associated Press.* December 29, 2008.
	"When rescue workers from the Red Cross and the Palestinian Red Crescent arrived at the site, they found 12 corpses lying on mattresses in one home, along with four young children lying next to their dead mothers, the Red Cross said. *The children were too weak to stand* and were rushed to a hospital, the agency said." Craig Whitlock. "Red Cross Reports Grisly Find in Gaza." *The Washington Post.* January 8, 2009.

Frame of Representation	Examples from Article Sample
Israeli Suffering	"But *Israeli officials said more than 50 people, half of them children, were treated for hysteria and shock.*" Ashraf Khalil. "Palestinian Attacks on Israel from Gaza Intensify." *The Los Angeles Times.* December 25, 2008.
	"*In Israel, 17 people have been killed in attacks from Gaza since the beginning of the year, including nine civilians—six of them killed by rockets—and eight soldiers,* according to Israel's Foreign Ministry." Ibrahim Barzak. "Israel Calls Gaza Assault a 'War to the Bitter End'." *The Associated Press.* December 29, 2008.
	"*Three Israeli civilians and a soldier were killed by rocket fire earlier in the campaign.*" Griff Witte. "Israel Hits U.N.-Run School in Gaza." *The Washington Post.* January 7, 2009.
Palestinian narration, rational	"'*We need our liberty, we need our freedom and we need to be independent. If we don't accomplish this objective, then we have to resist. This is our right,*' the official, Abu Marzook [said]." Ibrahim Barzak. "Israel Calls Gaza Assault a 'War to the Bitter End'." *The Associated Press.* December 29, 2008.
	"'*Hamas as an institution is not really sustaining casualties,*' said Ziad Asali, president of the American Task Force for Palestine. '*The people of Gaza are the ones who are paying the price.*'" –Steven Lee Meyers. "The New Meaning of an Old Battle." *The New York Times.* January 4, 2009.
Palestinian narration, radical	"*The residents of the south will stay in the bomb shelters for a long time, and the threats of an Israeli military offensive don't scare us because we are more prepared than ever,*" the [Izzidin al-Qassam Brigade] statement said." Ashraf Khalil. "Palestinian Attacks on Israel from Gaza Intensify." *The Los Angeles Times.* December 25, 2008.
	"'*We [Palestinians] say in all confidence that even if we are hung on gallows or they make our blood flow in the streets or they tear our bodies apart, we will bow only before God and we will not abandon Palestine,*' [Ismail Haniych] said." Taghreed El-Khodary. "Israelis Say Strikes against Hamas Will Continue. *The New York Times.* December 28, 2008.
Israeli narration, rational	"'Israel *"will answer quiet with quiet,*' Mr. Regev said, '*but will answer attacks with a response designed to protect our people.*'" Isabel Kershner. "Gaza Rocket Fire Intensifies." *The New York Times.* December 25, 2008.
	"Mr. Regev said the point of the fighting was '*to reach a situation where there will be quiet in the south and international support for that quiet.*'" Ethan Bronner. "Israeli Attack Splits Gaza." *The New York Times.* January 5, 2009.
	"At a hastily arranged State Department ceremony, Livni described the [cease-fire] deal as '*a vital complement for a cessation of hostility*' in the troubled region." Associated Press. "Israel Truce Vote Today." *The Chicago Sun-Times.* January 17, 2009.

Frame of Representation	Examples from Article Sample
Israeli narration, radical	"'The guiding principle behind the … operation is … *we are moving in with full force, shooting everything we have, including artillery,*' Alex Fishman, an Israeli military affairs correspondent, wrote Sunday in the newspaper Yediot Aharonot. '*We'll pay the international price later for the collateral damage and the anticipated civilian casualties.*'" Richard Boudreaux and Rushdi Abu Alouf. "Nowhere to Go, Gazans Stay Home." *The Los Angeles Times.* January 5, 2009.
	"[Said Ehud Olmert] *If our enemies decide that they haven't had enough … Israel will be ready and will feel free to continue to respond forcefully. I don't recommend that they or other terrorist groups test us.*" Joshua Mitnick. "Israel Agrees to Unilateral Cease-fire." *The Washington Times.* January 18, 2009.
Israeli restraint/precision	"*Israel had withdrawn its troops and settlers from the coastal strip in 2005,* only to see its border communities come under frequent attacks with crude rockets fired by Hamas and smaller Palestinian groups." Richard Boudreaux. "Israel Pounds Gaza, Pledges More Strikes against Hamas." *The Los Angeles Times.* December 28, 2008.
	"The Israeli military said *its soldiers fired in self-defense after Hamas fighters launched mortar shells from the school.* The United Nations condemned the attack and called for an independent investigation." Griff Witte. "Israel Hits U.N.-Run School in Gaza." *The Washington Post.* January 7, 2009.
Palestinian aggression	"Hamas, *an Islamic militant group backed by Iran whose charter calls for the Jewish state's destruction,* won the Palestinian Authority's parliamentary elections in early 2006." Richard Boudreaux. "Israel Pounds Gaza, Pledges More Strikes against Hamas." *The Los Angeles Times.* December 28, 2008.
	"Despite Israel's relentless bombardment of Hamas-affiliated targets, *rockets continued to fly out of Gaza on Sunday, with more than 20 launched into Israel.*" Griff Witte. "Israelis Push to Edge of Gaza City." *The Washington Post.* January 12, 2009.
Israeli aggression	"*Israel's intense bombings—more than 300 airstrikes since midday Saturday—reduced dozens of buildings to rubble.* The military said naval vessels also bombarded targets from the sea." Ibrahim Barzak. "Israel Calls Gaza Assault a 'War to the Bitter End'." *The Associated Press.* December 29, 2008.
	"*In unleashing a series of punishing attacks in Gaza last week,* Israel clearly aimed to hand Hamas a defeat from which it could not recover anytime soon." Steven Lee Meyers. "The New Meaning of an Old Battle." *The New York Times.* January 4, 2009.
Palestinian restraint/precision	"On Wednesday, Israel and *Hamas observed a three-hour pause in fighting to allow the delivery of humanitarian aid such as food, fuel and medical supplies into Gaza.*" Theodore May. "Ambulance Trip from Gaza a Harrowing Ride." *USA Today.* January 8, 2009.

UK print news media

Frame of Representation	Examples from Article Sample
Palestinian Culpability	"*Israel's onslaught is a reprisal for a week-long barrage of rocket and mortar attacks from Gaza.* Israel says it had to safeguard the lives in towns bordering the strip." Donald Macintyre. "Israel Prepares to Invade Gaza." *The Independent*. December 29, 2008.
	"Israel sent hundreds of tanks to Gaza's border and mobilised 7,000 reservists last night as it geared up for a possible ground assault *to end rocket attacks on its southern towns.*" James Hider. "Israel Masses Forces for Ground Assault on Gaza." *The Times*. December 29, 2008.
	"without doubt, *this invasion was systematically and skilfully provoked by fanatics elected by the Palestinians to run Gaza.*" Trevor Kavanagh. "Peace is the Last Thing Hamas Want." *The Sun*. January 5, 2009.
Israeli Culpability	"Israel stood defiant last night in the face of *mounting international condemnation*, as it vowed to continue a massive bombing offensive against key targets in the Gaza Strip that left 205 dead and 700 others injured." Toni O'Loughlin. "Air Strikes in Gaza Kill 225 as Israel Targets Hamas." *The Observer*. December 28, 2008.
	"Palestinian militants today *fought back against* a new wave of air raids pounding the Gaza strip by firing rockets deeper into Israel than ever before." Kiran Randhawa. "Defiant Palestinians Fire Rockets Deeper into Israel." *The Evening Standard*. December 29, 2008.
	"Palestinians fighters based in southern Lebanon *may be preparing to retaliate for the assault on Gaza* by striking across the border and opening a second front against Israel." Andrew Wander. "Palestinians Threaten Second Front to the North." *The Daily Telegraph*. December 30, 2008.
Palestinian Suffering	"Gaza City was a *ghost town of funeral tents* and nervous bread queues yesterday as shocked residents ventured out of their homes under Israel's massive firestorm only to carry out the bare necessities of life: buying food and *burying their dead.*" Azmi Keshawi. "Hospitals Face Catastrophe as Israeli Firestorm is Unleashed." *The Times*. December 29, 2008.
	"Witnesses at Shifa Hospital, the largest in Gaza, described seeing the wounded arriving for treatment with horrific injuries. *Some had limbs torn off, while one man had lost part of his torso. So strong was the flow of blood from the wounded that the hospital's floors were smeared red.*" Tim Butcher. "Palestinians Cower as Darkness and Fear Come to Gaza." *The Daily Telegraph*. January 5, 2009.
Israeli Suffering	"Their missiles have hit targets up to 23 miles away from the Hamas-ruled territory, leaving two dead and 15 injured. *An Israeli was killed today in the southern city of Ashkelon, 10 miles north of Gaza, in a rocket attack that wounded seven others.*" Kiran Randhawa. "Defiant Palestinians Fire Rockets Deeper into Israel." *The Evening Standard*. December 29, 2008.
	"*One Israeli soldier was killed near Jabalya in the first hours of the invasion. A further 32 were injured. A total of five Israelis – three civilians and two soldiers – have been killed since last Saturday when the Israeli campaign began.*" Rory McCarthy. "Thousands Flee Guns and Shells as Israel Tightens Grip on Gaza." *The Guardian*. January 5, 2009.

Frame of Representation	Examples from Article Sample
Palestinian narration, rational	"'*We are going to defend ourselves, defend our people and defend our land,*' Moussa Abu Marzouk, the deputy head of the Hamas politburo, told AP. '*We need our liberty, we need our freedom and we need to be independent.*'" Rory McCarthy. "Gaza Air Strikes: Israel Says its Army is Fighting a War to the Bitter End Against Hamas." *The Guardian*. December 30, 2008.
	"'*Now there is more hate and radicalism in the Gaza streets,*' one young Gazan told The Times by telephone from the apartment where he and his family were huddled, only venturing out to queue for hours for bread in the city's almost bare shops." James Hider. "Hamas Braced as Israel Pledges an All-Out War to Topple Regime." *The Times*. December 30, 2008.
Palestinian narration, radical	"The shopkeeper said he sent his son, 9, to buy cigarettes minutes before the air strikes began and now could not find him. '*May I burn like the cigarettes, may Israel burn,*' Masri moaned." Marie Colvin. "Israeli Jets Kill 'at least 225' in Revenge Strikes on Gaza." *The Sunday Times*. December 28, 2008.
	"'*You entered like rats. Your entry to Gaza won't be easy. Gaza will be a graveyard for you, God willing,*' Ismail Radwan, a Hamas spokesman said on the group's television station." Rory McCarthy. "Thousands Flee Guns and Shells as Israel Tightens Grip on Gaza." *The Guardian*. January 5, 2009.
Israeli narration, rational	"'The objective at this stage is to destroy the terrorist infrastructure of Hamas *in ... order to greatly reduce the quantity of rockets fired at Israel,*' said Major Avital Leibovich." Marie Colvin. "Israeli Tanks Roll Gaza to Crush Hamas." *The Sunday Times*. January 4, 2009.
	"Mr. Barak [Israeli Defence Minister] ... said ... 'We have refrained from acting for years and now *it is our duty to give our citizens what every citizen of the world deserves – peace, quiet, and security.*'" Staff Reporter. "42 People Killed at Gaza School." *The Sun*. January 6, 2009.
	"Uri Dan, a security co-ordinator for Nir Oz, a kibbutz which lies just 5km from Gaza ... said. 'We live next to the Palestinians and we will have to continue living with them. *You should live with your fellow human being as a neighbour, not as a wolf.*'" Ben Lynfeld. "Plea to Stop War from Victims of Rocket Salvoes." *The Independent*. January 17, 2009.
Israeli narration, radical	"Earlier this week, Israel's cabinet approved a possible operation that could last several days. '*We have enormous power, we can do things which will be devastating* and I keep restraining myself and keep restraining my friends all the time and I tell them: let's wait . . . give them another chance,' Israel's prime minister, Ehud Olmert." Toni O'Loughlin. "Israeli Far Right Gains Ground as Gaza Rockets Fuel Tension." *The Guardian*. December 27, 2008.

Frame of Representation	Examples from Article Sample
Israeli restraint/precision	*"One perfectly aimed missile demolished the Hamas-controlled Rafah police station."* Marie Colvin. "Israeli Jets Kill 'at least 225' in Revenge Strikes on Gaza." *The Sunday Times.* December 28, 2008.
	"The Israeli military said it would allow 80 lorries of humanitarian aid and vital fuel supplies into the Gaza Strip" Staff Reporters. "Gaza is a 'Catastrophe'." *The Sun.* January 5, 2009.
	"Gaza City 2009 is not Stalingrad 1944. *There had been no carpet bombing of large areas, no firebombing of complete suburbs. Targets had been selected and then hit, often several times, but almost always with precision munition*s." Tim Butcher. "Gaza Has been Hit Hard, but Has it Made Any Difference?" *The Daily Telegraph.* January 21, 2009.
Palestinian aggression	*"Hamas has pounded Israel's neighbouring southern townships with 36 rockets, 30 of which were fired on Wednesday, hitting a waterpark, a house and a factory.* There were no serious casualties. The rest fell in open areas. *Seventy mortars were also fired."* Toni O'Loughlin. "Israeli Far Right Gains Ground as Gaza Rockets Fuel Tension." *The Guardian.* December 27, 2008.
	"Just outside Sderot, *mortar rounds smashed to the ground about 50 yards from journalists* perched on a vantage point at Nir Am." Kim Sengupta. "'This is a War that We Have to Fight.'" *The Independent.* January 5, 2009.
Israeli aggression	*"Israeli missiles have wrought unprecedented destruction in Gaza, reducing whole buildings to rubble."* Kiran Randhawa. "Navy Joins Bombardment of Hamas Terrorist Bases." *The Evening Standard.* December 29, 2008.
	"It has never been like this before. *The assault is coming from the sky, the sea, and the ground. The explosion of shells, the gunfire from the tanks and the missiles from planes and helicopters are incessant. The sky is laced with smoke, grey here, black there, as the array of weaponry leaves its distinctive trail."* Hazem Balousha. "Gaza: Tanks, Rockets, Death, and Terror." *The Guardian.* January 5, 2009.
Palestinian restraint/precision	*"Last summer, Hamas initiated and accepted the terms of a six-month ceasefire between them and Israel."* Jeremy Greenstock. "Shooting Must Stop, Talking Must Start." *The Mirror.* January 13, 2009.
	"Hamas has offered a one-year, renewable truce on condition that all Israeli forces leave Gaza within a week and that all the border crossings with Israel and Egypt are opened which last night looked increasingly unlikely." Rupert Hamer. "War is Over." *The Sunday Mirror.* January 18, 2009.

Appendix F

Print news media articles analyzed in
covering the Gaza War

US print news media

An Eyeful in Gaza: Jan. 4–10. (2009, January 11). *The New York Times*, p. 2.

Barzak, I. and Christopher Torchia. (2009a, January 11). Israel Drops Bombs, Leaflets; Pursues offensive as Egypt Hosts Cease-fire Talks. *The Chicago Sun Times*, p. A14, *[The Associated Press]*.

Barzak, I. and Christopher Torchia. (2009b, January 21). It's over in Gaza; Israel, Hamas Announce Truces without Reaching Long-term Goals. *The Chicago Sun Times*, p. 20.

Barzak, I. and Jason Keyser. (2008a, December 30). Palestinians Hit Back; Hamas Shows Mettle with Counterattack after Days of Israeli Bombs. *The Chicago Sun Times*, p. 13 *[The Associated Press]*.

Barzak, I. and Jason Keyser. (2008b, December 31). Israel May Stop Bombing – if Hamas Halts Rockets. *The Chicago Sun Times*, p. 16.

Barzak, I. and Jason Keyser, (2009a, January 1). Next: Ground Offensive; Israel Runs Out of Air Targets, Gets Ready to Invade. *The Chicago Sun Times*, p. 10. *[The Associated Press]*.

Barzak, I. and Jason Keyser. (2009b, January 4). Incursion into Gaza; Israeli Ground Troops Clash with Palestinian Militants in Intensified Effort to Halt Rocket Attacks. *The Chicago Sun Times*, p. A13.

Barzak, I. and Jason Keyser. (2009c, January 5). Israelis Cut Off Gaza City. *The Chicago Sun Times*, p. 19.

Barzak, I. and Karin Laub. (2008, December 29). Israel Mobilizes Army as Assault Widens. *The Chicago Sun Times*, p. 17.

Barzak, I. and Karin Laub, (2009, January 9). 257 Children Dead; Israel Bombs as Hamas Hides with Civilians. *The Chicago Sun Times*, p. 25 *[The Associated Press]*.

Barzak, I. and Matti Friedman. (2009, December 29). Israel Calls Gaza Assault a 'War to the Bitter End'. *The Associated Press*.

Barzak, I. and Steven Gutkin. (2009, January 8). Israel, Hamas Hurry up Attacks; May Want to Get Strikes in before Truce. *The Chicago Sun Times*, p. 22 *[The Associated Press]*.

Borzou, D. and Raed Rafei. (2009, January 9). Conflict in Gaza: A Family's Tragic Encounter; Second-Front Worries; After Rocket Fire, Patrols Boosted in Lebanon; Palestinian Groups May Be Trying to Draw Hezbollah into Battle. *The Los Angeles Times*, p. A8.

Boudreaux, R. (2009a, January 6). Civilian Toll Grows; Israeli Forces Reach Gaza City; Twenty Children Die and Three Soldiers are Killed by 'Friendly Fire' as Troops Fight their Way into Urban Areas. *The Los Angeles Times*, p. A6.

Boudreaux, R. (2009b, January 20). Palestinian Authority is Left Weakened: The Moderate Government Appears Ineffective and Marginalized after Israel's Gaza Assault. *The Los Angeles Times*, p. A6.

Boudreaux, R. and Rushdi abu Alouf. (2008, December 28). Israel Pounds Gaza, Pledges More Strikes against Hamas; The Militant Group Urges a New Uprising as 271 Palestinians Are Killed. *The Los Angeles Times*, p. A1.

Boudreaux, R. and Rushdi abu Alouf. (2009a, January 5). At the Scene; Nowhere to Go, Gazans Stay Home; Some Scrambled to Stock up Supplies as Israeli Troops Neared; Five Died When Shells Hit a Main Market. *The Los Angeles Times*, p. A4.

Boudreaux, R. and Rushdi abu Alouf. (2009b, January 12). Israeli Offensive; Injuries Linked to Incendiary Shells; Israelis Hit Gaza City on 3 Sides; the Drive is Met by a Fierce Hamas Response. *The Los Angeles Times*, p. A6

Boudreaux, R. and Fayed abu Shammaleh. (2009, January 15). Progress Toward a Truce; Hamas Eases its Cease-Fire Terms; As the Gaza Death Toll Tops 1,000, the Militant Group Offers a new Deal Aimed at Ending its Battle with Israel. *The Los Angeles Times*, p. A5.

Bronner, E. (2009a, January 4). Is Real Target Hamas Rule? *The New York Times*, p. 1.

Bronner, E. (2009b, January 5). Israeli Attack Splits Gaza; Truce Calls Are Rebuffed: Death Toll Passes 500 – City Is Surrounded. *The New York Times*, p. 1.

Bronner, E. (2009c, January 15). Egypt Cites Progress Toward Truce as Gaza Toll Exceeds 1,000. *The New York Times*, p. 6.

Bronner, E. and Alan Cowell. (2009, January 22). Israel Completes Gaza Withdrawal. *The New York Times*.

Bronner, E., Michael Slackman, Taghreed El-Khodary, and Steven Erlanger. (2009, January 21). Israel Slows Withdrawal from Gaza. *The New York Times*. p. A8.

Burai, A. and Jeffrey Fleishman. (2009, January 7). Calls for Gaza Truce Mount after School Hit; Thirty Palestinians Die at the Site Israel Says Militants Fired from. *The Los Angeles Times*. p. A1.

Cowell, A. (2009, January 9). Gaza Children Found with Mothers' Corpses. *The New York Times*.

Daragahi, R. B. and Raed Rafei. (2009, January 9). After Rocker Fire, Patrols Boosted in Lebanon; Palestinian Groups May be Trying to Draw Hezbollah into Battle. *The Los Angeles Times*, p. 8.

de Montesquiou, A. (2009, January 23). Guns Silent as Gaza Edges Back to Normalcy. *The Associated Press Online*. Retrieved April 18, 2009 from www.ap.org.

El-Khodary, T. (2008, December 28). Israelis Say Strikes against Hamas Will Continue. *The New York Times*. p. A1.

El-Khodary, T. and Ethan Bronner. (2008, December 28). Israel Say Strikes Against Hamas Will Continue. *The New York Times*.

El-Khodary, T. and Isabel Kershner. (2008, December 29). Israel Keeps up Assault on Gaza; Arab Anger Rises. *The New York Times*. p. A1.

Erdbrink, T. (2009. February 3). Hamas Chief Thanks Iran for Support While on Regional Tour. *The Washington Post*, p. A10.

Finer, J. and Craig Whitlock. (2009, January 22). As Constraints on Gaza Ease, New Reports of Misery. *The Washington Post*, p. A10.

Friedman, M. and Ibrahim Barzak. (2009, January 18). Israel Declares Cease-fire; No Pullout for Now – Militants Vow to Keep Fighting until Troops Leave. *The Chicago Sun Times*, p. A19.

Greenberg, J. (2009, January 17). Under International Pressure, Israel Declares Cease-Fire as Hamas Vows to Keep Fighting. *The Chicago Tribune*.

Gross, R. C. (2009, January 1). Eliminating Hamas from Gaza Strip Won't Be Easy. *The Washington Times*, p. A04.

Israel Gambles in Gaza. (2008, December 30). *USA Today*, p. 8A.

Jordans, F. (2009, January 8). ICRC: Israel Delayed Access to Wounded for Days. *Associated Press Online*. Retrieved April 18, 2009, from www.ap.org.

Kershner, I. (2008, December 18). Israel: Palestinian Militants Fire Rockets from Gaza. *The New York Times,* p. 16.

Kershner, I. (2009a, January 2). In a Broadening Offensive, an Israeli Strike Kills a Senior Hamas Leader. *The New York Times*, p. 6.

Kershner, I. (2009b, January 16). Israel Shells UN Site in Gaza, Drawing Fresh Condemnation. *The New York Times*, p. A1.

Kershner, I. (2009c, January 19). Rebuilding Begins Upon a Wobbly Truce. *The New York Times*, p. 11.

Kershner, I. (2009d, January 23). Hamas to Start Paying Gaza Residents Compensation and Reconstruction Aid. *The New York Times*, p. 8.

Kershner, I. (2009e, January 29). U.S. Envoy Urges 2 Sides To Fortify Gaza Truce. *The New York Times*, p. 14.

Kershner, I. (2009f, February 3). New Gaza Exchanges Strain Fragile Truce. *The New York Times*.

Kershner, I. and Taghreed El-Khodary. (2008, December 25). Gaza Rocket Fire Intensifies. *The New York Times*.

Kershner, I. and Taghreed El-Khodary. (2009a, January 4). Israeli Tanks and Troops Launch Attack on Gaza. *The New York Times*. p. A1.

Kershner, I. and Taghreed El-Khodary (2009b, February 4). Palestinians and Israelis Exchange Fire; Egyptian-Backed Peace Talks Grind On. *The New York Times*, p. 6.

Kershner, I. and Taghreed El-Khodary (2009c, February 5). Agency Says Hamas Took Aid Intended For Needy. *The New York Times*, p. 10.

Keyser, J. (2009, January 12). Israel Accused of Using Phosphorus Shells; Military Says it Sticks to Law in Making Smoke Screens. *The Chicago Sun Times*, p. 14 *[The Associated Press]*.

Khalil, A. (2009, January 21). UN Chief Tours Gaza, Israeli Town; Ban Calls Destruction in Palestinian Territory 'Shocking'. In Sderot, He Calls Rocket Attacks on Civilians 'Appalling'. *The Los Angeles Times*, p. A3.

Khalil, A. and Rushdi Abu Alouf. (2008, December 25). Palestinian Attacks on Israel from Gaza Intensify. *The Los Angeles Times*.

May, T. (2009a, January 8). Ambulance Trip from Gaza a Harrowing Ride. *USA Today*, p. 8A.

May, T. (2009b, January 19). Gaza Residents Venture into Streets, Begin Daunting Task of Clearing Debris. *USA Today*, p. 8A.

Meyers, S. Lee. (2009, January 4). The New Meaning of an Old Battle. *The New York Times*, p. WK1.

Michaels, J. and Theodore May. (2009, January 22). Israeli Troops Exit Gaza; Residents Try to Rebuild; Relief Aid Pours into Region as Shortages Persist. *USA Today*, p. 2A.

Mitnick, J. (2008a, December 28). Israel Hammers Hamas in Gaza; Retaliatory Air strikes Kill 230; Fighting Deadliest in Decades. *The Washington Times*, p. A01.

Mitnick, J. (2008b, December 30). Israel Postures to Reshape Truce; Troops Line Gaza Border, Slam Hamas for Third Day. *The Washington Times*, p. A01.

Mitnick, J. (2008c, December 30). Israel Risks Repeat of Lebanon 2006; Invasion Backfired then, so this Time Israelis Don't Brag. *The Christian Science Monitor*, p. 13.

Mitnick, J. (2009a, January 4). Israel Charges into Gaza Strip; Infantry, Armor Escalate Attack on Hamas to 'Complete Mission'. *The Washington Times*, p. A01.

Mitnick, J. (2009b, January 9). United Nations Halts Relief Work in Gaza. *The Christian Science Monitor*, p. 25.

Mitnick, J. (2009c, January 11). Israel Warns of Escalating Siege of Gaza; Protesters Urge Cease-Fire. *The Washington Times*, p. A01.

Mitnick, J. (2009d, January 16). Amid Broad Israeli Support for Gaza War, a Rare Dissenting Voice. *The Christian Science Monitor*, p. 4.

Mitnick, J. (2009e, January 19). Hamas Agrees to Cease-fire; Israelis Begin Withdrawal. *The Washington Times*, p. A07.

Mitnick, J. (2009f, January 18) Israel Agrees to Unilateral Gaza Cease-fire; Vows to Defend Itself. *The Washington Times*, p. A01.

Mitnick, J. and Betsy Pisik. (2009, January 16). Israel Kills Key Hamas Leader; Hits U.N. Building, Besieges Gaza City. *The Washington Times*, p. A15.

Prusher, I. (2009a, January 12). What's the Endgame for Israel and Hamas in Gaza? *The Christian Science Monitor*, p. 1.

Prusher, I. (2009b, January 20). Gaza Fighting Pauses, But is the War Over? *The Christian Science Monitor*, p. 1.

Prusher, I. (2009c, January 28). Crux of Gaza Cease-Fire: Border Crossings. *The Christian Science Monitor,* p. 6.

Rivera, R. (2009, January 4). Times Square Rally Protests Fighting in Gaza. *New York Times.* p. A24.

Raghavan, S. (2009a, January 1). Israel Rejects Proposal for 48-Hour Truce; Ground Incursion Looms as Hamas's Rockets Hit Farther. *The Washington Post*, p. A10.

Raghavan, S. (2009b, January 14). At Cairo Hospital, Injured Palestinians Increasingly Voice Support for Hamas. *The Washington Post*, p. A10.

Raghavan, S. and Dan Eggen. (2009, January 3). Hamas Provoked Attacks, Bush Says; President Accuses Group of Adding to Civilian Deaths from Israeli Strikes. *Washington Post*, p. A08.

Raghavan, S.and Islam Abdel Kareem (2008, December 31). Hospital in Gaza City Engulfed by Suffering; Facility Short of Staff, Supplies for Wave of Injured. *The Washington Post*, p. A11.

Raghavan, S. and Reyham Abdel Kareem. (2009a, January 2). On Both Sides of the Border, Wounded Bodies and Minds; Fear Defines Conflict as Much as Missiles, Bombs and Blood. *The Washington Post*, p. A10.

Raghavan, S. and Reyham Abdel Kareem. (2009b, January 6). At Gaza Hospital, Chaos and Desperation; Israel's Strategy Of Dividing the Strip Hinders Relief Efforts. *The Washington Post*, p. A09.

Raghavan, S. and Reyham Abdel Kareem. (2009c, January 7). For Battered Gazans, Few Places Left to Hide; 'People Are Terrorized by This Situation… They Are Trapped,' U.N. Official Says. *The Washington Post*, p. A10.

Reuters. (2008, December 26). Israel Issues an Appeal to Palestinians in Gaza. *The New York Times*, p. 15.

Santana, R. (2009, January 3). Israeli Strikes on Hamas Enter Second Week; Thousands March in Opposition to Assault. *The Chicago Sun Times*, p. 2 *[Associated Press]*.

Soltis, A. (2009, January 3). It's Truce or Dare in the Gaza Strip – US Calls for Cease-fire as Rockets Rain. *The New York Post*, p. 6.

Stockman, F. (2009, January 17). Pact Targets Gaza Rocket Smuggling US Agreement with Israel Will Provide Funds. *The Boston Globe*, p. A3.

Strobel, W. (2009, January 3). World Powers Ponder How to Guard a Cease-fire; Even as Bombs hit Gaza, Leaders Mull Border Issues, International Force. *The Houston Chronicle*, p. 17.

Tavernise, S. (2009, January 18). In Home and on Streets, a War that Feels Deadlier. *The New York Times*, p. A14.

The Associated Press. (2009a, January 9). A Look at the Islamic Militant Hamas Group. *The Associated Press*.

The Associated Press. (2009c, January 17). Israel Truce Vote Today; U.S. Signs Deal to Help Cut off Weapons to Hamas. *The Chicago Sun Times*, p. 14.

The Associated Press. (2009d, January 20). UN Chief Demands Probe into Deadly Israeli Attacks. *Associated Press Online*. Retrieved April 18, 2009 from www.ap.org.

War in the Middle East; A Safe Place to Call Home Is at Heart of Latest Conflict. (2009, January 14). *The Washington Post*, p. C12.

Watson, T. (2008, December 29). Key Events in Gaza since 2005. *USA Today*, p. 2A.

Whitlock, C. (2009a, January 6). Israel Rejects Intensified Push for Cease-Fire. *The Washington Post*, p. A01.

Whitlock, C. (2009b, January 8). Red Cross Reports Grisly Find in Gaza; Israel Accused of Blocking Aid to Wounded. *The Washington Post*, p. A01.

Whitlock, C. (2009c, January 14). Hamas May Survive Offensive, Israel Says; Group Is Weakened, Military Officials Assert; Goal Is to Apply Pressure and Force a Truce. *The Washington Post*, p. A10.

Whitlock, C. (2009d, January 15). Progress Reported in Gaza Truce Talks; Palestinian Toll Exceeds 1,000. *The Washington Post*, p. A14.

Whitlock, C. (2009e, January 21). Control of Gaza Subject Of Debate; Many Wonder if Fatah Will Assume Leadership Role. *The Washington Post*, p. A03.

Whitlock, C. and Jonathan Finer. (2009, January 19). Israel Begins Pullout; Gazans Survey Debris; Hamas Joins Truce but Warns of Renewed Fighting. *The Washington Post*, p. A14.

Whitlock, C. and Reyham Abdel Kareem (2009a, January 11). Combat May Escalate In Gaza, Israel Warns; Operation in Densely Packed City, Camps Weighed. *The Washington Post*, p. A12.

Whitlock, C. and Reyham Abdel Kareem. (2009b, January 20). In the Silence, Gazans Take Stock; Remains Retrieved; Survivors Recount Attack on Family. *The Washington Post*, p. A16.

Whitlock, C. and Sudarsan Raghavan. (2009, January 10). Israel, Hamas Reject Efforts to Reach Truce. *The Washington Post*, p. A09.

Witte, G. (2008, December 31). Behind Gaza Operation, an Uneasy Triumvirate. *The Washington Post*, p. A01.

Witte, G. (2009a, January 2). Senior Hamas Leader Killed; Israelis Stand Ready to Invade Gaza by Land. *The Washington Post*, p. A01.

Witte, G. (2009b, January 6). Wounded Israeli Troops Yearn to Be in the Fight; Families Also. *The Washington Post*, p. A10.

Witte, G. (2009c, January 11). The View From Israel: Victors in a Necessary War. *The Washington Post*, p. A12.

Witte, G. (2009d, January 12). Israelis Push to Edge of Gaza City; Move Could Signal a Long Urban Battle. *The Washington Post*, p. A01.

Witte, G. (2009e, January 13). Israel's Top Leaders Weighing Their Next Steps in Gaza, *The Washington Post*, p. A10.

Witte, G. (2009f, January 28). Violence Erupts at Gaza Border as U.S. Envoy Arrives in Region. *The Washington Post*, p. A08.

Witte, G. (2009g. February 7). U.N. Halts Aid to Gaza In Dispute With Hamas. *The Washington Post*, p. A10.

Witte, G. and Sudarsan Raghavan. (2009, January 7). Israel Hits U.N.-Run School in Gaza; 40 Die at Shelter That Military Says Hamas Was Firing From. *The Washington Post*, p. A01.

UK print news media

Balousha, H. and Chris McGreal. (2009, January 5). Gaza: Tanks, Rockets, Death and Terror: A Civilian Catastrophe Unfolding: Incessant Bombardment, No Electricity, No Water, and the Hospitals Full to Overflowing—How Gaza Was Torn Apart. *The Guardian*, p. 2.

Balousha, H. and Toni O'Loughlin. (2009a, January 2). Gaza: Cemeteries: Besieged Palestinians Battle to Find Burial Spaces. *The Guardian*, p. 17.

Balousha, H. and Toni O'Loughlin. (2009b, January 19). Gaza Crisis: 'This is What Hamas Promised – Just Destruction'. *The Guardian*, p. 17.

Barry, M. (2009, January 10). These Fine Folk are Dying. They Need Help Now. *The Mirror*, p. 12.

Benn, T. (2009, January 1). Return to 1967 Borders is Only Hope. *The Mirror*, p. 6.

Blair, D. (2009, February 9) Hopes High for Israel Ceasefire with Hamas. *The Daily Telegraph*, p. 14.

Butcher, T. (2008a, December 27). Pressure Grows in Israel for Gaza Action; Aid Allowed In. *The Daily Telegraph*.

Butcher, T. (2008b, December 27). Egypt Reinforces Gaza Border Guards as Tensions Rise Over Rocket Attacks. *The Daily Telegraph*, p. 25.

Butcher, T. (2009a, January 1). Palestinians Able to Strike Deeper into Israel. *The Daily Telegraph*, p. 13.

Butcher, T. (2009b, January 2). Aid Groups Accuse Israel of Playing Down Gaza Suffering. *The Daily Telegraph*, p. 17.

Butcher, T. (2009c, January 5). Palestinians Cower as Darkness and Fear Come to Gaza. *The Daily Telegraph*, p. 5.

Butcher, T. (2009d, January 21). Gaza Has been Hit Hard, but Has it Made Any Difference? *The Daily Telegraph*, p. 22.

Cockburn, P. (2009, January 20). Gaza Was Demolished in Three Weeks. Rebuilding it Will Take Years. *The Independent*, p. 26.

Colvin, M., Tony Allen-Mills, and Uzi Mahnaimi. (2008, December 28). Israeli Jets Kill 'at Least 225' in Revenge Strikes on Gaza; Children Among Victims; First test for Obama the Stink of Death Hangs Over 'Black Saturday'. *The Sunday Times*, p. 1.

Colvin, M. And Uzi Mahnaimi. (2009, January 4). Israeli Tanks Roll Gaza to Crush Hamas; Calls for Ceasefire. *The Sunday Times*.

Drury, I. (2009, January 19). Brown Peace Talks as Gaza Truce is Tested. *Daily Mail*, p. 4.

Even I'm Scared... 2,500 Miles Away; Gaza, the Secret Hell. (2009, January 10). *The Mirror*, p. 12.

Fierce Words Over 'Nazi Link' to Gaza. (2009, January 11). *The Sunday Times*, p. 12.

Flynn, B. (2008, December 31). Air Blitz 'Just the 1st Stage'; Israel's Warning to Hamas. *The Sun*, p. 4.

Frenkel, S. (2008, December 27). Girls Die as Militants' Rockets Fall Short. *The Times*, p. 44.

Fricker, M. and Ryaen Parry. (2009, January 1). Siege City; No Let-Up from Israel as Gaza Death Toll Hits 400. *The Mirror*, p. 11

Gaza: A Week of Conflict. (2009, January 4). *The Observer*, p. 20.

Gaza Hit by Israeli Air Strikes. (2009, January 28). *The Sun*, p. 15.

Greenstock, Sir Jeremy. (2009, January 13). Shooting Must Stop, Talking Must Start; after 18 Days of Siege, Israel Prepares Final Assault. *The Mirror*, p. 6.

Guardian Reporters. (2009, January 2). Assault on Gaza: Israel vows to fight Hamas 'to bitter end': Jets target official buildings, 'weapons stores' and university. *The Guardian*, p. 10.

Hamas Kills Palestinian Children in Israel Attack. (2008, December 27). *The Daily Mail*, p. 10

Hamer, R. (2009, January 18). War is Over; Israel Halts Onslaught, but Can Gaza Peace Last? *The Sunday Mirror*, p. 7.

Harris, E. (2009a, January 19). Israel Begins Gaza Pull-Out. *The Evening Standard*, p. 26.

Harris, E. (2009b, January 20). 'Mortar fire' Claim Threatens Ceasefires in Gaza. *The Evening Standard*, p. 20.

Hider, J. (2008, December 30). Hamas Braced as Israel Pledges an All-Out War to Topple Regime. *The Times*, p. 6, 7.

Hider, J. (2009, January 5). Elite Israeli Forces Cut Region into Three in Drive to Eliminate Hamas. *The Times*, p. 6, 7.

Hider, J. and Sheera Frenkel. (2009, January 24). White Phosphorus Was Used in Gaza, Ministry Says; Israel. *The Times*, p. 50.

Israel Threatens to Send Military Back into Gaza. (2008, December 26). *The Daily Mail*, p. 10.

Kavanagh, T. (2009, January 5). Peace is the Last thing Hamas want. *The Sun*.

Lynfield, B. (2009, January 17). Plea to Stop War from Victims of Rocket Salvoes. *The Independent*, p. 32.

Macintyre, D. (2009a, February 7). UN Halts Aid to Gaza after Hamas Seizure. *The Independent*, p. 30.

Macintyre, D. (2009b, February 13). Israel Allows Valentine Carnations Out of Gaza. *The Independent*, p. 26.

Mail Foreign Service. (2008, December 26). Israelis' Threat to Invade Gaza Over Hamas Attacks. *The Daily Mail*, p. 10.

McCarthy, R. (2008a, December 29). Israel Considers Ground Attack as it Mobilises More Troops; Olmert: Fighting in Gaza Will Be 'Long and Painful'. *The Guardian*, p. 1.

McCarthy, R. (2008b, December 31). Gaza Air Strikes: Press Freedom: Foreign Media Challenge Gaza Entry Ban. *The Guardian*, p. 5.

McCarthy, R (2009a, January 2). Israeli bomb kills Hamas leader and six of his family. *The Guardian*, p. 1.

McCarthy, R. (2009b, January 3). Factional divide rules out show of solidarity from the West Bank: Despite a week of bombing, the long-standing rift between Hamas and Fatah prevents a united front against Israel. *The Guardian*, p. 6.

McCarthy, R. (2009c, January 3). Gaza: Israeli attacks: 'Critical emergency' after air strike every 20 minutes. *The Guardian*, p. 7.

McCarthy, R. (2009d, January 5). Gaza: Hamas: Struggle for Self-Defence and the Struggle for Palestinian Primacy. *The Guardian*, p. 5.

McCarthy, R. (2009e, January 6). Gaza: Fighting: Civilian Toll Soars as Troops and Tanks Press into Gaza. *The Guardian*, p. 5.

McCarthy, R. (2009f, January 30). Gaza: Dozens Believed Dead in Reprisal Attacks as Hamas Retakes Control: Suspected Collaborators Shot During and after War. *The Guardian*, p. 28.

McCarthy, R. and Ewen MacAskill. (2008, December 30). Gaza Air Strikes: Israel Says its Army is Fighting War to the Bitter End against Hamas: Defence Minister Rules Out Fresh Ceasefire with Hamas: Closure of Border Area May Signal Ground Offensive. *The Guardian*, p. 6.

McElroy, D. (2009a, January 6). The Offensive; Street Battles Break Out in Gaza City. *The Daily Telegraph*, p. 4.

McElroy, D. (2009b, January 30). US Targets Hamas Border; Police. *The Daily Telegraph*, p. 15.

McElroy, D. and Tim Butcher. (2009, January 6). Aid; I Saw Utter Devastation, Says UN Chief. *The Daily Telegraph*, p. 4.

McGreal, C. (2009a, January 4). Why Israel Went to War in Gaza. *The Observer*, p. 19.

McGreal, C. (2009b, January 11). Israel Set to Escalate Gaza Campaign. *The Observer*, p. 9.

Mendick, R. (2009, January 5). Family of 7 Killed as Israel Sets Out to Split Gaza City from Rest of Territory. *The Evening Standard*, p. 8.

Parker, N. (2009, 8 January). Miracle Saves Brit Blown Up by Hamas. *The Sun*.

Randhawa, K. (2008a, December 29). Defiant Palestinians fire rockets deeper into Israel; Hamas commander may have been killed in strike. *The Evening Standard*, p. 4.

Randhawa, K. (2008b, December 29). Navy joins bombardment of Hamas terrorist bases: (1) Israel blasts Palestinian militants for third day (2) 'This is the beginning of a successful operation. The idea is to change realities on the ground' Israeli Foreign Minister Tzipi Livni. *The Evening Standard*, p. 4.

Raymond, B. and Padraic Flanagan. (2009, January 7). 42 Killed after Israeli Shells Blast UN School. *The Express*, p. 10.

Rockett, K. (2008, December 28). Gaza's Grief: 205 Dead in Biggest Israeli Raid in 40 Years. *The Sunday Mirror*, p. 8.

Sun Staff Reporters. (2009a, January 5). Gaza is a 'Catastrophe'. *The Sun.*

Sun Staff Reporters. (2009b, January 6). 42 People Killed at Gaza School. *The Sun.*

Sun Staff Reporters. (2009c, January 10). 'Israel Nearing Gaza Goals'. *The Sun.*

Tisdall, S. (2009, January 2). Assault on Gaza: Analysis: World Has Little Leverage. *The Guardian*, p. 11.

U.S. Signs Deal to Help Gaza Truce. (2009, January 17). *The Daily Mail*, p. 11.

Ward, V. (2009a, January 6). 13 Dead in Family Homes as Gaza Attack Rages on the Siren Wails and We Run. *The Mirror*, p. 9.

Ward, V. (2009b, January 9). The Lowest Act; As Gaza Burns, Two Families on Opposite Sides Pray for Their Sons Shelled Children Left Wounded for Days as Israelis 'Block' Red Cross. *The Mirror*, p. 16.

Ward, V. (2009c, January 10). We Have Enough Fuel for 2 Days. When it's Gone, 6 Babies Will Die; Gaza Doc's Grim Power-Cut Warning. *The Mirror*, p. 11.

Ward, V. (2009d, January 14). Two Weeks for Vital Gaza Aid; Exclusive Desperate Wait for Supplies. *The Mirror*, p. 12.

Williams, D. and Matthew Kalman. (2009, January 6). 14 More Children Killed in the Terror of Gaza. *Daily Mail*, p. 8.

Yarranton, L. (2009, January 10). Worse to come for Gaza as Israel warns of increase in attacks. *The Sunday Mirror*, p. 8.

Appendix G

The flotilla attack, in-text frames of representation

US print news media

Frame of Representation	Examples from Article Sample
Gaza Blockade as Legal, Legitimate	"The Israeli government hoped a siege would *keep weapons out of Gaza* and create public antipathy toward the Hamas-run government." Scott Wilson. "Israel Says Free Gaza Movement Poses Threat to Jewish State." *The Washington Post.* June 1, 2010.
	"*The Israeli blockade* – which activists were trying to pierce Monday when nine died in a melee at sea with Israeli commandos – *is designed to deny weapons to the Islamist Hamas group* and weaken its authority." Janine Zacharia. "Getting what they need to live, but not thrive." *The Washington Post.* June 3, 2010.
	"*Israeli officials say the restrictions, imposed in 2007, are necessary to prevent weapons from entering the coastal enclave and to isolate Hamas,* the militant Palestinian group that controls Gaza and refuses to recognize Israel's right to exist." Edmund Sanders. "Israel Acts Cautiously in Round 2." *The Los Angeles Times.* June 6, 2010.
Gaza Blockade as Illegal, Illegitimate	"'*Israel is finding it increasingly difficult to explain the rationale behind the blockade to the rest of the world,*' said an editorial published Friday in the Israeli newspaper Haaretz. The price of lifting the siege, the paper wrote." Edmund Sanders. "Gaza Aid Flotilla Anticipates High-Seas Standoff with Israel." *The Los Angeles Times.* May 29, 2010.
	"*The White House considers Israel's blockade of Gaza to be untenable* and plans to press for another approach to ensure Israel's security while allowing more supplies into the impoverished Palestinian area, according to senior U.S. officials." Ethan Bronner. "U.S. taking Gaza deaths as cue for policy shift." *The International Herald Tribune.* June 4, 2010.

Frame of Representation	Examples from Article Sample
Flotilla/Activists as Legal, Humanitarian	"The cargo ships are carrying an array of donated goods not allowed into Gaza, *including cement, prefab homes, lumber, window frames, paper for printing school books, children's toys, a full dentist's office, electric wheelchairs and high-end medical equipment*, Ms. Berlin said." Erin Cunningham. "Large Aid Flotilla to Test Israeli Blockade of Gaza." *The Christian Science Monitor.* May 26, 2010.
	"*The boats carried medicine, food, school and construction materials, and other non-military items*, as well as human rights activists and lawmakers from Europe and Turkey." Scott Wilson. "Israel Says Free Gaza Movement Poses Threat to Jewish State." *The Washington Post.* June 1, 2010.
	"The ill-fated *aid flotilla bound for Gaza this week bore food, medicine and toys*." Janine Zacharia. "Getting what they need to live, but not thrive." *The Washington Post.* June 3, 2010.
Flotilla/Activists as Illegal, Provocative, Violent	"Israeli naval ships seized a *protest flotilla* carrying humanitarian aid to the Gaza Strip on Monday, killing at least 10 people and injuring several dozen, the Israeli military said." Edmund Sanders. "Israel Seizes Flotilla; 10 Activists Die." *The Los Angeles Times.* May 31, 2010.
	"*Footage provided by both passengers and the Israeli military show activists beating Israeli commandos*, but human rights groups have come out against what they say was Israel's 'excessive use of force.'" Erin Cunningham. "After Israeli Raid, Freedom Flotilla Aid Starts to Flow to Gaza." *The Christian Science Monitor.* June 1, 2010.
	"The U.N. Security Council on Tuesday condemned a deadly Israeli raid on a *so-called aid flotilla* bound for the Gaza Strip even as pro-Palestinian activists planned to send another ship in an attempt to break the Israeli blockade." Ashish Kumar Sen. "U.N. Panel Condemns Israelis' Ship Raid." *The Washington Times.* June 2, 2010.
Israeli Violence, Aggression	"Israel faced intense international condemnation and growing domestic questions on Monday after *a raid by naval commandos that killed nine people, many of them Turks, on an aid flotilla bound for Gaza*." –Isabel Kershner. "Deadly Israeli Raid Draws Condemnation." *The New York Times.* May 31, 2010.
	"Then, in 2009, *shortly after Israel's assault on Gaza killed about 1,400 Palestinians and laid waste to a tiny territory already devastated by poverty and violence*, Erdogan electrified the Arab world with an outburst of well-timed criticism". Megan K. Stack. "Israel Flotilla Raid Deals a Blow to Ties with Turkey." The Los Angeles Times. May 31, 2010.
Hamas/Palestinian Violence, Aggression	"*In an effort to cripple Hamas, which has launched rocket attacks from the strip*, Israel imposed widespread restrictions on imports and exports." Barry Paddock. "Blockade Spurred by Hamas Takeover." *The Daily News.* June 1, 2010.
	"*Hamas and other groups fired rockets from the territory toward Israeli towns* until Israel launched a large-scale offensive against the strip in December 2008, an operation that killed more than 1,000." Janine Zacharia. "Israel Considers Loosening its Blockade of Gaza Strip." *The Washington Post.* June 17, 2010.

Frame of Representation	Examples from Article Sample
Israeli Restraint, Generosity	"In recent months, *Israel has relaxed some restrictions, recently permitting trucks with limited amounts of clothing and cement to enter.*" Edmund Sanders. "Gaza Aid Flotilla Anticipates High-Seas Standoff with Israel." *The Los Angeles Times.* May 29, 2010.
	"*Israel has a long tradition of conducting painstaking investigations,* usually led by a former Supreme Court judge – a position seen as being above politics – after controversial Israeli military operations." Joshua Mitnick. "Israel to Set Up Inquiry on 'Freedom Flotilla' Raid." *The Christian Science Monitor.* June 11, 2010.
Humanitarian Crisis in Gaza	"International organizations working in Gaza have warned of growing hardship. Deprived of raw materials, local industry has been severely damaged, and *the Gaza economy has collapsed.*" Helene Cooper and Isabel Kershener. "Obama Pledges New Aid for Gaza and West Bank." *The New York Times.* June 10, 2010.
	"The ICRC said the 3-year-old closure *'is having a devastating impact on the 1.5 million people living in Gaza'* and urged Israel to 'put an end' to it." "Israel Launches Internal Probe in Aid-Ship Raid." *Newsday.* June 15, 2010.
No Humanitarian Crisis in Gaza	"*Gazans readily admit they are not going hungry.* But that, they say, is the wrong benchmark for assessing their quality of life." Janine Zacharia. "Getting what they need to live, but not thrive." *The Washington Post.* June 3, 2010.
	"In Israel, there are shopping malls and traffic lights. *In Gaza, donkey carts and herds of goats cross the road. Young boys pick through the debris of bombed-out buildings to salvage construction materials.*" Edmund Sanders. "Gaza's Plight a Crisis with a Difference." *The Los Angeles Times.* June 13, 2010.
Hamas/Palestinian Culpability for Gaza Crisis	"How *Hamas commandeered previous aid deliveries.*" Erin Cunningham. "Israel's Concern: Gaza Aid Flotilla will Help Hamas." *The Christian Science Monitor.* May 27, 2010.
	"Some Israelis oppose lifting restrictions unless Hamas, which refuses to recognize Israel's right to exist, releases Israeli soldier Gilad Shalit, who has been held in Gaza since 2006. His capture helped prompt Israel's blockade." Edmund Sanders. "Israel Agrees in Principle to Ease Gaza Blockade." *The Los Angeles Times.* June 18, 2010.
Diplomacy Crisis, Israeli Culpability	"*Israel's raid on an aid flotilla that sailed out of Turkey may have eviscerated, at least for the foreseeable future, any lingering remnants of goodwill among the political elite of Turkey* — a country long prized by the Jewish state as its most stalwart Muslim ally." Megan K. Stack. "Israel Flotilla Raid Deals a Blow to Ties with Turkey." The Los Angeles Times. May 31, 2010.
	"*The raid put relations with Turkey, once one of Israeli's best friends in the region, into a deep freeze* and drawn calls from the European Union for an immediate end to the blockade." Joshua Mitnick. "After Gaza Flotilla Raid, Israel Close to Easing Gaza Blockade." *The Christian Science Monitor.* June 16, 2010.
Diplomacy Crisis, Turkish Culpability	"Mr. Phillips said *Turkey's willingness to allow pro-Hamas activists to launch the flotilla from its ports is part of a new foreign policy strategy.*" Rowan Scarborough. "Turkey's Shift Spurs Concern on Hill." *The Washington Times.* June 14, 2010.

UK print news media

Frame of Representation	Examples from Article Sample
Gaza Blockade as Legal, Legitimate	"Militarily, *Israel's blockade of the tiny Gaza Strip was designed to starve Hamas of the weaponry it needs to attack Israel."* Kevin Toolis. "Fuse Lit for a New War in Mid East." *The Mirror.* June 2, 2010.
	"Building materials have been banned because of Israeli concerns that militants would use them to construct fortifications." David Charter; James Hider. "Israeli Blockade is Eased but Critics Cast Doubt on Inquiry into Flotilla Raid." *The Times.* June 15, 2010.
Gaza Blockade as Illegal, Illegitimate	*"Humanitarian aid is in theory allowed in, but UN agencies and charities claim that the Israelis have banned any items that are humanitarian in nature but could be put to alternative use."* Ian Black, Haroon Siddique, and Afua Hirsch. "Gaza Flotilla Assault: The Blockade." *The Guardian.* June 1, 2010.
	"Four years into a blockade mounted ostensibly to prevent weapons from being smuggled into the enclave, this claim, too, is utterly specious." "Gaza: From Blockade to Bloodshed." *The Guardian.* June 1, 2010.
	"The blockade amounts to a collective punishment against the 1.5million civilian population." Kevin Toolis. "Fuse Lit for a New War in Mid East." *The Mirror.* June 2, 2010.
Flotilla/Activists as Legal, Humanitarian	"Besides building materials, medical supplies, *the ships are carrying paper for schools as well as a complete dental surgery. Crayons and chocolate are also on board for Gazan children."* Harriet Sherwood. "Gaza Aid Flotilla to Test Israel's Blockade." *The Guardian.* May 26, 2010.
	"The convoy was carrying construction materials, electric wheelchairs and water purifiers for Gaza's people." "Gaza: From Blockade to Bloodshed." *The Guardian.* June 1, 2010.
	"The humanitarian aid being brought to Gaza included 550 tonnes of bagged cement, 20 tonnes of printing paper, 25 tonnes of school supplies and books, 12 tonnes of toys and 150 tonnes of medical equipment." Justine McCarthy; Philip Connolly. "Israelis to Deport Gaza Aid Crew." *The Sunday Times.* June 6, 2010.
Flotilla-Activists as Illegal, Provocative, Violent	"In his first newspaper interview since the Israeli navy halted a *pro-Palestinian activist flotilla* on Monday, Mr Blair called for a strategy for Gaza which 'isolates the extremists and helps the people and not one that operates the other way round'." Donald Macintyre. Blair urges Israel to Ease Gaza Blockade. *The Independent.* June 4, 2010.
	"Israeli officials have said that the *soldiers acted in self defence after they were attacked by passengers who beat them with metal poles, knives and later even shot at them with two pistols they took from the commandos".* Dina Kraft. "Israel to Block Irish-owned Gaza Aid Ship." *The Daily Telegraph.* June 5, 2010.

Frame of Representation	*Examples from Article Sample*
Israeli Violence, Aggression	*"Thousands of homes and businesses were destroyed during the three-week Gaza war in 2008-9."* Harriet Sherwood. "Gaza Flotilla Assault: Where Did the Aid Go?" *The Guardian.* June 4, 2010.
	"Another activist, Kevin Ovenden, from Newham, east London, *said he saw a man who had pointed a camera at the soldiers shot dead through the forehead.*" Justin Vela; Chris Irvine. "Homecoming Britons Tell of Raid on Gaza Flotilla." *The Daily Telegraph.* June 4, 2010.
	"Israel's brutal assault on the international aid flotilla bound for the Gaza Strip has united the outside world in agreement on one thing." "This Cruel and Ineffective Blockade of Gaza Must Be Brought to an End." *The Independent.* June 5, 2010.
Hamas/Palestinian Violence, Aggression	"Amid the increasing tensions, Israel carried out an airstrike in Gaza killing three of an *Islamic militant group who had been firing rockets into southern Israel.*" Gavin Cordon. "30 Britons Locked Up in Shoot-Out Crisis." *The Daily Post.* June 2, 2010.
	"He stressed more than once that the world needed to understand Israel's deep-seated security concerns and the fact *that Gilad Shalit, who has been held for almost four years by Gaza militants*, was a 'huge issue' for the Israeli public." Donald Macintyre. "Blair Urges Israel to Ease Gaza Blockade." *The Independent.* June 4, 2010.
	"The meeting came as *an Israeli policeman was shot dead and two others were injured* while their vehicle was driving in the Hebron area." Donald Macintyre. "Blair Urges Israel to Ease Gaza Blockade." *The Independent.* June 15, 2010.
Israeli Restraint, Generosity	*"Israel agreed to deliver the aid* after the flotilla attack ended in the deaths of nine pro-Palestinian activists." Harriet Sherwood. "Gaza Flotilla Assault: Where Did the Aid Go?" *The Guardian.* June 4, 2010.
	"Israel bowed to international pressure yesterday when *it agreed to reopen crossing points into Gaza for everyday goods.*" David Charter; James Hider. "Israeli Blockade is Eased but Critics Cast Doubt on Inquiry into Flotilla Raid." *The Times.* June 15, 2010.
Humanitarian Crisis in Gaza	*"Unemployment has soared and blackouts have become common. UN statistics show that around 70% of Gazans live on less than $1 a day, 75% rely on food aid and 60% have no daily access to water."* Ian Black, Haroon Siddique, and Afua Hirsch. "Gaza Flotilla Assault: The Blockade." *The Guardian.* June 1, 2010.
	"The result for Gazans is widespread malnourishment. The embargo on fuel has created chronic shortages of electricity. The blockade on construction materials means that three-quarters of the homes and buildings destroyed in the 2008/2009 Israeli invasion have not been rebuilt. Gaza's sanitation system is close to collapse." "This Cruel and Ineffective Blockade of Gaza Must Be Brought to an End." *The Independent.* June 5, 2010.
No Humanitarian Crisis in Gaza	"He added: '*There is no humanitarian crisis in Gaza*, and despite the Hamas leadership's war crimes and rocket fire, Israel is conducting itself in the most humanitarian manner, and is allowing the entrance of thousands of tons of food and equipment into Gaza.'" Harriet Sherwood. "International: Israeli Navy Prepares for Action as Activists' Flotilla Nears Gaza." *The Guardian.* May 29, 2010.

Frame of Representation	Examples from Article Sample
Hamas/Palestinian Culpability for Gaza Crisis	*"Hamas has turned away from Gaza a consignment of aid – including wheelchairs – transferred from the commandeered flotilla,* partly on the grounds that it was incomplete, with Israel excluding construction materials like cement and piping from the original cargo." Donald Macintyre. "Blair Urges Israel to Ease Gaza Blockade." *The Independent.* June 4, 2010.
	"The de facto Hamas government in Gaza has refused to accept truckloads of aid offloaded from the flotilla raided by Israeli forces." Harriet Sherwood. "Gaza Flotilla Assault: Where Did the Aid Go?" *The Guardian.* June 4, 2010.
Diplomacy Crisis, Israeli Culpability	*"Diplomatic relations between Turkey and Israel have deteriorated since the Israelis launched a three-week war on Gaza in 2008-09."* Harriet Sherwood. "Gaza Aid Flotilla to Test Israel's Blockade." *The Guardian.* May 26, 2010.
	"It is not simply the fury that [Israel] has created in Turkey, which will only grow as the bodies of its dead are buried." "Gaza: From Blockade to Bloodshed." *The Guardian.* June 1, 2010.
Diplomacy Crisis, Turkish Culpability	*"Israel's diplomatic problems were highlighted last week when the United States, its closest ally, broke with 50 years of policy to back a UN resolution calling for international inspection of Israel's top-secret nuclear facility near Dimona.* Despite President Obama later criticising the resolution for singling out Israel, *commentators interpreted it as a slap in the face."* Matthew Kalman. "Flotilla Sets Sail to Beat Gaza Blockade." *The Daily Telegraph.* May 31, 2010.
	"Turkey, which unofficially supported the flotilla, led the criticism, calling the action a 'bloody massacre.'" Gavin Cordon. "30 Britons Locked Up in Shoot-Out Crisis." *The Daily Post.* June 2, 2010.
	"Over the weekend, *Iran suggested that its Revolutionary Guards could escort aid flotillas to Gaza.* Such threats are widely seen as bluster and have even been criticised by Hamas, the Iranian-sponsored movement that controls Gaza." Adrian Blomfield. "Iran raises Gaza threat by vowing to challenge Israel's blockade." *The Telegraph.* June 7, 2010.

Appendix H

Print news media articles analyzed in *flotilla attack: Israel's blockade of Gaza and naval assault of the flotilla in the printed news*

US news media

Arsu, S. (2010, June 4). New Ship Heads to Gaza, and Israel Vows to Stop It. *The New York Times*, p. 8A (*The Associated Press*).

The Associated Press. (2010, June 18). Israel to Loosen Blockade on Gaza. *Newsday*, p. 46A.

Berton, J. (2010, June 2). 4 Bay Area Activists Reported Safe in Israel. *The San Francisco Chronicle*, p. 1A

Bronner, E. (2010a, June 4). U.S. Taking Gaza Deaths as Cue for Policy Shift; New Approach Is Needed, Aides to Obama Sat, as Israel Warns of Conditions. *The International Herald Tribune*, p. 1.

Bronner, E. (2010b, June 13). Gaza, Through Fresh Eyes. *The New York Times*, p. 3.

Bronner, E. (2010c, July 1). Cargo of Turkish Aid From Flotilla begins Arriving in Gaza by Land. *The New York Times*, p. 4A.

Bronner, E. and Cooper, H. (2010, May 31). Raid Complicates U.S. Ties and Push for Peace. *The New York Times*, p. 8A.

Bronner, E. and Kershner, I. (2010, June 3). New Israeli Tack Needed on Gaza, U.S. Officials Say. *The New York Times*, p. 1.

Bronner, E. and Tavernise, S. (2010, June 4). Days of Planning Led to Flotilla's Hour of Chaos. *The New York Times*, p. 1A.

Cooper, H. and Kershner, I. (2010, June 10). Obama Pledges New Aid for Gaza and West Bank. *The Washington Post*, p. 14.

Cowell, A. and Kershner, I. (2010, June 2). Pressure Mounts on Israel After Raid; Egypt Opens its Border with Gaza and Activists Begin a New Sea Mission. *The International Herald Tribune*, p. 4.

Cowell, A. and MacFarquhar, N. (2010, June 1). U.N. Security Council condemns 'Acts' in Israeli Raid. *The New York Times*.

Croghan, L. (2010, June 15). Pols Antsy About Gaza Activists' Visit. *The Daily News*, p. 17.

Croghan, L. and Einhorn, E. (2010, June 14). Food For Gazans OK. *e Daily News*, p. 17.

Cunningham, E. (2010a, 26 May). Large Aid Flotilla to Test Israeli Blockade of Gaza. *The Christian Science Monitor*.

Cunningham, E. (2010b, 27 May). Israel's Concern: Gaza Aid Flotilla Will Help Hamas. *The Christian Science Monitor*.

Cunningham, E. (2010c, June 1). After Israel Raid, Freedom Flotilla Aid Starts to Flow to Gaza. *The Christian Science Monitor*.

Fleishman, J. (2010, June 1). After Raid, Egypt Opens Border with Gaza Strip. *The Los Angeles Times*, p. 7.

Greenberg, J. (2010, July 1). U.S. Envoy Watches as Israel Allows More Good to Enter Gaza. *The Washington Post*, p. 6A.

Grossman, D. (2010, June 2). Gaza Naval Raid – a Folly Foretold. *The Los Angeles Times*, p. 15A)

Hacaoglu, S. and Lavie, M. (2010, June 3). Israel Refuses to Lift Blockade; Netanyahu Says Ban Prevents Hamas Attacks; Calls Criticism of Raid 'International Hypocrisy'. *Newsday*, p. 24A.

Israel Faces Deepening Tensions With Turkey over Raid, and Bond With U.S. Frays. (2010, June 4). *The New York Times*, p. 7A.

Israel Intercepts Gaza Flotilla; Violence Reported. (2010, May 30). *The New York Times*, p. 8A.

Israel Launches Internal Probe in Aid-Ship Raid. (2010, June 15). *Newsday*, p. 33A.

Israel: Officials Brace for the Gaza Flotilla, with the Navy – and PR. (2010, May 26). *The New York Times*.

Kershner, I. (2010a, May 28). Defying Blockade, Cargo and Passenger Vessels Head for Gaza. *The New York Times*, p. 10A.

Kershner, I. (2010b, May 29). Gaza Flotilla Organizers Protest Israeli Response to Their Mission. *The New York Times*, p. 6A.

Kershner, I. (2010c, May 31). Deadly Israeli Raid Draws Condemnation. *The New York Times*, p. 1A.

Kershner, I. (2010d, May 31). Israel Intercepts Boats Heading to Gaza; Violence is Reported. *The New York Times*, p. 8A.

Kershner, I. (2010e, June 3). Israel Signals New Flexibility on Gaza Shipments. *The New York Times*.

Kershner, I. (2010f, June 4). Israel Shifts Approach to Gaza. *The New York Times*, p. 4.

Kershner, I. (2010g, June 4). Second Set of Activists Steams Toward Gaza. *The New York Times*, p. 7A.

Kershner, I. (2010h, June 5). Israel Seeking 'New Ways' to Allow Gaza Aid; Cargo Must Be Inspected, Government Insists, But Goods Should Get Through. *The International Herald Tribune*, p. 6.

Kershner, I. (2010i, June 5). Israeli Military boards Gaza-Bound Aid Ship. *The New York Times*.

Kershner, I. (2010j, June 5). Second Group of Activists Is Headed Toward Gaza. *The New York Times*, p. 7.

Kershner, I. (2010k, June 8). 4 Palestinian Drivers Killed Near Gaza by Israeli Navy. *The New York Times*, p. 8.

Kershner, I. (2010l, June 10). Israel Widens Supplies Allowed into Gaza. *The New York Times*.

Kershner, I. (2010m, June 18). Israel to Ease Land Blockade of Gaza and Allow the Entry of Food. *The New York Times*, p. 12.

Kershner, I. (2010n, June 21). In Concession, Israel Relaxes Gaza Blockade. *The New York Times*, p. 1A.

Kershner, I. and MacFarquhar, N. (2010, June 1). Pressure Mounts on Israel as Activists Vow to Test Blockade Again. *The New York Times*, p. 10A.

Kessler, G. (2010, June 4). American teenager among Those Killed In Israeli Raid of Aid Flotilla. *The Washington Post*.

Kessler, G., Wilgoren, D. and Zacharia, J. (2010, June 4). Gaza-Bound Aid Ship Rachel Corrie Expected to Arrive Saturday. *The Los Angeles Times.*

Kessler, G. & Wilson, S. (2010, June 3). U.S. Warned Israel Before Raid; Administration Urged 'Caution and Restraint' Regarding Aid Boats. *The Washington Post,* p. 1A.

Kraft, D. (2010, July 1). Turkish and Israeli Officials Meet Secretly on Raid Crisis. *The New York Times,* p. 6A.

Kumar, A. (2010, June 2). U.N. Panel Condemns Israeli's Ship Raid; Gaza Activists Weigh Sending New Shipment to Challenge Blockade. *The Washington Times,* p. 7.

Landler, M. (2010, June 1). After Flotilla Raid, U.S. Is Torn Between Allies. *The New York Times.*

Lake, E. (2010, June 24). U.S. Urges Flotilla Backers to Deliver Gaza Aid by Land; Aims to Avert Clash With Israel. *The Washington Times,* p. 8

Laub, K. (2010a, June 6). Israel Seizes Ship to Gaza; Nonviolent Takeover Contrast to Previous Raid; Aid Vessel Carrying Nobel Laureate, Activists. *Newsday,* p. 30A (*The Associated Press*).

Laub, K. (2010b, July 6). Israel Easing Gaza Land Blockade. *Newsday,* p. 33A.

MacFarquhar, N. (2010a, May 31). Security Council Debates Criticism of Israeli Raid. *The New York Times.*

MacFarquhar, N. (2010b, June 19). U.N. Leader Criticizes Israeli Plan for Inquiry. *The New York Times,* p. 5A.

Mitnick, J. (2010a, 28 May). Gaza Aid Flotilla: Why Israel Expects To Lose the PR War. *The Christian Science Monitor.*

Mitnick, J. (2010b, May 31). Israel's Deadly Gaza Flotilla Raid Sparks Diplomatic Crisis. *The Christian Science Monitor.*

Mitnick, J. (2010c, June 4). As MV Rachel Corrie Draws Nearer, Israel Mulls Easing Gaza Blockade. *The Christian Science Monitor.*

Mitnick, J. (2010d, June 11). Israel to Set Up Inquiry on 'Freedom Flotilla' Raid. *The Christian Science Monitor.*

Mitnick, J. (2010e, June 14). Israel Announces Gaza Aid Flotilla Inquiry. *The Christian Science Monitor.*

Mitnick, J. (2010f, June 16). After Gaza Flotilla Raid, Israel Close to Easing Gaza Blockade. *The Christian Science Monitor.*

Mitnick, J. (2010g, June 17). Israel Eases Gaza Blockade, Allowing Building Supplies and Ketchup. *The Christian Science Monitor.*

Mitnick, J. (2010h, June 21). Israel's Easing of Gaza Blockade Doesn't Address Banking, Travel Rules. *The Christian Science Monitor.*

Mourners in Turkey Honor Slain Aid Ship Activists. (2010, June 3). *The Associated Press.*

Paddock, B. (2010, June 1). Blockade Spurred By Hamas Takeover. *The Daily News,* p. 4.

Parsons, C. (2010, June 10). Obama Pledges Aid for the Palestinians; His Meeting at the White House With Abbas Focuses More on the Gaza Blockade Than Mideast Peace. *The Los Angeles Times,* p. 5.

Peled, J. (2010 June 2). A Bloody PR Stunt. *USA Today,* p. 8A.

Reuters. (2010, June 14). Netanyahu announces Inquiry Into flotilla Raid; Investigation of Siege on Gaza-Bound Ship Will Include Two Foreigners. *The Washington Post,* p. 11A.

Richter, P. (2010, June 2). Gaza Flotilla Raid; Raid Throws a Wrench in U.S. Agenda. *The Los Angeles Times,* p. 6A)

Sanders, E. (2010a, 29 May). Gaza Aid Flotilla Anticipates High-Seas Standoff with Israel. *The Los Angeles Times.*

Sanders, E. (2010b, May 30). Showdown Looms As Aid Flotilla Heads Toward Gaza. *The Los Angeles Times*, p. 4A.

Sanders, E. (2010c, May 31). Israel Seizes Flotilla; 10 Activists Die. *The Los Angeles Times*, p. 1AA.

Sanders, E. (2010d, June 1). Israel Criticized Over Raid on Gaza Flotilla. *The Los Angeles Times*.

Sanders, E. (2010e, June 3). Netanyahu Ignores Calls for Investigation of Aid Flotilla Raid. *The Los Angeles Times*, p. 4.

Sanders, E. (2010f, June 5). Israelis Intercept Aid Ship without Bloodshed. *The Los Angeles Times*.

Sanders, E. (2010g, June 6). Israel Acts Cautiously in Round 2; Fallout From a Deadly Raid Continues, Though Another Ship Is Seized Without Incident. *The Los Angeles Times*, p. 3A.

Sanders, E. (2010h, June 10). Israel Permits Snack Foods to Enter Gaza. *The Los Angeles Times*, p. 5.

Sanders, E. (2010i, June 13). Gaza's Plight a Crisis With a Difference; The Situation Under the Blockade Defies the Usual Categories, Aid Officials Say. *The Los Angeles Times*, p. 1.

Sanders, E. (2010j, June 14). Israeli-Led Panel Will Probe Raid. *The Los Angeles Times*, p. 5.

Sanders, E. (2010k, June 15). Israelis Are Conflicted About Probe. *The Los Angeles Times*, p. 3.

Sanders, E. (2010l, June 18). Israel Agrees in Principle to Ease Gaza Blockade. *The Los Angeles Times*, p. 6.

Sanders, E. (2010m, July 6). Israel Revises List of Banned Gaza Items, More Goods Are Permitted, But Critics Say Vital Supplies Are Still Blocked. *The Los Angeles Times*, p. 5A.

Sanders, E. (2010n, June 21). Israel to Ease Gaza Embargo. *The Los Angeles Times*, p. 3A.

Scarborough, R. (2010, June 14). Turkey's Shift Spurs Concern on Hill. *The Washington Times*, p. 1.

Shear, M. D. (2010, June 10). Obama Seeks New Approach on Gaza; He Calls for Israeli Blockade to Consider Aid as Well as Security. *The Washington Post*, p. 9A.

Siemaszko, C. (2010, June 1). Pro-Palestinian Activists Claim They Did Not Attack Israeli Soldiers First During Raid on Aid Ship. *The Daily News*.

Siemaszko, C. and Yaniv, O. (2010, June 2). Bibi Bashes Bashers. Bloomberg Joins Netanjahu in Defending Commando's Attack on Gaza-Bound Ship. *The Daily News*, p. 17.

Silverman, E. & Martinez, J. (2010, June 1). Botched Raid Riles World. Israeli Commandos Kill Nine in Gaza Flotilla. Bibi Defends Actions, But Protests Mounting. *The Daily News*, p. 2.

Sisik, R. (2010, June 4). U.S. Squeezes Israel to Ease Blockade of Gaza. *The Daily News*, p. 14.

Slackman, M. (2010, June 2). In Bid to Quell Anger Over Raid, Israel Frees Detainees. *The New York Times*, p. 4A.

Slackman, M. and Tavernise, S. (2010, June 2). Turkish funds Helped Group Test Blockade. *The New York Times*, p. 1A.

Slackman, M. and Tavernise, S. (2010, June 3). Turks' Gifts Gave Flotilla Activists New Life; Aid Group's Millions 'Shifted The Balance' And Put Israel on Notice. *The International Herald Tribune*, p. 6.

Stack, M. K. (2010, May 31). Israel Flotilla Raid Deals a Blow to Ties with Turkey. *The Los Angeles Times*.

Stelter, B. (2010, June 1). Videos Carry On the Fight Over Sea Raid. *The New York Times*, p. 1A.

Tavernise, S. (2010, June 3). Thousands in Turkey Mourn Victims of Israeli Raid. *The New York Times*, p. 8A.

Times Wire Reports. (2010, June 29). Top Officials to Testify in Inquiry on Flotilla Deaths. *The Los Angeles Times*, p. 5A.

Werner, E. (2010, June 10). Obama Looks to Aid Gaza, West Bank. *Newsday*, p. 8A.

Wilson, S. (2010, June 1). Israel Says Free Gaza Movement Poses Threat To Jewish State; Aid Flotilla Was Run by Member Charity with Alleged Ties to Islamists. *The Washington Post*, p. 6A.

Zacharia, J. (2010, June 3). Getting What They Need to Live, But Not Thrive. *The Washington Post*, p. 1A.

Zacharia, J. (2010a, June 4). Israel's Netanyahu Maintains Defiance Amid Criticism Over Gaza Blockade. *The Washington Post.*

Zacharia, J. (2010b, June 15). Israeli Raid Leaves Egypt in Awkward Spot. *The Washington Post*, p. 6A.

Zacharia, J. (2010v, June 17). Israel Considers Loosening Its Blockade of Gaza Strip. *The Washington Post*, p. 10A.

Zacharia, J. (2010d, June 18). Israel Will Allow More Goods Into Gaza Strip; Sea Blockade Remains Over Reports of Further Aid Ships Arriving Soon. *The Washington Post*, p. 18A.

Zavis, A. (2010, June 7). Israel Supporters Rally in L.A.; Crowds Back the State, Saying Criticism of Its Raid on a Gaza-Bound Flotilla Is Unfair. *The Los Angeles Times*, p. 1AA.

UK news media

Aid Chief's Israel Call; Gaza. (2010, June 12). *The Mirror*, p. 27.

BBC Monitoring Europe. (2010, June 1). Palestinian Delegation in Cyprus Condemns Assault on Gaza Flotilla. *BBC.*

BBC Monitoring Middle East. (2010a, May 29). Palestinian Gaza Flotilla Activists Threaten Hunger Strike. *BBC.*

BBC Monitoring Middle East. (2010b, May 31). Egypt Condemns Israeli Attack on "Freedom Flotilla," Offers Condolences – TV. *BBC.*

BBC Monitoring Middle East. (2010c, June 4). Hamas, Palestinian Islamic Jihad Hold Rallies in Support of Flotilla. *BBC.*

BBC Monitoring Middle East. (2010d, June 5). Hamas Says Israel's Interception of Gaza Ship "Barbaric Piracy". *BBC.*

BBC Monitoring Middle East. (2010g, June 25). Israel to Increase Truckloads into Gaza to Pre-Blockade Level. *BBC.*

Bardon, S. (2010a, May 31). Irish Politicians in Gaza Aid Ban. *The Mirror*, p. 5.

Bardon, S. (2010b, June 7). Blocked, Seized and Sent Home. *The Mirror*, p. 17.

Bardon, S. (2010c, June 15). Israel to Investigate Boat Raid Massacre. *The Mirror*, p. 16.

Bardon, S. (2010d, June 18). Israel Backs Down over Gaza. *The Mirror*, p. 2.

Beattie, J. (2010, July 28). Cameron: Gaza is a Prison Camp. *The Mirror*, p. 4.

Black, I. (2010a, June 2). Humanitarian Aid: Egypt Opens Border with Gaza. *The Guardian*, p. 5.

Black, I. (2010b, June 3). Gaza Flotilla Assault: Israeli Blockade: Netanyahu Defiant as Pressure Builds to Lift Siege. *The Guardian*, p. 11.

Black, I. (2010c, June 7). Iran Offers Escort to Next Gaza Aid Convoy. *The Guardian*, p. 2.

Black, I. (2010d, June 11). Spain Seeks EU Backing on Plans to Lift Gaza Blockade. *The Guardian*, p. 22.

Black, I. (2010e, June 18). Israel's Easing of Gaza Blockade Dismissed as Inadequate. *The Guardian*, p. 25.

Black, I. (2010f, June 29). Turkey Bans Israeli Military Flight from Airspace as Freeze Deepens. *The Guardian*, p. 18.

Black, I., Hirsch, A. and Siddique, H. (2010, June 1). Gaza Flotilla Assault: The Blockade. *The Guardian*, p. 5.

Black, I., Booth, R. and MacAskill, E. (2010, June 4). Gaza Flotilla Assault: Turks Killed by 'Israeli Angel of Death' Given Heroes' Funeral. *The Guardian*, p. 14.

Blomfield, A. (2010a, June 2). Abbas Move Keeps Door Open on Peace Process. *The Daily Telegraph*, p. 17.

Blomfield, A. (2010b, June 8). Iran Adds to Gaza Tension with Threat to Challenge Blockade. *The Daily Telegraph*, p. 14.

Blomfield, A. (2010c, June 18). Israel Set to Ease Gaza Blockade. *The Daily Telegraph*, p. 22.

Blomfield, A. (2010d, July 26). Israel to Co-Operate with Flotilla Inquiry. *The Daily Telegraph*, p. 13.

Blomfield, A. and Waterfield, B. (2010, June 15). Gaza Blockade May be Eased within Days after Inquiry Deal. *The Daily Telegraph*, p. 16.

Bloody Blockade. (2010, June 14). *The Mirror*, p. 24.

Blunden, M. (2010, June 7). Israel Shoots 'Terror Divers' off Gaza. *The Evening Standard*.

Bluden, M. and Lydall, R. (2010, June 2). Gaza Activists Tell of Terror as Israelis Let Off Gas and Bombs. *The Evening Standard*.

Booth, R. (2010a, June 3). Gaza Flotilla Assault: Protest Generation. *The Guardian*, p. 10.

Booth, R. (2010b, June 4). Gaza Flotilla Assault: The Next Flashpoint. *The Guardian*, p. 14.

Charter, D. and Hider, J. (2010, June 15). Israeli Blockade is Eased but Critics Cast Doubt on Inquiry into Flotilla Raid. *The Times*, p. 36, 37.

Churchers, J. (2010a, June 1). '19 dead' as Israelis Storm Supply Ships. *Daily Post*, p. 2.

Churchers, J. (2010b, June 1). Shoot-Out: Dead as Israeli Commandos Storm Aid Ship. *Daily Post*, p. 17.

Coghlan, T. and Hider, J. (2010, June 25). Women Armed with 'Faith' Plan Aid Voyage. *The London Times*, p. 3.

Connolly, P. and McCarthy, J. (2010, June 6) Israelis to Deport Gaza Aid Crew. *The Sunday Times*, p. 1, 2.

Cordon, G. (2010, June 2). 30 Brits Locked Up in Shoot-Out Crisis. *Daily Post*, p. 19.

Dixon, C. (2010, June 3). Gaza Britons Dumped in Turkey With No Cash. *The Express*, p. 15.

Fitzmaurice, M. (2010a, June 4). The Rachel Corrie Will Not Reach Gaza. *The Mirror*, p. 19.

Fitzmaurice, M. (2010b, June 5). The Danger Zone; Gaza Blockade Freedom Flotilla. *The Mirror*, p. 16, 17.

Fitzmaurice, M. (2010c, June 15). Trimble to Join Israeli Probe into Massacre. *The Mirror*, p. 14.

Gabbatt, A. (2010, June 5). Gaza: MV Rachel Corrie: Aid ship heading for Gaza despite Israeli warning. *The Guardian*, p. 29.

Gaza Aid Ship Backs Away. (2010, July 15). *The Daily Telegraph*, p. 14.

Gaza Campaigners Say Aid Workers Could Fight Deportation. (2010, June 7). *Daily Post*, p. 16.

Gaza: From Blockade to Bloodshed. (2010, June 1). *The Guardian*, p. 28.

Gaza: In Numbers. (2010, June 5). *The Guardian*, p. 28.

Gaza: State of Siege. (2010, June 27). *The Guardian*, p. 32.

Green, T. and Macintyre, D. (2010, June 5). Israel Warns Gaza-Bound 'Rachel Corrie' to Stop. *The Independent*, p. 4.

Greenhill, S. (2010, June 3). Exit the Peace Ship Prisoners. *Daily Mail*.

Hall, M. (2010, July 28). Fury as Cameron Calls Gaza a 'Prison Camp'. *The Express*, p. 4.

History of Gaza Strip. (2010, June 6). *Sunday Mirror*, p. 25.

I Feared for My Life as Israelis Stormed Boat. (2010, June 4.) *The Mirror*, p.17.

Irvine, C. and Vela, J. (2010, June 4). Homecoming Britons Tell of Raid on Gaza Flotilla. *The Daily Telegraph*, p. 19.

Israel Kicks Out Seven Aid Sailors. (2010, June 7). *The Mirror*, p. 19.

Israel Plans Probe into Flotilla Raid. (2010, June 14). *The Mirror*, p. 14.

Israel Raid Probe. (2010, June 14). *The Sun*, p. 23.

Israel Vows to Stop Irish Ship Bound for Gaza. (2010, June 5). *Daily Mail*.

Kalman, M. (2010, May 31). Flotilla Sets Sail to Beat Gaza Blockade. *The Daily Telegraph*, p. 13.

Kolirin, L. (2010, June 21). Israel to Ease Land Blockade of Gaza Strip. *The Express*, p. 9.

Kraft, D. (2010, June 5). Israel to Block Irish-Owned Gaza Aid Ship. *The Daily Telegraph*, p. 17.

Macintyre, D. (2010a, May 30). Gaza Flotilla Delayed After Mystery Faults Hit Two Boats. *The Independent on Sunday*, p. 36.

Macintyre, D. (2010b, June 4). Blair Urges Israel to Ease Gaza blockade. *The Independent*, p. 14.

Macintyre, D. (2010c, June 14). Trimble to Observe on Israeli Inquiry into Flotilla Attack. *The Independent*, p. 14.

Macintyre, D. (2010d, June 15). Israel Agrees 'in Principle' to Ease Blockade, Says Blair. *The Independent*, p. 28.

Macintyre, D. (2010e, June 18). Israel Urged to Do More as Gaza Blockade is Eased. *The Independent*, p. 28.

Macintyre, D. (2010f, June 21). Blair Takes Heart from Israeli Offer to Relax Gaza Blockade. *The Independent*, p. 30.

May, M. and Tierney, P. (2010, June 3). Defiant Brian: Israel You're Going Cowen; Taoiseach Demands Passage to Gaza. *The Sun*, p. 8.

McGreal, C. (2010, June 2). Gaza Flotilla Assault: United Nations: Israel Should Lead Investigation, Says US. *The Guardian*, p. 5.

McLean, J. (2010, June 5). Israeli Soldiers Put a Gun to My Head but I Still Want to Go Back. *The Sun*, p. 33.

Meneely, G. (2010, June 15). Trimble to Join Gaza Inquiry. *The Sun*, p. 9.

Murphy, J. (2010, June 14). Gaza Blockade Is Close to Being Lifted, Says Blair. *The Evening Standard*.

Newton Dunn, T. and Wheeler, V. (2010, June 1). Bloody Disastrous. *The Sun*, p. 4, 5.

Nicks, G. (2010, June 1). Fears for Brits in Aid-Ship Massacre. *Daily Star*, p. 17.

O'Keeffe, M. (2010, June 3). We'll Storm Irish Aid Ship; Gaza Conflict Showdown Near. *The Mirror*, p. 11.

Prince, R. (2010, July 28). Gaza is Like a Prison Camp, Says PM. *The Daily Telegraph*, p. 10.

Richards, V. (2010, June 2). Let Us All Go; Gaza Scots Plea. *Daily Star*, p. 18.

Shabi, R. (2010, June 4). Gaza Flotilla Assault: Israeli Politics: Palestinian Member of Knesset Faces Death Threats for Taking Part in Aid Flotilla. *The Guardian*, p. 14.

Sherwood, H. (2010a, May 26). Gaza Aid Flotilla to Test Israel's Blockade. *The Guardian*, p. 17.

Sherwood, H. (2010b, May 29). International: Israeli Navy Prepares for Action as Activists' Flotilla Nears Gaza: Organisers of Eight-Ship Fleet Predict Standoff: Protesters on Board Face Detention and Deportation. *The Guardian*, p. 36.

Sherwood, H. (2010c, June 4). Gaza Flotilla Assault: Where Did the Aid Go? *The Guardian*, p. 15.

Sherwood, H. (2010d, June 6). Anger at Israeli Seizure of another Gaza Aid Boat. *The Observer*, p. 4.

Sherwood, H. (2010, June 10). Obama Announces $400m Aid for Palestinians and Says Better Approach Needed to Gaza Situation. *The Guardian*, p. 17.

Sherwood, H. (2010e, June 14). Obama Backs Israeli Internal Inquiry into Assault on Flotilla. *The Guardian*, p. 22.

Sherwood, H. (2010f, June 21). Israel Bows to Pressure and Agrees to Ease Gaza Blockade. *The Guardian*, p. 1.

Sherwood, H. (2010g, July 12). Israeli Navy on Alert as Libyan Ship Heads for Gaza. *The Guardian*, p. 18.

Smyth, C. (2010, June 14). Trimble to Act as Observer in Israel's Aid Flotilla Inquiry. *The Times*, p. 30.

Spencer, R. (2010, June 21). Israelis to Let Civilian Supplies into Gaza. *The Daily Telegraph*, p. 15.

Spillius, A. (2010, June 10). US Urges Israel to Help Gaza Inquiry. *The Daily Telegraph*, p. 16.

Stewart, C. (2010a, June 3). Passengers on Flotilla Had Al-Qa'ida Links, Claims Israel. *The Independent*, p. 6.

Stewart, C. (2010b, July 1). Pyjama Photo Forces Netanyahu into U-Turn on Gaza Flotilla Inquiry. *The Independent*, p. 26.

Stewart, C. (2010c, July 28). Cameron Uses Turkish Visit to Launch Ferocious Attack on Israel. *The Independent*, p. 14.

Teibel, A. (2010, June 17). Israel to Ease Land Blockade of Gaza Strip. *The Evening Standard.*

Tevlin, R. (2010a, June 2). If Any Harm Comes to Any of Our Citizens There Will Be Serious Consequences; Taoiseach Warns Israel. *The Mirror*, p. 9.

Tevlin, R. (2010b, June 8). I'll Be Back; Brave Mairead Gaza Vow. *The Mirror*, p. 6.

Tevlin, R. (2010c, June 8). We'll Be Back; Deported Activists in Promise to Keep up Gaza Campaign. *The Mirror*, p. 19.

Traynor, I. (2010, June 15). Israel Will Ease Gaza Blockade, Blair Tells EU. *The Guardian*, p. 17.

This Cruel and Ineffective Blockade of Gaza Must Be Brought to an End. (2010, June 5). *The Independent*, p. 42.

Toolis, K. (2010, June 2). Fuse Lit for a New War in Mid East. *The Mirror*, p. 6.

Williams, D. (2010, June 2). Turkish Navy to Back Next Convoy. *Daily Mail*.

Young, L. (2010, June 2). Hundreds Protest in City over Israeli Raids. *Daily Post*, p. 2.

Index